Mission-Critical Microsoft® Exchange 2000

Mission-Critical Microsoft® Exchange 2000: Building Highly Available Messaging and Knowledge Management Systems

Jerry Cochran

Digital
Press

Boston • Oxford • Auckland • Johannesburg • Melbourne • New Delhi

Library of Congress Cataloging-in-Publication Data
Cochran, Jerry, 1964-
  Mission-critical Microsoft Exchange 2000 : building highly available messaging and knowledge management systems / Jerry Cochran.
    p.   cm.
  ISBN 1-55558-233-8 (pbk. : alk. paper)
  1. Microsoft Exchange server. 2. Client/server computing. I. Title.
QA76.9.C55 C63   2000
005.7'13769–dc21   00-047512
                                                                          CIP

The publisher offers special discounts on bulk orders of this book.
For information, please contact:
Manager of Special Sales
Butterworth–Heinemann
225 Wildwood Avenue
Woburn, MA 01801-2041
Tel: 781-904-2500
Fax: 781-904-2620

For information on all Butterworth–Heinemann publications available, contact our World Wide Web home page at: http://www.bhusa.com.

Transferred to Digital Printing, 2011

Printed and bound in the United Kingdom

To God, from whom all blessings flow,
and
to Petronella, for daring to love a computer nerd

Contents

Foreword

As an undergraduate, I studied history. One of the most important lessons I learned was that history is cyclical—if you wait long enough it is bound to repeat itself. I'm struck by this thought as I look back on the events that took place between my joining the Exchange team, prior to the first Microsoft Exchange Server announcement in June of 1994, and the release of Microsoft Exchange 2000 Server in October 2000.

In 1994, Microsoft introduced Microsoft Exchange Server 4.0. We thought of this as a revolution of sorts. Exchange was the first true client–server e-mail server designed for the enterprise. It was going to change the way people thought about e-mail, and give customers a reason to give up their existing shared file mail servers. And, we thought, it may just change the way people literally view e-mail as well.

We learned rather quickly, however, that moving customers to Exchange wasn't going to be easy. It wasn't that they wanted to keep their existing systems. On the contrary, every customer we spoke to was eager to move to something that was more reliable and more manageable. Still, as the old saying goes, "The devil you know is better than the devil you don't." The combination of a new e-mail server and a new operating system, Windows NT, created as many questions as answers. Realizing this, we began to spend a great deal of time developing expertise and resources to help customers plan how to do an effective deployment.

As was the case six years ago, we are once again ready to release a combination of products that we think will change the way people think about and use e-mail and collaboration software—Exchange 2000. But today the market has changed dramatically. No longer is e-mail just a neat way to speed communication between coworkers. Instead it is a critical component in the way companies do business both inside their enterprises and between organizations. E-mail and collaboration have broken down physical and temporal boundaries, much like the telephone and fax machine did previously, and have made decision making almost immediate. In fact, for many companies, including Microsoft, e-mail is at least as important, if not more, than the telephone. Anything less than complete reliability and availability is unacceptable.

Exchange 2000 Server is the e-mail and collaboration infrastructure customers demand. It is a great leap forward in reliability, manageability, and scalability. The Web Storage System does more than just integrate Internet protocols; it weaves the Internet into the basic fabric of the server. Combined with the improved capabilities of Windows 2000 and the Active Directory, Exchange 2000 is providing a messaging and collaboration solution that more than delivers.

As was the case with the introduction of Microsoft Exchange Server 4.0, moving to Exchange 2000 and Windows 2000 will not be easy. Now, more than ever, it is important to spend ample time and resources planning a deployment. There are Active Directory issues to consider; administrative, routing, and security group plans to be had; even new topology recommendations to be made. During the past three years of development, a lot of time has been spent on and much energy building expertise has gone into developing Exchange 2000. I am proud to say that we have more partners, courseware, and books dedicated to this product than to any previous release. Customers who need and want help will be assured they can get it.

So why is this book special? In my office I have a copy of nearly every book written about Exchange since Exchange 4.0. There are books about planning and deployment, books about management, books that explain how to configure connectors between Exchange and other systems, and books about how to develop applications for Exchange and Microsoft Outlook. Among them this book is unique. *Mission-Critical Microsoft Exchange 2000* is more than simply a book about deployment. It takes the extra step of explaining how to deploy Exchange such that it provides five-9s of reliability and availability. It is an invaluable resource for anyone deploying Exchange 2000, from the smallest company to the largest ASP.

This book is also special in that it is based on best practices developed by Compaq. From the earliest days of Exchange, Compaq (and Digital before that) has dedicated considerable resources to an Exchange practice. Today Compaq has 7 million seats under direct contract, and it has deployed many more, earning the designation "Prime Integrator for Exchange." By reading this book, you become the beneficiary of Compaq's experience.

As an amateur historian—and the last member of the server marketing team to have worked on each version of Exchange—I see a number of parallels between 1994 and today. Yes, the product we are shipping today in many ways holds little resemblance to the product we announced six years back. And yes, market dynamics have changed considerably. But one thing remains constant: Everyone who has worked on designing, developing, testing, documenting, and marketing Exchange 2000 is committed to delivering the highest quality product available. We continue to be 100% committed to providing our customers with the resources they need to successfully deploy and use this product. And we remain as enthusiastic now as we were back then.

We think you will be happy with the results.

Stan Sorensen
Group Product Manager, Server Applications
Microsoft Corp.

Preface

An Observed Vacuum of Knowledge

When I was approached with the opportunity to write this book and began to synthesize some ideas, my first thoughts were around the fact that, all too often, we don't plan for mission-critical deployments in the world of client/server computing. In my experience, the focus seems to be on performance, scalability, and the applications themselves and not on achieving maximum uptime. When I began work with Microsoft Exchange Server in 1996, version 4.0 was just released and many corporate customers were waiting in anticipation for Microsoft's entry into the client/server messaging and GroupWare market. Prior to this, Microsoft had only Microsoft Mail—a leading shared file-based e-mail product. A customer I was working with at the time quickly began to assess his requirements and plan a huge deployment of Exchange Server throughout his enterprise.

Among the key priorities of this customer's organization was the need to understand and characterize Exchange Server 4.0 performance. At the time, version 3.51 of Windows NT Server was the current shipping version from Microsoft. The customer was also in the midst of the initial deployment stages for Windows NT. In addition, the organization was trying to understand the key deployment issues for the operating system as well as applications such as Exchange Server. Since their focus and priority were on performance and scalability of Exchange Server 4.0, this organization committed substantial resources and began a project to understand and characterize Exchange Server performance and scalability.

This project began with a careful process of analyzing client access patterns to Exchange Server and characterizing the workload these servers could anticipate once deployed within the organization. Substantial resources were invested analyzing current e-mail applications, conducting user e-mail usage surveys, and capturing data from existing corporate mail gateways in an effort to comprehend every aspect of the performance management and deployment equation. Since the organization had chosen to deploy Windows NT and Exchange Server on Compaq hardware platforms, they also engaged Compaq to help them perform extensive capacity planning and performance analysis exercises at one of Compaq's facilities in Houston, Texas. An incredible amount of work went into developing an expert understanding of the performance requirements for deploying Exchange Server to a large population of users spread out over the entire world.

This stellar effort resulted in a deployment of Exchange Server to a population of almost 200,000 users on server platforms supporting 1,000 users per server. Furthermore, actual performance data captured during the initial stages of deployment were very close to what had been expected beforehand. The results of the extensive workload characterization, capacity planning, and performance analysis activities had given the organization a pretty accurate picture of what they could expect once their Exchange Server deployment went into production use. They were also able to determine, in advance, the hardware requirements and configuration needed to support the determined guideline of 1,000 users per server. The fruits of their labor were accurate performance models with which the organization could develop and manage service-level agreement (SLA) commitments made to the user population and management.

The point of my story is that in all of the tremendous efforts around predeployment planning for Exchange Server, the organization focused solely on performance planning and management (not that these aren't important) and did not do enough to anticipate disaster recovery and high availability requirements for Exchange Server. The same extremely painstaking and successful measures that had been taken on the performance and scalability side had not been taken on the disaster recovery and high availability fronts. In fact, the organization left disaster recovery measures for Exchange Server up to a separate team within the company that was responsible for disaster recovery but had no expertise with Exchange Server or investment in the ongoing deployment within the organization. The end result was a well-tuned Exchange Server deployment that provided little tolerance for the impending disasters to be encountered down the road. I suspect this organization was not alone in this oversight.

Assumptions

When preparing to write this book, I took the approach that you, the reader, already would know quite a lot about Exchange Server and that you would be looking to extend your knowledge and to get another perspective in the area of high availability and mission-critical system deployment. In fact, you may already have read Tony Redmond's *Microsoft® Exchange Server for Windows 2000* and want to continue your exploration of Digital Press's Exchange Server bookshelf. There are many excellent books on Exchange Server available from Digital Press and other publishers. I was looking to provide something that can complement the excellent resources already available from authors such as Tony Redmond, Greg Todd, Paul Robichaux, Sue Mosher, and several others. I wanted to give you a perspective that was not necessarily lacking in other resources, but would extend and drill down further on important high availability topics for Exchange deployment.

In so doing, I purposely neglected certain topics that I consider important but not necessarily relevant to the intended purpose of this book. Exchange 2000 is a huge and complex product that has many technologies and components that go into its making. However, I have tried to focus on core technologies such as Exchange's Extensible Storage Engine (ESE), which directly impacts important availability issues like disaster recovery, storage management, security, and clustering. More time and pages invested in providing a complete Exchange 2000 technology tutorial would have resulted in a tome of extraordinary volume. I will leave that task to other able-bodied authors. In fact, in the future look for the many great books completely canvassing Exchange technology from Digital Press. For my part, I simply considered the topics most important for mission-critical Exchange deployments.

Compaq and Exchange

Compaq (and now Digital, as part of Compaq) has been involved with Exchange Server from day one. Compaq's involvement has been both as a partner to Microsoft and as a customer deploying Exchange Server worldwide. Compaq has invested heavily in technology for servers and storage, integration and solutions development, and services to become the leading provider of platforms, solutions, and services for Exchange Server. For Windows 2000 and Exchange 2000, Microsoft has awarded Compaq its "Worldwide Prime Integrator" status based on Compaq's commitment and investments in these technologies. To date, Compaq has well over 7 million seats of Exchange under its deployment and services contract and has been designated Microsoft Global Services Partner of the Year by Microsoft for the year 2000.

Compaq also has consistently worked to test and integrate server and storage technology with Exchange Server to ensure optimal deployment of Compaq technology for Exchange customers. Many Compaq individuals represent the best and the brightest in the industry when it comes to Exchange. Compaq has over 1,000 mail and messaging consultants with specific Exchange deployment expertise. Microsoft frequently relies on Compaq for speakers at conferences such as Microsoft Tech Ed and the Microsoft Exchange Conference. The end result is that no other vendor brings more to the table in terms of value add for Exchange deployments. Compaq not only makes platforms for Exchange but also has the integration, support, and service organizations to back them up. In short, because of its passion and focus on Exchange product technology, no other company outside of Microsoft provides the environment that Compaq does for living and breathing Exchange on a daily basis.

Clearly, my employment at Compaq provides me with an excellent opportunity to learn and grow in my knowledge of Exchange. As the past manager of Compaq's Exchange Solutions Engineering team in Redmond, Washington, and now as a Principle Consultant for Compaq Global Services, I act as an on-site technical liaison to the Exchange Server Development team at Microsoft. I have been on site at Microsoft since 1996 and have had a unique opportunity to watch Exchange Server grow and mature from the inside. My team is focused on providing integration of Compaq's technology with Windows NT/2000 and Exchange Server. Compaq's servers have the leading market share of installed base for Exchange deployments and my focus is drilling down into server, storage, and other Compaq technologies and using them to solve customer-specific Exchange deployment issues. More recently, I joined Compaq's Global Services organization and worked in the Applied Microsoft Technologies Group that is part of the Chief Technology Office (headed by Tony Redmond). High availability is a key issue and has been a focus of my team and my work at Compaq for quite some time now.

Besides the raw testing of technologies in the Exchange environment, we at Compaq also get the opportunity to run our own Exchange site with a clustered Exchange server supporting a production user population. This gives us a real-world scenario in which to apply some of our ideas. Capping off our experiences are frequent customer engagements that address the real issues facing a wide range of customer deployments of Exchange. The end result is great exposure to the issues that face you, the reader/user, and others who are planning, deploying, administering, and managing Exchange Server deployments. My hope is that I can share as much of the information as possible.

Acknowledgments

First and foremost, I must thank God for the gifts and talents He has given me. In my continuing faith, God has blessed me beyond my wildest dreams, with success in career and in endeavors such as my writing activities. Any successes, any talents, any glory, I owe all to God; all shortcomings are my own.

My wife, Petronella (Nella), has provided me with tremendous support and encouragement throughout the course of this project. From the first mention of the opportunity to take on such an endeavor, she has been a tireless cheerleader and constant source of motivation, helping to ease the load of life's pressures while undertaking such a monumental effort. Her love, devotion, and tender heart would inspire any man to be the man God wants him to be.

I thank my Parents, Bill and Diane Cochran, for their love and support, and for raising me right and impressing upon me certain values that have enabled me to become the man I am—not without flaws, but without many regrets. I thank my parents for bringing me up in a Christian home, for instilling a strong work ethic in me, and for giving me the knowledge that I can do anything in this world my heart chose to do.

I would like to acknowledge my management team at Compaq. They have supported me throughout in my efforts in this project.

Without their encouragement and without their providing me with an environment in which to learn, grow, and develop, this endeavor would not have been possible. Over the year spent writing this book, Compaq has been very patient with me and liberal in approving the extended vacation periods necessary to complete such a project. Also, I have recently joined the Technology Leadership Group within Compaq Global Services and have been lucky enough to enjoy the support and camaraderie from that organization as well. Many thanks go to Tony Redmond, Don Vickers, and the Applied Microsoft Technologies team of Compaq Global Services. I'm glad to be part of the team.

I must also acknowledge the larger community of expertise that exists within Compaq. Compaq over a thousand messaging consultants who are the best and brightest at what they do. There are many in-company mechanisms for sharing information regarding Exchange and Microsoft technologies, and these many debates and discussions among a huge team of experts have most certainly influenced me and contributed to my own knowledge base.

Thanks to the Solutions Engineering team at Compaq, John Hargreaves, Steve Tramack, Chung Tam, Ralph Boehm, Gary Ketchum, Evan Morris, and Jeff Masors, who are a tremendous pleasure to work with. I hope I have been the team leader and manager they needed me to be. I thank them for their support and for "picking up the slack" for me when my vacation and travel schedule became horrendous.

I would also like to acknowledge and thank those who encouraged my writing and got me started down the path to publication: Greg Todd, for giving me my first opportunity to write for publication; and Tony Redmond, the man once declared an Exchange "god" by attendees of the Microsoft Exchange Conference, for his constant encouragement and support of my writing. I owe him a tremendous debt of gratitude. To the staff at *Windows 2000 Magazine*—Karen Forster, Karen Nicholson, Gayle Rodcay, Warren Pickett, and Amy Eisenberg—I offer thanks for their unwavering support of my writing and for giving me the opportunity to write for the best Windows and Exchange-focused publication in the business.

At Digital Press, thanks go to the entire staff. Special thanks go to Phil Sutherland, Pam Chester, and Theron Shreve, for their support and encouragement during the course of this project, and for their constant "bravos" and coaching. Used to writing short articles and papers, I definitely needed their coaching and their confidence in me to make it through this sizable effort.

Exchange Server is a product developed in one of the most innovative environments at Microsoft. Over the last several years, since its inception, Exchange has continued to reach greater heights. Many of the techniques and technologies that I leverage for discussions in this book would not be possible without the intense degree of focus of the Exchange Server Product unit at Microsoft. While Microsoft is often criticized for various reasons (especially by jealous competitors and knowledge-barren Department of Justice lawyers), I have always found my interaction and partnership with Microsoft to be gratifying. To the folks in the Microsoft Exchange Product Unit, I owe a tremendous debt of gratitude. Eric Lockard, Stan Sorenson, Gordon Mangione, Doug Stumburger, Charles Eliot, Mark Ledsome, Perry Clarke, David Howell, David Madison, Marc Allen, Mark Wistrom, Nat Ballou, Tim Kiesow, Laurion Burchall, Larry LeSuer, Greg Chapman, Phil Hupf, Ken Ewert, Patrick Walters, Denise Smith, Jen Fowler, and Linda Hirsh all deserve thanks for answering all my technical questions, for giving me their support, and for giving my team and me insider status in the best and brightest development team at Microsoft.

Jerry Cochran
jerry.cochran@compaq.com
August 2000

Mission-Critical Exchange

1.1 Mission-Critical Defined and Understood

> **mission-critical:** *A term applied to various systems on which the success of an organization or project depends. The loss of a mission-critical system results in unacceptable operational, functional, or financial harm to the organization or project.*

1.1.1 And Size Doesn't Matter

It should be noted upfront that the term *mission-critical* need not apply specifically or solely to large systems or even large Exchange deployments. Certainly, larger deployments in larger organizations may have millions of dollars of revenue per day riding on the availability of their messaging and knowledge management systems. However, in the eyes of a small/medium business owner or IT manager, a small deployment of 50 users may be equally important to his existence. Moreover, since a large portion of the total deployed Exchange servers in the market reside in small/medium businesses, we must not limit our discussions or focus to include only large deployments. Mission-critical refers not to the size of our messaging system but to the importance of our data and the medium itself. Therefore, even small and mid-sized companies can have a need for and deploy mission-critical Exchange servers. It is not the size that matters—both large and small Exchange deployments need the tools, concepts, and methods I will discuss throughout this book.

Planning and implementing mission-critical systems is like buying insurance for your home or car. We accept the fact that, at some point along the road, something may happen, and we will have to file a claim. It doesn't pay to have an "It won't happen to me" attitude. We select our insurance vendor in terms of price and service but also in terms of our confidence that we will be without our home or vehicle for a minimal amount of time. As part of this insurance-selection process, we also look for a policy that will protect us from liability. Maybe if downtime were treated more seriously and made more of a business requirement, we would do a better job of setting service-level requirements and putting plans in place to meet them. Unfortunately, not all organizations treat disaster recovery and high availability planning as a business requirement.

Many see downtime and outages for their Exchange servers as something that will most likely happen to the other guy. The other problem is that, in order to "do it right" for any environment, you must have qualified staff and lots of money. On a yearly basis, Comdisco does a survey, called the Comdisco Vulnerability Index, of the largest IS shops in the world. According to this survey in 1997, only 12% had an effective disaster recovery and system availability program in place for their most key business-critical enterprise applications. In another study by the Gartner Group, only about 20% of companies running web-based e-commerce sites have proactive reliability plans in place. In 1998, a similar study by IBM Recovery Services showed that number to be only about 8% or less. This illustrates to me how businesses have generally neglected the whole process of ensuring mission-critical environments. This may be simply because many organizations are so resource constrained because it is a very resource-intensive and time-consuming process.

As we endeavor down the path of building mission-critical Exchange Server deployments, we must inevitably begin by defining exactly what is meant by mission-critical. We must also address some-times-overused terms such as *availability* and *reliability* in that same vein. Disaster recovery planning and implementation within the context of messaging systems must be addressed in terms of the key topics and goals important to administrators, planners, and implementers of Microsoft Exchange Server environments. Since any enterprise-wide distributed application, including Exchange Server, can be perceived as mission-critical, we need to establish what the reasons, objectives, and steps are for disaster recovery planning exercises. In this chapter, I will look at what is meant by mission-critical and its various facets applied to an Exchange server deployment. Next we will discuss how to evaluate the risks in your Exchange server environment. This risk-assessment process for your Exchange server environment will serve as a valuable precursor in determining your availability requirements for your Exchange Server deployment. Finally, we will look at defining service-level agreements (SLAs) for availability in an Exchange environment.

1.1.2 How Did "Mission-Critical" Become So Important to Exchange?

In the days (in the not-so-distant past) of Exchange Server version 4.0 as well as version 5.0, the information store was limited to 16GB. Thus, the maximum amount of mail storage (the private information store) that a single server could hold was 16GB. The public information store was also subject to this limit. This hard limitation in software was imposed by Microsoft's desire to get an already-delayed product (version 4.0) shipped, and it provided Exchange Server's first recognized scalability limitation. This limitation was soon encountered by many implementers eager to deploy thousands of users per server who quickly realized that the 16GB limit also effectively limited the number of users one could deploy on an Exchange server. If an administrator desired to give each Exchange user 30MB of mail storage, a simple calculation revealed that only around 500 users could be supported on any one Exchange Server. What was alarming about this was that both the hardware and software could support much higher user loads from a pure performance point of view. The end result was that scalability was limited by an administrative parameter—maximum mailbox size.

The 16GB limit also made disaster recovery operations fairly simple since 16GB per server was the maximum that would need to be backed up or restored. This information store limitation in Exchange Server 4.0 and 5.0 presented would-be implementers with few challenges as far as disaster recovery was concerned. Sixteen gigabytes could easily be backed up and restored within reasonable timeframes and well within the capabilities of the existing hardware and software technologies available at the time. For example, software products like Computer Associates' (then Cheyenne) ArcServe or Seagate's (now Veritas) Backup Exec products provided backup agents for Exchange Server. With hardware vendors shipping standard DLT drives that could easily backup 5GB to 10GB per hour or more, there seemed to be no real issues with Exchange server disaster recovery. The focus seemed to be still on performance and scalability and how Exchange Server could scale not only on a per-server basis but organizationally as well.

Enter Exchange Server version 5.5. Exchange Server version 5.5 was shipped in two flavors: Standard Edition and Enterprise Edition. Exchange Server 5.5 Enterprise Edition shipped in November of 1997 with one of its most touted features being an unlimited information store capacity. While the Standard Edition still maintained its limitation of 16GB, Enterprise Edition was advertised with an unlimited store capacity. While this limitation was technically 16TB, Microsoft was confident that Exchange Server storage limitations would now be subject to hardware limitations and no longer be software-based. Exchange Server customers were elated, as many were experiencing constant frustration when hitting the 16GB barrier on their Exchange servers. With 16TB, they were hopeful that they could now scale to thousands of users per server.

The shipment of Exchange Server 5.5 Enterprise Edition was timed closely to Intel's shipment of the Pentium Pro processor (although not through any orchestrated effort by Microsoft and Intel). However, with this and other technology advancements in the Intel x86 and Compaq Alpha server space (as well as scalability improvements in Windows NT 4.0), Exchange Server implementers had high hopes that both the hardware and software capabilities would provide a basis for consolidation of their Exchange Server populations. Servers supporting only 500 or 1000 users could now be combined on single, high-end hardware platforms running Exchange Server 5.5 Enterprise Edition that could handle user loads of 2,000, 5,000, or even 10,000 users per server. Organizations deploying Exchange Server could now drastically reduce their management and administrative overhead and could provide the lower total cost of ownership that their CIO had been asking for—life would be good!

Unfortunately, these dreams were not realized for Exchange Server deployments. In my experience, the typical Exchange Server deployment is still limited to around 2,000 to 3,000 users per server or less due to backup and restore limitations. To make matters worse, hardware vendors continue to demonstrate that today's hardware technologies, along with Exchange Server 5.5 and Exchange 2000, will support well over 30,000 users per server from a purely benchmarked performance point of view. Recent 8-processor benchmarks for Exchange Server leave Exchange Server implementers craving the consolidated deployment "nirvana" they had dreamed about. Why haven't things panned out? The answer and subject of this book is disaster recovery and high availability. Deploying mission-critical servers involves more than just meeting performance and scalability goals. It involves understanding, anticipating, and accounting for all the factors that allow a server to provide mission-critical service.

1.1.3   Exchange as a Basis for Future Technology

Another reason our discussions in this book are very applicable and pertinent is that what we know and (sometimes) love as Exchange Server or Exchange 2000 today will form a basis for many key Microsoft technologies in the future. New to Exchange 2000 is the much-touted Web Storage System. The Web Storage System is the embodiment of recent evolutions in Exchange storage and database technology that allows native Internet content to be quickly and efficiently accessed directly out of the Exchange database with minimal conversions. Content is available to various clients natively regardless of their protocol. Content can be accessed as a simple URL, as a Win32 API call, or simply by mapping a drive directly into the Web Storage System. The Web Storage System will be the basis for future knowledge management and portal products from Microsoft. For example, Microsoft's Site Server product will evolve and eventually use the Web Storage System as its storage mechanism. Microsoft's forthcoming Document and Search Server (code-named "Tahoe") will also leverage the Web Storage System. In fact, many future Microsoft products will either ship with a lite version of the Exchange 2000 Web Storage System or require that Exchange 2000 be installed. Microsoft's storage future is highly dependent upon Exchange 2000's Web Storage System. In the future, there will be two types of data that we deal with—structured and semi-structured data. SQL Server will be the technology that Microsoft relies on to manage structured data. The Web Storage System will manage semi-structured data. It is based on this future importance of Exchange 2000's storage and the Web Storage System that we see the significance behind deploying mission-critical Exchange servers. If we can achieve high levels of reliability with our Exchange deployments today, we will be positioned well as we move into the future and more of our organization's data becomes managed by this technology.

1.1.4 Taking Windows NT/2000 Seriously

In postulating and strategizing my approach to the problem of deploying mission-critical Exchange Servers, one foundational thought that should not be overlooked occurred to me. Are we taking Windows NT/2000 deployments seriously? Stay with me here. Prior to my present life in the world according to Microsoft, my roots were in the oddly married Digital VMS and Novell NetWare environment. Prior to that, I had a brief touch (although I don't usually admit it) in the IBM AS/400 environment. So the thought occurred to me: What if Exchange Server ran on the OS/400 or VMS operating system in the world of minicomputers and mainframes? In my associations with these environments, years of experience and learning from mistakes had gone before me. In other words, disaster recovery, reliability, management, and other proven techniques for guaranteeing system availability were taken for granted in the mainframe or minicomputer world. The procedures and practices had been practiced and honed to razor-sharp perfection over the last 20 years that these systems have been used in line-of-business computing activities. Organizations have run their businesses on these systems for years and have invested in the promise that they will be up and running when they need them.

Microsoft Windows NT/2000 for mission-critical line-of-business computing is a relatively new paradigm. This begs my question regarding the level of reverence we give to ensuring that these systems are available for the business-critical computing tasks we give them. Messaging, collaboration, and knowledge management applications are not free from these requirements. While it is true that some organizations may be able to get by without e-mail for a short period of time, collaborative and knowledge management applications are being implemented to replace key business processes that an organization cannot live without. Table 1.1 illustrates how the outages of certain types of business-critical processes and activities can cost organizations substantial amounts of money.

Table 1.1   *Typical Cost of Downtime by Business Type*

Business Activity	*Average Hourly Cost of Downtime*
E-commerce/brokerage site	$6,400,000
Credit card transactions	$2,600,000

Table 1.1   *Typical Cost of Downtime by Business Type (continued)*

Business Activity	Average Hourly Cost of Downtime
Catalog sales	$90,000
Package shipping and transport	$28,000

Source: Contingency Planning Research, Inc.

The other factor in this equation is hardware. Are we still treating our mission-critical server's hardware running Windows NT/2000 as PCs? Just over 10 years ago, Compaq introduced the first "server" called the Systempro. Until that time, desktop computers were simply turned on their side and put into the data center as servers running operating systems such as Novell NetWare or Banyan Vines and were used for file- and application-sharing tasks, most of which were not that mission-critical. With the advent of the PC server, we weren't really sure what to do with these devices. They were the same as our desktop computers (although some like the Compaq Systempro even had multiple processors) but also different. Being part of that revolution, I remember struggling with my desktop PC being used as a server and being frustrated with the fact that many of the taken-for-granted luxuries of the minicomputer environment were nowhere to be found here. At the time, there was no such thing as RAID disk arrays or redundant power supplies for my little NetWare fileserver. In addition, major availability technologies such as VAX/VMS Clusters and Compaq NonStop® Himilaya (both of which I think are really cool . . .) were nowhere to be found in my somewhat limited PC server world.

As far as disaster recovery, most Windows NT administrators and system operators have been left to figure this out on their own. I have many repressed memories of being paged at 10:00PM by the help desk to let me know that my fileserver had crashed and then spending the entire night trying to figure out how to get it back up in operation. At the time, tape drives and disaster recovery software were just becoming available for the PC server world. In the meantime, my friends back in the "glass house" found it humorous that I had crossed over into the dark side to find nothing but virgin territory when it came to building mission-critical systems.

My point here is that PC servers and operating systems like Novell's NetWare and Microsoft's Windows NT are, in relative terms, infants to the world of mission-critical line-of-business computing. The challenge we face for deploying mission-critical Exchange servers lies in understanding this issue and discovering how we can take tried and proven technologies for increasing system reliability and uptime and apply them to Exchange server deployments that *are* mission-critical in nature. As more and more business processes are moved to this environment and as new technologies for leveraging Exchange Server (such as knowledge management) are discovered, defined, and deployed, this issue will have to be addressed. Maybe the very thing preventing operating systems like Windows NT from "enterprise-level" acceptance is our failure to take them seriously.

1.1.5   The Vacuum for Information

All of this has left a terrible, deep-down groaning in the bellies of Exchange Server administrators and implementers everywhere. Even Microsoft's own documentation for Exchange Server disaster recovery and reliability has been somewhat lacking in the past. In fact, it wasn't until recently (Exchange 5.5) that Microsoft recognized that customers were in dire need of such assistance. Since then, Microsoft has been valiantly adding to the body of information available on this subject. Microsoft has begun to provide additional tools such as books, white papers, utilities, and additional Microsoft ATEC (Authorized Training and Education Center) courses that are targeted to meeting the growing need for knowledge for administrators and implementers. Microsoft has also recognized the need to work more closely with hardware vendors such as Compaq, Dell, HP, IBM, EMC, and Network Appliance.

With the Exchange 2000 release, a major design goal was to address this key area of concern—reliability. The Exchange 2000 release contains many improvements in storage management, backup and restore, clustering, and administration and management that will help organizations deploy mission-critical Exchange servers. Also, despite the fact that we will look deep into Exchange Server in this book and illustrate some weaknesses or identify potential areas for reliability improvements, most research indicates that Exchange still compares well to other messaging systems in terms of reliability (as shown in Table 1.2 from Creative Networks, Inc.).

Table 1.2   *Availability—Exchange and Domino Compared*

	Microsoft Exchange	*Lotus Notes/Domino*
Total downtime per year (hours)	27.2	75.2
Operation hours (yearly)	8,760	8,760
Availability (uptime)	99.7%	99.1%

Source: Creative Networks, Inc., 1998

Hardware manufacturers also recognize the tremendous opportunity to leverage their technology to improve Exchange Server reliability. In my work at Compaq managing our solutions engineering efforts around Exchange, this has been the major focus in our projects over the last year or two. Also, vendors besides Compaq such as EMC, Network Appliance, and others have recognized an opportunity as well. With so much attention on the need to make Exchange deployments more bulletproof, these vendors have targeted storage and backup solutions directly at filling this void. As organizations look to increase uptime for Exchange, they are also looking to their hardware and integration partners to assist them. In fact, in my work at Compaq, I work under the assumption that my customers will select their hardware vendor for Exchange based largely on the solutions, services, and deployment expertise for Exchange that the vendor brings to the table—not on the hardware by itself.

Service vendors have jumped on the Exchange high availability bandwagon as well. Compaq is the largest Exchange services provider with over six million Exchange users under deployment contract. In that extensive experience, the tremendous need for Exchange reliability has also been recognized. Illustrating this point, the top Exchange service providers like Compaq, Wang Global Services, IBM Global Services, Software Spectrum, and others have begun to offer services such as disaster recovery and high availability assessments to their Exchange customers. These services are designed to assess and identify the areas of vulnerability of a particular Exchange deployment and to assist the customer in assessing risks, developing plans, leveraging technology, defining service-level agreements, and the many other tasks that go into designing mission-critical deployments for Exchange Server.

The evolvement of Exchange Server from its early days of version 4.0 to the current release, Exchange Server 2000, has been somewhat responsible for creation of the current scenario. When the primary focus of Microsoft and hardware vendors was ensuring scalability for Exchange Server, Microsoft made great strides in providing code that would support thousands of users from a performance point of view. Also, storage barriers have been shattered with the advent of the 16TB (a.k.a. unlimited) store in Exchange Server 5.5 Enterprise Edition and parallel developments to increase storage capacity from hardware manufacturers. This has lead to a desire to deploy as many users on an Exchange Server as possible. Unfortunately, the ideal scenario has not materialized due to huge gaps between the number of users deployable from a performance viewpoint and the number of users deployable from a disaster recovery and reliability viewpoint. Microsoft's Windows NT and PC hardware platforms have contributed to this problem as well. The best practices, procedures, and discipline rooted in the days of "big iron" mainframes and minicomputers have not completely filtered down to this arena yet. This situation is improving, however, because Microsoft, hardware vendors, and third-party service providers have recognized that, first, there is tremendous void of information here, and second, there is a lot of money to be made in filling that void. As any author of technical material will attest, this isn't a Stephen King–like, money-making type of deal. However, motivated by the professional development opportunity, the filling of this information void for Exchange Server disaster recovery, reliability, and high availability was a primary goal in the endeavor of this book.

1.2   Assumptions about the Reader

At this point, I should pause and share my assumptions about the reader's knowledge and background. My assumption here is that you are already very familiar with the basics of Exchange Server and the history of the evolution of Microsoft's most successful piece of Back-Office. I assume, since you are reading this book, that you are taking the next steps in your knowledge of Exchange and are trying to complement your existing understandings about setup, deployment, administration, and management of Exchange with additional information about how to achieve the highest levels of reliability. You may also be looking for recommendations on best practices and for ideas on how some new or alternate technologies may be leveraged to reduce downtime. If you would like more detail on the basics, you can refer to some excellent references on Exchange Server that are available from Digital Press and other publishers. These can provide a basis for much of the information I will discuss. Table 1.3 highlights some of my top picks for Exchange Server reference materials. These references are more general in focus on administration and deployment for Exchange and provide solid discussions of many points on which I will not elaborate in this book.

Table 1.3   *Additional Suggested Reading for Microsoft Exchange Server*

Title	*Publisher*	*ISBN Number*	*Author*
Microsoft Exchange Server for Windows 2000	Digital Press	1-55558-224-9	Tony Redmond
Exchange Server 5.5 Unleashed	SAMS	0-672-21383-2	Greg Todd et al.
Notes From the Field: Managing and Maintaining Microsoft Exchange Server 5.5	Microsoft Press	0-7356-0528-9	Microsoft Press Microsoft MCS
Notes From the Field: Deploying Microsoft Exchange Server 5.5	Microsoft Press	0-7356-0529-7	Microsoft Press Microsoft MCS

Mission-Critical Microsoft Exchange 2000 seeks to explain and provide solutions for this most serious issue in Exchange Server deployments. The book will look at all of the various issues that administrators face when striving to ensure maximum reliability and disaster tolerance for Exchange Server. Exchange Server database technology, along with best practices for ensuring reliability and disaster recovery, will be covered in-depth. The content will span existing Exchange Server versions through 5.5 but will focus on new developments, techniques and technology available in the Exchange 2000 release. Topics such as disaster recovery planning and execution, high availability technologies such as clustering and high-end storage solutions, anti-virus and corruption prevention, proactive management techniques, operations and user training, etc., will be discussed in detail. The goal for *Mission-Critical Microsoft Exchange 2000* is to provide a comprehensive reference and guide for successful deployment of highly reliable, disaster-resilient Exchange Servers with the utmost levels of data protection.

1.2.1   Who Should Read This Book

- *Exchange deployment planners, implementers, and administrators*—Individuals responsible for planning, deployment, and operations activities for Microsoft Exchange Server within small, medium, and large enterprise corporate environments. These individuals have a foundational knowledge of Windows NT and Exchange Server but are seeking to augment this with Exchange Server-specific detail pertaining to disaster recovery and high availability. Due to the high visibility of disaster recovery and high availability within the Exchange environment, this market segment is extremely thirsty for this information.

- *Consultants, VARs, and integrators*—Channel and services-oriented organizations that specialize in Exchange Server deployments and that provide Exchange Disaster Recovery Services for corporate customers. These organizations are seeking reference material on this topic to provide expertise for their systems engineering and consulting teams in order to differentiate their services from competitors.

- *Press, analysts, and educational and industry research organizations*—Individuals or organizations conducting research or analysis focus on this subject matter. In particular, university-based computer science and management information systems courses dealing with disaster recovery strategies and techniques.

1.3   Inside Mission-Critical

Let us start down the path by looking at the definition of mission-critical as applied to Microsoft Exchange Server. In my mind, a mission-critical system running Exchange Server has several facets that should be included in our definition. These facets include reliability, scalability, security, manageability, and interoperability. Figure 1.1 identifies the major components of a mission-critical Exchange Server system or deployment.

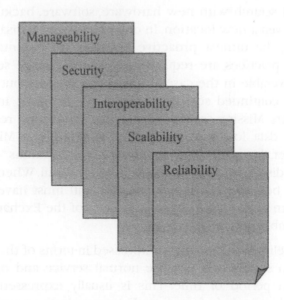

Figure 1.1
*Facets of a
mission-critical
system*

Manageability

Security

Interoperability

Scalability

Reliability

1.3.1   Reliability

When one considers the elements of a mission-critical server, the
first and most obvious is reliability. Reliability is, quite simply, the
ability to survive any interference with normal operations. Also, the
degree of interference does not always need to be catastrophic. For
example, in March of 1999, organizations worldwide fell victim to
the "Melissa" virus shutting down messaging systems everywhere.
While Melissa did not specifically destroy any data, it prevented
many users from accessing their messaging systems because these
systems were either shutdown by support staff as they scrambled to
remove the virus from information stores or were unavailable
because of the mail storms created as a result of the virus in action.
In this example, Exchange Server information stores did not need to
be restored from tape (in most cases), and once the virus had been
eradicated from the system, it was restored to normal operation. The
other extreme, however, is the scenario in which your Exchange
server or group of servers is completely destroyed, leaving nothing
but a memory. Recovering from a disaster of this type means starting

from scratch with new hardware, software, backup sets, and possibly even a new location. In order to tolerate a disaster of this magnitude, the utmost proactive planning, documentation, testing, and best practices are required. Reliable Exchange servers need to be recoverable in the case of a catastrophic loss but also need to provide continued services when even the most minor interruption occurs. Mission-critical servers also need to be resilient against not only data loss but also data corruption. For Microsoft Exchange Server, this most often manifests as the infamous "-1018 Error" that I will discuss in later chapters in more detail. When Exchange Server data becomes corrupted, support staff must have some options to return to the last known good state of the Exchange Server private or public information store.

Reliability is normally expressed in terms of the probability that a given system will provide normal service and operation during a given period of time. This is usually expressed as a percentage within a period of one year. For example, the e-mail system achieved 99.99% reliability in 1999. Many are not sure what this really means. In addition, we often hear the terms "four nines" or "five nines" of reliability thrown around today. One rule of thumb that I have often heard is that "five nines" (99.999%) translates to five minutes per year. That is one method of quick reference but Table 1.4 may explain this a little better.

Table 1.4   *Reliability and Downtime—24×7 (365 days per year or 8,760 hours)*

Availability/Reliability ("Nines")	*Downtime*
90% (one nine)	876 hours (36.5 days)
99% (two nines)	87.6 hours (3.65 days)
99.9% (three nines)	8.76 hours
99.99% (four nines)	3,153 seconds (52.55 minutes)
99.999% (five nines)	315 seconds (5.25 minutes)
99.9999% (six nines)	31.5 seconds

The U.S. government, IEEE, and many standards organizations have guidelines for calculating reliability for electronics and computer systems as well. Table 1.5 provides some basics for calculation of system availability that are used industry-wide.

Table 1.5   *Reliability Formulas*

Measure	Formula/Equation
Failure rate (b)	$b = 1/MTBF$ Where: MTBF = (mean time between failure)
Reliability (R)	$R = e^{-bT}$ Where: e = natural logarithm b = failure rate T = time (period to be measured)
Reliability of parallel systems (Rp)	$R_p = 1 - [(1-R1) \times (1-R2) \times \ldots (1-Rn)]$ Where: R1...Rn = reliability (R) of each system in parallel
Reliability of series systems (Rs)	$R_s = R1 \times R2 \times \ldots Rn$ Where: R1... Rn = Reliability (R) of each system in the series

Source: MIL-STD and IEEE

Closely tied to reliability is recoverability. When we discuss recoverability for Exchange Server, it is assumed that the server has already become unavailable. Thus, we have a need to recover it. A reliable Exchange Server must have a high degree of recoverability. Recoverability need not only address such subjects as reinstalling software and restoring data from tape, it must also address whatever is necessary to get users up and running as soon as possible after a failure. Better yet, recoverability should endeavor to restore normal operation before users are even aware of the outage. For example, as long as a user has access to his inbox and can send and receive mail, he could be considered recovered. An example of this could be a scenario in which an Exchange server's information store becomes corrupted. One angle of attack on this problem could be to immediately move as many mailboxes as possible to a spare backup Exchange server. Once the move is complete, these users are back in operation, in many cases experiencing little or no loss in productivity. While no actual recovery in the form of a restore from tape occurred, the system achieves a higher degree of availability than simply starting over and restoring the database from tape.

Recoverability should be viewed in the same light as fault tolerance versus fault recovery. Fault-tolerance technologies such as RAID disk arrays, ECC memory, redundant power supplies, clustering, etc., provide a means to tolerate faults that occur without causing downtime. ECC memory, for example, can detect and correct single- and double-bit memory errors by including some extra bits (i.e., 72 vs. 64 bits) in the memory subsystem that can be used to verify the integrity of the data being read from system memory. Thus, if one or two bits are incorrect, the memory system can correct the error without the system crashing. Another example is redundant network interface cards (NICs). Server vendors like Compaq provide technologies that allow two NICs in a server to function as backups to each other called NIC Teaming. If the primary NIC fails or experiences a cable fault, the secondary NIC will transparently pick up where the primary left off—all without interrupting the operation of the server.

Fault tolerance is very important, but you also need a second line of defense—fault recovery. Fault recovery is exhibited as a method of ensuring that the system will rapidly recover in the event of a critical fault that could not be tolerated. For example, PC-based servers available today do not provide online processor redundancy similar to what is available in Compaq's Himalaya NonStop® systems. The next best thing, however, is the ability to quickly recover in the event that one processor in a multiple-processor system fails. In the past, if a processor failed, the system would simply halt, and an administrator would need to diagnose and repair the failed processor before returning the system to normal operation. Today, however, many server vendors provide the capability for offline processor recovery. Offline processor recovery quickly recovers the server in the event of a processor failure. When the processor fails, the system BIOS senses the condition and reboots the system with the bad processor disabled. The end result for multiprocessor systems is that, if one CPU fails, the system will reboot and return to normal operation on the remaining good processors. In this case, a fault was not avoided, but the system was quickly recovered.

Recoverability also extends into backup and restore operations. In the event that no other option exists, an Exchange server needs to have the capability to be recovered from tape in the most expedient manner. In later chapters, we will discuss methods, tools, and best practices for ensuring expedient recovery of Exchange servers. These methods are not limited to tape-based restoration, however. With so many alternate technologies available, such as snapshots and data replication, these tools can also be employed as additional measures for increasing the recoverability and ultimately the availability for Exchange server deployments.

Reliability (and recoverability) is the cornerstone of mission-critical servers. An understanding of how to measure reliability will be crucial later on when we discuss service-level definitions and analyze Exchange Server downtime causes. It is important to understand that reliability for an Exchange Server is determined by many factors. A surprising fact is that hardware failures account for fewer root-cause cases of server downtime for Exchange Server as well as many other mission-critical applications. Root causes such as software errors, operational issues, and personnel account for more system downtime than hardware does. According to Strategic Planning Research, Inc., less than 20% of computer system downtime is caused by equipment failures. Data from OnTrack International and other sources shows similar trends. The most significant cause—human error—can be attributed to poor planning and procedures, lack of training, and a myriad of other human factors. Throughout this book, I hope to emphasize this point and provide some of the education that we as Exchange Server designers, implementers, operators, and administrators need to reduce this factor and its impact on mission-critical Exchange Server deployments.

1.3.2   Scalability

Most hardware vendors who have an interest in the huge Exchange Server deployment opportunity that has developed in the last several years have invested in the resources and personnel required for producing and publishing performance, scalability, and benchmarking information for Microsoft Exchange Server. With the release of Exchange Server 5.5 and subsequently Exchange Server 2000, the published performance results have experienced a vast leap. Figure 1.2 illustrates the substantial performance improvements that the most recent versions of Microsoft Exchange Server have yielded.

As is evident in Figure 1.2, Microsoft has solved the most relevant performance issues related to Exchange Server with the most recent versions. Recent improvements in hardware technology such as

Figure 1.2
*Exchange
Server
performance
based on MMB
benchmarks*

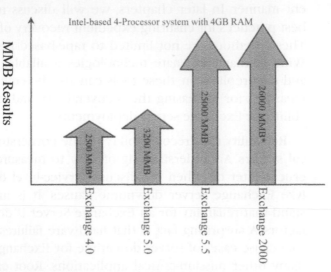

Intel-based 4-Processor system with 4GB RAM

MMB Results

2500 MMB* Exchange 4.0

3200 MMB Exchange 5.0

25000 MMB Exchange 5.5

26000 MMB* Exchange 2000

* Results extrapolated and normalized based on common MMB measurement.
MMB did not exist for Exchange 4.0 and MMB2 has replaced it for Exchange 2000.

Intel Pentium III Xeon, 8-processor systems, and disk subsystem advances (along with operating system improvements from Windows NT 3.51, 4.0, and now Windows 2000) have also contributed to performance and scalability improvements for Exchange Server.

The benchmarks do not tell the whole story, however. When hardware vendors set out to provide Exchange Server benchmarking information, the focus is on optimal performing systems. As a result, published benchmarks are performed using top-of-the-line hardware configurations that represent the latest available server platforms from each vendor. Since before Exchange Server 4.0 shipped, I have been involved with Exchange Server benchmarking activities for Compaq Computer Corporation. Early on in our efforts to provide customers with performance information around Microsoft Exchange Server, I sought to provide performance results that were based only on what I called *customer-deployable scenarios*. Customer-deployable scenarios translate to providing benchmarks based on server configurations that organizations would actually use when deploying Microsoft Exchange Server. For example, most organizations may not deploy their Exchange servers with 4GB of RAM installed on every box. A less obvious example would be configuring a disk subsystem for RAID5 instead of RAID0. Ideally, to achieve maximum performance, one would configure a disk subsystem used for benchmarking for RAID0 since it provides the best performance in the majority of environments. In my benchmarking activities at Compaq, I sought to produce only benchmarks based on RAID5 or RAID0+1 disk arrays. RAID5 suffers heavily in a write-intensive environment like that of Exchange Server. My goal, however, was to use RAID5 since most organizations would use RAID5 or RAID1/0+1 when designing and deploying their Exchange servers. While RAID5 does not yield the highest performance, it does provide data protection and offers a reasonable trade-off between performance and data protection. Thus, my thought process was that benchmarks for Exchange Server based on these "real-world" server configurations would be much more useful and credible to organizations that were using the information I produced for making key Exchange Server deployment decisions.

My thinking had one small flaw—never neglect the marketing implications of your benchmarking activities. Soon my competitors from other companies like Digital Equipment Corporation (obviously, previous to Compaq's acquisition), Hewlett-Packard, and others were providing better benchmark numbers than mine based on server configurations utilizing RAID0 disk subsystems. This was understandable since RAID0 can provide as much as 40% more (depending on a number of factors) I/Os per second than the same number of disk drives configured as RAID5. The matter of using RAID0 versus RAID5 was discussed with Microsoft and the other hardware vendors, and the decision (with which I reluctantly agreed) was made that RAID0 benchmarks for Exchange Server would be allowed providing that the vendor specified that RAID0 provided no data protection capabilities in the event of disk failure. The result was that benchmark results climbed higher and higher as vendors including Compaq abandoned my dream of customer-deployable scenarios in favor of publishing the highest possible result.

In October of 1998, Microsoft formalized the Exchange Server benchmarking business by releasing the MAPI Messaging Benchmark (MMB). MMB not only was a defined workload based on Microsoft's LoadSim tool, it also was a process and set of guidelines that hardware vendors must follow in order to publish valid results based on a consistent and reproducible methodology. Microsoft's goal in promoting the MMB specification was to level the playing field of benchmarking for Exchange Server by asking vendors to adhere to the guidelines and audit process that Microsoft felt was necessary to ensure that meaningful benchmarks were published for Exchange Server. Microsoft also hoped to shift the focus of Exchange benchmarking from users per server to a more abstract notion such as what the Transaction Performance Council (TPC) had achieved in the relational database environment with benchmarks such as TPC-A, TPC-B, TPC-C, TPC-D, etc.

The concern that Microsoft had (and still has) was that hardware vendors were publishing benchmark numbers that were much higher than the actual deployment numbers. For example, at the time, the highest benchmark result was Compaq's ProLiant 7000 with 15,000 medium users per server. In practice, organizations were deploying far fewer users per server than the benchmark indicated was possible. The problem was twofold. First, the medium user profile for LoadSim did not necessarily reflect the actual workload profile for a typical corporate MAPI user. In some cases, the LoadSim medium user was too heavy, and in others, it was too light. In certain areas such as server CPU utilization and memory usage, the LoadSim medium user accurately loaded the Exchange server. In other areas such as disk I/O and network utilization, it was not even close to what production Exchange servers were experiencing. Exchange benchmarks also lacked consideration for key deployment factors such as capacity, disaster recovery, and high availability.

Servers cannot be mission-critical in nature if they can't handle the demands of large user loads and the growth trends in system capacity that accompany them. For Exchange Server, scalability has recently taken a back seat to reliability. Although it's not the focus of this book, I would be remiss if I did not discuss Exchange Server performance and scalability in relationship to mission-critical systems. In Chapter 9 (Bringing It All Together with Proactive Management), we will also discuss performance management, which is the key to achieving scalable servers that respond to growth in user capacity. When discussing scalability, it is important to look at it in terms of a two-sided coin. Side one, the most-thought-of, is performance scalability. Simply put, as the server's workload increases, how does the server respond and meet this demand? The other side of the coin is capacity scalability. Capacity scalability involves the degree to which a server can meet the ever-increasing demands for more—more disk space, more information stores, more messages, more attachments, more directory entries, etc. Table 1.6 illustrates some different components of performance versus capacity scalability.

Table 1.6   *Comparing Performance Versus Capacity Scalability*

Performance Scalability	Capacity Scalability
I/Os per second	Information store size
Instructions per second	Directory size
Transactions per second	Mailbox size
Messages per second	Users per server
Megabytes per second	Messages per folder

More traditionally, scalability is viewed in terms of the additional work that can be done by adding more resources. The additional resources are items like more processors, memory, disks, threads, processes, and buffers. The additional work could be in the form of more users, transactions, messages, or megabytes. For Exchange Server, scalability is manifested in many ways. Scalability may be the number of users that a given hardware platform will support. Alternately, scalability may be the degree to which the Exchange directory (for Exchange 5.5) or the Active Directory (in the case of Exchange 2000) is able to grow. This is not a crucial point, but it's one worth mentioning. Depending on your context and frame of reference, scalability means different things to different people. Nonetheless, scalability is an essential element of mission-critical servers.

1.3.3   Using Benchmarks Wisely

It is important to understand that MMB benchmarks are designed to give Exchange Server implementation planners some baseline references for understanding the capabilities of hardware platforms from a single vendor as compared to other competing hardware vendors. The most important aspect of benchmark interpretation is an understanding of how to compare different results. This is true not only for messaging applications but for everything from SPECMarks to WinMarks to TPC as well. When interpreting these benchmarks in terms of Exchange Server scalability, four rules of thumb should be kept in mind.

First, compare only results based on similar methodologies and user profiles. It is unwise to compare the popular TPC-C benchmark for Online Transaction Processing (OLTP) applications to the TPC-D benchmark for decision support applications. Applying this analogy to the messaging benchmarks, it would be unfair to compare the NotesBench results to the LoadSim/MMB results. It would also be unwise to compare LoadSim results based on different profiles such as comparing 1,000 medium users to 1,000 heavy users. The workloads and user profiles in each of these benchmarks are different. Compare results only when you are sure that a user from result A is similar to a user from result B.

Second, compare only results based on similar operating system architectures. Comparing results for benchmarks run on the Windows NT/2000 operating system to those run on a NetWare or UNIX platform is inappropriate. Results from competing messaging server vendors (such as Lotus) are often conducted on platforms supporting alternate operating system architectures (such as UNIX, AIX, and OS/400) that support 64-bit addresses and up to 64GB of RAM. These operating systems are very different from Microsoft Windows NT/2000, and as a result, comparisons are not necessarily valid. Compare only results for Exchange Server on Windows NT to like results.

Third, compare only results based on similar hardware configurations. While it is important for end users to compare results from vendor to vendor, it is not appropriate to compare dissimilar configurations. For example, a 15,000 MMB result from Vendor A was performed on a system supporting 16 drives configured in a RAID0 configuration for the information store. Vendor B published results that show 1,000 more users on a seemingly comparable server platform to Vendor A's result. Digging deeper, we find that Vendor B used a 24-drive disk subsystem, while Vendor A achieved its results with only 16 drives. In this example, the additional I/O capacity of six more disk drives easily accounts for the additional 1,000 users. We can find differences in most published results—remember to look closely! Compare results that are based on similar hardware configurations, and more importantly, compare them to those you would deploy in your own environment.

Finally, the fourth rule is to consider price versus performance when comparing results. Many published benchmark results touting tens of thousands of transactions per second or users per server are achieved utilizing gargantuan hardware configurations. You should consider not only whether these are customer-deployable scenarios but also the relative price/performance ratio when comparing results. The question to ask is, "Do you get a 20% performance benefit at 100% increased cost?" Consider not only price/performance but also the total cost of ownership (TCO) for a specific vendor's solution. This encompasses all that a particular vendor has to offer. Many other hardware vendors simply sell boxes. Comparing apples to apples and interpreting messaging server performance benchmarks requires diligence and an understanding of what is really "under the covers." It is important for implementers and planners to not get caught in marketing hype surrounding the world of published benchmark results for Exchange Server. More importantly, MMB or MMB2 results are not the only measure of Exchange Server scalability. The subject of Exchange Server scalability alone could warrant an entire book devoted to the subject. In the context of building mission-critical Exchange Servers, scalability should not be overlooked simply because disaster recovery and reliability issues seem more at the forefront.

For Exchange 2000, Microsoft has plans to support the MMB2 workload for MAPI users. MMB2 (developed by Compaq) will consist of a much different user workload profile resulting in heavier resource utilization on the server. This is accomplished by modifying the workload profile in LoadSim. Task frequencies, mix, and durations are adjusted in order to generate more accurate loads on individual server resources such as disk and processor. In addition, the actual message and attachment files will be modified. The result will be a more realistic loading of the Exchange server during benchmark runs. The goal for MMB2 will be to have benchmark results in line with actual deployment users per server.

Another important point regarding benchmark results is that, with Exchange 2000, it is expected that more companies will begin to deploy non-MAPI clients such as IMAP, POP3, and browser-based (HTTP) clients. As these new clients become mainstream for Exchange server deployments, new methods and standards for benchmarking will have to be developed. At this writing, several hardware vendors along with Microsoft are working on industry-standard Internet protocol-based messaging benchmark suites. Once developed, Microsoft and other messaging vendors will encourage these results be published in addition to MMB and MMB2 results. The hope is that, in the future, benchmark results for Exchange Server will bear a closer relation to actual deployments. Scalability and performance have been adequately demonstrated for Exchange Server in its four-year history as a product. In my opinion, this is an area in which implementers of Exchange are less concerned. While scalability remains a key concern, disaster recovery and other facets of mission-critical servers often overshadow.

1.3.4   Security

The next facet of mission-critical Exchange Servers is security. An entire portfolio of reliability and scalability best practices and tools will not be enough if your messaging system is not secure. Secure messaging systems must be bulletproof in terms of virus, sabotage, denial of service, and other forms of attack. Chapter 8 (Don't Overlook Security as a Powerful, High Availability Measure) will be devoted to this key element. For a mission-critical messaging server, there are several perimeters that must be defended. These include gateways, networks, message stores, and clients. Gateways provide an opening for mail storm attacks, viruses, and other forms of attack. The network wire is open to "snooping," "spoofing," and "sniffing." Message stores and mailboxes are potentially open for unauthorized persons to access and viruses to destroy or infect. Client systems can be a point of access or the point of origin for viruses and unauthorized persons to access the entire system. Mission-critical servers must provide mechanisms to defend these perimeters. Exchange Server provides many security mechanisms and tools for preventing these attacks. Table 1.7 highlights some of the most common security breeches and denial-of-service attacks and the built-in tools that Exchange has to protect against them.

Table 1.7   *Built-in Security Mechanisms for Exchange Server*

Attack	*Perimeters*	*Exchange Protection*
Virus	Gateway, message store, and client	None (third party)
Sniffing	Message store, network, and gateway	Message encryption

Table 1.7   *Built-in Security Mechanisms for Exchange Server (continued)*

Attack	Perimeters	Exchange Protection
Spoofing	Message store, network, and gateway	Digital signatures
Mail storm/SPAM/UCE	Gateway	IMS/SMTP configuration

Unfortunately, security is often overlooked when designing mission-critical servers. With so much focus on reliability, disaster recovery, and scalability, implementers are often hard-pressed to allocate planning cycles to address security issues. Contributing to the problem, tools and mechanisms to address security issues have only recently become available for Exchange Server. Prior to version 5.5, only minimal mechanisms were available in Exchange to protect against the most common forms of attack. In addition, many organizations do not have security expertise in-house and often must rely on expensive consultants to deploy some of the more advanced security measures required.

1.3.5   Manageability

Personally, I believe that proactive management techniques are the key component to highly available Exchange Servers. Many shortcomings in other areas, such as reliability, scalability, and security, can be overcome or compensated for by applying the right management tools, methodologies, and philosophies to your deployment. These can be characterized as follows:

- *Technical knowledge*—A good understanding of the technology that Microsoft Exchange Server uses and that surrounds it, such as Windows NT/2000. Good training and access to an environment for experimentation (such as a lab) are the keys to the ability to understand Exchange Server in order to perform proactive management. Utilizing industry sources such as magazines, white papers, and support databases can also be invaluable in this area.

- *A systems approach*—This is an understanding that any management solution is a careful balance between things you have some control over (i.e., hardware, OS, network) and those that are somewhat more elusive (i.e., control over users and outside issues that cause problems). This is the ability to look at the "big picture" when making decisions about your Exchange Server deployment. Again, a proactive approach is what is called for here.

- *Planning and design*—The Windows NT/2000 and Exchange Server environment can be very complex. Effective planning, design, and pilot activities must take place before deployment in order to identify and resolve problems before production. It is a lot easier to resolve issues during the design phase than during the production phase of any information technology deployment.

- *Configuration management*—The Exchange Server environment offers many variables. Key to any successful deployment is the ability to manage and control these variables. The most successful Exchange Server deployments actively manage and monitor these variables. These are items such as registry tuning, drivers, OS and application variations, service packs, hotfixes, firmware updates, etc.

- *Establishment of service-level agreements and performance management*—It is often commonplace for organizations to manage performance in a reactive manner (i.e., when users complain). The Windows NT and Exchange Server environment offers rich capabilities in this area. In addition, many third parties such as BMC and NETIQ, (and others) offer management tools that aid in the proactive management of Exchange servers. The definition of service-level agreements (SLAs) is an effective method of measuring performance proactively. SLAs prompt the monitoring of various performance characteristics within the Exchange Server environment in order to measure the degree to which these service levels are being met. We will discuss the definition and establishment of service-level agreements in the next chapter. The establishment of service-level agreements is also a key driver for other aspects of manageability such as problem management and performance management.

Through the use of proactive management practices, I have seen many organizations drastically reduce Exchange Server downtime. Proactive management calls for the preceeding items—technical knowledge, high-level approach, planning and design, configuration management, and the establishment of criteria in which to assess your success (SLAs).

A thesis for this book sums up my point (more on this in Chapter 9). Only through understanding and proactive planning, design, and implementation can a system such as Exchange achieve mission-critical capabilities. Furthermore, success comes only through a thorough understanding of Exchange itself, as well as the technologies we can employ such as disaster recovery, storage, clustering, and management to increase system reliability. In addition, if the first and only focus of our system planning is on performance, scalability, and server sizing, we can hardly expect a system to achieve a high degree of uptime.

1.3.6   Interoperability

We would be foolish to think that an Exchange Server deployment (or any client/server system, for that matter) operates in a vacuum. There are not only many other messaging system choices but also protocols, transports, and standards by which these systems operate. The term *interoperability* comes from this scenario. Interoperability means that a system has to communicate effectively with clients, servers, and systems that surround it. Take SMTP or X.400, for example. Although these standards have been widely implemented by a host of vendors, not all systems are perfectly compatible. Luckily, in the case of Exchange Server, Microsoft has performed valiantly in terms of providing basic compatibility among systems using these standards. Better still, there are various compatibility tuning options and parameter settings that allow for ironing out most rough spots encountered along the way. Interoperability is a key facet of a mission-critical messaging system. Without the ability to interoperate seamlessly with other messaging, directory, and networking systems, an Exchange Server deployment would be an island—unable to reach beyond it's own barriers of incompatibility. Messaging systems have several areas of key importance where interoperability in concerned. Table 1.8 summarizes these areas.

Table 1.8   *Key Areas of Interoperability for Mission-Critical Messaging Systems*

Interoperability Factor	Standards and Protocols
Client	MAPI, POP3, IMAP, HTTP, SMTP
Mail transport	X.400, SMTP, RPC

Table 1.8   *Key Areas of Interoperability for Mission-Critical Messaging Systems (continued)*

Interoperability Factor	Standards and Protocols
Security	X.509, SSL, S/MIME, TLS, E/SMTP, Kerberos
Directory services	DAPI, LDAP, X.500, ADSI
Network services	TCP/IP, IPX/SPX, RPC

Microsoft Exchange Server fares very well in the area of interoperability out of the box. In addition, Exchange also provides configuration options in various components to achieve a high degree of interoperability with other systems. Microsoft is also very active in the various working groups within organizations such as the Internet Engineering Task Force (IETF), both in proposing new standards as well as in working to improve or adopt emerging standards that impact both Windows NT/Windows 2000 and Exchange Server. Interoperability has become a mandatory requirement for vendors of messaging and collaboration servers. Most organizations do not support a completely homogeneous environment and do not tolerate vendors who promote these environments. In addition, as businesses and organizations more and more turn to the Internet as a place of doing business and sharing information, none can afford to deploy any mission-critical systems that do not support a high degree of interoperability.

1.4   How This Book Is Organized

Over the last several years, as I have talked with organizations and individuals deploying Exchange Server into mission-critical environments, it has become ever so apparent that no complete work or body of knowledge is available that addresses this topic in its entirety for Microsoft Exchange Server. Microsoft and other sources provide bits and pieces of this information but fail in completeness and accuracy. Also, even though much of this information is available, there is no comprehensive resource that brings all of the issues together and addresses them in the context of Exchange Server. The information and technologies also change at a rapid rate that is often difficult for most deployments to keep pace with. The goal and mission for this book is to provide a complete and accurate resource for

Exchange Server deployment personnel to use in their daily activities. My hope is that the material provided will truly provide a basis for deploying mission-critical Exchange within any organization.

The book is organized into three main sections that helped me manage my thought processes during the course of this project. My hope is that this organizational method will also be translated into your understanding as you approach, plan, implement, and evolve these best practices and techniques for your Exchange environment. Figure 1.3 illustrates the organization of this book as an approach to building mission-critical Exchange environments from the ground up with each layer resting on the foundation of the previous.

Figure 1.3
*Building
mission-critical
Exchange
Servers*

Building Mission Critical Exchange Servers

Foundation Layer			
Mission Critical Defined	Analyzing Downtime	Exchange Server Storage and Database Technology	Exchange Server Disaster Recovery Technology
Technology and Practice Layer			
Disaster Recovery Best Practices	Storage Technology	Cluster Technology	Security Technology
Management Layer			
Proactive Management and Administration			

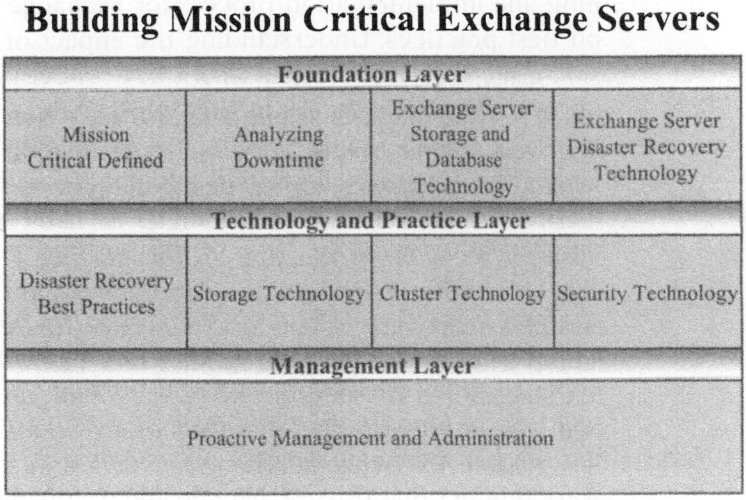

The first section is the foundation layer. The chapters in this section form a basis for proceeding through the entire book. They start with the definition of what mission-critical means to an Exchange deployment and show you how to analyze, assess risk and downtime, and set service-level requirements that meet your organizational needs for reliability of your messaging, collaboration, or knowledge management system, the basis of which Exchange Server will form.

Any foundation layer would not be complete without providing a detailed understanding of Exchange Server technology such as the database engine and disaster recovery technology. We will take an in-depth look at the Exchange Server database fundamental technology that is key to beginning any discussion on Exchange reliability or disaster recovery. This first section will prepare you for later discussions on backup and restore and for when technologies such as clustering or data replication are applied in later sections.

The next section is the technology and practices layer. This section will be the "meat and potatoes" of my discussions about providing solid disaster recovery for Exchange Server. First, there is a discussion of how Exchange Server disaster recovery is accomplished and the methods provided by Microsoft for Exchange Server backup and restore. Next, I will address the disaster recovery planning and implementation process for Exchange Server with a focus on best practices. Understanding the impact of growth in any mission-critical environment is also a key concern. Many organizations do not adequately factor in this impact when developing disaster recovery plans, sizing servers, or estimating deployment costs. Finally, this section will provide a comprehensive look at the various hardware and software technologies available for Exchange Server disaster recovery at the time of this writing. This will address storage, clustering, snapshots, and data replication technologies that are available from various vendors to increase the reliability and recoverability of applications such as Microsoft Exchange Server. Using the enhancements of section two will provide an understanding that will help to identify the next level of investment available for ensuring reliable Exchange servers. An overview of the selection of software product that provide backup and restore support for Exchange as well as the hardware devices they support will be provided. This section will bring together the myriad of information available on best practices, tools, technologies, and procedures for Exchange disaster recovery and high availability.

The final section of this book (the management layer) deals with proactive management technologies and techniques that should be applied by every IS organization—not just Exchange Server deployments. With the first two sections as a foundation, this section builds on these layers by discussing the importance of security and proactive management for achieving mission-critical environments. The focus of this last section is to identify how administrators and implementers can be more proactive about ensuring reliability for Exchange Server. This section would not be complete without a look at security issues and protection from malicious activities such as viruses and denial-of-service attacks. Proactive management and administration techniques, along with establishment of solid configuration and change management practices, will comprise the core of the section. In fact, one of the fundamental theses for this book is that management practices can have the most significant effect on Exchange Server reliability and high availability.

Mission-critical Exchange servers are a reality today. However, much of the onus for ensuring reliability and meeting service-level agreements falls on the Exchange deployment planners, implementers, and administrators. Microsoft alone can not provide all the tools that one needs for disaster-tolerant and reliable Exchange servers. By partnering with Microsoft and third-party hardware, software, and service vendors, the highest levels of uptime can be achieved for Microsoft Exchange Server deployments. My hope is that this book provides a starting point and basis for successful implementation of *Mission-Critical Microsoft Exchange 2000*.

2

Analyzing Downtime Outages

As I charge down the path of building a mission-critical Exchange deployment, it wouldn't be prudent to start without a discussion and investigation into downtime and outages for Exchange Server. If your messaging system has become mission-critical, the cost of downtime can be devastating to an organization. These costs can come in the form of lost revenue, lost opportunity, failed service-level agreements (SLAs), and/or noncompliance/performance penalties. This does not even consider the fixed costs that an organization must pay whether its employees are working or not. What can be the most damaging are the losses that are incalculable such as the loss of customer relationships or satisfaction. When your customers and business partners are affected by an outage in your messaging system, they may perceive a poorly run organization that they are not excited to do business with. As a result, our discussions around outage and downtime should begin in the business context. In other words, what does downtime of your Exchange deployment cost the company? The higher the costs, the more dollars are justified for deploying high availability measures and investing in personnel and procedures. The more successful an organization is in delivering the levels of reliability required, the faster a return on investment can be realized.

In this chapter, we will look at the enemy of mission-critical systems—downtime. It is important that we have a consensus on how downtime is to be measured and the affect this will have on how the Exchange deployment is viewed by users and management. I will not treat downtime as a simple concept but as a complex series of components. My thesis here is that, by understanding the internals of a downtime event, organizations can reduce the overall event and provide a means of continuous process improvement. Finally, the understanding of downtime and its measurement can help organizations set reasonable goals for achieving mission-critical operation. Understanding, measuring, and determining the cost of downtime is the key to making business case arguments for further investments in mission-critical technologies and services.

2.1   How Do You Measure Downtime?

Often taken for granted or misunderstood is the measurement of downtime for computer systems. We mistakenly assume that everyone measures downtime for Exchange Server in the same fashion. Typically, we conclude that downtime is the total number of hours that the server is unavailable. For example, as I discussed in Chapter 1, if the server was down for 8.76 hours or less in one year, we conclude that 99.9% availability was achieved. However, not all organizations measure downtime in the same manner.

One common alternative to a simple measure of server inaccessibility is the *lost client opportunity* method. With this method, the number of times a client or user attempts to perform a function and is unable to is tracked. In other words, when your Exchange server is down, you cannot access e-mail. Instead of tracking the number of hours that your Exchange server is unavailable, you could track lost client opportunities to do work. This method of measurement is derived from the telephone system and other "dial-tone" services in which system users expect the system to be available when usage is attempted. If your organization views the e-mail system in a similar manner as the telephone system, this method of downtime measurement may be appropriate for you. Essentially, whether you are measuring actual server downtime or lost client opportunities, the same downtime is being measured. However, when you are looking at downtime statistics, one method may yield different results than another. When you are looking at the amount of time a server is down, there is not necessarily any element of client service factored in. When lost client hours or opportunities are measured, client service is the primary concern. In order to determine which method of measurement is appropriate for your organization, let's take a look at both methods of measuring downtime for a hypothetical one-hour downtime event (during a one-month period) that impacts an Exchange server supporting 2,000 users.

2.1.1   Method 1: Simple Server Downtime

This method simply measures how many hours a particular server was down without regard to how many users a server supports or the lost services for those users. The amount of downtime for a server is compared against the total service hours in one year (8,760 hours for yearly 7×24 operations or 720 hours for a 30-day month). Dividing the downtime hours by 8,760 provides this comparison. The result is the commonly used "nines of availability."

Server Availability

720 hours – 1 hour = 720 hours = 99.86%

2.1.2   Method 2: Lost Client Opportunity

This method directly considers the client services affected by a server outage. Using this approach, the number of users each server supports becomes more important. In our hypothetical scenario, the server has a user load of 2,000. When calculating availability for the server, the user load is included. The number of users is multiplied by the total lost service time, yielding a total lost service measurement. The total service is then divided by the total service opportunity for the system or some other period. In my experience, organizations will use a service interval such as 1 million or 100,000 hours. This method will yield results that are based on the lost client opportunities for the service period (720 hours for our hypothetical scenario). The resulting measure is a figure of lost client opportunity (hours) for the total client-service period.

Server Availability

$(720 \times 2000) - (1 \times 2000)/(720 \times 2000) = 99.86\%$

As you can see, a simple measurement using either method will yield the same result. Both measurements yielded a 99.86% availability measure for the server. However, using a deployment-wide measurement such as lost opportunity hours per 1 million hours can yield very different results because individual server metrics are masked as the focus shifts from server outage to client service hours and opportunity. Figure 2.1 shows how this measurement may look for a large deployment scenario measured monthly with a sample period of 1 million workstation hours.

Figure 2.1
*Lost client
opportunity
downtime
measurement
data*

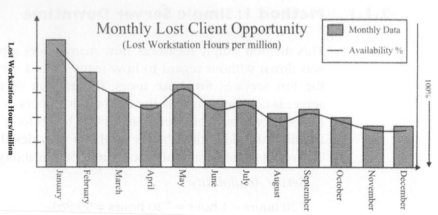

Although the preceding discussion may seem like splitting hairs, the method you choose to track and view downtime data for your deployment is important. This is of particular importance when you are being held accountable for SLAs for availability. As a system manager, you may want to select the measurement method that most closely matches how your SLAs are defined and that fits best into the traditional measurements used historically in your organization.

In order to determine what the availability requirements are for your Exchange deployment, you need to understand several key issues. The process of planning and architecting a system that delivers the required levels of availability includes these steps:

1. Understand the cost of downtime for your messaging system.

2. Understand the anatomy of downtime for your Exchange deployment.

3. Access the causes of downtime in your Exchange deployment.

4. Set service-level agreements.

5. Architect the system with steps 1–4 in mind.

2.2   Step 1: What Is the Cost of Exchange Downtime?

Step one of the process focuses on understanding what happens to your organization when the messaging system goes down. This can run the gambit from catastrophic to inconvenient. This may also vary by department or business activity. For example, some departments may be able to do without the ability to send e-mail for several hours or longer. Other departments, such as customer service, shipping, or supply-chain management, may require constant use and access to e-mail as well as collaborative applications that may be deployed using Exchange. In addition, as more business processes are automated and made available as collaborative or knowledge management applications, the Exchange system will become more mission-critical. In order to measure the cost of downtime, you need to know the answer to this question: "Who gets hurt and how badly?" Obviously, I can't answer this question for each and every organization. However, there is some research available for Exchange Server from various organizations that can shed some light on the cost of Exchange downtime in a general sense. Creative Networks, Inc. (CNI), published a study in 1998 called *Benchmark TCO: Microsoft Exchange and Lotus Notes/Domino in the Enterprise* that explained reliability and the cost of downtime for Exchange Server and Lotus Notes/Domino environments. Table 2.1 summarizes some of the report's findings where downtime is concerned.

Table 2.1   *Downtime Incidents and Duration for Microsoft Exchange and Lotus Notes/Domino*

	Microsoft Exchange	*Lotus Notes/ Domino*
Unscheduled or unplanned downtime incidents per month	2.0	3.2
Length of typical downtime incident (minutes)	97	35
Total downtime per month (minutes)	136.0	375.9
Total downtime per year (hours)	27.2	75.2

Source: Creative Networks, Inc., 1998

I found two things to be notable in this study. First, Exchange deployments were found to experience significantly fewer unscheduled or unplanned downtime incidents in a typical month. Closely related was the fact that Exchange also experiences less total downtime per month and per year than Lotus Notes/Domino. The second point is even more important for our discussion. Although Exchange deployments experience fewer incidents and less total downtime, incidents in the Exchange environment tend to last longer. According to Table 2.1, the length of a typical incident for Exchange is 97 minutes versus 35 minutes for Lotus Notes/Domino.

When moving through step 1 (the cost of downtime), you will need to answer the questions about who is affected and how much it costs your Exchange deployment. The areas to look at are processes, programs and projects, revenue, people, and operations. For processes, vital business processes might be interrupted, lost, corrupted, or altered if your Exchange deployment falters. Such processes might include order and supply-chain management, financial reporting, transaction-notification systems, manufacturing systems, human resources, etc. When downtime affects programs or projects, both long-term and short-term revenue can be impacted. Also, key important customer and/or employee transactions or activities can be missed. In the age of "e-business" or "@business," if customers cannot access systems of which messaging is a key component, they may not come back, and they will most likely end up with your competitors.

People can also be impacted when systems are unreliable. I have not had direct exposure to messaging systems that directly provide life-sustaining medical systems, but I can easily envision a day when these systems will rely on messaging and knowledge management technologies like those provided by Exchange. Imagine, however, a 911 call center that relies on some sort of messaging system for different aspects of this vital service. From an operations point of view, it is not hard to see how an operations staff managing the daily activities of an organization could be impacted by the loss of the messaging system. The organization could potentially grind to a halt when this staff finds itself without required data or with lost information and key reports incomplete or corrupted.

To illustrate a real-world example, one of my side activities is writing a weekly electronic-newsletter column that is e-mailed to over 60,000 subscribers. This newsletter contains time-sensitive information and also relies on sponsorship for support. Exchange is used as the messaging system that handles the mailing of this newsletter each week. If the system went down and the newsletter did not get out, readers would be disappointed, and sponsors may discontinue their support. This is a very real revenue impact on the company that publishes the newsletter.

Getting back to some research data, CNI also found that the impact of downtime on the end user for Microsoft Exchange was less than in the Lotus Notes/Domino environment. Table 2.2 summarizes the overall cost impact per end user. Keep in mind that this research data in based on respondents' feedback to surveys and interviews and may not reflect the actual measure for your own organization.

Table 2.2   *Impact of Downtime on an End User Basis*

	Exchange Server	Notes Domino
Downtime per year (hours)	27.2	75.2
Likelihood of end user impact	33.9%	31.9%
Productivity loss if impacted	25.7%	20.7%
Annual downtime–induced productivity loss (hours)	2.37	4.86
Annual per-user cost of downtime–induced productivity loss	$43.66	$93.37

Source: Creative Networks, Inc., 1998

In addition to productivity losses caused by downtime, revenue can also be impacted. In their research, CNI calculated the annual revenue loss per end user. For Microsoft Exchange Server, CNI found that $127.85 per end user was the average downtime revenue loss for an organization surveyed. This compared well with Lotus Notes/Domino, which was roughly double that figure. In other words, the per-user cost of downtime annually for Exchange is about $171 ($43.66 + $127.85), according to CNI's 1998 research study. Again, these numbers may be different for your organization. However, calculations such as these cited from CNI's research might give you an idea of some areas you could investigate. Organizational loss can be measured by much more than money alone. However, in most cases, your management will be motivated by money. It is important for you to evaluate the various areas of your organization that are most impacted by the loss of a messaging system. For some organizations, this will be simply an annoyance. For others, the loss of e-mail, calendaring, or other Exchange-provided services could be more serious. Spend some time accessing each area and assigning the costs associated with the loss.

2.3   Step 2: Understand the Anatomy of Exchange Downtime

Before you can properly assess downtime causes for your Exchange deployment, you must be able to recognize that downtime is not simply a mysterious "black box." By black box I mean that downtime is not just a singular event in which the internals of the event are hidden. Downtime for any environment, including Exchange, is actually a series of incidents and activities that can be exposed and individually analyzed. In other words, it is possible to open up and view the internal components of the black box of downtime. Figure 2.2 illustrates this concept.

Figure 2.2
The black box of Exchange downtime

The Black Box of Downtime

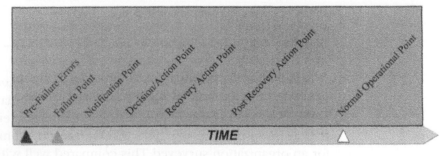

If one looks at an outage event for Exchange, there are actually many subevents that compose the entire outage. If a single outage lasts for eight hours, be assured that the eight-hour period can be divided into smaller units that can be individually analyzed. On the time continuum of a downtime event, understanding the components that make up the downtime can be a key to reducing the overall duration of an outage. For example, suppose that your Exchange server is down for four hours. During the four-hour period, one hour is spent diagnosing the problem, two hours are spent finding a good backup tape, and the remaining hour is spent actually restoring from tape. Understanding that two hours were spent searching for a good backup tape would be an important data point in your search to decrease downtime for your deployment. In another scenario, suppose the server was down for three hours before any of the operations staff was notified. In this scenario, this knowledge would indicate that effective outage-notification measures could have trimmed as much as three hours from the total outage period. Let's take a look at the typical components within the black box of downtime for Exchange.

2.3.1 Prefailure Errors

Prefailure errors are indicators and conditions that point to an impending problem that will result in downtime. These indications are not always obvious, and not all system administrators or operators may understand their significance. They can come in many forms such as hardware events, software indications, performance degradation, or other benign indicators. For example, one common occurrence in the Exchange environment that I would classify as a prefailure error is the infamous "-1018" error. This error occurs when the Exchange database engine encounters a problem with pages in the database. The error (or its subsequent errors) is logged to the application event log when encountered. This error is a precursor to much bigger problems and indicates that the database (or portions of it) is corrupt (more on this in later chapters). This error is usually only logged during backup operations or online maintenance. If this error is ignored (in my experience, it is ignored all too often), you may continue to operate your Exchange server—worsening an already corrupted database. In addition, you may place a false sense of security on your backups. If a -1018 error is encountered during online backup, the backup operation is terminated. If best practices for proactive scanning of event logs are not in place, no one would be the wiser about the backup not being successful. I have seen many organizations go for days or even weeks being unaware that the last good backup was completed weeks ago. The awareness of various errors that are indicators of more serious problems, later resulting in downtime or causing additional downtime, gives operators the ability to assess impact on users and the business risk associated.

By establishing best practices that provide a look into the prefailure component of downtime, you allow insight into how overall downtime can be reduced or eliminated. For Exchange Server, the leading shortfalls encountered with understanding the prefailure component include:

- No proactive error checking and monitoring
- No ability to correlate error events with downtime
- No predictive or root cause analysis capability
- No ability to link hardware and software errors
- Lack of tools or improper use of tools

Overall, an understanding of this component can have the most impact on your ability to proactively manage around Exchange deployment downtime. We will discuss this key component in greater detail in Chapter 9, "Bringing It All Together with Proactive Management."

2.3.2 Failure Point

The actual failure point is where the downtime clock begins to tick. For Exchange, this can be triggered when a user calls the help desk complaining that he can't access his server. Conversely, the operator or Exchange administrator may be notified of the failure point when a management application shows an Exchange service failure or a configured Exchange server or link monitor alerts him of an incident. Of course, if an organization does not implement management tools, the user's call to the help desk will be the first word. In many cases, the failure point may not be the point of notification. Also, many times, the root cause of the failure may not be the object of monitoring tools or capabilities. In many cases, the failure point and the next component—the notification point—can be treated as a combined event.

2.3.3 Notification Point

This is an important component of the larger black box of downtime. This is the point at which human intervention is applied to the situation. An operator or administrator takes notice of whatever event has occurred and then must take action. This may include scrambling to determine the root cause, consulting the operations procedures, or calling Microsoft Product Support Services. What happens at this point of the outage can be critical in minimizing the duration. If operators are not properly trained or ignore procedures, the length of downtime may be extended. If no ability exists to determine root cause or if no resources exist to escalate the problem, support staff will struggle to get the system operational and may waste valuable time or make matters worse. Problems that are often encountered with the notification point component include:

- No response to notification
- Inability to troubleshoot fault condition
- Poor or inaccurate procedures
- Poor support staff training
- Ineffective escalation procedures
- Incorrect support information from vendors

2.3.4   Decision/Action Point

Once again, the actions and decisions of operators and administrators can drastically impact the duration of an outage event for your Exchange deployment. The decision point component of downtime has little to do with the software, hardware, or any other system component. Unlike many of the other components of downtime, the decision point, for the most part, is strictly reliant upon the support staff. Therefore, the duration of downtime is largely impacted by how well equipped they are to manage the situation. This is the point in the downtime event when an environmental cause must be rectified, defective hardware or software must be replaced, troubleshooting must begin, or recovery procedures must be initiated. The error condition must be analyzed and resolved. Troubleshooting skills and system knowledge are key during this period. Again, training and experience as well as procedures and best practices will come into play here. If support staff makes the wrong decision at this point in an outage, downtime will increase. In a worst-case scenario, a bad decision could also result in permanent data loss and could cost the organization even more than the actual downtime event. Some common problems or failures at this point include:

- Lack of documentation, training, and procedures for support staff
- Corrective action fails to properly resolve the issue
- Incorrect information from vendor support
- Operator chooses an incorrect action
- Failure to recognize the correct condition

2.3.5   Recovery Action Point

The recovery action point assumes that the actual root cause has been determined and resolved. For example, if a power supply on a server has failed and is replaced, the server can be restarted and any necessary recovery steps initiated. In another example, if you have a failed disk drive on which the Exchange information store is placed, the information store must be recovered once the failed disk drive has been replaced (assuming no RAID capability). This may also be the point at which diagnostic and repair tools such as ESEUTIL and ISINTEG are utilized. In many cases, this is the point at which a restore from backup media occurs. However, this may be as simple as a server reboot and allowing Exchange to perform a soft recovery. Issues like support-staff training, documentation, procedures, and decision-making abilities will impact the duration of this downtime component in much the same way as they can impact other components of downtime. In addition, staff intervention or second-guessing the recovery process has great potential to be detrimental to the system. Problems that can occur at this stage in the downtime timeline include:

- Backup media is missing, corrupt, or incomplete
- Backup hardware or software is inoperable
- Poor procedures, documentation, or training
- Improper interference in the recovery process
- Improper use of recovery or diagnostic tools

2.3.6 Postrecovery Action Point

Once recovery of an Exchange server is complete, there are, in many cases, several operation points that follow. These actions are usually taken before the server is made available for end user services. For example, after you restore an information store from backup, you may want to run some integrity-checking tools like ISINTEG, ESEFILE, or ESEUTIL. This step may be an extra measure to ensure that the original problem that caused data loss or corruption has been rectified. Another postrecovery step that is a common practice is the initiation of a postrecovery backup. By performing a postrecovery backup of your information stores, you can ensure that the databases are error free. Remember that a normal backup operation checks every page of the database for corruption. Running postrecovery backups is a good best practice to adopt as part of normal postrecovery procedures. Other common postrecovery checks include verifying server connectivity; ensuring that all services are started; verifying third-party software; and checking directory, public folder, and free/busy replication activity for the recovered server. Issues that sometimes cause problems during postrecovery include:

- Omission of a postrecovery backup
- Improper use of tools
- Poor training and procedures
- Failure to resolve the original root cause

2.3.7 Normal Operational Point

The downtime clock stops ticking once the recovery operation reaches the point when normal operations can be declared. At this point, clients should be able to access the services they had been denied during the outage. The point of resumed normal operations is where all system administrators want to get as soon as possible when an outage occurs. This is also the point at which incident documentation should be done. This includes a complete report of the failure and the activities that occurred at each point in the outage (a postmortem). The incident-reporting and -documentation process should be the beginning of an operational feedback loop that drives a process improvement program for your Exchange deployment. Without this feedback loop and improvement program, common problems and issues that occur during an outage are never reported. As a result, these issues continue to extend the downtime periods as personnel run into the same problems each time a crisis occurs. While the point of normal operational resumption may not seem like an important part of an outage (everyone is just glad to get the Exchange server back up and running), it may be one of the most important points where process improvement is concerned.

I have taken the time here to step you through the individual components that make up the entire downtime incident for one reason. Only through an understanding of what a downtime incident is actually composed of can we devise methods of reducing downtime. Too often, we look at the black box of downtime and are afraid to look inside. Many organizations I work with are frustrated by the amount of downtime they have for their overall Exchange deployment. They often see a downtime incident for Exchange and credit (or debit) the entire incident to the Exchange software or their hardware vendor. Many times, I have seen downtime incidents that last for many hours that result in Exchange Server getting a bad rap. For example, in one case I was involved in, the Exchange information store was found to be corrupt and had to be restored from backup. The recovery process lasted over eight hours, resulting in a huge downtime incident charged against the messaging system's team. When looking deeper into this incident, we found that several things contributed to the total of eight hours of downtime. First, the problem was not recognized until an hour into the outage (the notification point). Once the problem was determined, an inexperienced staff scrambled to get the necessary backup tapes required to perform the restore. However, after beginning the restore process, it was determined that the backup was not good. In fact, the last successful backup had occurred three days earlier. Since the staff was not well trained and procedures were not well documented, there was a delay in finding the correct backup tapes from three days earlier. Overall, approximately four hours was spent trying to identify and locate the last known good backup of the downed Exchange server. Once the correct tape was located, the recovery operation began, and the server was fully recovered in about three hours. However, since the last good backup tape was three days old, three days worth of messaging data was lost.

This extreme case in point serves to illustrate how several components of downtime took excessive amounts of time. By looking at downtime as a series of components instead of a singular event, we can start to identify problem spots. These problem spots can be analyzed further and targeted for process improvement in order to reduce the overall outage period. In my example, if better notification methods had existed, the operational staff could have responded quicker. In addition, if backup verification procedures had existed for validating each day's backup, three days worth of data would not have been lost. You can be certain that this particular organization quickly recognized the need to look at the notification, decision/action, and recovery points within the overall outage in order to eliminate the tremendous amount of unneeded downtime that occurred in this incident. By looking deeper into the outage and not treating it as a simple and single component, we can look for ways to increase system availability.

2.3.8 Recovery-Point Focus versus Recovery-Time Focus

High availability means different things to different people. As I have discussed, at the pinnacle, we have continuous availability or non-stop computing. What is your definition of high availability for your Exchange deployment? Perhaps you don't need a full "five nines" (99.999%), but you would like to get as close as you can. Regardless of your needs, you need to consider the difference between focusing on recovery point versus focusing on recovery time. Over the years, we have consistently seen the reliability of systems components increase. However, downtime still happens, software crashes, hardware fails, and data can be lost.

A recovery-point focus means that your primary concern is being able to recover your system to an exact point in time or system state, and there is no tolerance for data loss. With a recovery-point focus, the disaster-recovery planner is concerned with the ability to recover to a specific system transaction point without data loss. What is the impact when you measure your operations using a recovery-point standard? If you aren't able to pick up where you left off, will it be inconvenient, damaging, or completely catastrophic? With a focus on recovery time, you are concerned with continuous operations and care most about the time it takes to restore the system to operational status. The big question is this: Do you need fast recovery, recovery to the exact system state prior to the failure, or both?

For Exchange, we could contrast recovery point and recovery time with this example. A recovery-time focus would favor simply getting the server back in operation and would be less concerned with whether the users' mailbox data was intact. The end result would be that users can send and receive mail as soon as possible, but data in their mailbox may not be immediately available. With a recovery-point focus, the importance might be placed on recovering mailbox data to an exact point preceding a failure with less concern for quickly restoring system operation. Obviously, when planning for a real-world situation, disaster recovery specialists must strike a balance between a focus on recovery point and recovery time. For an Exchange deployment, we would like to have our users back online with access to their messaging data as soon as possible—both recovery point and recovery time are important. However, the two focal points can be in direct competition with one another. The ability to ensure recovery-point capability may impact the ability to ensure a rapid recovery time. The focus you choose or, more likely, the balance you strike will be important as you plan your recovery procedures and strategy for Exchange. Using the criteria of recovery point and recovery time will help you determine what is most important in your attempts to reduce downtime for your Exchange deployment.

2.4   Step 3: Assessing the Causes of Downtime for Exchange

For each Exchange deployment, the causes of downtime may vary. Also, the leading causes of downtime for Exchange may depend on how well you understand the technology, plan, and implement your operational procedures. Finally, the architecture and design of Exchange Server, itself, may somewhat contribute to the leading causes of downtime.

For most mission-critical environments, the leading causes of downtime fall into four key areas, as illustrated in Figure 2.3. These areas are software, hardware, operator, and environment.

2.4.1   Software

Bugs, configuration errors, performance problems, and other issues with software can cause significant downtime for any environment.

Figure 2.3
Categorizing the causes of downtime

Software	Hardware	Operator	Environment
Operating System	Server	Human Error	Power
Device Drivers	Storage	Sabotage	Fire
Name Resolution	Memory	Denial of Service	Weather
Authentication	Network	Monitoring	Earthquake
Malicious Code	Backup Devices	Administration	Heat
Applications		Security	Terrorism

Software causes of downtime can also fall into many areas such as the operating system, drivers, applications, tools, etc. Problems in any of these areas can render a server unavailable. For Exchange Server, software problems, in my experience, usually come as a result of configuration errors. Since Exchange Server is a very complex system, there are many opportunities for configuration problems. Likewise, third-party applications and drivers can also be a source of much grief for administrators. For Exchange, third-party software such as hardware device drivers, anti-virus scanners, management agents, fax servers, connectors, etc., are well-known culprits. All too often, these types of software are frequently found to have issues such as memory leaks and other problems that can result in downtime for Exchange. Microsoft is not without fault either. We are all painfully aware of the continuous wave of service packs and patches that Microsoft must provide to address issues discovered in the Windows NT/Windows 2000 operating systems or Exchange Server. Although we are often frustrated when software bugs are discovered, Microsoft is no worse an offender than any other developer. Left unchecked and/or misunderstood, software problems can be a significant contributor to system downtime. In practice, we often find that measures such as regularly scheduled system reboots become part of operational procedures in an attempt to compensate for shortcomings and problems with the operating system, third-party software, or Exchange Server itself.

What's important to understand here is that we must accept this as a reality of the technology we are using and seek to understand how and why software can be a significant cause of downtime. Only then can we plan and implement methods of reducing our exposure to the occurrence of software problems.

2.4.2   Hardware

Hardware is another area in which problems and issues can cause downtime. Working for a hardware manufacturer and dealing daily with the impacts of hardware on overall system reliability, I have become painfully aware of this issue. What is most interesting about hardware failures is that, according to most research, hardware is rarely cited as the leading cause of downtime. In fact, software is a more likely culprit where the causes of downtime are concerned. The hardware platform that runs Exchange Server is not a single device but a collection of interoperating devices. The problem with hardware is that all components are mostly subject to the laws of physics, which we have no control over. The server on which you run Exchange is composed of electronic circuits and mechanical devices that, over time and use, can breakdown and degrade. For example, a hard disk drive is a magnetic platter (or several platters) rotating at speeds up to 15,000RPM. A device like this is bound to fail. Not coincidentally, hard disk drives are the most likely component to fail in a server, followed by memory, power supplies, and fans. Again, while we cannot prevent hardware failures from occurring, we can take steps to reduce the impacts of such failures by building systems that are tolerant to these faults. Another key point here is that most hardware also contains software—usually called firmware. The system board on a server contains firmware or BIOS (Basic Input/Output System) for controlling low-level hardware operations. Likewise, devices such as disk drives and controllers also contain firmware "micro-code," which controls the operation of these devices. In my experience, firmware problems are the cause of device failure all too often.

Although hardware manufacturers are continually improving technology, there is little hope of eliminating the possibility of hardware device failures. Best results are usually achieved by aligning your organization with a hardware vendor that is in the top tier and that has excellent service and support offerings as well as solid experience and expertise with Exchange Server and Windows NT/2000. A key point to consider about hardware failures is that we can design and manage our systems in a manner that significantly reduces or possibly even eliminates hardware as a cause of system downtime.

2.4.3 Operator

Next we come to the operator. Unfortunately, all of the research I have seen points to the operator (the human factor in the equation) as the leading cause of downtime for mission-critical systems. A recent study by OnTrack Data International showed that as much as 32% of the causes of downtime are due to human error. How often I hear stories of people clicking the mouse when they shouldn't have, hitting the wrong key, tripping over a cable, selecting the wrong options, or just plain not knowing what to do. It isn't that people are stupid (I know you are thinking of someone in particular right now...); they often just aren't well trained or have incorrect procedures or instructions to work from. For example, many operators have never actually performed a server recovery until they are faced with a real-world crisis and have to perform flawlessly under pressure. If these operators have practiced disaster recovery drills many times beforehand, many potential mistakes that an inexperienced operator will make in a crisis can be avoided. Knowing that operator error is the leading cause of downtime is half the battle, however. The hope is in the fact that this potential cause of downtime is the one you have the most control over. Proper planning, procedures, and training can do wonders toward eliminating operator error as a cause of downtime.

2.4.4 Environment

The last category of downtime causes is environmental. The environment includes everything that is outside of or connected to the system. Environmental causes of downtime are things like power failure and conditioning, heating and cooling, destruction, physical security, a host of other external occurrences that can directly cause a system outage. One of my favorite tales that illustrates a problem with physical security is one in which a system administrator entered the computer room at night, shut down each server, and removed a 128MB memory module from each. This did not create a problem on most servers since nobody seemed to notice that the additional memory was gone (evidently, most of the servers had plenty of free memory). However, for the database server, the missing 128MB of RAM soon became noticeable. When month-end reports and summaries were generated, the server would run out of memory, grind to a halt, and finally crash. Upon closer examination, it was discovered that the missing memory was sorely needed once a month when system activity peaked during monthly report runs.

The most extreme examples of environmental conditions causing system outages are natural and man-made disasters that result in total system destruction. While impossible to plan for, these incidents do require some thought in your disaster recovery planning. Also, technologies are available that can tolerate such disasters that are a very real threat in the world we live in. Most environmental causes of downtime are tamer, however, and can be compensated for with countermeasures. These include issues with power or heating/cooling. It is within our control to provide adequate heating and cooling for data centers and to provide power conditioning and backup. Most of these issues are eliminated through solid data center design practices. Even so, I have seen issues with power and heating and cooling cause problems in even well-designed data centers. While working (in a past life) in an MIS department that had a state-of-the-art data center, I found myself troubleshooting an elusive problem with memory modules and disk drives failing at rates too high to be a coincidence. Upon further investigation, we discovered that our very expensive UPS was indeed providing a continuous but also "dirty" supply of power for the data center. The bad power (full of spikes and slumps) had taken its toll on our equipment. The memory modules and disk drives were most susceptible to the issue and began to fail at a rapid rate. Once the power condition problem was resolved, the failures began to taper off. While environmental conditions are not the leading cause of outage, they are often the leading contributor to outage duration.

It is important to understand here that within each of these four areas (software, hardware, operations, and environment) are many potential causes of downtime. For your organization, you must determine which of these are your leading causes of downtime since every organization is different. Understanding the potential issues that could possibly cause downtime in your environment is critical to the process of planning and implementing mission-critical systems. Armed with the knowledge of your leading causes of downtime, you can take the next steps toward architecting systems that resolve your leading issues. For example, if you determine that hardware is the single largest contributor to downtime, you can design and purchase systems that eliminate or reduce these issues. If you determine that operator error is your biggest issue, you are empowered to take steps to provide better training, documentation, procedures, and experience for your operations staff. Whatever your leading causes of downtime are, the advantage is given to those organizations that can understand them and take steps toward their eradication.

2.5 Step 4: Defining Mission-Critical Service-Level Agreements

One final key to providing continuous availability for your Exchange deployment is the ability to set some guidelines for determining whether the system is meeting the organization's business objectives for implementing the system in the first place. E-mail has become a key mission-critical application within most organizations, but just how much service degradation can the organization tolerate before the messaging system becomes a hindrance instead of a business advantage? The means of translating business objectives and requirements for any system is usually provided in the form of SLAs. SLAs come in various forms and can be established for every facet of system function and operation. For an Exchange deployment, SLAs help management determine whether the system is delivering the services that the organization desired when investing in the system in the first place. SLAs also assist system managers in ensuring that the business services they have committed to are being delivered. SLAs come in many forms and can touch many areas of operation for an Exchange deployment. Table 2.3 shows the types of SLAs that can be established for message systems. Table 2.4 highlights some common SLAs that are used for messaging systems to ensure optimal functionality and maximum availability.

SLAs are the only means we have of ensuring that the messaging system is delivering business value to the organization. Without SLAs it is difficult to provide consistent functionality and service availability. Also, system managers have no criteria on which to base staffing, procedures, and training. The obvious goal should be to provide messaging services as close to 100% of the time as possible. But

Table 2.3   *Service-Level Types*

SLA Type	Description
Performance SLA	Established to measure how the system performs and to provide an acceptable user experience. Examples include message delivery, response time, replication periods, message rates, bytes rates, etc.
Recovery SLA	Established to provide guidelines for maximum tolerable downtime. Can be set for Server, Mailbox, or even message recovery. Also may measure system failover times. Can also be used to drive or set recovery windows to disaster recovery operations.
Security SLA	Established to provide goals for ensuring system security. Can focus on intruder detection, viral and denial-of-service detection and attacks, or encryption and other secure service performance.
Interoperability SLA	Established to ensure maximum interoperability with heterogeneous systems such as gateways and legacy systems. Could include conversion metrics, message rates, error rates, or delivery times.
Management and administrative SLA	Established to measure administrative and management activities such as user maintenance and account service. May include service timeouts or response time guidelines.

Table 2.4   *Service-Level Agreement Examples*

SLA	Description	Example
Message delivery time	Established on a site and/or organizational basis to ensure that message delivery does not exceed limits set by business requirements	95% of messages delivered within 10 minutes (global); 99% of messages delivered within 30 minutes (global)
Message rate	Sets a guaranteed transaction rate for a messaging system	100 message opens/sec; 50 messages submitted per minute
Information store recovery period/rate	Sets maximum tolerable time for restoring an entire information store	4 hours per IS; 30GB/hour
Mailbox recovery period	Sets a guideline for ensuring that an individual mailbox can be recovered in a timely manner	1 hour
Connector message rate	Sets a guideline for ensuring that a site, X.400, SMTP, or routing group connector can meet message-delivery rates	5,000 messages per day; 10MB/hour

Table 2.4   *Service-Level Agreement Examples (continued)*

SLA	Description	Example
Virus detection rate	Sets a guideline for ensuring that virus-protection methods are effective	99% viral detection rate
Account service timeout	Ensures that user-account servicing is performed within reasonable period	24-hour turnaround
Replication timeouts	Ensures that directory, public folder, and other replication activities occur within time guidelines	24-hour global replication consistency
System availability	Ensures that the system is available	99.99% uptime; lost workstation hours/1M

uptime is not the only focus of SLAs. We can also use SLAs to provide a high degree of user experience and functionality by setting SLAs for performance, recovery, and administration. SLAs are an essential part of helping to define your operational procedures for your system. SLAs tie closely to proactive management and administration techniques and practices. We will discuss SLAs in more detail in Chapter 9.

2.6   The Final Step: Architecting Mission-Critical Exchange Servers

We have now covered the preliminaries needed to develop an understanding of how downtime is defined. In addition, we discussed the importance of determining the cost of downtime for your organization and how this will determine your tolerance for and ability to counteract the potential for downtime. We have looked at the anatomy of downtime and have opened the black box in order to point out that downtime is not just a simple event that takes place beyond the control of system operators. Downtime is a series of events and points at which there are opportunities for process improvement. Armed with thorough knowledge of the components that make up an outage, we can better prepare for downtime and can ensure that it is minimized. Also, it is important that we first understand how our organization will measure downtime, as there are several techniques available and your method should be whichever method most closely meets your business requirements. We have also discussed and categorized the causes of downtime into four areas: software, hardware, operator, and environment. Finally, we can set realistic SLAs that will allow us, as system managers, operators, and planners, to provide the level of service that the business requires. In the chapters to follow, I will discuss technologies. Not only will I discuss technology for Exchange Server but also the hardware and software solutions and technologies that allow us to plan, build, and operate Exchange deployments that are more tolerant to failure and that achieve high levels of availability. So now, let us set off on the most challenging part of our task—architecting mission-critical Exchange servers.

3

Exchange Database Technology Foundations

No discussion on disaster recovery or high availability best practices should begin before understanding the underlying technology for which these practices will be implemented. Microsoft Exchange Server is a complex application server that is not a monolithic architecture. There are many components of Exchange Server that interact and fulfill specific functions in order to deliver the complete system that is Exchange Server as we know it. In this chapter, I will look deeper into the Exchange database technology and neglect the rest of Exchange Server. This is due to the fact that, in my opinion, the focus for high availability for Exchange is on the database engine and how Exchange stores and recovers data. I will attempt to drill down deeper into some key technical concepts, such as Exchange database architecture and design, that will provide a basis for later topics around disaster recovery and reliability.

3.1 Storage Paradigms

Key to our discussions around disaster recovery and high availability for Exchange 2000 Server are the differences in how user data is stored in Exchange 2000 compared to its predecessors. In previous versions of Exchange Server, a single monolithic information store was available to administrators for storing user data. This single store was comprised of two components—a private information store and a public information store. From a file system perspective, the information store consisted of two files—PRIV.EDB and PUB.EDB—in versions of Exchange prior to Exchange 2000.

For Exchange Server 5.5 and previous versions, although limited in some ways, the information store was a simple concept to understand. Each server's information store was made up of the public and private information stores. The public information store housed the

Exchange Public Folder hierarchy, whereas the private information store was where user data in the form of mailboxes was stored. Figure 3.1 illustrates the components and layout of the Exchange Server 5.5 information store.

Figure 3.1
The Exchange Server 5.5 information store architecture

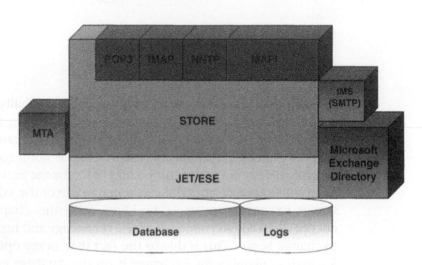

From one point of view, Exchange Server 5.5 and previous versions were much easier to get a handle on since there was one public and one private information store.

The purpose of the information store is to implement messaging storage semantics for the various clients that need access based on the respective API they support. In Exchange Server 5.5 and prior versions, the information store is implemented in one process—STORE.EXE. The store process provides clients such as Microsoft Outlook and others with a method of manipulating, storing, and visualizing data such as the form of an inbox, folder, message or attachment. Embedded in the information store process (in Exchange Server 5.5 and previous versions) are the various client access protocols such as MAPI, POP3, and IMAP. This allows clients running any of these protocols to have direct, high-performance access to their data without the overhead of going through any additional layers. Also, part of the store process is the database engine (called JET or ESE), which we will discuss in detail later in this chapter. The combination of both subprocesses into a single process provides clients with a mapping from a logical abstraction layer of message data (inbox, messages, folders, and attachments) to a layer of physical data storage (database pages and files). This is provided in the most optimal fashion and at reduced system resource overhead.

This monolithic store approach in earlier versions of Exchange Server, although simple, created many issues for administrators. First, since all users on a particular server store their mail in the private information store (PRIV.EDB), there is little flexibility in storage allocation on a server. In addition, this single file continues to grow larger over time as more users are added to the server and as existing users accumulate more mail in their respective mailboxes. As this single information store grows over time, disaster recovery issues begin to surface. For example, when the server is initially deployed, backup and restore service-level agreements (SLAs) (recovery time) for the server may be relatively easy to meet since the planned disaster recovery procedures can accommodate the initial size of the information store. However, as the information store grows, backup and, more importantly, restore times may tend to "creep" to longer and longer time periods until the existing disaster recovery measures can no longer meet required SLAs.

Another problem relates to the integrity-checking measures that Exchange provides to ensure that the database is not corrupt. While Exchange provides a higher level of database integrity (implemented in the database engine and discussed in more detail later in this chapter) than most of it competitors, the fact that Exchange Server will terminate operations when corruption is encountered can be problematic. This results in the entire information store on a server (on which all user data is stored) having to be restored from backup. This can result in significant downtime as all users on the server are without access until the restore operations are complete. With no flexibility in storage and a monolithic information store, the number of users exposed to such an outage can be a limiting factor in planning and deploying the number of users on a given Exchange server. The monolithic information storage approach is one of the most significant contributors to total deployment outage in an Exchange deployment. Microsoft's competitors know this weakness well and have regularly exploited it in their marketing campaigns. While this can be a significant problem, I have not found any of Microsoft's competitors offering alternatives that are without their own issues.

3.2   Redefining Storage in Exchange 2000

The issues and problems with a single database approach in previous versions of Exchange Server have definitely taken their toll on Microsoft Product Support Services (PSS). Disaster recovery, database maintenance, database corruption, and other related issues have made up a huge portion of the PSS customer caseload for Exchange. In fact, there have been numerous occasions in which these issues have topped the charts for all Microsoft BackOffice products. In response to customer feedback and their own support organizations, Microsoft set out to address storage limitations and issues from previous versions of Exchange in Exchange 2000. One of the most significant changes in Exchange 2000 is how storage is allocated and managed. A new concept called a storage group (SG) has emerged.

Figure 3.2
Exchange 2000
storage design

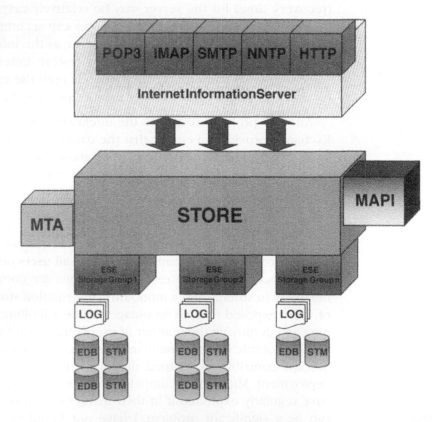

Besides the absence of a directory service database in Exchange 2000 Server, there are also some other significant differences where database technology is concerned. The concept of a storage group is introduced in Exchange 2000 Server. A storage group is defined as the combination of an instance in memory of the Extensible Storage Engine (ESE), which runs as a subprocess of STORE.EXE, and the set of database and log files within that storage group. While Exchange Server 5.5 and previous versions only supported a single instance of the database engine, Exchange 2000 Server now supports multiple instances of ESE running (in the process context of STORE.EXE) on a server at the same time. In other words, multiple storage groups can be configured on an Exchange 2000 Server server. An SG manages a group of databases all sharing the same set of log files. Storage groups run instantiated within the STORE process of Exchange 2000 Server. Exchange 2000 Server is limited to four storage groups per server in the Enterprise edition and one storage group in the Standard edition. The capability to configure additional storage groups (up to 15) will be added in later releases of Exchange Server and when Win64 is available. An additional SG instance is reserved by the STORE process for use for recovery operations on the server. The SG also handles all backup operations for the databases it manages, making an SG the typical unit of backup for Exchange 2000 Server. It is also the unit of failover for Exchange virtual server clustered configurations of Exchange 2000 Server. We will discuss these points in more detail in Chapter 7. The advent of multiple instances of the database engine presents a significant paradigm shift from previous versions of Exchange Server for administrators and system implementers. Not only does it bring substantial improvements in scalability, reliability, and flexibility, it also makes the previously simpler task of information store management (in previous versions) more complex.

Closely related is another significant technology advance in Exchange 2000 Server, the support for multiple databases per storage group. Again, in versions prior to Exchange 2000 Server, only one information store instance was available. This instance supported one private and one public database per server. With Exchange 2000 Server, not only are multiple SGs available, but multiple databases per SG are also supported. Technically, each storage group can host up to six configured databases (MDBs). However, only five databases can be configured since utilities like ISINTEG need an available database for use as temporary storage. This means that the limit for a single Exchange 2000 Enterprise server at initial release is 20 databases (4 storage groups × 5 databases). Upon creation, each database (MDB, which is a file pair that includes the *.EDB and *.STM files) requires approximately 8MB to 9MB of disk space plus about 10MB RAM overhead on the Exchange server. The multiple-database approach has many advantages. For example, you could host multiple different departments or even different companies on separate database files within one SG or in separate SGs. In addition, you can host special users, such as your CEO or CIO, on their own private database, providing security and increased management.

The most significant advantage that multiple databases offer is in the area of reliability and server scalability. As previously discussed, the single most limiting factor of Exchange Server scalability (the number of users per server) in the past has been disaster recovery concerns. Since the number of users per server is tied to how large the information store will grow and how quickly backup and restore can be performed, server configurations have not grown beyond 2,000 to 3,000 users for most deployments. Also, the typical size of the information store for Exchange Server 5.5 deployments has not typically exceeded 40GB to 60GB for the reliability and disaster recovery reasons previously cited. This problem was the driving force behind Microsoft's design of multiple information store instances and multiple databases in Exchange 2000. With the flexibility that these features bring, reliability and scalability can become more of a reality with Exchange 2000 Server. For example, with multiple databases per server, a single 50GB database could be split into five 10GB databases. Exchange 2000 Server supports up to five databases per storage group. As mention earlier, a sixth database per SG is reserved for utilities like ISINTEG. In the previous example, by splitting a large database into smaller partitions of user data, more reliability options are available to administrators. The reason for this is that (using this example), since each database is only 10GB in size, backup and restore of each take less time to accomplish. Also, since Exchange 2000 Server always reserves an SG instance for recovery, restore operations can be performed while the server is up and running, and multiple current operations can occur simultaneously. The restore of a single database can be performed much more rapidly than an entire storage group. If one of the 10GB databases becomes damaged or corrupt, it can be restored while the other four databases are online servicing users.

In another scenario, suppose 5,000 users are distributed across five databases (with 1,000 users per database). While one database is offline for restore (dismounted), 1,000 users are impacted. Meanwhile, the other 4,000 users still have access to their data. In contrast, for Exchange Server 5.5, all 5,000 users have to utilize a single database. If the database becomes corrupted or damaged, all users are affected and unable to access to their data until the entire database was restored. The advantages and benefits of the storage technology advances in Exchange 2000 Server will become increasingly more apparent as we continue discussions around disaster recovery, management, and administration later in this book. Table 3.1 highlights some important reasons and applications for implementing multiple storage groups and databases.

Table 3.1   *Reasons for Multiple Databases or Storage Groups*

Why Multiple Databases?	*Why Multiple Storage Groups?*
Eliminate large monolithic mailbox stores by partitioning into smaller databases.	Partitioning multiple organizational divisions on a server.
Partition data by workgroup, department, or cross-functional teams.	Disaster recovery scheduling or service-level agreements.
Large public folder, knowledge management, or portal applications.	Performance or capacity requirements.
VIP mailboxes—separate out special users for security, performance, or disaster recovery reasons.	NNTP server requiring circular logging that can only be configured at the storage group level.
Partition data that is content or full-text indexed for a subset of users of an application.	Implementing clustering deployment where the storage group is the unit of resource failover.
Partition data by service-level agreement conformance.	Current storage group has reached the limit of six configured databases (MDBs).
Data design to achieve high single instance storage ratios.	In an ISP scenario where hosting of multiple organizations per server is required.
Reduce backup and restore times	Clustering requires the flexibility of multiple storage groups since they are the unit of resource failover for the virtual server.

3.3   Exchange Database Files

The Exchange Server ESE database engine uses five key file types during all operations. Table 3.2 identifies each of these file types and their purposes. We will discuss the properties data file (*.EDB), the streaming data file (*.STM), the transaction log file (*.LOG), and the checkpoint file (*.CHK) types in this chapter. Since the patch file (*.PAT) is particular to backup and restore operations, we will defer discussion of this file type until the next chapter.

3.3.1   The Streaming Store

The streaming data file (*.STM) is a new file type introduced with Exchange 2000 Server. The STM file is an important database file in that it provides a storage location for Internet MIME formatted content. The STM file is well suited for content such as voice, video, and other multimedia formats that require data to be streamed. Microsoft developed the STM file in order to provide an alternative to storing streaming content in the traditional Exchange database file (*.EDB). The EDB file is not well suited to this type of content, and Microsoft felt that a new file type was required to provide optimal performance for applications utilizing content of this type. Content stored in the STM file is broken into 64KB chunks (16KB/4KB pages) and is stored in clustered runs similar to those of a file system such as NTFS. Storing content in this manner allows the data to be read rapidly in a large block (64KB) random I/O fashion whenever possible (typically accessed in I/Os as large as 32KB). Page header information including checksums for content stored in the streaming file is maintained in the EDB file. The STM file provides a significant advancement in Exchange Server's ability to store a wide variety of data. This feature will be of particular importance to future knowledge management, workflow, and content-indexing applications and technologies.

Table 3.2   *Important Exchange Server Database Files*

File Type	File name	Purpose
Log file	E0*n*.LOG, E0*nnnnnnn*.LOG	5MB file in which transaction log records are stored. Files are used in both soft and hard database recovery operations.
Patch file	PRIV*n*.PAT, PUB*n*.PAT, etc.	Used during backup, restore, and recovery operations. Patch files contain database pages that were split during online backup.
Checkpoint file	EDB.CHK	The checkpoint maintains information about the location in the transaction logs that was last committed to the database.

Table 3.2 *Important Exchange Server Database Files (continued)*

File Type	File name	Purpose
Database file	PRIV*n*.EDB, PUB*n*.EDB, DIR.EDB, etc.	The database file stores all user data in the form of 4KB pages. This file is only consistent when all outstanding transactions have been applied. (note: DIR.EDB is only used in versions prior to Exchange 2000)
Streaming database file	PRIV*n*.STM, PUB*n*.STM	New to Exchange 2000 Server, the streaming file stores native MIME content from Internet clients. Structure is 4KB pages in 64KB block runs (16/4KB pages).

3.4 Storage Group Allocation and Data Distribution

At the time this book is published, widespread deployment of Exchange 2000 will still be very much in the planning and initial deployment phases for most organizations. Therefore, many best practices and design techniques for Exchange 2000 storage groups and databases have not been established yet. However, there are some basic expectations for storage group design and configuration that I will discuss here. These are mainly based on what we know of Exchange Server to this point as well as some best practices that apply simply because Exchange Server is still "just a database engine at heart."

3.4.1 Separate Sequential from Random I/O

In Exchange 2000, there are three key files within a storage group for which we should concern ourselves—EDB, STM, and LOG files. From the early days of deploying transacted storage technologies, we have learned that locating log files separate from database files is a good practice. For Exchange 2000, the log files are accessed in a highly sequential fashion. The EDB and the STM files, on the other hand, are accessed with very random patterns (random I/O). With earlier versions of Exchange, we learned that, for optimal performance, management, and disaster recovery, we should place the transaction logs on a volume that performs sequential I/O in an optimal fashion. The EDB files were placed on a separate volume that was optimized for random I/O. In Exchange 2000, our scenario is further complicated by the fact that we not only can now add a new file to the mixture (the STM file), we can also have multiple storage groups and databases on a single server. How can these former best practices be applied to our new scenario in Exchange 2000?

The answer may not be as complicated as it seems. While Exchange 2000 does add some degree of complexity to storage design for our Exchange servers, we can still hold fast to our prior techniques. First, we should continue to separate random from sequential I/O. For Exchange 2000, this means that we will probably want to have a dedicated volume for every log file group (per storage group) on a server. For example, on a server with three storage groups, each configured with four databases per storage group, the anticipated best design would be one that provides a separate physical array (volume) for every database file set (EDB + STM file) and an additional array per storage group for the log files. Figure 3.3 illustrates this example. For each log file group, a RAID1 consisting of two disk drives is configured. For each database set, a RAID0 + 1 or RAID5 array is configured. The result is a server configured with 15 separate physical drive arrays to support the Exchange storage group requirements (3 arrays for log files plus 12 arrays for the databases). This is just one example, but it follows established best practices that are well known in most Exchange deployments. Certainly, all storage groups and databases could be allocated on a single volume or array, but optimal performance and manageability will be sacrificed. Table 3.3 provides some basic guidelines for placement of the Exchange 2000 database files for optimal performance

Table 3.3   *Storage Design Best Practices for Exchange 2000 Database Components*

Database Component	*Storage Design Best Practices*
Storage group transaction logs	Sequential I/O in 4KB blocks: Dedicate a RAID1 or 0+1 array to each storage group for transaction logs.
Property store (*.EDB)	Random I/O in 4KB blocks: Dedicate a RAID1, 0+1, or 5 array to each storage group for the property store. Can be combined with streaming store if no or few Internet protocol clients are supported. For MAPI clients, combine with streaming store. For heavily I/O environments, a separate array for each property store in a storage group (up to five can be configured) may be necessary.

Table 3.3   *Storage Design Best Practices for Exchange 2000 Database Components (continued)*

Database Component	Storage Design Best Practices
Streaming store (*.STM)	Mostly random I/O in 32KB blocks: Dedicate a RAID1, 0+1, or 5 array to each storage group for the streaming store. Can be combined with the properties store if no or few Internet protocol clients are supported. For MAPI clients, combine with property store. For Internet protocol clients in heavily I/O environments, a separate array for each streaming store in a storage group may be necessary. However, this will double storage requirements in a cluster.

Figure 3.3
*Server
Configuration
for Exchange
2000*

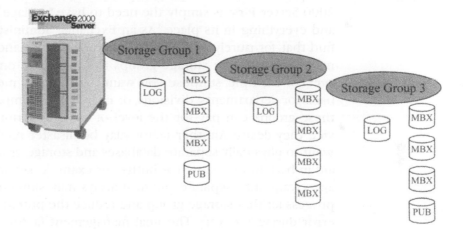

Another variation in storage allocation concerns the STM file. In deployments that make heavy use of the streaming store, it may become necessary to allocate a dedicated physical array for the STM file. Examples of applications that may require this include newsgroup servers (NNTP) and those environments in which native Internet protocols such as SMTP, POP3, and IMAP dominate the clients that are supported by the server. Since Internet clients natively use MIME content that is stored directly in the streaming store, heavy usage may justify separate storage allocation. As more Exchange 2000 servers are deployed and the streaming store is more heavily utilized, common I/O patterns for this file type will be better understood. It is likely that I/O patterns will be random (32KB blocks) in nature even though the file is organized in a highly sequential manner. Since most corporate deployments use MAPI as the default protocol and MAPI clients do not utilize the streaming store, I don't expect that most deployments will need to take the additional step of allocating a separate array. It is presented here, however, as a possibility that may benefit future deployments and applications for Exchange 2000.

3.4.2   For Management's Sake

There are other management factors that influence the allocation and placement of storage groups and database files for Exchange 2000 Server. First is simply the need to have "a place for everything and everything in its place." As an Exchange administrator, you may find that, for purely management and not performance reasons, you may wish to locate storage groups and databases on separate storage. For example, suppose you want to provide a means of charge-back for departments, divisions, or even entire companies in which these groups can pay for the level of storage, performance, or service they desire. Another factor may be disaster recovery. You may want to physically separate databases and storage groups in order to aid in backup or restore (or both). For example, separation of a storage group onto separate physical arrays may simplify the recovery process for that storage group and reduce the potential for operator error during recovery. The final management factor may be one of security. Your organization (or one you host) may have specific security requirements that force you to allocate dedicated storage for its data. In addition, you may have an administration model that requires you to have separate administrators for particular storage groups (defined by administrative groups in Exchange 2000). All of these management factors may produce various reasons and practices for the management and allocation of storage groups and databases in Exchange 2000. In addition, as Exchange 2000 becomes more widely deployed and future applications further leverage the capabilities of Exchange 2000 storage, we will see addition best practices and creative management techniques emerge.

The concepts of multiple databases and storage groups are very important innovations in Exchange 2000. A thorough understanding of the concepts discussed will be key for effective management and administration of the data that Exchange stores. Spend some time familiarizing yourself with defining, allocating, and designing storage for Exchange 2000. This knowledge will also provide a solid basis for our discussion in Chapters 4 and 5 on disaster recovery. Underlying our logical view of Exchange data, which is made up of storage groups and databases, is the database engine technology itself. In the next section, we will discuss the history of the Exchange database engine as well as its concepts, components, and methods of ensuring highly reliable and recoverable data storage.

3.5   Exchange Database Technology

An important prerequisite to assessing, planning, and implementing high availability or disaster recovery for any mission-critical system is a thorough understanding and in-depth knowledge of the application in question. This knowledge allows us to answer the questions and make the right decisions necessary for ensuring high levels of reliability and recovery. In my opinion, the key part of Exchange Server impacting disaster recovery and high availability that we must comprehend is the underlying store and database technology. Understanding the Exchange Server information store and how it stores, accesses, and manipulates user data is fundamental to building mission-critical Exchange Server deployments. So how does Exchange Server store your messages? Figure 3.4 illustrates how various database tables and subtables provide users with a view of an inbox, messages, folders, and attachments.

As Figure 3.4 shows, there is a Folders table that has one row for each folder in the information store. Note that since the private and public information stores are separate databases, data is not shared or intermingled between the two. Next, there is one Message table with a message body for each message in the database. Since Exchange Server supports a feature called single instance storage, each message residing in multiple user mailboxes is only stored in the Message table one time. In other words, no matter how many users you send a message to on an individual information store, there will be only one copy of the message stored in the information store. The advantages of single instance storage are obvious and result in substantial opportunities for reduced storage requirements

Figure 3.4
*The Exchange
database
logical view*

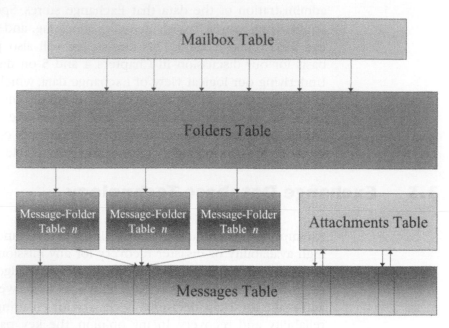

when compared to some other messaging systems in which a copy
of a message is stored for every recipient to which it is sent. The
Message Folder table is a structure that exists for every folder in the
information store that maintains a sort order and holds a row for
every message that resides in the folder. The Message Folder table
does not actually store the message since all messages are already
stored in the Message table. The Message Folder table simply uses
the message ID as a pointer (or key) to the Message table. The last
fundamental, logical information store structure is the Attachments
table. The Attachments table, as the name implies, holds all message
attachments. Once again, with the single instance storage feature,
each attachment is only stored once per database regardless of how
many recipients actually have the attachment as part of their mailbox. In the case of attachments, even greater advantages can be
seen for single instance storage. At least you can rest in the knowledge that the 20MB PowerPoint presentation your boss sent to his
entire team is only stored once per server.

The trick with all of the various tables that make up the Exchange
information store database is to organize these structures into some-

thing usable to even the most novice user and to present it all as a mailbox and folder view. This is accomplished in a high-speed and optimal manner through the use of views and indexes. Views allow you to change the way you look at different folders in your mailbox on the Exchange Server. Views are created and built on the fly based on the user's needs. For example, if I want to see all the messages in my inbox by sender (FROM:) in alphabetical order, the operation is simple. Under the covers, however, Exchange Server is creating or, most of the time, reusing a specific view to allow me to see my messages this way, and it does so in a very high-speed fashion that has minimal resource impact on the server. Indexes allow the entire information store database to be quickly and efficiently navigated. Indexes are also updated and created dynamically within the information store. For example, since my inbox is actually made up of several different tables, as I discussed above, Exchange server needs to quickly respond to my requests when I am manipulating messages within my inbox. When I double-click on a message, the server must pull together the message header, body, and any attachments and send them to my client (in my case, Outlook) for presentation. If the message has an attachment, Exchange Server must quickly find that attachment in the Attachment table when I need it. Indexes allow this to happen in the most efficient manner. Let's look at two examples of common client tasks that the Exchange Server information store must perform and the individual actions that occur in the background. Two common tasks are receiving a message and moving a message. Figures 3.5 and 3.6 illustrate the steps taken for each of these tasks by the Exchange Server Store process and underlying database engine.

Microsoft designed Exchange Server to be a highly reliable messaging server platform that would provide continuous operation, high transactional throughput, rapid recovery, and the atomic operational capability of a relational database system. There were philosophical concepts kept in mind during the design phases of the Exchange Server database technology. One key thought kept at the forefront of designers' minds was, "What if the database crashes?" Exchange Server had to be able to recover quickly and completely. Also, the database had to provide for 7×24 operation and the ability to perform backup operations without shutting down the services. In later versions of Exchange Server, the designers also sought to

Figure 3.5
*Message
Receive actions
for Exchange
Server Store*

Receive Message (MAPI Client)

BEGIN TRANSACTION

1. Locate recipient inbox records in Folders Table

2. Insert message body in Message Table

3. Insert message header in Message-Folder table for each recipient

4. Increment message count/unread count of Folders Table

COMMIT TRANSACTION

Figure 3.6
*Message Move
actions for
Exchange
Server Store*

Move Message (MAPI Client)

BEGIN TRANSACTION

1. Locate source and destination records in Folders Table for each recipients

2. Insert message header in Message-Folder Table for destination folder

3. Delete message header in Message-Folder Table for source folder

4. Increment message count in destination folder row of Folders Table

5. Decrement message count in source folder row of Folders Table

COMMIT TRANSACTION

make the Exchange database engine as self-tuning as possible—eliminating previous issues related to static memory allocation and design rigidity. Finally, the designers understood that the most critical component of performance for Exchange Server would be I/O operations and the efficiency of how they were performed by the database engine.

These philosophies and design points lead Exchange Server developers to select Microsoft's Joint Engine Technology (JET) as the database engine technology on which to base Exchange Server. JET was an outgrowth of technology that Microsoft had used in other products such as Microsoft Access and Foxpro/Foxbase (formerly owned by Borland). JET had two variants—JET "Red" and JET "Blue," which Microsoft at one point had planned on converging into a single technology. JET Red is the variant that has evolved into the current Access product, and it is used in various other places on the client side such as Microsoft Office. JET Red is a single user database engine that was designed to run standalone on an end user's workstation (as in the case of Microsoft Access). JET Red is not well suited for multiuser access and is not relevant to our discussion. On the other hand, JET Blue was used to develop the Exchange Server database technology. Since JET Blue was a multiuser variant, it was much better suited to an environment such as Exchange Server. Although Exchange Server is based on JET Blue, it has greatly evolved over the last several years and is hardly recognizable to its original form. In fact, in Exchange Server 5.5, Microsoft renamed the JET variant that Exchange used to Extensible Storage Engine (ESE) because ESE represented significant new technology (a major rewrite) compared to previous JET versions. This was also done for marketing reasons since customers and competitors often cited JET technology as a weakness and shortcoming of Exchange Server. By severing ties to JET, Microsoft had hoped to establish Exchange Server's database engine in a class by itself. This was only successful to a certain degree since ESE's roots are still mired in the negative connotations of JET and Microsoft Access. Nevertheless, the marketing aspects and issues are not pertinent to our cause. Realistically, JET/ESE technology in Exchange Server has evolved so far from its original form that any arguments over what to call the technology are a waste of valuable brain cells.

Table 3.4   *Evolution of ESE/JET Technology Variants*

JET Blue Version/ Variant	Description
JET NT (JET*.DLL), JET Exchange (EDB.DLL)	Original Exchange database engine technology used in versions 4.0 and 5.0 and also for NT services such as the Windows Internet Naming Service (WINS).
ESE97 (ESE.DLL)	Shipped with Exchange 5.5, providing major performance and reliability improvements over previous versions.
ESE98 (ESE.DLL)	Available in Exchange 2000, further refining and enhancing Exchange database technology.
ESENT (ESENT.DLL)	Available with Windows 2000 as the Active Directory core database engine. ESENT for Windows 2000 is based on ESE97. Future ESENT versions will be based on ESE98.

3.5.1   Industry Standard Core Technology

Whether you refer to the underlying database technology for Exchange Server as JET or ESE, an understanding of this technology is an important foundation for our discussion of disaster recovery and reliability later in this book. The ESE supports two core database files for Exchange 2000—the property store and the streaming store. The property store (EDB file) is based on a fundamental relational database structure used throughout the years in the computer industry called Balanced Tree Database Structure, or B-Tree for short. The B-Tree structure is not something that Microsoft invented but a fundamental structural data design conceived years before in the halls of computer science academia.

3.5.2   B-Tree Database Structure

B-Tree technology is based on the concept of a data tree. A tree is a data structure that consists of a set of data nodes that branch out at the top from a root node. If you think about this, it is more like an upside-down tree. The root node is the parent node of all nodes in the tree, and all nodes have only one parent. Also, nodes can have from zero to *n* child nodes under them. Another type of node in this structure is a leaf node. A leaf node is a node that has no children (no nodes beneath it) where data is typically stored. Within a data tree structure there can also be subtrees, which consist of the structure that exists below a certain node—thus, its subtree. The last important structure in a tree is the pointer. One way to implement data trees that allow for quick navigation of the tree is to place a field in each node called the pointer. The pointer is a field containing information that can be used to locate a related record. Often, most nodes have pointers to both their parent and all child nodes. Figure 3.7 illustrates the concept of data tree structures used in database technology for data storage and organization.

Figure 3.7
Database tree
structure

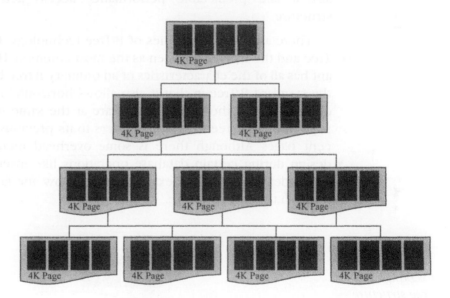

Data trees are viewed and manipulated in terms of several properties. First is the *degree* of a tree. This is also called the branching factor or fan-out by database design gurus. The branching factor is the maximum number of children allowed for each parent node. In general, trees with a large branching factor are broader and shallower structures. Trees with small branching factors have the opposite effect on their structure. For Exchange, ESE will allow each page to store over 200 page pointers per 4KB page, providing for a very high fan-out (translating to high performance). This ensures (in theory) that any piece of data in a large database can be accessed with no more than four disk I/Os (three pointer pages to navigate plus the data page itself). When a database engine accesses tree structures, tree depth has the greatest impact on performance. The breadth of a tree has less of an effect on the speed at which data in trees is accessed. Tree depth is the number of levels between the root node and a leaf node (lowest level) of a data tree structure. When the depth of a tree is uniform across the entire tree structure (i.e., the distance is the same from the root node to each leaf node), the tree structure is referred to as a Balanced Tree (B-Tree). In a B-Tree structure, all leaves are the same distance from the root. This ensures consistent and predictable performance access across the entire structure.

There are several varieties of B-Tree technology; the standard B-Tree and the B+Tree are seen as the most common. The B+Tree variant has all of the characteristics of an ordinary B-tree but differs from the standard B-Tree in that it also allows horizontal relationships to other nodes in the structure that are at the same level. Each data page in the B+Tree has page pointers to its previous and next adjacent pages. Although there is some overhead incurred with this design during certain database operations like insert, split, merge, and index creation, the extra pointers allow for faster navigation through the tree structure.

Figure 3.8
Exchange ESE B-Tree structure

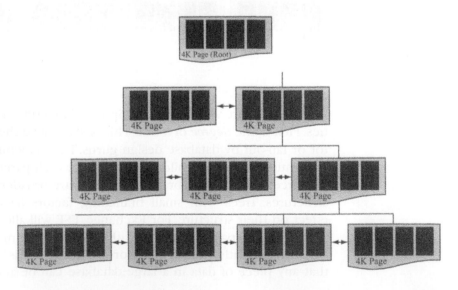

Microsoft Exchange Server's ESE uses the standard B+Tree implementation (with some modifications to get some extra features). Keep in mind that the structures I describe here are standard technologies defined and refined by computer scientists and software engineers for many years. The particular implementation that Microsoft uses for Exchange Server is based on these technologies but may vary based on designers' goals at Microsoft as Exchange has been developed and evolved. Applied to Microsoft Exchange Server, balanced tree technology is the best fit for the complex, semistructured data requirements of a messaging and collaborative application server. This is a key point since I continually hear speculation from different sources wondering when Microsoft will migrate Exchange Server to SQL Server database technology. The flaw in this speculation is that SQL Server is not as well suited to storing semistructured data. Microsoft SQL Server's data-storage strengths lie in structured data storage in which indexes are more static and the data changes less frequently. Applied to Exchange Server, the SQL Server technology would not fair well in an environment where data changes continuously and indexes and data views must be created and re-created dynamically. While Microsoft may someday merge these two database engine technologies into one suited to both application and data storage needs, I don't foresee ESE's replacement by SQL Server technology. In fact, Microsoft's strategy for collaborative, workflow, and knowledge management technologies is to use both database engine technologies—SQL Server for structured data and ESE for semistructured data. What the future holds is uncertain as SQL Server technology may evolve to handle both data types well.

To return to our discussion of ESE technology used by Exchange Server, let's dig deeper into how this technology is used to store messaging data. ESE stores all Exchange Server data in a B-Tree structure. An individual table within the Exchange Server information store is simply a collection of B-Trees. The B-Trees are indexed to provide fast and efficient access to data on disk by minimizing the number of disk I/Os required to access the database. An Exchange Server ESE B-Tree database is organized into (4KB) pages. These pages contain either data or pointers to other pages in the database. For faster access, Exchange Server caches these 4KB database pages in memory. The structure of the ESE page is illustrated in Figure 3.9.

Figure 3.9
*Exchange
Server ESE page
structure*

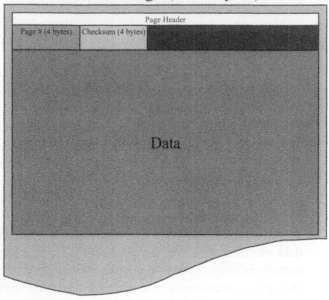

Each 4KB page is comprised of a header portion and a data portion. The content of the page header includes a 4-byte checksum, a 4-byte page number, flags, and a timestamp (known as DBTime). We will discuss the importance of the header information to ensuring the integrity of the Exchange Server databases later in this chapter. Exchange Server arranges the B-Tree structures in the database in a fashion that provides for shallow B-Tree structures. This is achieved with a "high-fan-out" design that ensures that the B-Tree structure is purposely broad and shallow. With the goal of achieving a fan-out greater than 200 (meaning 200 pages across), a shallow B-Tree structure of less than four levels deep can usually be achieved. Again, this helps reduce disk I/O by increasing cache hits for pages in the ESE page cache and makes page access as efficient as possible. Dynamic buffer allocation (discussed later in this chapter) does this wonder by caching most of the internal nodes of the B-Tree, thereby greatly enhancing access to any page in the database.

3.5.3 B-Tree Indexes

Another key structure for the ESE is the index. Indexes allow users to quickly access and view database records using whatever key they desire. ESE allows the creation and deletion of indexes dynamically. The combination of these key database structures provides Exchange Server with high-performance access to user data while minimizing disk I/O requirements. When you need to have flexibility of access and views of your data while not sacrificing performance, you utilize indexes. In B-Tree technology, an index is just another B-Tree that maps a primary key for viewing the data in a particular way. A secondary index simply maps a secondary key onto a primary key. Indexes are useful for the semistructured data environment of messaging and collaborative applications. For example, if you modify your folder view in the Exchange client (typically Outlook), Outlook uses MAPI to request that the database engine build a new index (a secondary index) of your data in the information store. This is why there is typically some delay as the new index is created. When unutilized, secondary indexes (which are B-Tree structures themselves) are maintained for seven days and then are aged out of the database. One of ESE's strengths is that it allows these indexes to be created without taking the database offline (other database engines require that indexes be created while the data is offline). ESE uses the version store cache to keep track of database transactions that modify tables during the index creation. When the index creation is complete, ESE updates the table. The use of online secondary index creation is a major competitive advantage for Exchange over its competitors.

3.5.4 Long Value B-Trees

In certain cases, a column in a table may be too large to fit into a single 4KB database page. One example of this is a message with a body longer than 4KB (held in the PR_BODY column of the message table). Exchange Server provides for this case through the use of a Long-Value B-Tree (LV). Long -Value B-Trees take these large data segments, breaks them into 4KB chunks (approximately, since there is overhead for the page header), and store them as a special long value data type. If data needs to be stored in an ESE page that is to too large (4KB) to fit into a single B-Tree data page, ESE breaks the data into pieces of almost 4KB (allowing room for headers and over-head) and stores the data in a separate Long-Value B-Tree. In the data B-Tree, there will be a pointer (the LID) to the Long-Value B-Tree. Using a Long-Value Identifier (LID) and offset that can be accessed on a table-wide basis allows for efficient access to these chunks.

ESE saves space by allowing multiple database records to share the same long value (the single instance storage benefit) such as a message body for a message sent to multiple recipients. ESE accomplishes this by storing a reference count for each long-value record. Once the reference count reaches zero, the long-value can be deleted. Long-values are an important and powerful feature of ESE. As such, tools like ESEUTIL will inspect and fix long-value references (using the /p "repair" option) and will also detect long-values that have been dereferenced (called orphaned) but not deleted (using the /x integrity/repair option). ESEUTIL will not remove orphaned long-values from the database. However, in Exchange 2000, orphaned long-values will be deleted during online maintenance.

To summarize thus far, the design of Exchange Server, as we have seen, is based on standard database technology available for years. The system relies on an embedded database engine that lays out the structure of the disk for Exchange and manages memory. The database engine technology used in Exchange is also used "under the covers" by other services in the Windows 2000 operating system, such as the Active Directory. In the case of the Active Directory, ESE is implemented in the Local Security Authentication Subsystem (LSASS) utilizing the ESENT.DLL (ESENT uses 8KB pages, however). The Exchange Server database engine caches the disk in memory by swapping 4KB chunks of data, called pages, in and out of memory. It updates the pages in memory and takes care of writing new or updated pages back to the disk. This means that, when requests come into the system, the database engine can buffer data in memory so it doesn't have to constantly go to disk. This makes the system more efficient because writing to memory is "cheaper" (or faster) than writing to disk. When users make requests, the database engine starts loading the requests into memory and marks the pages as "dirty" (a dirty page is a page in memory that has been written with data). These dirty pages are then later written to the information store databases on disk.

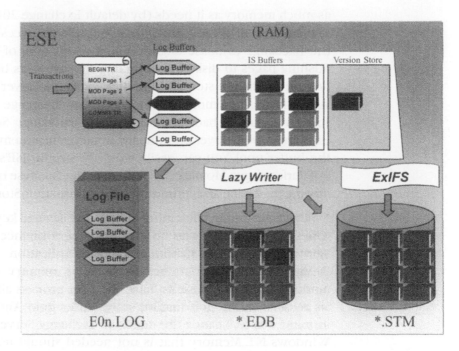

Figure 3.10
*How Exchange
server database
transactions
are committed*

3.5.5   Dynamic Buffer Allocation

Prior to Exchange Server 5.5, the buffer cache that the database engine used to hold its pages (called the information store buffer pool) was of a fixed size. If Exchange Server was thrashing and needed more memory, the administrator had to install more memory on the system and then run the Exchange Server Performance Optimizer to retune the system. To make matters worse, previous versions could only use a maximum of about 20,000 of these buffers or about 80MB (20,000 buffers × 4KB). With Exchange Server 5.5, however, the development team made some design changes to the way the database engine uses memory. They built dynamic buffer allocation into the database engine so that the database engine dynamically grows or shrinks depending on how much memory is available and whether there is pressure from other services running on the system. If memory is not being used by other services in the system, such as Microsoft Internet Information Service (IIS), ESE will take up as much memory as it needs (by default Exchange 2000 limits this to a maximum of 900MB of RAM). When other services need memory, the Exchange database engine will give up some of its memory by flushing pages to disk and shrinking the size of its buffer. The number of information store buffers that Exchange Server allocates is the single highest memory consumer on an Exchange Server (unless someone has a bad memory leak). Exchange Server 5.5 and Exchange 2000 Server continually monitor the system and the size of the buffer pool. You can easily view the size of ESE's buffer pool in NT Performance Monitor by looking at the Database object and monitoring the cache size counter for the Information Store Instance.

Dynamic buffer allocation (DBA) had several key design goals. Chief among these was to maximize performance for Exchange Server. Next was to maximize memory utilization on the system. Designers could see no reason to leave memory on the system underutilized and chose to have the store process allocate as much as possible to the information store buffer pool. Another goal kept in mind was to balance the needs of Exchange Server with those of Windows NT. Memory that is not needed should not be used, and finally, when memory is released, it should be released quickly. The Exchange Server database engine very efficiently utilizes the DBA feature to dynamically tune the information store buffer pool. This is most beneficial when the Exchange Server is also running other services such as Microsoft SQL Server. When first available in Exchange Server 5.5, DBA was a bit alarming to some Exchange administrators. This was due to the fact that the STORE process immediately allocated all available memory on the server. In contrast, previous versions of Exchange Server would leave substantial amounts of memory unused. This created quite a stir and appeared to some as though Exchange Server 5.5 had sprung a memory leak. System manager education eventually overcame this misconception. Today, for Exchange Server 5.5 and Exchange 2000 Server, the manifestations of DBA have become accepted and are a welcomed mode of operation for Microsoft Exchange Server. DBA makes optimal use of server resources while maximizing performance.

Although caching data in memory is the fastest and most efficient way to process data, it means that while Exchange Server is running, the information on disk is never completely consistent. The latest version of the database is in memory, and since many changes in memory haven't made it to disk yet, the database and memory are out of sync. If there are any dirty pages in memory that haven't been flushed and written to disk yet, the databases are flagged as inconsistent. Therefore, while Exchange Server is running normally, the databases are technically inconsistent. The only time that Exchange databases are truly in a consistent state is when all the dirty pages in memory are flushed to disk following a graceful shutdown or dismount of the database in which no errors occurred. Based on this, you can see that, if something goes wrong, the database must be recovered. If you lose the contents of memory because of a server outage before the data is written to disk, you're left with an inconsistent database. To protect against this problem, Exchange Server provides a way to recover from this situation. This is where transaction logging comes in. I will discuss transaction logging more in later sections.

3.5.6   It's about Reliability

While the performance features of the Exchange Server database engine are key to the server scalability, reliability, and recoverability are of paramount concern. Exchange Server is often referred to as a transaction-based e-mail system and the information store as a transactional database. So what does that mean anyway?

A *transaction* is defined as a set of changes, such as inserts, deletes, and updates, to a database in which the system obeys the following absolutes known as the ACID properties:

- *Atomic:* Either all the operations occur or none of them occur.
- *Consistent:* The database is transformed from one correct state to another.
- *Isolated:* Changes are not visible until they are committed.
- *Durable:* Committed transactions are preserved in the database even if the system crashes.

The database engine "commits" a transaction only when it can guarantee that the data is "durable," meaning that it is protected from crashes or other failures. The database engine will only successfully commit data when there is confidence that transactions have been flushed from memory to the transaction log file on disk.

For example, to move an e-mail message from one folder, such as *Inbox,* to another folder called *Important,* Exchange Server must perform the following logical operations (at the physical database level, it is much more complex than these three logical steps).

1.   Delete the e-mail message from Inbox.

2.   Insert the e-mail message into Important.

3.   Update the information about each folder to correctly reflect the number of items in each folder and the number of unread items.

Because these operations are done within the boundary of a single transaction, Exchange will perform all or none of these operations. As a result, it doesn't matter which order Exchange Server performs the operations. The message can be deleted safely from Inbox first because the system knows that the delete will only be committed if the message is also inserted into Important. Because of transaction-based system qualities, even if the system crashes, it is guaranteed that Exchange Server will never lose an e-mail message while performing any operations on it. In addition, Exchange Server will never end up with two copies of an e-mail message that was moved. Hopefully, your bank uses similar technology when making changes to your checking account.

3.5.7   The Version Store

The version store is a component of the ESE transaction process that gives Exchange the ability to track and manage multiple concurrent transactions to the same database page. This provides the isolation and consistency ACID attributes that ensure consistent transactions to the database. The version store exists only in memory (refer to Figure 3.10) and is a list of page modifications. When a transaction starts, the original page is stored in the version store cache in memory. This allows concurrent session threads to read the contents of the original page even though a current transaction has not committed. In fact, the transaction may never commit, which is why it is important to have saved the original page contents (providing for a rollback). If a transaction needs to be rolled back, the version store contains a list of all operations performed, and ESE simply needs to "undo" these operations in order for rollback to be complete. The version store also protects against page write conflicts by detecting when two sessions attempt to modify the same page. In this case, the version store will reject the second modification. ESE's version store guarantees that sessions (i.e., users) will see a consistent view of the database and that reads to the database are repeatable. When a session begins a transaction, it always sees the same view—regardless of whether the records in view are being modified by other sessions. The version store is able to discern which view of a record a session should see. The version store is key to ESE's ability to meet the requirements of the ACID properties for transaction-based systems.

3.5.8   How Transaction Logging Works

Most administrators will agree that the database files are an important aspect of data recovery. But transaction log files are equally important because they reflect server operations up to the second. With Exchange Server, the database files are written to as server I/O bandwidth allows via a checkpointing mechanism that flushes dirty database buffers to disk. The transaction log files contain information that the database files don't. As a result, the transaction logs are critical to recovery of your Exchange Server. Without them, the Exchange Server databases will be inconsistent and, most likely, unusable. ESE technology uses what is called *write-ahead logging*. Write-ahead logging is a valuable tool since system failures are bound to occur. Failures in hardware such as disk drive failure, system errors, or power failures are a given. Transaction logging allows the Exchange Server database to remain consistent despite crashes. With write-ahead logging, transactions and data are written to the log files first. Since the information store buffer pool also has database pages cached in memory, these pages are updated in memory but are not immediately written to disk. Since transactions are appended to the log files sequentially, I/O is very fast.

Exchange uses transaction log files to keep track of the information in memory that hasn't yet made its way to the database on disk. Transaction log files are a sequence of files whose purpose is to keep a secure copy on disk of volatile data in memory so that the system can recover in the event of a failure. If your system crashes and the database is undamaged, as long as you have the log files, you can recover data up to the last committed transaction before the failure. As a best practice, log files should be placed on a dedicated disk or array so that they aren't affected by any problems or failures that corrupt the database.

Transaction log files also make writing data fast since appending operations and data sequentially in a log file takes less I/O bandwidth than writing randomly to a database file. When a change is made to the database, the database engine updates the data in memory and synchronously writes a record of the transaction to the log file. This record allows the database engine to re-create the transaction in the event of failure. Then the database engine writes the data to the database on disk. To save disk I/O, the database engine doesn't write pages to disk during every transaction; but instead, it batches them into larger I/O operations. With Exchange 5.5 this batched checkpoint operation resulted in an I/O pattern that is rather "spike-like" in nature. For Exchange 2000, algorithms have been implemented that smooth out the checkpointing operations, resulting in a more evened I/O pattern. Logically, you can think of the data as moving from memory to the log file to the database on disk, but what actually happens is that data moves from memory to the database on disk (refer to Figure 3.10). The log files are optimized for high-speed writes, so during normal operations, the database engine never actually reads the log files. It only reads the log files if the information store service stops abnormally or crashes and the database engine needs to recover from the failure by replaying the log files.

The transaction logs are generated and accessed in sequential order called *generations*. Each transaction log file in a sequence can contain up to 5MB of data. When the log file is full, it rolls over to a new log file by creating an interim file called EDBTMP.LOG, saving the current E0n.LOG to the next generational sequence and renaming EDBTMP.LOG to E0n.LOG. To track transaction log files, ESE associates each log file with a generation number. For example, when Exchange 2000 Server starts for the first time, it creates a log file called E00.log for the first storage group (EDB.LOG in previous versions) with a generation number of 1. Additional storage groups' default transaction logs are enumerated E01.LOG, E02.LOG, etc. When that log file is full and the database engine rolls over to a new log file, the new log file becomes E00.log with a generation number of 2 (or the next in sequence), and the old E00.log file is renamed E00nnnnn.log. This sequence number is in hexadecimal format. This continues until the next sequence of log files starts. If you shut down the server and lose all the log files, when you restart the information store, the database engine will create a new sequence of log files starting with a generation number of 1. Since log files can have the same name, the database engine stamps the header in each file in the sequence with a unique signature so it can distinguish between different series of log files. Also within each log file are hard-coded paths of the database files that the log is associated with along with other information such as timestamps and generation information. Figure 3.11 shows a dump of the header of a transaction log file using the ESEUTIL utility with the /ML parameter (ESEUTIL /ML).

Figure 3.11
*Exchange
Server
transaction log
file header
format*

```
1Generation: 23 (0x17)
    Checkpoint: (0x17,15,1D9)
    creation time: 11/23/1999 13:59:39
    prev gen time: 11/23/1999 13:45:58
    Format LGVersion: (7.3703.1)
    Engine LGVersion: (7.3703.1)
    Signature: Create time:09/28/1999 12:15:23 Rand:3246416 Computer:
    Env SystemPath: F:\exchsrvr\mdbdata\
    Env LogFilePath: F:\exchsrvr\mdbdata\
    Env Log Sec size: 512
    Env (Session, Opentbl, VerPage, Cursors, LogBufs, LogFile, Buffers)
    (    272,   37800,    2320,   12600,      84,   10240,   65421)
    1 f:\exchsrvr\mdbdata\priv1.edb
      dbtime: 97021 (0-97021)
      objidLast: 206
      Signature: Create time:09/28/1999 12:15:27 Rand:3272303 Computer:
      MaxDbSize: 0 pages
      Last Attach: (0x16,1F9C,1FF)
      Last Consistent: (0x16,1F93,1B7)
    2 F:\exchsrvr\mdbdata\pub1.edb
      dbtime: 572673 (0-572673)
      objidLast: 5363
      Signature: Create time:09/28/1999 12:15:49 Rand:3308205 Computer:
      MaxDbSize: 0 pages
      Last Attach: (0x16,1FA1,1A1)
      Last Consistent: (0x16,1F9B,17A)
    Last Lgpos: (0x17,15,1EC)
```

If you were to dig deeper into the inside of a transaction log file, you would also find the most important parts of the log files—log records. Log records contain transactional information and commands like BeginTransaction, Insert, Delete, Replace, Commit, and Rollback. Records of low-level, physical modifications to the database are also stored. Figure 3.12 gives an illustration of the format of log records contained within a transaction log file.

At a high level, delivering one piece of mail seems to be a rather simple operation. However, under the covers, it is a complex operation that involves many low-level operations to the database. Also, since a typical Exchange server under load is handling hundreds or thousands of operations from multiple users simultaneously, the

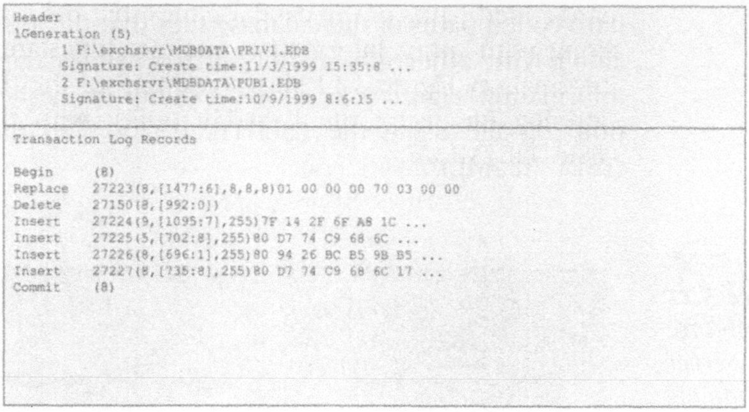

Figure 3.12
*ESE transaction
log file structure*

```
Header
1Generation (5)
      1 F:\exchsrvr\MDBDATA\PRIV1.EDB
      Signature: Create time:11/3/1999 15:35:8 ...
      2 F:\exchsrvr\MDBDATA\PUB1.EDB
      Signature: Create time:10/9/1999 8:6:15 ...

Transaction Log Records

Begin     (8)
Replace   27223(8,[1477:6],8,8,8)01 00 00 00 70 03 00 00
Delete    27150(8,[992:0])
Insert    27224(9,[1095:7],255)7F 14 2F 6F A8 1C ...
Insert    27225(5,[702:8],255)80 D7 74 C9 68 6C ...
Insert    27226(8,[696:1],255)80 94 26 BC B5 9B B5 ...
Insert    27227(8,[735:8],255)80 D7 74 C9 68 6C 17 ...
Commit    (8)
```

operations performed by these transactions are interleaved within the transaction log file. When an Exchange server database page is modified, the following operations occur:

1.   The timestamp on the database page is updated.

2.   A new log record is created in memory that includes the timestamp.

3.   The page is modified.

4.   When modification operations are complete, a commit occurs.

5.   Once a commit operation occurs, all log records are flushed to the disk.

6.   The database page on disk is updated once the transaction log records have been flushed to disk via the checkpoint process and sufficient I/O bandwidth is available.

The implications of physical logging of every transaction applied to the database are that the database must be in the correct state in order for recovery operations to work. What would happen if something were to go wrong in the database recovery scenario? What if log files were missing or if the wrong version of the database were restored? What would be the effect of a corrupt log file? For example, what if a log record performed a delete operation but the data had never been inserted? In another scenario, what if the most current log file generation (E00.LOG) were accidentally deleted? It is possible that some recent transactions in a previous log file that had already been flushed to the database could have been undone in the current log file. If E00.LOG were deleted, these roll-back operations would never be executed. Thus, the Exchange server database could potentially become corrupted. This emphasizes the importance of proper database maintenance and the need to not interfere with or second-guess Exchange Server's transactional integrity mechanisms.

3.5.9 Logging File Record Checksumming

We know that the transaction logs protect the database from permanent corruption by allowing transactions to be replayed in the event of a failure. In addition, the database itself has an integrity checksum on every 4KB page. So what protects the logs? In Exchange 2000, each record in a log file has a checksum. The LRCK (log record checksum) can cover a range of data both before and after its position in the log file.

ESE creates the checksum by XORing every 4 bytes in the range (backwards and forwards), all fields in the LRCK, and the generation number of the log file. The generation number of the log file is included when calculating the checksum so that when circular logging is enabled, ESE will reuse an old log file and will not interpret the old records as valid. Each checksum is verified during backup and recovery. If a checksum fails during one of these operations, the operation will stop, logging an event in the application event log with an event ID of 463, indicating the failed checksum record location. During recovery, if an LRCK fails to match the data it covers, it can be for one of two reasons, either a torn write at the end of the current log file (E0n.LOG) or data damage somewhere else in the log file sequence. ESE handles these two situations differently.

- *Torn write*—Before ESE can act on a failed LRCK, it must first work out where the data damage is. To enable ESE to do this, each log file is filled before use with a data pattern known as the *log-file fill pattern*. If ESE is replaying transactions in E0n.log, ESE looks for the recognizable fill pattern beyond the LRCK range. If the fill pattern is the only data found beyond the point of the failed LRCK range to the end of the log file, then ESE can safely make the decision that the invalid data was caused by a torn write at the end of the log file sequence and that there are no log records beyond this point. ESE will log an event ID 461 to indicate that it has hit this condition.

- *Data damage*—If, however, ESE either is not replaying transactions from E00.log or finds data other than the recognizable
  log-file fill pattern in E00.log beyond the failed LRCK data
  range, there must be more records in this log file. In this case,
  data that the disk subsystem had confirmed to be successfully
  written to disk is now no longer not matching its checksum.
  ESE will log an event ID 464 or 465 to indicate this condition.

The log file checksums can be manually verified using ESEUTIL /
ml; this performs a quick (i.e., less than a second) integrity check
verifying each checksum. This additional level of integrity checking
further enhances an already robust system in the Exchange database
engine for ensuring that user data is intact. No other messaging
server product that I am aware of provides the levels of integrity
checking of Exchange 2000.

3.5.10 Reserved Log Files

Finally, within each storage group or ESE instance, reserve transaction logs are also maintained. These files (named RES1.LOG and
RES2.LOG) are needed in the event that disk space on the volume
holding transaction logs runs out. While these files rarely get used,
they provide an important safeguard against the potential condition
that results when disk space on the transaction logging volume is
not monitored and runs out. These reserved log files are kept in the
default directory where the other log files for a storage group are
stored. If the database engine is in the process of renaming the current E00.LOG to the next log generation and there is not enough
disk space to create a new E00.LOG (NTFS returns an out of disk
space to ESE), the reserve log files are then used and are renamed to
the current generation number. This fail-safe measure is only acti-
vated in that the event of an emergency. Once Exchange Server is
aware that there is not disk space available to create new log files,
the storage group instance must be shut down. When this happens,
ESE will flush any transactions in memory that have not yet been
committed to the database (dirty buffers) to a log entry in RES1.LOG
or RES2.LOG. The reserve log files provide a location for transactions
that may be "in flight" during this premature shutdown to be written. Once complete with this flush operation, the storage group can
be safely taken offline, and administrative action must occur (e.g.,
increase disk space). Also, in this event, the ESE instance will shut
down and record this event in the system event log. On an

extremely busy server with large amounts of memory, it could be possible that not all outstanding transactions can be safely stored within the confines of RES1.LOG and RES2.LOG. Remember that each log file is only 5MB in size. While this possibility exists, it is quite remote in nature since, by design, Exchange attempts to minimize the number of outstanding transactions in memory. However, this possibility should serve as a good example of the importance to overall server health of proactive monitoring of available disk space and other measures.

3.5.11 The Checkpoint File

Since not all transaction log files are needed to recover a database, database systems provide a method to quickly comprehend which log files are required. This mechanism is the checkpoint file. The checkpoint file tells ESE which log files are needed to recover from a crash. The checkpoint file simply keeps track of the data contained in the log files that hasn't yet been written to the database file on disk. The database engine maintains a checkpoint file called E0N.CHK for each log file sequence (per storage group in Exchange 2000). The checkpoint file is a pointer in the log sequence that maintains the status between memory and the database files on disk. It indicates the point in the log file from which the database engine needs to start the recovery if there's been a failure. In fact, the checkpoint file is essential for efficient recovery because, if it didn't exist, the information store would have to attempt recovery by starting from the beginning of the oldest log file it found on disk and then checking every page in every log file to determine whether it had already been written to the database. The database engine can recover without the checkpoint file but it will take much longer because all transaction logs must be scanned to search for transactions that have not been written to the database. This process, of course, is very time consuming, especially if all you want to do is make the database consistent.

3.5.12 Circular Logging

Exchange supports a feature called *circular logging.* The circular logging feature is left over from the days when server disk space was at a premium. Back in the early days of Exchange, there was some concern about running out of disk space and less concern about recovering data. As a result, to maintain a fixed size for log files and to prevent the buildup of log files, circular logging was enabled by default. This means that once five log file generations have been written, the first file in the sequence is reused. The database engine deletes it and creates a new log file in the sequence. By doing this, only enough data is on disk to make the database consistent in the event of a crash. This still provides ESE with the ability to perform a soft recovery, but it makes hard recovery (restore from backup) impossible.

If you're concerned about protecting your data, the first thing you should do is turn circular logging off on your Exchange server. For Exchanger 2000, circular logging is disabled by default. While circular logging reduces the need for disk space, it eliminates your ability to recover all changes since your last backup if your information store is corrupted due to a hardware failure. This is because circular logging only maintains enough log files to ensure transactional integrity when recovering from nonhardware failures. Circular logging negates the advantages of using a transaction-based system and sacrifices the ability to recover if something goes wrong with the system and the contents of memory are lost. As a result, it's not recommended for most deployments.

Circular logging works in much the same way as normal logging except that the checkpoint file is no longer just an optimization feature; it's essential for keeping track of the information that has been flushed to disk. During circular logging, as the checkpoint file advances to the next log file, old files are reused in the next generation. When this happens, you lose the ability to use the log files on disk in conjunction with your backup media to restore to the most recently committed transaction. When (and only when) circular logging is enabled for Exchange 2000, writes to the streaming store (*.STM files) are not transaction logged. This saves disk I/O to the transaction logs when transactions are committed. One exception to this is during backup operations when writes to the streaming store are always logged. If you're concerned about log files consuming your disk resources, there's a better way to clean up your log files— simply perform regular online backups. Backups automatically remove transaction log files when they're no longer needed.

3.6   How Exchange 2000 Stores Incoming Data

Exchange 2000 now supports the ability for content to be stored in the database based on the type of native format of the client. In previous versions of Exchange Server, all incoming content was stored in Microsoft Rich Text Format (RTF) and was viewed as MAPI properties in the database (*.EDB file). In previous versions of Exchange, when non-MAPI clients sent or retrieved data from the Exchange information store, content was converted to a useable native form (such as MIME). This resulted in an increased processing load for Exchange servers as they performed this conversion process (called IMAIL).

Exchange 2000 now provides a native content store for Internet protocol clients using the MIME (Multipart Internet Mail Extension) format. This store is the streaming store, or STM file. As discussed earlier in this chapter, the streaming store has no B-Tree overhead and is simply a flat data structure consisting of 4KB pages grouped into 16 page runs that is ideal for storing MIME content and binary large objects (BLOBs). In order for all types of clients to have access to data in the Exchange databases (EDB + STM file pair), Exchange 2000 supports a feature known as *property promotion*. Property promotion allows data held in the streaming file to have some of its key properties (such as sender, date sent, date received, subject, etc.) promoted to the properties store, allowing folder and index views of the data stored in the streaming file. Property promotion is based on where the data came from and where it is stored. Table 3.5 documents how Exchange 2000 carries out property promotion. In general, the rule is that the "last writer" determines how and where the data is stored.

Table 3.5   *Exchange 2000 Property Promotion Rules*

Content Received From	Promotion Rules
MAPI client	Content stored in properties store (EDB). If a non-MAPI client asks for this message, Exchange will perform a conversion from MAPI to Internet format. The conversion is not persisted (moved to the streaming store).
Internet client	Level 1 conversion: Content is stored in the streaming store (STM), and certain headers are promoted as properties to the EDB file.

Table 3.5   *Exchange 2000 Property Promotion Rules (continued)*

Content Received From	Promotion Rules
	Level 2 conversion: If a MAPI client requests a property of the message (such as subject), Exchange will promote all of the header information into the property store.
	Level 3 conversion: If the MAPI client requests the attachment data, a near-duplicate message is created in the property store. If the MAPI client modifies the message, the streaming store version is discarded.

3.6.1   Exchange Installable File System

Exchange (ExIFS) 2000 features the much-touted Installable File System (IFS), which turns Exchange 2000 into a file repository for most any application. IFS provides direct access to the STM file at a file-system level. This enables Win32 applications and Server Message Block (SMB) applications to directly access the Exchange information store by exposing item- and folder-level information store objects as a simple file or share. For maximum benefit of IFS, it should be combined with other Exchange 2000 information store features such as document property promotion, full-text indexing, or Web client (HTTP) support. When used in conjunction with these features, Exchange 2000 becomes a file server with capabilities beyond even those available with Windows 2000 and NTFS. For example, a browser-based client could query the Exchange information store for object properties or perform full-text searches much easier than was possible with earlier versions of Exchange Server.

On every Exchange 2000 server, the M: drive (by default) is automatically mapped with a share name of "Exchange." Users can access the Exchange information remotely over the network by simply mapping a drive. IFS provides access to two hierarchical levels of the Exchange information store—Public Folders and Mailbox. Public folder items can be listed using the standard DIR command or view and can be manipulated with Windows Explorer and other standard interfaces and commands. The mailbox level is provided by the MBX folder. This is the root for all mailboxes on the Exchange 2000 server. Mailbox folder names are not viewable by default, but with proper access, users can view these as well. ExIFS is new to Exchange 2000, and the real significance has yet to be discovered.

Exchange 2000 deployment rollout and applications leverage this feature. This powerful feature also requires the utmost in management and security attention. To summarize, the ExIFS is a method of providing complete file system semantics for the Exchange information store objects. ExIFS is implemented as a kernel mode device driver (ExIFS.SYS) for high performance and reflects Win32 file system calls to the Exchange Store (via ExWin32.DLL), thereby exposing Win32 file system APIs (i.e., CreateFileEx, ReadFileEx, etc.) as well as file system functions exported from Kernel32.DLL for both third-party developers and Microsoft software such as IIS. Via ExIFS, the contents of the Exchange databases are exposed as ordinary NTFS file objects.

3.6.2 The Information Store and ExIFS Work Together to Store Messaging Data

Figure 3.13 shows the relationship between the Exchange Store process (a subcomponent of which is ESE), the ExIFS, and IIS.

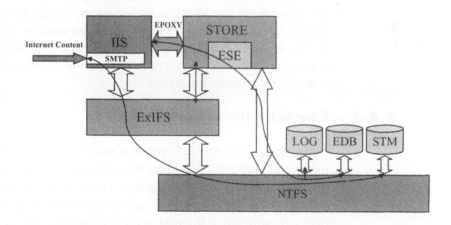

Figure 3.13
Exchange 2000 interaction between the store, ExIFS, and IIS

In previous versions of Exchange, incoming messaging data from services such as SMTP or NNTP was transferred using the NTFS file system as an intermediate step (in Exchange 5.5, this was done by transferring files in the IMSDATAIN directory to the MTS-IN folders). For Exchange 2000, more focus was given to Internet protocols, and therefore ExIFS was leveraged to allow IIS to view the streaming store as a collection of smaller "virtual files." Since IIS hosts all Internet protocols (in the form of virtual servers) for Exchange 2000, a protocol server such as SMTP will communicate via the Exchange/ IIS "Epoxy" layer (a shared memory message-passing construct), obtain file handles (provided by ExIFS) to these virtual files, and write incoming Internet content directly into the streaming store (STM file). Likewise, outgoing messages can be read directly from the STM file by IIS. A message then becomes a list of pages and properties (some of which are promoted to the property store). IIS is able to simply allocate pages from the virtual files (contained in the streaming store) via communication with the store process (which manages the database engine) and the ExIFS. Accessing the streaming store via ExIFS allows IIS to use standard Win32 file handlers to access content stored in Exchange 2000 databases. ESE maintains a list of pages in the streaming store that are available for use by IIS. The ExIFS driver queries this list, known as a *scatter-gather list*, when it needs to write information to the streaming store. When an IFS client (such as IIS) needs to write to the streaming store, ESE will allocate chunks of 16 4KB pages (64KB). This enables data to be streamed from the STM file in kernel mode (ExIFS is a kernel-mode driver) in large I/Os of 32KB. The combination of ESE and ExIFS allows Exchange 2000 to provide a high performance storage mechanism for both native Internet content and MAPI content that is also completely transaction based.

3.6.3   Content Indexing

The Exchange 2000 information store now supports the management and creation of indexes for common key fields such as *subject* or *message body* for fast searches and lookups. Previous versions of Exchange would search through every document in every folder in order to support a full-text search capability. This would drastically increase search times as databases grew larger. With the content indexing feature in Exchange 2000, every word in the database is indexed, making fast searches a reality regardless of the database size. Both the message content and attachment text can now be searched. In addition, advanced searches are now possible for content in both the EDB and STM stores using the property promotion feature of the information store. Searches can be performed on any document property such as *author.* Content indexing will be a very important feature as future document management and workflow applications for Microsoft and third-party vendors leverage the Exchange 2000 information store.

3.6.4   Is Single Instance Storage Sacrificed?

Since the very first versions, Exchange Server supported the single instance storage feature. With single instance storage, a message sent to multiple mailboxes is only stored once per database. While this feature was significant is reducing overall storage requirements on the server, it is difficult to realize this benefit in larger deployments and receive any practical benefits. In order to achieve a high degree of single instance storage (called a single instance storage ratio), you must attempt to allocate users by workgroup and provide a high degree of concentration in your user population. The idea is that the locality of users will achieve high single instance storage since messages, in theory, will be grouped by workgroup or other factors such as geography. In practice, we see that real-world deployments have trouble achieving the desired result since workgroups and organizations are highly dispersed. Exchange 2000 still supports single instance storage as well. However, based on our previous discussions of multiple storage groups and databases, you can see that a high degree of single instance storage will be an even more challenging goal to achieve with Exchange 2000. As long as messages are sent to users that reside on the same database, single instance storage is attainable. If not, the message (or any data, for that matter) is copied once to each database where recipients reside. If the databases are in different storage groups, then the additional overhead of multiple transaction logging is also added. To illustrate this, let's look at an example illustrated in Figure 3.14. Suppose a single storage group is deployed on a server. The storage group has four private and one public information stores (databases) configured. A single 1MB message is sent to 40 people configured as follows: 10 people are hosted by each of the 4 private information stores configured. In this configuration, the total amount of information store space required is 4MB—1MB on each private information store. An additional 1MB is also used because the message is also stored in the transaction log for that storage group. Without single instance storage, the message would have to be replicated to each individual user's mailbox, resulting in 40 copies of the 1MB message—a total of 40MB of information store space would be required.

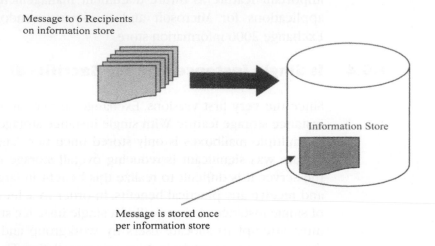

Figure 3.14
*Single instance
storage
illustration*

Message to 6 Recipients
on information store

Information Store

Message is stored once
per information store

Obviously, Microsoft marketers will still continue to tout the benefits of single instance storage. In addition, the competition has also recognized the benefits of this feature. In fact, IBM/Lotus has included single instance storage in Domino Release 5, released in March of 1999. Whenever possible, you might consider how you can take advantage of this feature in your Exchange deployment. In practice, however, I expect this feature to gradually fade into the background as it is difficult in practice to administer. While still of some value, the benefits will be less dramatic than originally planned.

3.6.5   Storage and the Exchange Database Are Key

I have taken the liberty in this chapter of significantly digressing into the roots and technologies around Exchange Server's database technology. I wanted not only to focus on Exchange 2000 features and functionality but also to highlight how the technology in Exchange has evolved within the industry and at Microsoft to provide the high-performance, reliable, recoverable, scalable, and manageable semistructured storage engine that we now see in Exchange 2000 Server. Remember, Exchange has roots in single user database technology much the same as Microsoft Access. However, never again the two shall meet. It is also important that we understand the significance of balanced tree database technology, upon which the Exchange database property store is based. This is proven technology used for years that Microsoft (believe it or not) did not invent. Hopefully, I have also illustrated how important new developments in Exchange 2000 such as storage groups and multiple databases will free us from the bondage of the monolithic store in previous versions of Exchange Server. The new features in the Exchange information store technology, such as the streaming store, multiple public folder trees, ExIFS, and the removal of the Internet protocols allowing for a front-end/back-end architecture for Exchange 2000 to be deployed, will be important to our later discussions on building reliable systems. Along with all these new capabilities and powerful features in Exchange 2000 come greater management complexities. This will require Exchange administrators to master these new features in order to deploy them properly. Key foundational knowledge must be comprehended in order to conduct further discussions about high availability and disaster recovery for Exchange. A thorough understanding of the new technologies provided in Exchange 2000 as well as the issues that have limited us in previous versions will help us build Exchange deployments that truly meet mission-critical standards.

4

Exchange Disaster Recovery Technology

If you recall the discussion of the "black box" of downtime from Chapter 2, you will remember that I pointed out that downtime is not a singular event but a series of individual outage components. My main emphasis was to point out that, by identifying and evaluating each individual component of a downtime occurrence, we can look for ways to reduce the overall time period of a downtime event. By looking inside of each outage point, we may be able to find possible points of process improvement that will substantially reduce or even eliminate periods of time that are unnecessary or too lengthy. In Chapter 2, I identified seven points or components of a typical outage. These were prefailure errors, the failure point, the notification point, the decision point, the recovery action point, the postrecovery point, and the normal operational point. Within each of these components of downtime we can find many subcomponents in which we may be able to find errors or oversights that, once addressed, can be substantially reduced or eliminated.

It is the recovery action point that we will focus on in this chapter. I believe that this component of downtime is responsible for the majority of the "chargeable" time within a downtime event. For example, I have seen many organizations rack up hours and hours of downtime simply because they did not have a good backup or because they interfered with Exchange Server's own recovery measures. I believe that lack of knowledge and poor operational procedures can create vast amounts of unnecessary downtime for an Exchange deployment. Therefore, I will gear this chapter toward a focus on Exchange disaster recovery technology for the specific purpose of reducing the amount of time an operations staff spends recovering an Exchange server. An understanding of what types of failures can occur as well as the scenarios in which disaster recovery will be performed is the first step. We must also understand, operationally, how the Exchange database engine recovers itself. Next we must understand the process flow of how Exchange 2000 performs backup and restore operations as well the types of backup techniques that are available. This is followed by a look at overall best practices, tips, and methods of disaster recovery–process improvement in Chapter 5. I will also take a brief look at some of the third-party backup applications and hardware products available for Exchange and the similarities and differences in their approaches. Finally, we will bring it all back together by discussing some sample scenarios that implement the practices and technique we've discussed. My hope is that this chapter on Exchange disaster recovery technology will provide you with meaningful insight into the recovery action point of the black box of downtime for Exchange Server and will help you identify methods of improving your processes, thereby reducing the amount of time spent recovering Exchange.

4.1   How Can an Exchange Server Fail?

There are basically two scenarios under which we engage in disaster recovery planning, testing, and operations. The first scenario is a server catastrophe. In this situation, your Exchange server has been completely lost due to some disaster incident such as fire, flood, earthquake, etc. This catastrophe requires that you completely recover your Exchange server from "scratch." In this situation, you must concern yourself with the operating system (Windows NT or Windows 2000), Exchange Server, and the information stores. For Exchange 2000, we also have two additional components—the Active Directory and the Internet Information Server (IIS) Metabase. In most situations, I don't anticipate Exchange administrators and operators will be responsible for disaster recovery planning for the Active Directory. However, since the Active Directory is really just JET/ESE "lite," Exchange gurus may be called upon to assist infrastructure staff (whom I would typically expect to own the Active Directory) with backup, restore, and maintenance planning for the Windows 2000 Active Directory (AD). Don't write the AD off, however, as you will need to understand how AD recovery operations on an Exchange server should be done. Whether you rely on the infrastructure staff or not, factoring the Active Directory into Exchange Server disaster recovery plans is a must. In most cases, however, I only expect AD recovery to be a factor in Exchange 2000 Server recovery if Exchange 2000 was acting as a Windows 2000 domain controller (DC) or Global Catalog (GC) server. This is a practice I would discourage if at all possible. Just ensure that you understand whether the Windows 2000 Active Directory is a factor during recovery of your Exchange servers. Most likely, you will find that a careful understanding of how Exchange databases rely on the Active Directory is required for complete recovery.

The IIS Metabase is another important piece that is new to Exchange 2000 disaster recovery planning. The IIS Metabase is part of the IIS that stores static configuration information for protocols and virtual servers. Exchange 2000, for example, will store information about the protocols it uses and the SMTP or other virtual servers that are configured for Exchange within IIS. Since IIS is now such an integral part of Exchange 2000, planning for IIS Metabase recovery is a vital component of disaster recovery that we didn't have to worry about with previous versions of Exchange (since they didn't depend on IIS). The final part of complete recovery for an Exchange 2000 server is the information stores. This involves one or more storage groups and any databases configured in those storage groups.

Recovering a complete Exchange 2000 server leaves us many things to think about. The second scenario we plan for is recovery of the Exchange information store. For Exchange 2000, the term "information store" expands in scope. In previous versions of Exchange, the information store simply included the public (PUB.EDB) and private (PRIV.EDB) information stores. Recovery of these two databases is not trivial, but it pales in comparison to the possible future recovery complexities in Exchange 2000. Since Exchange 2000 provides for multiple storage groups and allows you to configure multiple databases per sg, we now have much more to consider when planning for disaster recovery of an Exchange 2000 deployment. Our plans must include the ability to recover all storage groups and databases, an individual storage group, an individual database (MDB), one mailbox, or even a single message or document. Table 4.1 highlights the two basic recovery scenarios we face for Exchange 2000 and the factors and considerations for each.

Before moving further into how recovery operations work for Exchange 2000, let's pause to discuss the types of failures in Exchange that may require these operations to be performed. While Exchange Server is a continuously operational system that does not require the system to be taken down, there are some failures that

Table 4.1   *Exchange 2000 Recovery Scenarios*

Recovery Scenario	Components	Considerations
Complete server recovery	Windows 2000, Active Directory, IIS Metabase, Exchange 2000, Information stores	• Factor into plans and define ownership for Windows 2000 and AD disaster recovery planning • Add IIS Metabase to operational procedures • Update procedures for Exchange 2000 • Separate into another recovery component
Information store recovery	All SGs and MDBs, single storage group, single MDB, single mailbox, message or document	• Storage group size and layout • Number of storage groups and concurrency issues • Number of MDBs per SG • Recovery of SG or server? • Can you support this granularity?

will require the system to shift into a recovery mode of operation. The Exchange information store is the focus of our discussion. There are two basic types of failures that cause the information store to need recovery—physical and logical corruption.

4.1.1   Physical Database Corruption

Once Exchange passes data to the operating system (Windows NT/ 2000), it relies on the operating system, device drivers, and hardware to ensure that data is preserved. However, these lower layers do not always provide flawless protection of the data. Physical corruption to the Exchange database is the most severe form of failure you can experience because you are not able to repair the data and it must be recovered using your established disaster recovery measures such as restoring from tape backup. Physical corruption to the database can occur in several areas such as an internal page, index, database header, leaf (data) pages, or the database catalog (Exchange has two copies per database). If given a choice, I would prefer corruption of a secondary index or internal page. The reason for this preference is that corruption is limited in these circumstances, and the data itself is usually safe. Because of the seriousness of physical corruption, it is very important that these errors are detected and corrected as early as possible.

4.1.1.1   The Infamous −1018 Error

Most often, physical corruption for Exchange databases is announced by the occurrence of a −1018 (negative 1018) error. Additional errors such as those in Table 4.2 are also signs of physical database corruption.

Table 4.2   *Common Exchange Database Physical Corruption Errors*

JET/ESE Error	Indication
−1018 (JET_errReadVerifyFailure)	Data requested by the database engine (ESE) in a read operation to database is not valid. Either the incorrect database page was returned or the page failed CRC check.
−1022 (JET_errDiskIO)	The database engine (ESE) is unable to perform an I/O operation due to hardware, device driver, or operating system errors that have been returned.

When Exchange Server detects a physical corruption, the error is logged to the application log in Windows NT/2000. Most often, these errors are encountered during online backup or database maintenance. This is due to the fact that the database engine checks every database page during these operations. Each 4KB database page contains a header with information about the page. Within the header, both the page number and a checksum or cyclic redundancy check (CRC) is stored. When the database engine reads a database page, it first ensures that the page number it requested is the one returned by checking the page number in the header. Next, the CRC is validated. If either an invalid page number was returned or the CRC failed, the database engine will report an error. In previous versions of Exchange Server, the database engine would simply log a −1018 error to the application log and continue on. However, since Exchange Server 5.5 Service Pack 2 (and now in Exchange 2000), ESE will attempt a retry of the page in question. ESE will attempt to reread and check the database page up to 16 times before declaring the page as corrupt and logging the error (a good indication that your disk subsystem has a problem). In the event that this occurs, 200/201 series errors will be logged to the application log, indicating either that the database engine encountered a bad page but retried successfully or that it retried 16 times without success and the database must be recovered. If this occurs during online backup, the operation will be terminated. This ensures that a physically corrupted database is not backed up.

4.1.1.2   *Preventing and Repairing Physical Corruption*

The best method that I am aware of for preventing database corruption is to deploy Exchange on solid hardware configurations and to practice proactive management of your Exchange deployment (stay tuned for Chapter 9). In my experience, however, not all occurrences of physical corruption are caused by hardware (contrary to what Microsoft Product Support Services may tell you). In fact, up until Exchange 5.5 SP2, Exchange itself was a potential source of corruption. This was particularly true in earlier versions such as Exchange 4.0 and 5.0. However, Microsoft has done a significant amount of work and has collaborated with hardware vendors like Compaq to work to understand and reduce the occurrence of physical corruption. The retry instrumentation code (where ESE retries up to 16 times) was added in Exchange 5.5 SP2 and has significantly impacted the occurrence of –1018 errors by allowing the database engine to retry read operations. This ensures that the error was not caused by a transient condition, busy disk subsystem, or other benign condition.

Deploying rock-solid hardware does help, however. Implementing hardware-based RAID and ensuring that your hardware vendor of choice meets some basic criteria is important. Make sure your hardware vendor meets some basics such as the Microsoft Hardware Compatibility List (HCL). Your hardware vendor should at least be in the top tier of server vendors such as Compaq, Hewlett-Packard, IBM, or Dell. Also, your vendor should have some basic experience with Exchange. A good consulting practice focused on Exchange, or industry experts who know Exchange and the hardware are good indicators of a hardware vendor you can count on. Also, hardware vendors, like Compaq, frequently update their code in the form of drivers and firmware (ROMs) for servers and devices such as disk drives and controllers. Make sure you are following your vendor's recommendation about keeping up to date with the latest versions; this includes bug fixes and enhancements that address issues that could potentially cause corruption of your Exchange databases. I can't tell you how often I hear of Exchange downtime that is charged against the hardware when the fix in the form of an updated device driver or ROM was available from the hardware vendor. So often, these updates are not applied, and the result is disastrous. I will defer my "harping" on this subject to later discussions on configuration and change management in a later chapter. However, this is a key point in reducing physical corruption in Exchange databases as a result of hardware problems.

4.1.1.3 The Question of Write-Back Caching

Another question that frequently surfaces in the area of Exchange database corruption and hardware is the issue of write-back caching. Write-back caching is a tremendous aid to performance because it reduces the amount of time it takes to return a write completion status to the operating system, thereby improving application performance (as shown in Figure 4.1). Rather than waiting until each write I/O has been written to disk, the write-back cache accepts the data to cache and informs the system that the write has been completed.

Figure 4.1
The effect of write caching on disk I/O performance

Without Write Cache

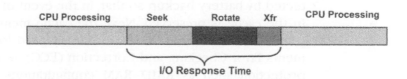

With Write Cache

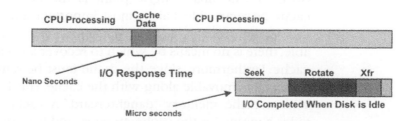

Write-back caching comes in two forms. First, disk drives have individual write-back caches located on the disk drive that can improve the performance of write operations. These caches are very dangerous since there is no protection or battery backup for cache memory located on the individual disk drive. Although drive vendors make this available (mostly for benchmarking and performance reasons), most server vendors I am aware of will turn write-back caching off at the individual disk drive level. If you are in doubt, ask your server vendor about whether it disables write-back caching at the drive level.

The second implementation of write-back caching is at the controller level. Many vendors have hardware-based RAID controllers with large amounts of write-back cache. These caches typically vary in size anywhere from 4MB to 16GB. In the extreme case of a cache as large as 16GB, you can see how important it is to have the cache protected. If the power or cache memory should fail, you could easily have megabytes of unwritten data in the cache lost. Most of the leading server vendors do provide protection for their caching RAID controllers. Of the third-party RAID controllers available, some provide protection while others do not. If in doubt, you should ensure that the controller you purchase for your Exchange servers meets the following three criteria points. First, the cache must be protected by battery backup so that, in the event of power failure, data in the cache is preserved. Next, the cache memory should also be protected. This means that the memory used for the cache implements Error Checking and Correction (ECC) or some other form of protection such as RAID RAM configurations. With RAID cache RAM, the memory banks are arranged in a fashion that implements protection in the form of mirroring (RAID1) or distributed parity (RAID5). One final criteria point is the necessity that controller cache be removable. This is most important during a controller failure. In the event of a controller failure, if the cache is not removable, there is no means by which to recover any data currently in the cache. Furthermore, since the cache must be removable, the batteries must be movable along with the cache. This is best implemented with a cache memory "daughtercard." A cache daughtercard provides a means for the cache memory and batteries to be part of the same assembly. When the controller fails, the cache daughtercard is simply removed and plugged into a replacement controller. Once the system is restored to operation, any data that was stored in the cache can be flushed to disk, thereby completing any outstanding write operations. It is very important that your caching RAID controller meet these minimum criteria. Other desirable controller features include the ability to configured the cache as read-ahead versus write-back and the ability to disable caching on a per-logical-drive basis. Once these criteria are met, you can safely deploy Exchange Server configured with write-back caching enabled.

Table 4.3   *Cache Controller Protection Attributes*

Controller Attribute	Description
Battery backup	The controller includes on-board batteries that maintain cache information in the event of a power failure.
Protected cache memory	The cache memory is configured with protection schemes such as mirroring or RAID parity and provides protection in the event of memory-component failure.
Cache "daughtercard"	Controller cache is contained on a pluggable card that is separate from the base controller. This allows the cache to be transferred to another controller in the event of controller failure.

Contrary to much misinformation, there has been no documented correlation between Exchange database corruption and write-back caching at the controller level. Over that last several years, several incorrect or misleading Microsoft KnowledgeBase (KB) or "Q" articles have been written that have incorrectly advised turning off write-back caching for Exchange Server. This error was due to the subtle differences between write-back caching at the disk drive level versus the controller level. Since most hardware manufacturers disable write-back caching at the disk drive level, the disk drive–level caching issue is moot. However, at the controller level, if the preceding criterion has been met, it is completely safe to deploy servers with write-back caching enabled for Exchange information store volumes. This is the best practice from a performance point of view as well. RAID5, in particular, will suffer huge performance penalties if write-back caching is disabled due to the overhead of the intense XOR computations required. However, performance will suffer for any RAID level when write-back caching has been disabled. The bottom line is this: Ensure that your RAID controller meets the three criteria points I discussed. If it does, enable write-back caching (I recommend setting the controller cache for 100% write) and enjoy the performance gains for which it was designed without fear of physical corruption of your Exchange databases.

When physical corruption of an Exchange database is encountered, your options for recovery and restoration are limited. There simply are not many options for repair of a physically corrupted database. You can use the ESEUTIL utility that comes with Exchange. However, this method technically does not repair corruption in the database. ESEUTIL essentially just identifies the bad page or pages and deletes them from the database. My recommendation is that you avoid using ESEUTIL in the event of database corruption. ESEUTIL does have a repair mode of operation (ESEUTIL /P) that allows the database engine to delete corrupted pages, but the result is just an operational server with missing data. The result is loss of user data or, in worse cases, the introduction of logical corruption. The only way to recover from physical corruption of an Exchange database is to restore from backup or use another disaster recovery measure. If you are able to restore the database to the last known good state (if your last backup operation completed successfully without errors, you can be assured it is good), you can then allow Exchange to perform recovery by playing through transaction log files and bringing the database to a consistent state. If you continually find your databases in a corrupted state, thorough hardware diagnostics will be necessary since the cause of corruption may be hardware related.

4.2   Logical Database Corruption

Logical corruption of your Exchange server database is problematic and is much more difficult to diagnose and repair than physical corruption. This is because logical corruption can be hard to identify and is often caused by problems in software such as Exchange, itself, or the operating system. With logical corruption, the user and administrator are typically unaware of an occurrence. To make matters worse, Exchange contains no built-in checking (like that available for physical corruption) to diagnose and alert you to logical database corruption. In addition, there are no specific symptoms that are identifiers of logical corruption. Usually, when an administrator is alerted to logical corruption, it may be too late for repair.

As previously mentioned, physical corruption may also cause logical corruption. Let me give you an example of this. Suppose a database page has become corrupt for whatever reason. In many cases, this page may just contain user data, and that data is simply lost. However, the rest of the database and its structure remains intact. Suppose, however, that the problem page contained B-Tree structure data or index information for the database. The loss of this page could render the entire database unusable since key structural information for the database has been lost. Logical corruption may manifest itself in other situations as well. Suppose, in another example, that a bug in the Exchange database engine incorrectly links tables contained within the database. The linkage between the many different tables contained in the information store and the indexes used is the key to storing semistructured data in Exchange in the fastest and most efficient manner. Logical corruption can render the entire dataset useless. If you encounter logical corruption (you may not recognize it as such), your troubleshooting skills will be quickly tested.

The saving grace here is that since Exchange 5.5, occurrences of logical corruption have virtually disappeared because the database engine has been continually refined and stabilized as various versions and service packs for Exchange have been rolled out. Also, in versions prior to 5.5, logical corruption could be introduced by replaying transaction logs incorrectly (such as in the wrong order or with a gap in the generational sequence). However, Exchange 2000 prevents this scenario by ensuring that the correct transaction logs exist before replay. While we have fewer statistics for Exchange 2000, I expect this to continue to be the case. Because logical corruption is so unpredictable and sometimes invisible in nature, it is important to focus your attention toward preventing it. Ensure that you keep close tabs on new service packs and hotfixes that Microsoft releases, which specifically address logical corruption issues that have been discovered. Since logical corruption is potentially so serious, Microsoft is quick to address issues when they are found and escalated through the support channels. However, if you are unaware of these issues or fail to implement critical fixes, you may end up a victim of logical corruption.

Another bright spot is the existence of tools that can repair logical corruption of Exchange databases. Since logical corruption may occur at either the information store level (tables, indexes, keys, links, etc.) or the database level (B-Tree structures, etc.), we must have tools that address each of these levels. The ISINTEG utility looks at the information store to check potential logical corruption at this level. ESEUTIL, on the other hand, checks, diagnoses, and repairs problems at the database level.

4.2.1   ISINTEG

ISINTEG is the Information Store Integrity Checker utility. ISINTEG
finds and eliminates errors in Exchange information stores. These
are errors that may prevent the database from starting or mounting.
They also can prevent users from accessing their data. ISINTEG has
many uses in restoring Exchange databases to normal operation but
should not be seen as a regular tool for information store maintenance. ISINTEG can only be of assistance in certain scenarios in
which a database has become damaged. ISINTEG works at the logical schema level of the Exchange information store. Because of ISIN-
TEG's focus on the logical level rather than the physical database
structure, it is able to repair and recover data that other tools like
ESEUTIL (which looks at physical database structure) cannot. When
looking at data from the physical database level, ESEUTIL may find it
to be valid since it looks for things like page integrity and B-Tree
structure. Data that appears valid to ESEUTIL from a physical view
may not be valid from the logical view of the database. For example,
data for various information store tables, such as the message, folder,
or attachments table, may be intact, but the relationships between
tables or records within tables may be broken or incorrect due to
corruption in the logical structure. This may render the database
unusable from a logical database schema point of view. ISINTEG can
potentially repair this logical schema corruption when other utilities
may not even be aware of the problem.

4.2.2   ESEUTIL

ESEUTIL defragments, repairs, and checks the integrity of the
Microsoft Exchange Server information store. In versions prior to
Exchange 2000, ESEUTIL could also be used on the directory database. Unlike ISINTEG, which is sensitive to the use and content of
data in the information store, ESEUTIL examines the structure of the
database tables and records. ESEUTIL looks at structural issues for
both the database tables and the individual records. In repair mode,
ESEUTIL deletes any corrupted pages found in the interest of getting
the database operational as quickly as possible. ESEUTIL is now
located in the \Program Files\Exchsrvr\bin directory. (Prior to
Exchange 2000, it was located in the NT System32 directory for
Exchange 5.5. For versions 4.0 and 5.0, it was located in the \Exch-
srvr\bin directory.) You can run it on one database at a time from the

command line. You should only use ESEUTIL if you are familiar with Exchange database architecture. The best bet is to use the tool with the assistance of Microsoft Product Support Services. Again, as in the case of ISINTEG, the use of ESEUTIL should not be a regular database-maintenance activity. The defragmentation option makes used storage contiguous, eliminates unused storage, compacts the database, and reduces its size. ESEUTIL copies database records to a new database. When defragmention is complete, the original database is deleted or saved to a user-specified location, and the new version is renamed as the original. If the utility encounters a bad record, it stops and displays an error. When defragmenting a database, the recommended requirement is disk space equal to twice the size of the database being defragmented. The defragment option of ESEUTIL is the /D switch along with the database name and other options.

ESEUTIL in Exchange 2000 has changed significantly because the nature and structure of Exchange 2000's databases has also changed. The most notable change is that the /IS, /ISPRIV, /ISPUB, and /DS switches are no longer supported. The information about the location of the databases and transaction log files is now stored in the Windows 2000 Active Directory (not the registry). Therefore, the information is not readily available to ESEUTIL, and the paths must be manually specified. The /S option has been added to allow you to specify a checkpoint file (*.CHK) that is in an alternative directory. The /L option provides a similar capability to specify and alternate locations for transaction log files. Several other changes to ESEUTIL have also been made for Exchange 2000. It is important that you understand all of the new switches and options for ESEUTIL before using it with Exchange 2000 databases. For more information on ESEUTIL parameters, switches, and options, use the ESEUTIL "/?" option shown in Figure 4.2.

4.2.3   ESEFILE

ESEFILE is tool written by the Exchange ESE development team for the specific purpose of checking the physical page integrity for the property store (EDB file). ESEFILE actually contains no ESE code but is simply a very light program that does nothing but page comparison and checksum validation. The main use of ESEFILE is to check individual databases for bad pages. ESEFILE uses Win32 file system APIs to read ESE pages directly from the EDB file. Each 4K page is read in sequential order, and the page number and the checksum is

Figure 4.2
*ESEUTIL
options and
parameters*

verified. Since ESEFILE contains no ESE code, it runs very fast. ESE-
FILE has three functions, as described in Table 4.4. ESEFILE must be
run with the database offline.

Table 4.4   *ESEFILE Functions*

ESEFILE Function	Description
File Copy - /C	ESEFILE can copy a database file of any size very quickly (up to two times the speed of the COPY or XCOPY command).
Page Compare/Checksum - /S (individual page - /D)	ESEFILE will read, compare, and checksum pages in the entire database or individual pages (/D option).
File Deletion - /U	ESEFILE can also provide a quick method of database file deletion.

The ESEUTIL, ESEFILE, and ISINTEG utilities are very powerful
programs. Left in the hand of an inexperienced administrator, these
tools can also be very dangerous. These utilities can help resolve logical and physical corruption that occurs with the Exchange information store databases. However, my recommendation and that of
Microsoft Product Support is that these tools be used only after
efforts to restore from an online backup have failed. In this case,
these utilities can get your Exchange server up and running again.
However, the price may be lost data since these utilities cannot mag-
ically re-create lost or corrupted data. Logical and physical corruption are typically the most common reasons that information store
recovery operations are performed. While there may be extreme catastrophic cases when the entire server must be rebuilt from scratch,

most of our disaster recovery scenarios will take place at the storage group or individual database level. In the next section, let's take a look at how Exchange Server recovers its databases.

4.3 JET/ESE Recovery Technology

Exchange's database engine is very powerful and provides high performance and robust service for storing semistructured data. However, the speed and ease at which Exchange can store user and business data is unimportant if the technology does not ensure recovery. Beginning with version 4.0, Exchange Server has also focused on providing a 7×24 platform that is highly recoverable. In the next section, wc will look at the technology behind Exchange Server's promise of recoverability. In Chapter 5, we will expand this discussion further by looking at the best practices with which we can apply this technology.

4.3.1 Soft Recovery

In many cases, Exchange Server is able to quietly recover when a server crashes and the contents of the database buffers in memory are lost. It does this by performing a *soft recovery*, a process that runs automatically when you try to start the information store after a failure. Soft recovery uses the log files and database files on disk instead of tape backup to recover from a failure. The checkpoint file that I described in Chapter 3 is used to identify the oldest transaction not flushed to disk, and the log files and records are replayed for the checkpoint forward. Any transaction operations in the log files that have not been committed are ignored. If your server crashes and the contents of memory are lost, the database file on disk is flagged as inconsistent in the database file header. Before you can restart Exchange Server and service users, the database must be made consistent again. Exchange Server uses soft recovery to simulate a clean shutdown by replaying pages from the log files on disk into the information store databases. Here is how soft recovery works: First, the database engine (storage group instance) checks that the E0n.LOG file exists. Next, the database engine reads the checkpoint file to determine which log file to start replaying. If the checkpoint does not exist, all log files are scanned to determine if any committed transactions have not been written to the database.

At the end of the operation, the database is effectively consistent again, and the Exchange Server information store can start normally. If, however, soft recovery doesn't work, there could be more serious problems with the system; you might be required to restore from backup.

4.3.2   Hard Recovery

Restoring from an online backup is a process similar to soft recovery. I refer to this as hard recovery since the databases and/or log files must be restored from backup. Exchange Server makes sure that all the files are put in the right place when using the backup APIs and brings the database up to a consistent state. In this scenario, when you restore data from tape backup, the restore process returns to disk all the files that were backed up. Next, the system attendant starts the information store. The information store checks the RESTORE.ENV file for the database (more on the RESTORE.ENV file later) and determines that the database has been restored from an online backup. The database engine then applies pages in the patch file (*.PAT) file to the database files (property store—EDB files). The RESTORE.ENV file tells ESE where to start replaying the transaction logs. It does not check for E0n.LOG. ESE then replays the log files specified by the RESTORE.ENV and plays through any other logs in the current database directory. Using ESEUTIL with the /C switch allows you to modify how Exchange 2000 uses the RESTORE.ENV file. The process of hard recovery is what is used when an Exchange server needs to be recovered from tape. In the next sections, we will look at backup and restore fundamentals for Exchange 2000.

4.3.3   Exchange 2000 Backup/Restore Fundamentals

With the changes and new options for Exchange 2000, the disaster recovery API that Microsoft provides as part of Exchange must undergo a bit of a facelift. The ESE (Extensible Storage Engine) database engine in Exchange Server has always made an online backup API available via two DLLs called ESECLIB2.DLL and ESEBACK2.DLL. (For Exchange 5.5, the DLLs are ESECLIB1.DLL and ESEBACK.DLL.) This API allows Exchange to stay operational and service users while backup operations are performed. In previous versions of Exchange, since there was only one ESE instance, restore operations were offline (the server is down until complete). However, since Exchange 2000 provides multiple ESE instances (storage groups), recovery operations can be underway within one storage group while another storage group continues to service users. This means the API must be adapted to allow for concurrent operations and to handle the fact that multiple SGs, MDBs, and log file sets must be managed. In addition, there is new stuff to back up in Exchange 2000 such as the Site Replication Service (SRS) and the Key Management Server (KMS). SRS and KMS were not included in backup operations for previous versions of Exchange.

Finally, the ESE Recovery API must allow for more granularity. You now are able to back up/restore an entire storage group (best practice) or an individual database (MDB). What's more, while a database was one file (*.EDB) in previous versions, it is now a set that includes both the EDB and the STM file. The API has undergone several changes in Exchange 2000 to accommodate these needs. In the next section, we'll take a look at how Exchange 2000 performs backup and restore operations. Microsoft Exchange Server provides a specific backup API to allow backup products, including NTBACKUP, to access the contents of the Exchange information stores while online. This sidebar includes a brief description of the Exchange backup API, together with an outline of the function calls used during a backup.

A Programmatic Look at Online Backup for Exchange

The following procedures outline a typical methodology to programmatically back up the information store databases. The procedure explains how to perform a full backup.

To perform a full backup of Exchange data

1. **The Backup/Restore Client**—Calls to the server application through application-specific functions to locate a server to connect to.

2. **HrESEBackupPrepare()**—Establishes an RPC to the server application and gets information about the databases.

3. **HrESEBackupSetup()**—Tells the server which instance to back up, which may disable shutdown.

4. **HrESEBackupGetDependencyInfo()**—Internally the server calls ErrESECBGetDependencyInfo() and passes back the information for the client to process.

5. **HrESEBackupOpenFile()**—To open the database for read.

6. **HrESEBackupReadFile()**—To read the database.

7. **HrESEBackupCloseFile()**—To close the database.

8. Loop back to Step 5 until all database files are read. (Note: For databases with an STM file, both files must be backed up separately in two different open/read/close sequences.)

9. **HrESEBackupGetLogAndPatchFiles()**—To get a list of log file names and patch file names.

10. **HrESEBackupOpenFile()**—To open the log/patch file for read.

11. **HrESEBackupReadFile()**—To read the log/patch file.

12. **HrESEBackupCloseFile()**—To close the file.

13. Loop until all log/patch files are read.

14. **HrESEBackupTruncateLog()**—To delete logs after backup.

15. **HrESEBackupInstanceEnd()**—To end the backup for the instance.

16. **HrESEBackupEnd()**—To disconnect from the server application.

4.3.4   Overview of the Exchange Backup API

The sidebar gave you an abstract of the Exchange backup API, in case you were wondering about the actual function calls and how it looks programmatically (you probably weren't). I think it is interesting to see it in relative simplicity. The Microsoft Exchange Server SDK provides functions for backing up and restoring data in the Microsoft Exchange Server information stores. These functions perform backups online, which means there is no need to stop the directory service or information store service to back up directory or information store data. Also, backup and restore operations can be performed remotely. Using these APIs, backup software vendors are able to perform online backups for Exchange Server data.

Table 4.5   *Files Needed to Call the Backup and Restore Functions for Exchange*

File Required	Purpose
ESEBACKMSG.H	Error codes
ESECLIB2.H	Header file for the backup/restore functions

Table 4.5   *Files Needed to Call the Backup and Restore Functions for Exchange (continued)*

File Required	Purpose
ESECLIB2.LIB	Static LIB of backup/restore functions
ESECLIB2.DLL	Backup/restore entry point DLL
MDBREST.DLL	Restore DLL for database files
SRSREST.DLL	Extensions for SRS restore
KMSREST.DLL	Extensions for KMS restore

4.3.5   Exchange Backup Types

The backup and restore functions provide three types of backup capabilities: full, incremental, and differential.

- A *full backup* (also called a normal backup) backs up the entire directory or information store and allows you to restore it from a single backup.

- An *incremental backup* backs up just the changes since the last full or incremental backup. These are simply the transaction logs that have accumulated since the last full backup. Restoring incremental backups requires the original full backup plus all the incremental backups (transaction logs) made since that time.

- A *differential backup* backs up the changes since the last full backup. Restoring a differential backup requires one differential backup and the original full backup.

Appendix B provides a full discussion of backup and restore functions and their specific uses.

Online backup operations are fundamental to Exchange Server and enable you to back up databases without shutting down the entire server to perform a file-by-file type backup approach (offline backup). While backup operations are in progress, all services continue to operate, and users can access their data on the Exchange server. Database pages that are cached in memory in the information store buffer pool continue to be updated and flushed to the database on disk. Transactions also continue to be written to the transaction log files, and the checkpoint file continues to advance.

All in all, the backup and restore technology for Exchange 2000 is very similar to previous versions of Exchange Server with one notable exception. Exchange 2000's advent of multiple storage groups and multiple databases (MDBs) has a substantial impact on how the Exchange backup API works. The types of backup available in Exchange 2000 are similar to previous versions. However, Exchange may support an additional backup type called Snapshot backup in the future. Table 4-6 compares the backup types available for Exchange 2000.

Table 4.6   *Exchange 2000 Backup Options*

Backup Type	Files Included	Logs Truncated?	Restore Steps
Normal (full)	MDB and log files	Yes	Last normal
Incremental	Log files	Yes	Last normal + all incremental
Differential	Log files	No	Last normal + last differential
Copy	MDB and log files	No	Archive or point in time purpose
Snapshot (future)	Implementation specific	Special	Special

4.3.5.1   Normal (Full) and Copy Backups

The *normal backup* (also referred to as a full backup) is the fundamental unit of operation for most Exchange deployments. Regardless of the strategy you select for backup, the normal backup type will be part of your operational procedures. With a normal backup, both the database files and the log files are copied to tape. In addition, the log files are truncated or deleted once they have been copied to the backup media. The truncation point for the transaction log files is the current database checkpoint location. The normal backup operation is also important to database integrity since only during a normal backup are the 4KB database pages checked for corruption (they are also checked during copy backups and online database maintenance as well). This is accomplished by verifying each page read to make sure that the page number requested is the page the database engine received. Next, each page's CRC information (contained in the page header) is verified to ensure that the data contained in the page is valid. The normal backup is also important to the ESE Page Zeroing feature, which I will discuss later in this chapter. To restore from a normal backup, you only need to restore the complete set and allow the ESE database engine to replay any log files required for the database to be in a consistent state.

Similar to the normal backup is the copy backup. A *copy backup* differs in that it does not truncate or purge log files once they have been copied to tape. In addition, the copy backup does not update database backup context information contained in the database file header. Copy backups are very useful for archival purposes or other scenarios in which you want to back up your Exchange databases but do not want to disrupt the normal backup schedule. A copy backup performs the same functions of integrity checking and page zeroing (if enabled) as the normal backup.

4.3.5.2   *Incremental and Differential Backups*

The backup process in the case of an incremental or differential backup type is somewhat different. Again, as in the case of a normal backup operation, the truncation point marks the beginning of backup. The current E0*n*.LOG file (*n* being the storage group number or designation) is renamed to E0*nnnnnn*.LOG, and a new generation is started in a new E0*n*.LOG. With the incremental and differential backup types, no database files are copied to tape. It is also worth mentioning that, since the databases are not copied, no page verification or checksumming is performed on the database to ensure integrity. This is a notable point when selecting which backup strategy you will use for your Exchange deployment. Since an incremental or differential backup only operates on the log files, if circular logging is enabled, neither incremental nor differential backup operations will be capable of providing complete recovery. Like a normal backup, an incremental backup will delete log files up to the truncation point once they have been backed up. This is the key point of difference between incremental and differential backups. To restore from an incremental backup, you will need your last normal (full) backup set plus any incremental backup sets that have been taken since. For Exchange 2000, you must indicate when the last backup set has been restored in order for the ESE database instance (storage group) to recover the database properly.

Like an incremental backup, the differential backup is also only concerned with transaction log files. The point of difference from an incremental backup is that a differential backup does not delete the log files at the truncation point (current checkpoint location). While log file truncation is marked by closing and renaming the current E0n.LOG to E0nnnnnn.LOG and creating a new E0n.LOG generation, the log files are left intact. To restore from a differential backup set, as was the case with an incremental backup, the last normal (full) backup set is required. Next, this is combined with the latest differential backup set. This is due to the fact that, since the differential backups have left log files intact throughout subsequent backup operations, the latest differential backup contains all log files backed up since the last normal backup set. As was the case with the incremental backup recovery operation, the last backup set must be indicated for the ESE recovery storage instance to properly recover the database or storage group.

4.3.5.3   "Brick-Level" vs. Normal Backup

Customers have requested the ability to restore a single message, folder, or mailbox since the earliest days of Exchange. This is not possible using the normal backup API because data is read from the database in 4KB pages and is written to tape in that manner. No contextual information is written along with the data, so a full restore is necessary before the data is reordered into mailboxfolder-item order.

Several backup software vendors have attempted to provide the necessary features to support single message restore in their Exchange-compliant backup products. This mode requires that data be written to backup media with all its contextual information intact, so the normal backup API cannot be used. Instead, a connection is made in much the same way as a normal MAPI client, and data is read out in mailbox order. This is referred to as a "bricked" backup. A bricked restore is one in which a single item (mailbox, folder, or other item) is extracted from the backup media and inserted into the information store. Restoring a single item is very much easier with this approach, but backup times are significantly longer due to the requirement to write out additional information. Typically, a bricked backup takes four to five times longer than a normal backup. I do not recommend that you use a bricked backup as the basis for your daily backup routine. Instead, if you use a product that supports bricked backup, consider using this feature once a week and use normal backup every other day. Another possibility is to use such a product feature for key personnel in the enterprise. Microsoft may never provide brick-level backup for Exchange, but many third-party products can provide some solution to this problem. With the ability to partition the information store into smaller units of manageability in Exchange 2000, brick-level backups may become less important.

4.3.5.4 *Individual Item Recovery*

Microsoft partly addressed the issue of single item recovery with the deleted items retention feature in Exchange 5.5 that has been carried over to Exchange 2000. The most common reason why people ask for single items to be restored is that they made a mistake when they deleted it in the first place. Deleted items retention means that items are "soft" deleted initially and then "hard" deleted after a set period has elapsed. Soft deletion means that the item is marked as deleted in the database and is hidden from view. Hard deletion means that the item is permanently removed from the database. During the time (the retention period) when the item is soft deleted, it can be recovered and recalled to view using an option on Outlook 97, Outlook 98, and Outlook 2000 clients (Outlook 8.0.3 onwards). If your organization has not implemented this feature, help desk or administration staff must perform recovery. I believe that the deleted item recovery feature implemented in Microsoft Exchange 5.5 covers most of the cases in which a restore has to be done. In addition, Exchange 2000 extends this feature by adding individual mailbox recovery as well. Many companies have set retention periods of between 7 and 14 days and have found that this eliminates the vast majority of requests for item recovery. However, you should be aware that implementing this feature would cause your database to grow. A conservative estimate is that you should expect an individual private information store database to grow by between 10 and 15 percent for a retention period of 14 days. This percentage will vary from organization to organization and will largely depend on the usage pattern of the messaging server. Regardless, you should plan to utilize a dedicated server for deleted item recovery in the situations in which Microsoft Exchange 5.5 is not yet deployed or if the item has been deleted outside of the deleted item recovery time window. This dedicated server must have sufficient disk space to hold the database being restored.

4.3.5.5   *A Word about Offline Backup and Restore*

When Microsoft developed Exchange Server, choices were made about the architecture and operation of the database engine, and an online API for backup and restore operations was developed. This ensured that the server could be operational 7×4 and that backup operations would not cause server outage. Microsoft has strongly educated Exchange implementers about the benefits and necessities of performing online backup operations. When calling Microsoft PSS, you will be hard-pressed to find a sympathetic ear if your only means of Exchange Server recovery is an offline backup. Microsoft has specific reasons for enforcing its recommendations for online backups. The main reason is that online backups, which utilize the ESE APIs, have awareness to the transactional nature of the Exchange database engine. If you simply treat the Exchange database as a file, no transactional integrity of the database is maintained. An online backup not only will back up the database but will also back up log files and provide log file truncation. In addition, online backups for Exchange provide management on the restore side as well. When restoring backup sets created using online methods, the database engine is able to provide recovery up to the very last transaction recorded by utilizing the log files. All around, online backups are a preferable method. I will also recommend against the practice of offline methods unless they are used as a mechanism for periodic archival or your databases.

Unfortunately, many have still chosen to use offline methods to backup their Exchange servers. In an offline scenario, all Exchange services are shut down in order to perform the backup or restore operation. Backup operations simply treat the Exchange information store databases as individual files in the file system. EDB and STM files would be backed up just like any other file on the server. This can be very problematic for several reasons. First, since an offline backup method does not utilize the ESE API, no integrity checking of the database is performed (unless manually with tools from Microsoft PSS). Remember, using an online method and performing a normal (or full) backup will verify each and every page of the database during the backup procedure. With offline methods, this is not available unless you were to manually verify each backup set using ESEUTIL or ESEFILE to check database integrity. Another problem with offline backup method for Exchange is that the operator must take responsibility for managing database transaction log files. The transaction log files are required for successful recovery of the database up to the point of the last transaction that occurred. Suppose, for example, you needed to recover your Exchange 2000 server (either an individual database or an entire storage group) in an offline backup scenario. If your backup was performed at midnight (12:00AM), you would have a consistent copy of the data for that point in time, assuming the services were stopped or an individual database (store) was dismounted. In our example scenario, suppose a failure condition occurred at 2:00PM (14 hours later) and you were forced to recover the database. If the failure was mild enough (such as database corruption), you would be able to restore the database files (EDB+STM) but would not be able to play through the existing log files that have accumulated (representing real user data) since the database files were backed up. The greatest potential for error exists in an offline scenario because, during the restore of an offline database, the database engine does not automatically play through the log files, as is the case in an online scenario. There are certainly ways to accomplish the task, but this must be accomplished through manual log file management and the use of scripts and "hacks" that attempt to mimic the online recovery operations. Realistically, there is no point in this exercise since that is the purpose for which Microsoft designed the online backup APIs.

While you may have been able to devise methods of safe recovery using offline methods in previous versions of Exchange, Exchange 2000 will make it virtually impossible to enjoy success using offline methods. In previous versions of Exchange, the fact that there was a single private and public information store (PUB.EDB and PRIV.EDB) made it possible (although still prone to error) to implement successful disaster recovery procedures based on offline methods. There were only two database files and one ESE database engine instance (storage group) in previous versions of Exchange. Consider Exchange 2000, however, in which you can configure up to four storage groups (even more in later releases) on a server—each with five databases. Further consider the fact that the database is now two files (*.EDB and *.STM) instead of one. Putting all of this together, you can see the difficulty in implementing a backup strategy based on offline methods for Exchange 2000 on a server with multiple storage groups and databases. Here's my bottom line for this discussion: I hope I have convinced you to stay away from an offline approach and to only use this method for periodic archival or as an added measure of protection that is *complementary* to online, API-based backups.

4.4   Exchange 2000 Backup Operation

Let's take a moment to walk through the process of what actually occurs in backup operations for Exchange 2000. This detail will assist you by providing an "under the covers" look at the internals of how ESE performs backup operations using its recovery API. Figure 4.3 illustrates this process flow. Earlier in this chapter, we looked at this from a programmatic point of view. Now let's explore backup operation from a process point of view.

Figure 4.3
*Exchange 2000
backup process
flow operation*

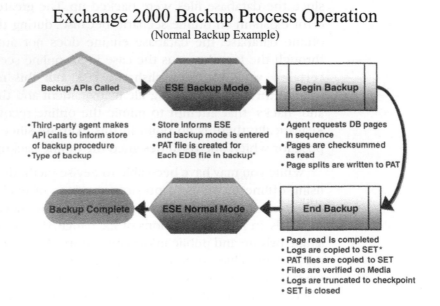

When backup operations are initiated, some process must call the ESE APIs (via ESECLIB2.DLL and ESEBACK2.DLL) to invoke the process. The process can be third-party backup software such as CA ArcServe, Veritas Backup Exec, or Legato Networker, and it must specify what type of backup is to be performed. In the case of incremental and differential backups, only log files are processed. For this discussion, let's focus in on a normal (full) backup in order to understand the full extent of the process. Once the APIs are called, the ESE (actually part of the Store process) informs the Store process

(STORE.EXE) that a backup operation is to be started; ESE must create a patch file for each. ESE must also truncate the transaction logging at the current transaction log in which the database checkpoint is currently located. This is done by closing E0n.LOG as a new generation (by renaming it to E0nnnnnn.LOG) and creating a new E0N.LOG. This is the point of truncation for the backup operation. Also remember that this is typically occurring for an entire storage group for Exchange 2000. A storage group may contain several (up to five) databases—all sharing a log file generational sequence. The next step in the process is for the backup agent to request that the database files be backed up. ESE does this by sending database pages (4KB) in batches of 16 (64KB). The pages are read in sequential order from the database. However, due to the B-Tree structure, these pages do not necessarily exist sequentially on disk. As the pages are read from the database (during a normal backup), the page number and checksum data for each page are validated for integrity. In the event that an error is found, the operation is discontinued to ensure that a corrupt database is not back up. Once all pages from the database have been successfully copied to tape (for both the property store and the streaming store), this step is complete. Remember that, when page split or merge operations to the database occur during the backup, these are written to the patch files for their respective property store. After the database files have been copied, the log files and patch files must be requested by the backup agent and written to media. The log files that are requested are those that occur in sequence before the truncation point discussed earlier. Once they are backed up, ESE truncates (deletes) the log files up to the truncation point since they have been committed to the backup. Once this is complete, the backup set is closed, the process completes, and the API returns to the agent—the operation is complete. Also, keep in mind that, if the backup type were simply an incremental or differential backup, only log files would be processed, and the steps involving the EDB, STM, and patch files would not be applicable.

4.4.1   The Poor, Misunderstood Patch File

Patch files (*.PAT) are special-purpose files used by the Exchange Server database engine on limited occasions. During online backup operations, the database file is written out 64KB at a time in a sequential fashion. In other words, the 4KB database pages are written sequentially in groups of 16 pages at a time (16 × 4KB = 64KB).

Since Exchange Server allows backup operations to be performed while the server is running and users are connected, it is possible that changes to pages in the already written (or backed up) section of the database will not be on tape. This case, however, is handled by Exchange since these changes will be stored in the transaction logs, which will be copied to the backup as well. Another case exists, however, in which a single 4KB page that resides in the portion of the property store (EDB file) already copied in the backup becomes full (i.e., all 4KB are used) as a result of transactions that have occurred since the backup was begun. In this case, the page must be split and a new page allocated in the B-Tree structure of the database (remember that the streaming store is not a B-Tree database structure and therefore does not require patch file measures). A similar situation occurs if pages must be merged. If the pages are involved in a split or merge operation occurring across the backup committed/uncommitted boundary, they cannot be handled by the transaction logs alone. Therefore, these operations must be written to a separate location in order for the property store database to remain consistent when it is restored from backup. Updates to pages in the portion of the database that has already been copied in the backup are stored in the patch file. There is a patch file created during online backup for each database. During recovery, the database engine will update the database with any pages that are stored in the patch file. Starting with Exchange 2000, Microsoft implemented the same level of integrity checking of each page in the patch file as is available for the property store. Each page in the patch file is verified using the checksum stored in the page header. Patch files are an important concept to understand concerning disaster recovery for Exchange Server. This entire discussion of patch files and their use is purely academic since the important point is that ESE takes care of everything for you.

4.4.2   Optional Page Zeroing Feature

During an online normal backup, another important feature is available. This is ESE Page Zeroing. Page Zeroing is the ability to "zero" each deleted page in the database. This is typically implemented as a security measure in which pages of the database that have been logically deleted in the database (i.e., a user deletes a mail message and it has been aged out of the deleted items cache) are overwritten to ensure that the data is truly deleted and cannot be recovered by would-be spies, hackers, or U.S Department of Justice staff members with too much time on their hands. ESE page zeroing became available in Exchange 5.5 Service Pack 2 (released in December 1998) and is an important feature for Exchange deployments desiring the highest levels of data security. ESE page zeroing for Exchange 2000 is enabled via an Exchange System Manager option (shown in Figure 4.4) and is available on a per-storage-group level.

Figure 4.4
Enabling ESE Page Zeroing in Exchange System Manager

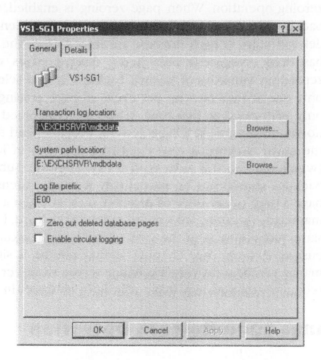

Microsoft chose to implement Page Zeroing as part of the backup process. More specifically, since this operation must touch the database and has nothing to do with the log files, Page Zeroing is done as part of an online normal backup operation. During a normal backup (when ESE Page Zeroing is enabled), as the database engine checks the integrity and copies pages to backup media, it will also "zero" delete pages in the database by writing a specific byte pattern to the page. Technically, the pages are not zeroed but contain a byte pattern known to the database as an empty page with no data. Regardless of the technicality, each deleted page no longer contains the original data and is safe from potential security threats.

As you might guess, ESE Page Zeroing can be a resource-intensive process for your Exchange Server. Additional overhead beyond what the backup operation already consumes is required to perform the zeroing operation. When page zeroing is enabled, the first normal backup operation will be the most resource intensive because all deleted pages in each database are zeroed. Once the initial operation has been completed, only newly deleted pages will need to be zeroed on subsequent normal backups. If you select a strategy of only one normal backup per cycle, all page zeroing operations are only performed at that time. If you are concerned about the additional overhead of ESE Page Zeroing, I recommend that you perform the initial backup of your databases at a time of low user activity (which may be the most typical case anyway). Subsequent normal backups should not be particularly resource intensive. Also, if you have a large occurrence of deletion, such as when a large number of mailboxes or public folders are moved or deleted, I recommend the same procedure as in the case of the initial backup previously discussed. Overall, Page Zeroing should not be a significant performance problem on your Exchange server. However, following these recommendations may make your life a bit easier in the long run.

4.5   Exchange 2000 Restore Operation

For restore operations, the process is a little more complex since ESE must manage concurrent operations and because current database and log files already exist (in some cases). Figure 4.5 illustrates the process flow for Exchange 2000 restore operations. Once again, an agent calls the recovery APIs (exposed by ESECLIB2.DLL and MDBREST.DLL) to start the process.

The store process informs ESE that restore operations for a particular database are to begin. For this to occur, the affected database must be dismounted by either the administrator (manually) or the backup/restore software (automatically). ESE then launches a recovery storage group instance of ESE that is actually the same as another

Figure 4.5
*Exchange 2000
restore process
flow operation*

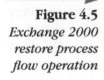

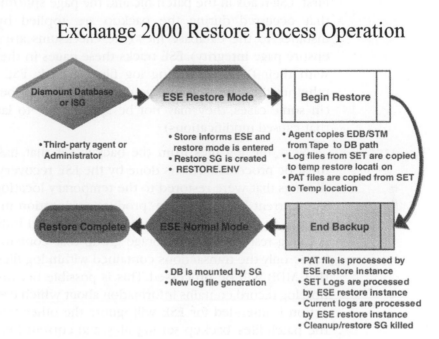

Exchange 2000 Restore Process Operation

storage group instance that exists for the period and context of the restore operation. The recovery instance writes a file called RESTORE.ENV to the default database directory. The RESTORE.ENV file tracks the current restore-in-progress information such as database paths and other information. The RESTORE.ENV file replaces the RestoreInProgress (RIP) registry key used in previous versions of Exchange. The next step is for the agent to begin restoration of the database(s) to the server database path. ESE does this by allowing the agent to directly open a file handle to the disk and copy the EDB and STM files. This is performed using standard Win32 API calls, not the Exchange API. Once complete, the log and patch files must be restored but with an important distinction. Since log files may already exist on the server for the storage group or database being restored, it would be unwise to restore the log and patch files to the same location. Before the restore begins, the operator is prompted for a temporary location to which to restore the log and patch files that are associated with the backup being restored. What happens next is very significant. The recovery storage group instance that was launched when the restore began now takes an active role.

First, ESE reads in the patch file and the page split/merge operations that occurred during the backup are applied by the recovery instance to the database files (the checksums are also verified to ensure page integrity). ESE tracks these pages in the page file along with their DBTIME. During log file playback, ESE will determine whether the page split/merge operations should be applied or not (in some cases, they may not be applied due to later transactions that caused modifications).

Next, the log files from the backup set that has been restored must be processed. This is done by the ESE recovery instance using the logs that were restored to the temporary location on the server. The current log files in the "production" location must also be processed. An important note here is that, when an individual database is being restored into a storage group that contains multiple databases, only the transactions contained within log files that pertain to that MDB will be processed. This is possible because each transaction log record contains information about which database the transaction is intended for. ESE will ignore the other transactions. Once the patch files, backup set log files, and current log files have been applied to the database, the job of the ESE recovery instance is complete. The recovery instance will do some cleanup work (such as deleting the RESTORE.ENV file), exit, and return control to the primary storage group instance, which then brings the database online. The restore operation is now complete.

4.5.1   A Word about Snapshots

Microsoft's original intention for Exchange 2000 was support snapshot technology as a method of backup and restore. As of this writing, Microsoft is still finalizing the specifics of how snapshot support will be implemented for Exchange. Also, snapshot supported is not expected until a later release of Exchange. When discussing snapshot support, it is important to understand that the term "snapshot" (more appropriately called a business continuance volume, or BCV) can mean different things depending on which hardware vendor you talk to. Compaq's storage technology defines a snapshot or BCV snapshot as a virtual block mapping to point-in-time data on disk. The snapshot is not a complete data set but a metadata pointer to the actual data. A BCV clone is an additional mirror set member that has been split off from the production mirror set. Compaq supports both a BCV clone and a BCV snapshot. On the other hand, what EMC calls a BCV snapshot is actually a BCV clone by Compaq's terminology. The vendor competitive issues are not important at this point, but it is important to understand that the terms "snapshot" and "BCV" can mean different things depending on your vendor of choice. Make sure you have a firm grasp on this technology before implementing it for Exchange.

I expect Microsoft to implement support for BCV technology in Exchange in a manner that allows technologies from vendors to easily integrate with Exchange backup and recovery procedures. As mentioned earlier, Microsoft is still working the specifics of BCV support of Exchange. I expect that BCV clone and snapshot support will be provided in Exchange by utilizing the BCV as the media where the database files reside. By using the BCV as a restore media, Exchange ESE will manage the transaction log files required to perform the complete recovery. In this scenario, the Exchange database engine (ESE) would dismount a database, causing all pages in memory to be flushed to the databases on disk. Next, a BCV (clone or snapshot) would be taken using the means a vendor provides. Since the databases are dismounted, they are consistent and do not need to have log files associated with them. This method would technically be an offline backup and restore technique. The BCV would function as the source of the Exchange database files that the ESE recovery instance (launched as part of a normal restore operation) would use, along with the necessary transaction log files to restore the Exchange data. Ideally, Microsoft will manage the entire process of utilizing BCVs as a recovery mechanism for Exchange. We will have to stay tuned until later in 2000 or 2001 to find out how support for BCV technology will be implemented in Exchange and integrated with the vendor product offerings available. Microsoft will most likely work with specific vendors to develop offline backup mechanisms for using BCVs. Longer term, I expect Microsoft to deliver full online backup solutions using specific vendor's implementations in a later version of Exchange beyond Exchange 2000. I also expect the procedures and practices to vary depending on the hardware vendor whose BCV technology you have selected. Both Compaq and EMC are actively engaged with Microsoft on-site, working on solutions for Exchange 2000. We will need to wait for the final release of snapshot support to be certain how this technology can aid in our disaster recovery for Exchange.

4.6   Power with Responsibility

With the advent of multiple storage groups and databases in Exchange 2000, the recovery API must be stretched to accommodate new scenarios. You must be able to perform backup and restore operations for the entire server, a storage group, or an individual database. In addition, since these operations can be performed concurrently, ESE must be able to handle this as well. Exchange 2000 offers a great deal of flexibility and additional availability that previous versions did not offer. For example, you could have four databases configured that are each hosting 1,000 users (a total of 4,000 users). You begin restore operations for one storage group or database without impacting the other storage groups. In our example, 3,000 users would be online accessing their data while the 1,000 users using the database being restored would be the only affected users. This, indeed, gives operators many more options and reduces the overall impact of restore operations. However, it also complicates procedures, requires better training, and has greater potential for error. Gather the knowledge you require to ensure that you are implementing solid disaster recovery plans for Exchange 2000. Understand the different backup strategies available for Exchange 2000 and select the one that best suits your organization. Also, keep in mind and stay tuned because many of the best practices and "tricks of the trade" for Exchange 2000 have not been discovered yet. The power of Exchange 2000 storage must not be realized without properly understanding the disaster recovery implications.

5

Exchange 2000 Disaster Recovery Best Practices

Providing rapid and safe recovery within desired service levels is a key part of building mission-critical Exchange deployments. Microsoft has continued support for previous methods and strategies for performing backup and restore operations but has evolved backup support in Exchange 2000 to support new features such as multiple storage groups and databases on a single Exchange 2000 server. With proper planning and the following recommended best practices, your organization can be prepared in the event of Exchange Server data loss. This data loss can span a wide spectrum from a complete server catastrophe to simply performing an individual message recovery. In this chapter, after having laid the technology foundation in the previous chapter, I will discuss some recommended best practices for successfully implementing disaster recovery for your Exchange deployment. Of course, these best practices must be tempered and tailored to your organization's specific needs. In addition, while many of the best practices developed for previous versions of Exchange Server still apply to Exchange 2000, many will be enhanced over time. Finally, since Exchange 2000 is a relatively new product and thus not widely deployed, many best practices for Exchange 2000 are yet to be developed and realized. With that said, the suggestions and tips I outline here will give any Exchange system manager a jump start in developing practices and procedures that will help ensure your Exchange deployment is both highly available and recoverable. For detailed recovery procedures, see Appendix A.

5.1 Best Practice #1: Understand Exchange Technology

I have devoted an entire chapter in this book to Exchange database technology. Understanding the underlying technology of the

Exchange database engine is a fundamental foundation for under-standing the backup and restore process. A close examination of the database engine and transaction logging will help you understand how Exchange server ensures that data remains intact and with the highest levels of integrity in the event of a system or component fail-ure. Along with a familiarity of the database engine, a thorough understanding of the concepts of storage groups and databases is key. Understanding which files the Exchange database engine uses is also extremely important. In Chapter 3, I discussed files such as property data (*.EDB), streaming data (*.STM), patch (*.PAT), and transaction log (*.LOG) which are all key components of backup and restore operations for Exchange. Without detailed knowledge of the various database engine components and their purposes, it will be difficult to design and operate systems with the highest levels of availability, scalability, and reliability. In the event that disaster recov-ery operations need to be performed, procedures and plans that comprehend how Exchange recovers its databases will be the key to rapid restoration of system operation.

Figure 5.1
Exchange Database transacted storage model

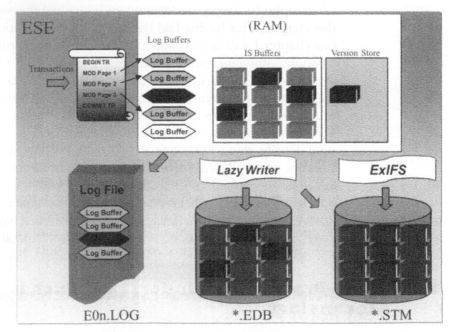

By understanding Exchange database technology, you will have a head start on backup and restore technology (the subject of Chapter 4). The most important concept in Exchange 2000 is the change from monolithic storage in previous versions of Exchange Server to multiple storage groups (ESE instances) and multiple mailbox and public folder stores (multiple databases called MDBs) within each storage group. You are able to back up and restore databases within a storage group either individually or as a group (i.e., the entire storage group). Also, remember that each storage group (and the databases configured in the storage group) shares a common sequence of transaction logs. Transactions logs are the critical component for data recovery in Exchange. When a database becomes damaged or corrupted, it is the transaction logs that allow a database to be recovered from a backup and restored to a consistent state. This knowledge of Exchange database technology and how recovery is accomplished is fundamental to success and is the reason I chose to present it at the top of the list of best practices for mission-critical systems.

5.2   Best Practice #2: Plan and Partition Data

One of the great new features of Exchange 2000 is the ability to segment or partition both public and user data into manageable units. In previous versions of Exchange Server, we did not have this luxury. As a result, the number of users per server we could support was limited by the size of the information store and the disaster recovery limitations imposed. With Exchange 2000, you have the ability to make some important decisions about how storage is allocated based on factors such as performance, recoverability, and management complexity. Since each storage group shares a set of log files, it is recommended for performance and management reasons that the log files be placed on separate disk devices from the database files. This is directly related to the nature of the I/O patterns for the individual database files. The transaction log files are accessed in a purely synchronous, sequential write pattern (except during replay). The property store (*.EDB) has an I/O pattern that is highly random in nature with small (4KB) synchronous reads and asynchronous writes. Somewhat unknown (due to lack of deployment experience) is the streaming store, which has an I/O pattern that will most likely be similar to the property store (random in nature with synchronous reads and asynchronous writes) but with a large I/O size of 32KB. The I/O access pattern for the Exchange database files, along with management considerations, is that key driver for partitioning and server design.

Since multiple databases can be configured within a storage group, you should design the size of each database within a storage group to be aligned with your recovery capabilities and time windows. For example, if your backup and restore facilities provide for a restore rate of 10GB per hour and you have a two-hour recovery window, it would be best to limit the size of each database to 20GB or less. You should maintain these databases to limits that facilitate reasonable recovery times. Microsoft is recommending that the entire storage group be backed up as a unit (as opposed to backing up each database in the storage group individually). This ensures simplicity in your backup and restore procedures since all databases within the storage group share the same transaction log sequence. Also, since all databases share the same transaction logs, the Exchange database engine will not truncate the transaction logs (during a full or incremental backup) until all databases in the storage group have been backed up. If you were to only back up individual databases, it is possible that log files would never be truncated, resulting in a greater potential for data loss.

When restoring data, you can restore a single database (MDB— *.EDB and *.STM files) without impacting other databases in the same storage group or in other storage groups. The other databases continue to provide services to clients. If other databases share the same physical storage devices such as a RAID array, there may be minor performance issues while databases are recovered. This issue, along with the potential for a loss of all databases sharing a single volume or array, makes a good case for separating databases onto separate physical disk devices for optimal performance and data protection. This partitioning of user data across multiple physical devices can isolate problems with hardware to a single database and only affects the users whose data resides there. To completely prepare for storage failure on an Exchange server, you should investigate data partitioning and plan to separate data into storage groups and databases. To add further protection, you can even back up the partitioned data to different backup media. Remember that the recovery limitation is on a per-storage-group basis. As long as you ini-

Figure 5.2
Illustration of partitioned vs. nonpartitioned data storage

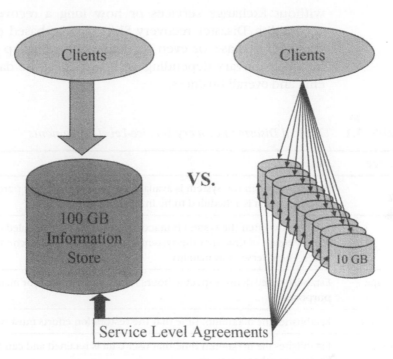

tiate separate backup and restore operations for each storage group, the Exchange database engine can operate on multiple storage groups at the same time. These parallel operations ensure that users who are not affected by an outage of one database can still access their data on another database. Taking advantage of these new features in Exchange 2000 and partitioning server data into manageable units of recovery and performance (based on SLAs) will allow you to meet and exceed those service levels and provide the highest levels of availability to your Exchange clients.

5.3   **Best Practice #3: Establish Disaster Recovery Service-Level Agreements**

I will discuss service-level agreements (SLAs) in more detail in Chapter 9. A SLA for a messaging system can exist in many forms. However, in the context of this section, the scope is limited to disaster recovery. This type of SLA typically defines how long a client can be without Exchange services or how long a recovery can take to accomplish. Disaster recovery SLAs may be based on an individual mailbox, database, or even an entire storage group. SLAs for restoring data will vary depending on how critical the data is to your clients and overall business.

Table 5.1   *Typical Disaster Recovery Service-Level Agreements*

SLA Coverage	Description
Availability	Establishes when the system is available for use. Measured in percentage of time that the system is scheduled to be in operation.
Reliability	Covers how often the system is inaccessible due to unscheduled outages. Measured in percentage of time that the system is operational during scheduled operational times. The inverse of availability.
Planned outage	Establishes and defines specific hours for planned outages for maintenance or other purposes.
Restoration time	Establishes the maximum time that the restoration efforts must not exceed.
Data retention period	Establishes the maximum time that user data is retained and can be restored via backup or other measures.
Message integrity	Guarantees that messages and attachments will arrive intact and not be corrupted as they travel throughout the organization.

After negotiating an SLA with your customers, you should test your operational procedures to verify whether or not they can meet the defined SLAs. If not, you will have to take steps to improve the performance of your procedures. This may be accomplished through improved data partitioning, faster performing server hardware, data partitioning, or distribution of your data across more Exchange servers. Since Exchange 2000 drastically improves the flexibility of storage design and allocation on an Exchange server, the ability to purposely and proactively design your information stores for optimal performance and reliability is provided. As previously discussed, Exchange 2000 allows you to configure up to 15 storage groups (a maximum of 4 is supported upon initial release of Exchange 2000) per server, each with up to 5 databases. This affords many more options than in previous versions of Exchange Server, which provided only a monolithic, single information store approach. Because of the flexibility available, administrators can now architect storage designs based on performance requirements as well as disaster recovery requirements or SLAs. Let's look at a couple of examples to illustrate this point.

First consider a scenario in which a customer (whether internal corporate IS or a consumer using the services of an ISP) has certain performance SLAs for message delivery or other metrics requiring a database to be located on a higher-performance disk subsystem. With the advent of storage groups and multiple databases in Exchange 2000, an administrator can configure a specific storage group or database on a dedicated storage array or storage area network that can provide a higher level of performance than others already configured on the server. This also lends itself very nicely to storage charge-back schemes in which clients/customers can pay for the level of performance they require. A single Exchange 2000 server could host many different storage groups, each providing the capabilities to meet one or many specific SLAs that clients require. The possibilities are only limited in degree by the amount of hardware you are willing to build around your Exchange server. In Chapter 6, I will address the topic of leveraging storage technology for Exchange and will discuss this in more detail.

In another scenario illustrating the best practice of designing storage based on SLAs, let's say a specific customer unit using Exchange 2000 services requires higher levels of availability, reliability, and recoverability. For example, suppose you are an Internet service provider that provides Exchange 2000 hosting services to a financial services company (just an example) that has fairly strict requirements for disaster recovery. The flexibility of storage allocation in Exchange 2000 allows for either storage groups or databases to be configured based on disaster recovery needs. For example, if the disaster recovery facility only allowed for backup rates of 30GB per hour and restore rates of 15GB per hour and the customer demanded a two-hour recovery SLA, you would have to find methods of partitioning or segmenting user data in such a manner that the SLA could be achieved. If the maximum restore rate available is 15GB per hour, an administrator may choose to limit the maximum database size to 20GB–30GB (allowing it to be restored within the two-hour window). This could be done with hard limits to the size of the information store or by limiting the number of users per information store. Since Exchange 2000 provides such a high degree of storage flexibility (multiple storage groups and multiple databases), the administrator has many options available to provide individual levels of services depending on the client's needs.

This best practice will be key as activities like server consolidation and multiple-organization hosting take place in Exchange 2000 deployments. Again, the keys to successfully implementing this best practice will be to understand how Exchange 2000 storage works and to seek opportunities to leverage it to meet customer requirements. The opportunities for creative storage management in Exchange 2000 are what Microsoft is counting on to provide high levels of scalability while, at the same time, delivering increased availability.

5.4   Best Practice #4: Select the Right Disaster Recovery Technology

There are a plethora of backup technologies, techniques, and strategies available in the Windows NT/2000 environment. From a technology point of view, choosing the right technology for your deployment involves both hardware and software. In addition, the storage technology you select for your Exchange deployment will have a significant impact on what options are available to you for disaster. From a best practices point of view, you will need to select the technology that best meets your unique requirements. Table 5.2 provides some basic criteria for selecting backup software. There are many different vendors available who offer excellent backup software products. Industry leaders such as Computer Associates (formerly Cheyenne) ArcServer IT, Veritas (formerly Seagate) Backup Exec, and Legato Networker are among the most often selected for Exchange deployments. Each vendor offers a different mix of features, device support, and cost. All have different trade-offs. For example, in my experience, Legato Networker provides the best heterogeneous operating system support but is weakest in hardware device support. Computer Associates' ArcServe product, on the other hand, has better device support but supports fewer operating system choices. All vendors have different strengths and weaknesses. You will need to select the vendor that best meets the needs of your Exchange deployment and disaster recovery requirements. As the Exchange system administrator, your organization may have already selected a standard, and you may not have the luxury of choosing.

Table 5.2   *Backup Software Vendor Selection Criteria*

Selection Criteria	Explanation
Client/server architecture	Client-server architecture applied to backup software results in a solution with two or more components. Some products use a two-tier or three-tier architecture for their solution; most important is the ability to back up on remote tape drives or, inversely, to back up locally remote server information.
Scheduling	Scheduling capability enables "lights-out" operations for the backup facility. For instance, a backup should be run at a given point in time with certain conditions. Such operations will require the ability to report backup status to a central management station.
Exchange API support	As explained earlier, the online backup capability resides in the implementation of a backup agent that uses the Microsoft Exchange Backup API to access to the database information. Online backups do not require Microsoft Exchange to be shut down for saving the information.
Tape management	Most software products provide some support for automatic tape labeling, including bar code generation, cataloging, and librarian functions for proper archiving and identification. This function is important when dealing with a large quantity of information to back up, for full or incremental backups.
Vendor support	How well the vendor supports its product offering including technical support, updates and patches, as well as platform support.
Performance tuning capability	The degree to which the software provides advanced tuning capabilities via the registry or other mechanisms that allow the software to be configured optimally for all scenarios.
Hardware device support	As new tape devices and other backup subsystems and media such as automated libraries and other devices are developed, how quickly a vendor provides support for these new devices is critical.
Operating system support	Since most organizations have more than one operating system deployed, support for multiple operating systems may be required so that the organization can utilize a single product for all disaster recovery needs including Exchange Server.
Disaster recovery management	Many vendors provide complete disaster recovery planning and other tools that provide total disaster recovery management and that allow complete recovery via a disaster recovery disk or other means.
Cluster and SAN support	Since clustering and storage area networks (SANs) add a degree of complexity to the environment, the ability of backup software to comprehend and support clustering and SAN scenarios is crucial.
Advanced technology support	Support for Redundant Array of Independent Tapes (RAIT), SAN-direct backup and restore, and other advanced techniques and technology should be a important consideration when selecting a backup software vendor.

In addition to selecting the backup software technology that best meets your organization-specific needs, you will need to put careful thought into the hardware technology choice to which you will marry that software. There are many options for devices to use as your media of choice for storing critical backup sets required to recover your Exchange servers. Quarter Inch Cartridge (QIC), Digital Audio Tape (DAT), Advanced Intelligent Tape (AIT), and Digital Linear Tape (DLT) are among the most popular options. However, each type of media has advantages and disadvantages. When selecting your media option (and therefore your hardware device option), many points need to be considered and weighed. In addition, each option will have a different cost point that must be justified. In some cases, the cost of the device and media may be relatively inexpensive but come at some cost in terms of reliability. In other cases, the most reliable option may also be the most expensive. Your choice for backup devices and media for your Exchange deployment will have to weigh all the technological, reliability, and cost factors against your organization's disaster recovery requirements. Table 5.3 includes some important criteria for selecting media and devices.

Table 5.3 *Backup Device/Media Selection Criteria*

Selection Criteria	Explanation
Vendor support	In the case of both backup devices and media, multiple vendors offer products. As in the case of backup software, the degree to which the vendor supports its product is important. Vendors should provide technical support and updates (such as firmware updates) for device hardware.
Configuration flexibility	Many vendors offer backup devices that can be configured in a variety of ways such as standalone, RAIT, or multistreaming. Flexibility of configuration provides more options for successful disaster recovery.
Capacity	Different device/media options have different capacities available. For example, DLT media comes in 10/20GB, 20/40GB, and 35/70GB capacities (in the future, SDLT will extend this even further). In addition, different levels of hardware and/or software compression are also available.
Interface	Devices may be offered with several interface options such as SCI, SCSI, or fibre channel attachment. Depending on growth and future flexibility needs, you may prefer one interface option to another.
Automation	Some devices are offered in the form of automation products such as carousels and libraries. If automation is key to your backup and recovery plans, selecting products that are offered in these form factors is a must.

Table 5.3   *Backup Device/Media Selection Criteria (continued)*

Selection Criteria	Explanation
Error detection/ correction	Technologies such as DLT, AIT, DAT, QIC, and others all offer varying degrees of error detection and correction capabilities. Understand what each technology offers and select the one best suited to your needs.
Cleaning duty cycle	Some technologies have very high cleaning duty cycles and require frequent cleaning and/or maintenance. QIC and DAT technologies are an example of this. DLT, on the other hand, requires less frequent cleaning and maintenance.
Head/drive life	The operational life of the tape drive and head will vary depending on the technology you choose.
Compatibility	QIC, DAT, and DLT have all evolved over several years and generations of technology. If you are archiving media or long periods, ensure that future devices will have compatibility for previous technology evolutions.
Cost	The cost of your technology choice will have long-term impacts. The cost of both devices and media will need to be considered.

I have always preferred DLT drives and array technology over DAT or QIC devices and media. While more costly, DLT offers superior capacity, reliability, performance, and drive and tape life than QIC or DAT options. While QIC and DAT may be less expensive and feasible for smaller deployments and organizations, they cannot match the strengths of DLT technology. DLT technology also offers more flexibility of configuration. DLT drives can be used standalone as individual drives or can be configured in RAIT arrays for increased performance, capacity, and reliability. A recent newcomer to tape technology is AIT. AIT provides many of the performance and reliability features that DLT provides but at a somewhat lower cost. The tape technology game is much like any other technology in that the various products and technology are engaged in an eternal battle of "leap frog" where technology benefits are concerned. Whatever your choice for backup media, make sure you understand the pros and cons of each technology and which is the bet fit for your Exchange deployment and organization's needs.

In the race to get high backup throughput, the alternative to fast and expensive tape drives is to use multiple DLTs. In fact, most vendors can support up to 28 DLT7000 tape drives or more, with resulting backup rates as high as 800GB/hr (unfortunately, not for Exchange). The backup and restore operations for Microsoft Exchange are single stream for the most part. The exception is when multiple storage groups are backed up simultaneously (which may have a net result of slower overall performance due to Exchange Server resource contention). It is not possible to back up several parts of the single-file databases at the same time. Using multiple tape drives requires selecting backup software that efficiently streams data to multiple tape drives in parallel. The common terminology is RAIT (Redundant Array of Independent Tape), and levels 0 and 5 (distributed parity) are commonly in use. Legato Networker, Cheyenne ARCserve, and Veritas Backup Exec are examples of backup software that handles multiple tape drives. I recommend only using RAIT5 or any RAIT with redundant parity; the data stream being strictly sequential, the generation of the parity will not degrade the performance to a large extent. Similar to multiple tape drive "striping" (using RAIT) are the benefits of multiple tape drive streaming. In this scenario, independent backup or restore operations to different data sets are performed simultaneously as multiple "streams." This can occur from separate storage groups on an individual Exchange server, or streams can come from multiple Exchange servers via the storage area network or the local area network. Tape drive striping or streaming are both excellent methods of increasing backup and restore speeds by allowing the concept of concurrency (either block concurrency or stream concurrency) in your Exchange backup and restore operations.

To compress or not to compress is an interesting question: It allows storing more information faster, but the rate at which an Exchange database, which is already somewhat compressed for text bodyparts, is compressed is not known. When in doubt, I suggest using compression whenever available, but you will need to make a choice between either software-based compression (done by the backup software) or hardware-based compression. The software-based compression has its advantages, such as transferring less data over the network in the case of client/server backup operations; on the other hand, the tape-level compression is done at the tape hardware level and is presumably faster than the software compression. Again, the CPU capacity of the client and the server will impact actual performance.

The products you select form the foundation of your disaster recovery capability. If you select products that limit your ability to provide adequate recovery of your Exchange servers, your disaster recovery service levels will not be achieved. A well-planned disaster recovery procedure will be worthless if the technology upon which you base the procedure does not deliver on its intended promises. Hopefully, you have the option of selecting the right backup software, device, and media in advance of putting your disaster recovery plan in place. Make every effort to thoroughly evaluate the vendors and technologies available using the previously discussed criteria above as well as criteria dictated by your own organizational or deployment needs. The balance you strike between criteria such as performance, reliability, and cost will enable you to build a solid disaster recovery plan for your Exchange deployment. This will help you meet your mission-critical SLAs.

5.5 Best Practice #5: Select the Right Backup and Recovery Strategy

Why back up? Today's hardware and software environments are increasingly reliable. Techniques have been developed to protect massive amounts of information. However, no solution is perfect, and there is always a chance that some form of failure will occur. The failure could arise in hardware, software, or through the fault of a human operator or administrator. For mission-critical applications, such as Microsoft Exchange Server, it is key to have a "safety net" so that production data and service can be restored in a minimal amount of time. Loss of data is very often associated with a crash or failure in the disk or storage subsystem. Hence, the important storage vendors in the industry have spent substantial investments to make improvements in terms of data protection. However, there are other ways in which information could be lost other than by a single disk crash:

- I/O subsystem failure
- System software failure
- Accidental or malicious deletion of information
- Destructive viruses
- Natural disasters
- Theft

A solid backup and restore strategy provides the basis for recovering information in a reliable manner. The backup type or combination of backup types you select can have a substantial impact on operational procedures, training, tape management, and restore times. It all comes down to tapes, time, and volume. Depending on which backup strategy you select, each of these will be affected. Table 5.4 shows the three basic backup strategies for Exchange 2000. Note that I don't include the snapshot option because I discussed thsi as a future option in chapter 4. The copy backup is not typically considered as disaster recovery operation for Exchange deployments but as an archival or point-in-time copy option.

Table 5.4   *Basic Backup Strategies for Exchange 2000*

Backup Strategy Option	*Description*	*Restore Trade-offs (Tapes, Time, and Volume)*
1. Daily normal backup	A normal (full) backup of all Exchange information stores is performed daily.	One tape, fixed period, fixed volume
2. Normal with daily incremental	A normal backup is performed on the first day of the backup cycle. For the following days, an incremental backup is performed.	Variable tapes (1-6), variable time, variable volume
3. Normal with daily differential	A normal backup is performed on the first day of the backup cycle. For the following days, a differential backup is performed.	Two tapes, variable time, variable volume

As one would expect, there are many trade-offs when selecting the right combination of backup types to include in your backup strategy for Exchange. The time required, the number of tapes, and the volume of data are all important considerations. If you select a daily normal backup, you gain the advantage of only having to deal with one tape, and the time and volume of data is usually fixed, allowing you to plan your recovery windows better. If you choose to perform a normal backup on the first day of your backup cycle and combine this with daily incremental backups thereafter, day one is similar to option 1. However, the subsequent days on which incremental backups are performed are much quicker because only the log files are backed up. The problem with option 2 is that recovery is more difficult to manage because multiple tapes are required and the process will take more time. Option 2 also has more exposure to operator error or media failure. Option 3 is a middle-ground approach between options 1 and 2. With this approach, a normal backup is taken on the first day followed by differentials on subsequent days. This ensures that only two tapes are required for recovery since tape one will have the normal backup from day one (database, logs, and patch files) and tape two will contain all the log files accumulated since. Since you only have two tapes, time, volume, errors, and chance of media failures are also reduced. You will need to consider these trade-offs when selecting the strategy that works best for your Exchange deployment. Keep in mind that the method you select will in large part determine the time it takes to recover Exchange. From a best practices point of view, most organizations I come into contact with have selected option 1 for obvious reasons. As the mission-critical nature of Exchange grows, the ability to limit the number of tapes, reduce errors and media failures, as well as simplify procedures becomes paramount. While options 2 and 3 are viable solutions, most savvy Exchange administrators have discovered the advantages of option 1 and have made it their best practice.

- *Daily normal*—The advantage of a daily normal backup is simplicity. It is by far the simplest schedule and the easiest option to manage when you need to restore your Exchange databases because you need only the last normal backup set. This approach is also far less prone to operator errors and tape-management problems due to its simplicity. One final advantage to daily normal backups is that the integrity-checking operations are performed each and every day to ensure that your database is not corrupt. Equally, this applies to ESE Page Zeroing, when enabled, and allows this operation to be performed daily, thereby potentially reducing system overhead. The only disadvantage to this approach is that it requires the entire volume of Exchange data to be backed up each day. Depending on the size of your Exchange databases, normal backups can be very time consuming and may not fit into daily backup "windows" available to your organization. Additionally, normal backup operations may require a tape swap each day due to management or capacity considerations.

- *Normal with incremental*—The obvious advantage of the normal with incremental approach is that it takes the least time, backs up the least amount of data, and has the least impact on system resources. This is due to the fact that, after the first normal backup in the cycle, each daily backup merely consists of the transaction logs that have accumulated since the last backup. The disadvantages are also apparent because in order to restore, between two and seven backup sets (on a weekly cycle) will be required. This can complicate tape management and operational procedures and can be quite prone to operator error. Also, since only one normal backup is performed each cycle, the advantages of integrity checking and ESE Page Zeroing are also lost.

- *Normal with differential*—The advantage of this approach is that, like the normal with incremental approach, less time, volume, and impact on the system are felt. In addition, a maximum of two backup sets will be required to perform a recovery—the last normal and the last differential set. Another side benefit of this strategy is that, throughout the week, multiple copies of the log files are stored because each differential backup is simply a cumulative of log files since the last normal backup. In the event that a log file from the current set is corrupt, another copy may be found on another differential backup set from a different day. The disadvantage to the normal with differential approach is that, each day, the differential backup set will be larger and take more time as log files accumulate over the duration of the cycle.

Whatever your strategy for recovering your Exchange Server data, it must meet your organizational requirements. In addition, your recovery strategy should include Exchange Server data viewed not only in terms of the entire information store or database but also as smaller increments of recovery such as an individual mailbox or even an individual item such as a message. In your planning, you will need to address how recovery for each unit (server, database, mailbox, or item) will be accomplished. Your practices and procedures can leverage several technologies in unison or individually to accomplish these tasks. Your backup and recovery strategy must also account and compensate for limitations in Exchange Server's capabilities. Since a maximum of four configured storage groups per server will be supported in the initial release of Exchange 2000, you will have to plan even more carefully. However, for future updates when the maximums are supported, this will likely not be a key concern. The key is to guide your recovery strategy-based on your SLAs. SLAs then drive your maximum disaster recovery windows, which in turn dictate your maximum data size and the technology you must use to provide disaster recovery.

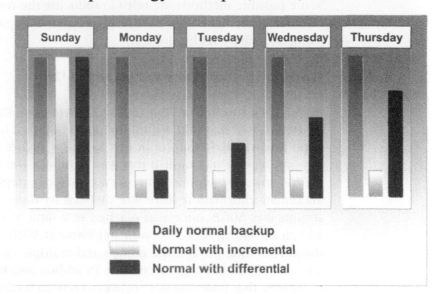

Backup Strategy — Tapes, Time, and Volume

5.6 Best Practice #6: Look for Ways to Shrink Disaster Recovery Windows

The rule here is that, if your backups take too long, your restores will too. The goal should be to reduce the amount of time it takes to restore your Exchange data. As Exchange deployments become more and more mission-critical, disaster recovery windows are constantly shrinking. I typically recommend that organizations target a four-hour recovery window for Exchange data. Since typical restore times are two times longer that the backup time, the maximum tolerable backup time is two hours. You must be able to perform backups on your data-recovery units within a two-hour period to be able to recover that data within four hours. There are several possible strategies to accomplish this. All involve a trade-off between the size of your recovery unit (i.e., how large is your

Exchange database) and the time it takes to back up and restore (usually dictated by your disaster recovery technology choice). Some possible methods include (1) reducing the recovery unit size, (2) increasing backup recovery performance capabilities, and (3) using alternative technologies.

5.6.1   Reducing the Recovery Unit Size

By reducing the size of your unit of recovery, you can manage disaster recovery of that unit within the limits imposed on you. Exchange 2000 is particularly helpful in this situation. Before Exchange 2000, the only way to accomplish this was to reduce the size of the information store by adding more servers to your deployment. If your maximum information store size dictated by disaster recovery constraints was 50GB, once you reached that limit, you would need to add an additional server to your deployment. With Exchange 2000's support of multiple storage groups and multiple databases per storage group, you have an alternative to adding another server. If you determine that your disaster recovery constraints limit you to a database size of 50GB, you simply add another database to an Exchange 2000 server when that limit is reached. Another way to accomplish this is to break down a deployment with few large information stores into many smaller information stores. For example, instead of an Exchange server with a single 100GB database, you could configure 10 10GB databases on a single server. Backup and restore of a single 100GB database may take many hours. However, backup and restore of 10 10GB databases concurrently (if the databases reside in separate storage groups) would take far less time.

Other techniques can help reduce the amount of data that must be backed up and restored as well. Periodic compression of databases can help in situations in which a large amount of data has been deleted from an Exchange database. Also, an Exchange archival solution can reduce the size of existing databases. Several third-party products offer archival functions that offer policy-based aging of user data out of the information stores. Enforcement of mailbox quotas and reducing deleted item retention can also decrease the amount of data that must be recovered. You may also choose to leverage personal store files (PSTs.) PSTs allow users to store data individually. When using PST files, however, you will need to set clear policies about whether or not disaster recovery measures will be provided by the organization for these user files. If so, you may not accomplish any reduction in the amount of data that must be recovered. There are many creative methods to reduce the size of your Exchange information stores. If you are successful in this effort, you will be rewarded with shorter backup and restore times, fewer tapes, and an overall reduction in your Exchange disaster recovery window.

5.6.2   Increasing Backup/Recovery Performance

Many times, this is much easier said than done. Depending on how you back up your Exchange server, you may be able to apply technology and better design principles toward this goal. Many Exchange deployments I come in contact with have limits to backup/restore performance that are imposed by either their technology choice or the architecture that technology operates within. If you have a single DAT tape drive attached to every Exchange server in your deployment, you are going to get a "ballpark estimate" maximum backup rate of about 1GB–2GB per hour. For DLT, that number increases to about 10GB–15GB per hour. For a database that is 50GB, the DAT device will never deliver the needed performance (~25 hours to backup and ~50 hours to restore). For the DLT tape drive, you may have acceptable backup rates (~3–4 hours) but the restore rates would be barely adequate (~5–6 hours). From an architecture viewpoint, you may have high-speed devices available but perform your backup and restore operations over a network instead of locally attached devices. In this case, the bottleneck could be the network, and a dedicated backup network backbone would be required. When attempting to reduce disaster recovery windows with performance enhancements, you will have to evaluate the relative cost versus performance trade-offs. While an 8-drive DLT array locally attached to every Exchange server may yield the ultimate in performance (Compaq has tested as high as 70GB per hour on backup), this solution is not cost-effective for a large deployment. However, in this example, you may be able to deploy several backup servers with DLT arrays or library devices and back up your Exchange server via a dedicated disaster recovery "backbone" network. This may strike a better price/performance balance while still accomplishing the goal of increased backup and restored performance. You can look to other areas to increase disaster recovery performance as well. The disk subsystem on your Exchange server is another key area that will impact backup and restore performance.

Upgrades to this important server subsystem can ensure that backup and/or restore performance is optimized. There are many areas to look at when attempting to increase performance of your disaster recovery operations for Exchange. The important point is to focus on where your current bottlenecks and limitation exist in your current strategy. By identifying where these bottlenecks exist, you can make sound, cost-effective decisions about which areas make the best sense for further enhancement and investment.

5.6.3   Using Alternative Technologies

In Chapter 6, I will discuss storage technology and the various features that can be leveraged to increase reliability for Exchange deployments. Technologies such as business continuance volumes (BCVs) and data replication can add to existing disaster recovery techniques and measures and can provide alternative recovery options. As an example, utilizing BCV technology can provide for another media that holds Exchange data in addition to the data that exists as part of your regular online backup. In a scenario in which BCVs are used, they could function as a backup volume (from which backups are performed) or could be used as a rapid-recovery measure in the event of database corruption or data loss. Since many of these alternative technologies are new, there are many caveats. I suggest that these technologies can provide some answers to the challenges of Exchange disaster recovery. However, I do not recommend that these options be used in lieu of established and Microsoft-supported measures. For example, I would not use BCV technology as a replacement for regular online backups. I do believe, however, that these technologies can be an important complement to existing practices and methods. In later releases of Exchange 2000 and when these technologies mature, I expect to see many of them used regularly and as the primary means of increasing backup and restore performance as well as functionality. In the meantime, approach with caution and stay tuned to Chapter 6, where I discuss these technologies in more detail.

By shrinking the amount of time it takes to accomplish disaster recovery, we can scale our Exchange deployments to larger user populations and data sets. There are several ways to approach this challenge. Reducing data, increasing performance, and leveraging alternative technologies are among the leading strategies. Whatever your approach, seek to identify ways to accomplish this and thereby enable your Exchange deployment to meet the ever-growing service-level requirements of mission-critical systems.

Figure 5.4
Using a BCV
with Exchange
2000

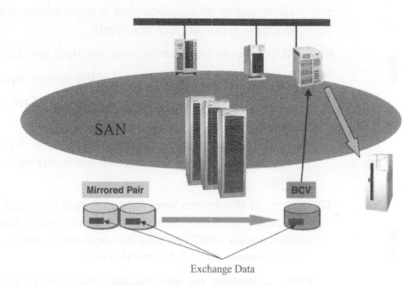

Using BCV Technology with Exchange

5.7   Best Practice #7: Develop an Exchange Disaster Recovery Plan

A solid backup plan should be in place when moving from a development or test environment to a production one. In the same way as you would never deploy untested software, the production phase of a project should never be entered into without a solid backup and restore plan. Best practices for Exchange deployments mandate the development of a backup plan as one of the essential steps in the design of a Microsoft Exchange infrastructure. In addition to protecting data as thoroughly as possible, the backup plan must reflect organizational requirements. Some of these requirements can be a driving factor in the hardware solution design. In the course of developing a backup plan, a series of questions should be addressed:

1. How often should the backups be performed?

2. What information should be backed up?

3. Which medium will be used (tape, disk, or BCV)?

4. What level of automation is required (unattended)?

5. How can it be ensured that any problems that occur are trapped, reported, and resolved?

6. What should be the retention, rotation, and archival policy?

7. In case of failure, how long will the restore operation take?

8. Is there a mechanism that makes sure if the backups are good?

9. How are the responsibilities defined to ensure that the backup operations are running smoothly and according to plan?

10. Are all the procedures documented thoroughly in such a manner that any member of the technical staff (including temporary staff) is able to perform backup and restore operations should the need arise?

These questions are just samples that may or may not apply to your environment. However, I strongly encourage you to consider them during the planning and design phases for each significant Exchange disaster recovery planning project. Any plan should also include and comprehend the entire system, not just Exchange. While you as an Exchange system manager may not have ultimate responsibility or accountability for all aspects of the system recovery (such as the Active Directory or Windows 2000), your plan needs to comprehend the complete system. For Exchange 2000, this includes Windows 2000 and Exchange 2000 but must also look at other components such as Internet Information Server (IIS) and third-party components as well. The disaster recovery plan must also consider each possible disaster scenario from the most minor incident (individual item recovery such as a message) to the most catastrophic event (such as fire, flood, theft, malicious activity, etc.). The plan must address backup procedures and methods, archival, tape management, rotation, personnel training requirements, and any resource requirements and staffing roles required. Once the plan has been developed, it must be thoroughly tested to ensure that the methods and procedures are valid for your environment. Don't rely on common MIS-generic disaster recovery planning for Exchange. Exchange is a specialized application that requires individual attention and a separate plan. The care that you take in developing and validating your disaster recovery plan for Exchange will have a direct correlation to how well the plan is executed and the level of availability you are able to achieve for your Exchange deployment.

5.8 Best Practice #8: Train Personnel and Practice Disaster Recovery

In larger, established companies, this is usually a given (but not always...). However, in small companies, this needs to be the rule as well. Training should start with the disaster recovery plan and the execution of that plan. Personnel should be trained in all aspects of the system. Understanding how the backup software works is not enough. Train operations personnel on Windows NT/2000, Exchange, and the hardware platform on which they run. If your Exchange servers are deployed in a SAN or a clustered environment, this added complexity must be well understood by those responsible for system recovery. Ensure that personnel know the intricacies of the Exchange database engine, transaction-based storage, and how recovery is performed. Engage Microsoft PSS and other knowledgeable support resources in the process of planning and training your staff. Ensure that those responsible are aware of support resources and how utilize them and how to escalate issues when things go wrong. When a problem does occur, make sure that each player in the recovery scenario understands his or her role.

The best training ground for personnel is a disaster recovery "fire drill." Not just one, however, lots of them. An Exchange system manager who drops a bomb on his recovery staff when there is no real emergency will be much better prepared when the situation is real. Finding out that your recovery procedures don't really work during an actual emergency is the worst time to get this news. Hopefully, the procedures have seen hours of QA and validation before this point. However, as an added measure, test your plan and procedures thoroughly. Murphy's Law says that it is a very real possibility that, when you most need something to work, it won't. Not only can your procedures be flawed (and therefore must be tested) but also, despite your best efforts and failsafe measures, your backup could be useless. Knowing how to handle an exception like this is much better addressed during a drill than a real-world crisis. Don't be afraid to periodically test your backups by restoring them onto a spare server or deployed recovery server. The more practice your operations staff has recovering Exchange data, the more likely it is that they will respond in an accurate and timely manner during a "live" outage. While validation of your procedures should work out most of these "bugs," Exchange fire drills are an invaluable practice to get into. Your organization should not neglect this important point and should implement a solid program to train all system managers, operators, and administrators on disaster recovery plans and procedures. This training program should include escalation procedures, recovery scenarios, and periodic disaster recovery drills that simulate all scenarios.

5.9   Best Practice #9: Disaster Recovery Management

Although we will never be able to prevent data loss and catastrophes or plan for all contingencies, there are some good disaster recovery management practices that should be part of your deployment routines to potentially help alleviate the problems when they occur.

The first item is the creation of an Exchange Server disaster recovery toolkit. The Exchange disaster recovery toolkit is unique to an Exchange deployment and should go beyond the typical kit that your organization may have for a Windows NT/2000 server. This toolkit must "add a layer" and provide tools for successfully recovering not only the operating system but also Exchange Server. The disaster recovery toolkit ensures that all materials and documentation are available when and where you need it in the event a disaster occurs. Some typical items that I recommend be included in your disaster recovery toolkit are as follows:

- *A server hardware configuration worksheet*—Provides documentation on how the server hardware components were installed and configured. Most important are hardware CMOS/ BIOS settings configured using the system configuration program. Critical to recovery is the configuration of the server storage including how disk devices are configured and RAID levels if applicable.

- *An operating system configuration worksheet*—Provides documentation on installation and configuration parameters needed to return the operating system to the same state it was before the disaster occurred. This should include any additional device drivers or utilities installed as well as registry settings that were modified from defaults. If the server is a Windows NT/2000 domain controller or Global Catalog server, the worksheet should contain any information settings pertinent to this configuration.

- *An Exchange Server configuration worksheet*—Provides information on Exchange-specific server configuration such as services installed and configurations. Critical to recovery operations is configuration data on how Exchange storage groups and databases are configured and allocated across server storage. Details on where log files and databases are stored will be critical to successful restoration to the last known good state. The Exchange worksheet should also contain data about any Exchange-specific configurations such as routing and administrative groups the server belongs to or Active Directory, SMTP, IIS, and X.400 connector settings.

- *A contact information worksheet*—Provides a source listing of proper individuals to contact in the event of an emergency or if specific configuration or security data is required. May also contain escalation procedures and contacts for both hardware and software issues encountered during recovery operations.

- *Recovery disks and CD-ROMs*—Should include all necessary software for successful installation, setup, and recovery of the Exchange Server including Windows NT/2000 emergency repair disk, hardware system configuration disks, device driver disks/CDs, and third-party software disks/CDs. May include Windows NT/2000 and Exchange Server CD-ROMs if they are not readily available.

These key components will form your disaster recovery toolkit for your Exchange deployment. In addition, your toolkit should also include any components specific to your deployment or organizational needs. The disaster recovery toolkit forms a solid cornerstone for excellent configuration management practices in your Exchange deployment. Configuration management with disaster recovery in mind will ensure that disaster recovery operations are performed efficiently and smoothly across the entire population of servers in an Exchange deployment. The following are some key points that are part of good configuration management practices. In Chapter 9, I will discuss configuration management in greater detail and beyond the limited scope of disaster recovery.

1.   Tightly control the configuration of all Exchange servers.

2.   Document all server configurations and keep a change log.

3.   Ensure that hardware device drivers and firmware updates are consistent across the deployment.

4.   Ensure that operating system and application service packs are consistently applied across the deployment.

5.   Use like hardware configurations for all Exchange servers.

6.   Deploy management software that provides configuration management capabilities.

Another solid practice for successful disaster recovery management is a good media rotation scheme. Here I am referring to the rotation of physical media to an off-site location and not to a backup strategy (full, incremental, differential, etc.). Many organizations rotate tapes to both on-site and off-site "vault" locations. The purpose of this is to protect the media from disasters like fire and flood at a primary business location. If you store your backup media in the closet and the building burns down, there will be no media available from which to perform recovery operations. When planning for Exchange disaster recovery, develop an off-site rotation scheme that provides protection from disaster as well as a good tracking mechanism for knowing where a particular media set is located. Some backup software applications will make recommendations and provide suggested routines and techniques for this practice. Don't leave out this often neglected part of successful disaster recovery planning.

Disaster recovery for Exchange is severely handicapped if the disaster recovery management practice of backup verification and validation is neglected. If you never are sure of whether your backups are good, you can never be certain that they can be used to recover your data come crunch time. Your ability to restore

Exchange data depends on the quality and usability of your backup sets. Many things can happen to a backup set between backup and restore that would render the set useless. Therefore, it is important to implement processes that will ensure that these backups are reliable. Performing disaster recovery drills with personnel may cover part of this. However, I would not solely rely on disaster recovery drills to provide this function. For complete assurance, you should form a triple-verification strategy. First, **verify the event**. It is important for you to know that the backup was successful and completed without any errors. As I discussed in earlier chapters, the Exchange database engine verifies every physical page of the database during backup (as well as every transaction log record during recovery) to ensure that corrupt data is not written to backup media. When problems are encountered, however, errors are only reported to the Windows NT/2000 event logs. It is important that you establish measures that will check both NT event logs and backup application logs to ensure that a backup completed without error. This should be done at every point at which a backup operation is completed.

The second phase is this triple-verification strategy is to **verify the data**. Verification of the data includes periodic restores of backup sets to another test or recovery server in order to ensure that the data was actually recoverable. Of course, you certainly cannot expect your operations staff to verify each and every backup using this method. However, you may want to establish a pattern or procedure of random sampling or rotation from server to server that allows you to identify potential problems proactively and to have the confidence that your disaster recovery measures will be successful. While testing the integrity of your disaster recovery procedures and facilities, you can provide invaluable training for your operations staff and can identify potential problems and issues before data is actually lost.

Finally, the third phase of our triple-verification strategy is to **verify the configuration**. Exchange API-based backups (online backups) do not provide protection for the operating system or server configuration data. This information is stored in three primary locations—the Active Directory, Internet Information Server, and the Windows NT/2000 registry. I recommend that you also develop a strategy for protecting this data as well. You may choose to perform periodic offline or file system backups of your Exchange server that include all of this data. However, I recommend that additional measures be taken as well. For the Active Directory data, most organizations will have multiple domain controllers and Global Catalog servers deployed that contain replicas of Active Directory data. In most cases, I do not recommend that your Exchange server be configured as a domain controller unless it is absolutely necessary. This will make recovery operations much simpler. Since the Active Directory is a "multimastered," replicated directory service, there may not be any need for the Exchange deployment personnel to worry about Active Directory data since it may be handled by a different organization. Also, in the event that a domain controller is lost, a new server can be added to the Active Directory and the information replicated (similar to the Exchange 5.5 directory database). If you are responsible for disaster recovery operations for the Active Directory, you should take every precaution and planning approach for Exchange and apply it to Active Directory recovery. You should perform regular backups to ensure that, if all Active Directory instances were lost, you would be able to recover your Exchange data. If you would like more information on Windows 2000 and Active Directory recovery procedures, see the Windows 2000 Server documentation and white papers available on Microsoft TechNet and the Windows 2000 Web site.

IIS data is also critical to Exchange 2000. Since Exchange 2000 relies on IIS for storing configuration data and servicing Internet client protocols such as IMAP, POP3, HTTP, and SMTP, you must provide measures to recover the IIS information. Since this information is stored in the IIS metabase, the simplest method is to back up the IIS metabase using the Configuration Backup option in the Internet Services Manager snap-in for Microsoft Management Console in Windows 2000 (shown in Figure 5.5).

Configuration data for Exchange 2000 is very important and steps need to be taken to ensure that your current configuration for each server in your deployment can be re-created. Without this information, you could spend days trying to re-create your server configuration from scratch. As you are developing your disaster recovery plans for Exchange 2000, don't forget to include this vital piece that will save you critical time.

One final important component of successful disaster recovery management is an archival strategy for your Exchange data. What is amazing to me is the degree of control you can achieve over your

Figure 5.5
Backup of the IIS configuration metabase via the Internet Services Manager

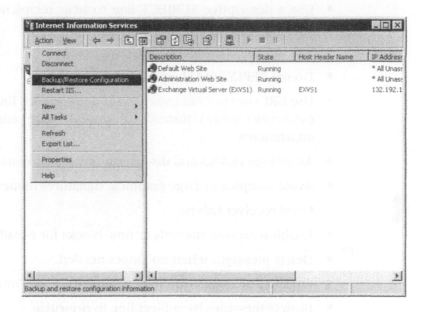

disaster recovery concerns by simply practicing some good archival and retention policies for your Exchange deployment. There are several ways to accomplish this level of control over the amount of Exchange server data that must be backed up and recovered. Good data archival and retention measures, in my opinion, start at the inbox. Educating users on how to reduce the amount of mail they and their peers must deal with is the first line of offense in combating bursting inboxes. E-mail users must be cognizant and considerate of the amount of mail they store and send. For example, sensitivity to the number and size of attachments can be a critical part of users' contributions to disaster recovery management. User discipline can only be accomplished through established polices and recognized good habits. The Gartner Group proposes several good habits for "Conquering E-mail Overload" in its November 1999 research report. These good habits can be categorized into sender and receiver habits and are provided here.

Good sender habits:

- Use distribution lists with caution.

- Be succinct and to the point in e-mail communications.

- Keep focused on the topic.

- Use a descriptive SUBJECT line to help recipients prioritize, file, and search.

- Use message tags and flags appropriately.

- Do not REPLY TO ALL unless necessary.

- Use URL (`http://server/file.doc`) or UNC links (`\\servershare`) instead of sending large and numerous attachments.

- Avoid long dialogs and discussion threads via e-mail.

- Avoid complex or large graphical signatures in messages.

  Good receiver habits:

- Establish regular intervals or time blocks for e-mail.

- Delete messages when no longer needed.

- Organize messages into folders outside of your inbox.

- Browse messages by subject line to prioritize.

- Eliminate unnecessary replies or acknowledgements.

- Delegate mailbox access when unable to retrieve messages.

- Use inbox rules sparingly and keep them simple.

- Avoid membership in unnecessary distribution lists or subscriptions.

Good e-mail user habits and awareness can aid immeasurably in controlling the amount of data stored on an Exchange server. By reducing data, you also impact disaster recovery and make it much easier and potentially faster for messaging data to be recovered.

When you've done everything to ensure that your users are disciplined in their e-mail use, the next line of offense is administratively imposed methods of controlling the amount of data stored in Exchange. Through the use of administrative settings such as mailbox size, attachment size, and others, an administrator can limit the amount of data a user is able to store, thereby forcing good habits and practices by users. In addition, through the use of add-ons to Exchange like the Exchange Mailbox Manager, the Exchange Archive Agent, and deleted item retention, system managers can control mailbox size (and therefore disaster recovery windows), provide basic message archival functions, and cache deleted items (in the event that messages are inadvertently deleted or need to be recovered without a full disaster recovery exercise). Another administrative option available in Exchange 2000 is administrative policies. Policies can be configured for a wide variety of controls and be applied based on membership or other global attributes. Setting sound policies and administrative limits on e-mail usage can have a drastic impact on disaster recovery. The following is one example of a published policy for e-mail usage that can be administratively implemented and controlled.

Table 5.5   *Sample E-mail Policy for an Organization*

ACME Corporation: Three-Tier E-mail Usage Policy	
Level I —standard user	40MB inbox limit 35MB warning/45MB send prohibit 7-day deleted item retention
Level II—heavy user	60MB inbox limit 55MB warning/65MB send prohibit 14-day deleted item retention Requires justification and manager approval
Level III—custom/VIP	Increase inbox limits of Levels I and II in increments of 10MB or 20MB Custom warning and send prohibit settings Custom deleted item retention settings Requires department head (director/VP) approval

The final measure or line of offense in controlling message store size is through the use of an advanced third-party product designed for this specific purpose. CommVault Systems (http://www.commvault.com), kVault Software (http://www.k-vault.com/), and SRA International (http://assentor.com) are three such companies that offer products that work with Exchange to provide advanced message-archival functions. Like the Microsoft Exchange Archiving Agent (for the low-budget minded), these products provide the ability to provide a hierarchical storage management (HSM) approach to archiving through the use of specialized hardware and software components that apply high performance, reliability, and security to this practice. While none of these products is by itself a panacea, they can provide a high-end solution that offers an effective means of archiving messaging and collaboration data if you are prepared to make the investment required. Whether you can afford only freeware (the Exchange Archive Agent) or the "Cadillac" of archival solutions, you should visit this option as you plan disaster recovery for your Exchange deployment. Through proactive measures to control and reduce the size of Exchange information stores, you can manage and maintain disaster recovery windows and meet associated service-level agreements. These measures as well as a well-thought-out disaster recovery toolkit, solid configuration management, verification of disaster recovery events, data, and configuration are the key to excellence in disaster recovery management.

5.10   Best Practice #10: Plan for Growth Impacts on Disaster Recovery

The growth in messaging and collaboration data is a huge issue confronting organizations that have deployed messaging systems like Exchange Server. Gartner Research projects that, through the year 2002, the number and size of messages will continue to grow at a compound annual growth rate (CAGR) of over 35 percent per year. In addition, since we are a global economy, business is being done at all hours, and the messaging system must be available around the clock. As a result, managers of these systems face the never-ending issue of growing information stores, shrinking disaster recovery windows, and more stringent disaster recovery SLAs. As part of your established best practices for your Exchange deployment, you will have to consider the impacts of growth on your disaster recovery plans. Without consideration of growth in our disaster recovery planning, burgeoning information stores will quickly surpass the capabilities of our disaster recovery measures and facilities. I like to plan conservatively here and anticipate as much as 100% growth every year. As an example, if the size of my databases is limited to 50GB based on disaster recovery constraints, I would either plan for 200% capacity in my DR facility (tape restore hardware and software rates), or I would limit my information stores to 25GB in anticipation of future growth. My conservative approach may be a bit extreme, but I would encourage you make your disaster recovery plans accordingly. Regardless of what degree of padding you choose to put in your plans, make sure you monitor how much of that buffer is being used on an ongoing basis. As you monitor growth, you can also adjust your disaster recovery procedures and facilities according to the rate of growth being observed. Avoid the pitfall of planning for growth but never verifying that growth occurs. Anticipating growth in your disaster recovery requirements should also be closely tied to growth planning of your information store. Since Exchange 2000 allows for greater flexibility in storage management, take advantage of this capability in your planning as well. All too often, growth is left out of the equation when deploying complex applications like Exchange Server. For your Exchange deployment, ensure that growth is factored into both your information store space planning and your disaster recovery planning.

Since Exchange 2000 is a relatively new product from Microsoft, it may be a little premature to claim complete knowledge on all best practices for Exchange 2000 disaster recovery. We do know that some things will not change. On the other hand, you can see that your disaster recovery (disaster recovery) procedures for Exchange will have to be revisited once you deploy Exchange 2000. From a disaster recovery planning perspective, you will need to understand the impact that new features such as multiple storage groups and databases will have on disaster recovery for Exchange. Your plans may be able to drop support for the Exchange directory but shouldn't neglect the Active Directory. In preparation for Exchange 2000, it's time to take a look at your disaster recovery plans and procedures. Also, don't forget configuration management. The complexities of laying out multiple databases and storage groups will call for a high degree of configuration control. From an operations perspective, understand the various scenarios under which you may have to recover Exchange. Practice for catastrophes as well as individual mailbox recovery. Also comprehend the complete system including hardware, drivers, patches, operating system, and other applications. If you are doing daily full backups now, you will probably want to continue for Exchange 2000. However, take a look at what snapshot technology might buy you. Closely related are your management practices for Exchange. Practice proactive performance, configuration, and problem management. Finally, keep in touch because many best practices for Exchange 2000 disaster recovery are yet to be discovered.

6

Leveraging Storage Technology

On our quest to build mission-critical Exchange servers and deployments, there are many keys and technologies in which we should invest. Understanding the technology, solid management practices, procedures, personnel/staffing, and training, etc., are some of the important points. We must look to all areas of hardware, software, and "peopleware" as we select where to focus our attention and investments. In my humble opinion, the single most significant area in which we can invest and educate ourselves is in the area of storage technology. I believe that storage technology is a fundamental piece (if not the most fundamental piece) of mission-critical Exchange servers.

When I think about storage technology for an Exchange server, I consider it to be central to keeping the server healthy and happy from a client and systems management perspective. The key to a highly available system is access to data with the highest level of performance and the utmost data protection and integrity. After all, if the data isn't available fast and with a guarantee of validity, the system has not served its intended purpose. Thus, storage technology is important in two areas—performance and data protection. My theorem is that, without solid storage technology, no Exchange server will rise to mission-critical status. To put it another way, no amount of management, training, and investment in other areas can help you if the underlying storage strategy for your Exchange server and across your entire deployment is weak. Therefore, the purpose of this chapter is to discuss some basic fundamentals of storage technology available at the time of this writing and how that technology can be applied to an Exchange 2000 deployment to achieve the highest levels of performance, scalability, reliability, availability, and manageability.

6.1   Storage Technology Basics

Let us first start with a discussion of the basics of disk subsystem technology. I will assume that you are somewhat familiar with this subject and will provide mostly an overview. In addition, since this book is focused on mission-critical Exchange servers, I will attempt to keep the discussion around storage aimed at that goal and not digress into detailed or even "religious" arguments concerning the pros and cons of various approaches and technologies. My goal will be mainly to "put on the table" the various technologies and products available.

Since the early days in the "PC" (Intel) server space when Compaq first announced and shipped the Compaq Systempro in 1989, storage subsystem technologies for servers have differed significantly from desktop and portable (single user) systems. Also, Compaq did not invent this differentiation between server and desktop system storage. Some tried-and-proven technology from the mainframe and minicomputer world was taken and applied to PC servers. This differentiation mainly centered around the difference between a individual disk drive or multiple drives attached to a system (sometimes called JBOD—Just a Bunch Of Disks in storage systems speak) and an array of disks configured as a single entity providing a higher level of performance and/or data protection. This differentiation essentially invented what we now know and use (or should be using) every day in our Exchange deployments. At the time (circa 1989), Compaq and other vendors used IDE (Intelligent Drive Electronics) type drives because of their superior performance, reliability, and price point for the PC server market. When server manufacturers began shipping systems for operating systems such as NetWare, OS/2, and UNIX, they provided intelligent controllers that made drive arrays available for these platforms. A *drive array* is very simply an array of individual physical disk drives. Physical drives are grouped together to form logical drives. Using drive array technology, the data can be distributed over a series of physical drives, providing higher performance. This is due to the fact that the distribution of the data across multiple independent drives (called disk striping) allows requests to each drive to be processed concurrently, yielding a higher I/O rate than drive configurations that are not configured in an array fashion. When multiple physical drives are grouped into a logical array, they appear to the host computer as a single disk drive equal in capacity to the sum of all physical drives in the array. However, the drawback to this approach is that the reliability of a drive array decreases based on simple statistics. Table 6.1 provides some reliability formulas commonly used to determine the reliability of a system or a device such as a disk drive. When an array of physical drives is configured, it becomes a series system (subject to the formula in the table following).

Table 6.1 *Reliability Formulas*

Failure rate (β)	$\beta = 1/\text{MTBF}$ Where: MTBF = (mean time between failure)
Reliability (R)	$R = e^{-\beta T}$ Where: e = natural logarithm β = failure rate T = time (period to be measured)
Reliability of parallel systems (R_p)	$R_p = 1 - [(1-R1) \times (1-R2) \times ... (1-Rn)]$ Where: R1...Rn = reliability (R) of each system in parallel
Reliability of Series Systems (R_s)	$R_s = R1 \times R2 \times ... Rn$ Where: R1...Rn = reliability (R) of each system the series

Source: MIL-STD and IEEE

In other words, the reliability of the array will be a function of the reliability of an individual drive and the number of drives in an array. For example, since drive reliability is typically measured as mean time between failure or MTBF, an array of four physical drives in which each drive has an MTBF of 100,000 hours would have a yearly reliability measurement of 70.44% using the following calculation.

Reliability of individual drive ($R = e^{-\beta T}$) = .9161 (91.61%)

Reliability of series system (drive array) = $(.9161)^4$ = .7044 (70.44%)

As you can see, as more drives are added to a logical array, although performance may increase, reliability decreases. Since a typical Exchange server may use 10 to 15 drives per array, the ramifications on reliability would not be worth the performance advantages gained by array technology.

Applying the preceding formulas further in a specific example, let's look at the most critical subsystem on an Exchange server, the disk subsystem. Not only is the disk subsystem the most critical in terms of reliability, it also can have the most drastic affect on reliability. Also, because disk failure rates are widely known, this makes an excellent example for applying the preceding reliability formulas. Most disk drives manufactured today have an MTBF (mean time between failure) as high as 500,000 hours or more. Less than 10 years ago, disk MTBF was at less than 100,000 hours for most IDE and SCSI devices. Over the last few years, the specified MTBF rating of hard disk drives has risen significantly. OEMs and other customers who purchase these drives from manufacturers such as Seagate, Quantum, and IBM have grown to expect much better reliability than they did just 10 years ago. Some manufacturers are even touting MTBF ratings as high as one million hours! Be aware, however, that there is a substantial difference between *theoretical* MTBF ratings and their *operational* equivalents. When manufacturers set out to design new disk drive products, they create reliability models for these products early in the development process.

These models however, are based on predictions and are theoretical. It is not until these products are developed, shipped, and put into production that field data on failure rates and root causes can be used to validate the models developed during the design phase. In addition, since a disk drive is actually made up of several components such as the head, platter, and associated circuitry, these models are much more granular than simple MTBF ratings for the entire disk drive. These models also lack the ability to factor in the other significant causes of drive failures such as design faults, firmware bugs, or failures induced in the manufacturing process. Mishandling, shipping damage, or the notorious "No Trouble Found (NTF)" are some other reasons for drive returns that are not factored into the theoretical MTBF ratings. From personal experience on the hardware side of things for the last 10 years, I have observed the many factors outside the MTBF ratings, such as firmware, manufacturing issues, and NTF, to be much more likely causes of disk drive failures. Table 6.2 provides an illustration of this from Quantum comparing operational versus theoretical MTBF ratings.

Table 6.2 *Operational vs. Theoretical MTBF*

Failure Root Cause	Operational MTBF	Theoretical MTBF
Handing damage	Not included	Not included
NTF returns	Included	Not included
Infancy failures	Included	Not included
Mfg. Process related	Included	Not included
Mfg. process test escapes	Included	Included
Random steady state failure	Included	Included
Firmware bugs	Included	Not included
Example disk drive product	188,005 hours	713,000 hours

Source: Quantum, Inc.

Since there really is no industry standard for how MTBF ratings are determined for various components of a server such as a disk drive, many of these ratings will vary from vendor to vendor. Also, it is important to remember that vendors use these ratings for marketing purposes and are interested in advertising the highest ratings possible. Operational MTBF is much more valuable but is not available from most vendors (for the preceding reasons). Adding to this is the fact that most server hardware vendors from which you buy your Exchange servers have different standards as well. For example, most hardware vendors have different qualification processes for when they use OEM disk drives from vendors like Quantum and Seagate. Quite often, OEMs like Compaq, Hewlett-Packard, and IBM have different firmware for disk drives due to integration needs such as specific reliability-monitoring techniques or support for management applications and utilities. For example, in order to support Compaq's Insight Manager (CIM) server management application and reliability features such as predictive failure alerting and monitoring, Compaq requires their drive vendors to add special firmware changes that otherwise are not available in generic drives from that vendor. As is quite obvious, there are many factors that determine disk drive reliability.

To digress on this subject further as an illustration of reliability calculation, let's use a disk drive with an MTBF of 500,000 hours. If you used this drive in an Exchange server with a single disk drive, the failure rate $(\beta)\beta$ would be calculated as: 1/500,000 or .000002. Thus, the reliability of the disk subsystem for that server (applying the formula from Table 6.1) is 98.2%. This means that, within a one-year timeframe (8,760 hours), we should only expect a failure approximately every 8,608 hours of operation of that subsystem (ignoring all other subsystems and causes for failure). This is *not* what I would call a mission-critical system.

To counteract the impact on reliability that drive arrays suffer from, some researchers at the University of California–Berkley (David Patterson and Garth Gibson) in 1988 conceptualized a technique called RAID. RAID stands for redundant array of inexpensive (later changed to independent) disks. RAID uses redundancy information stored in the array to prevent data loss, thereby offsetting the reliability issues of a simple drive array. In the initial paper introduced by Patterson and Gibson, there were only five RAID levels defined—RAID1 through RAID5.

Figure 6.1
Illustration of controller-based RAID configurations

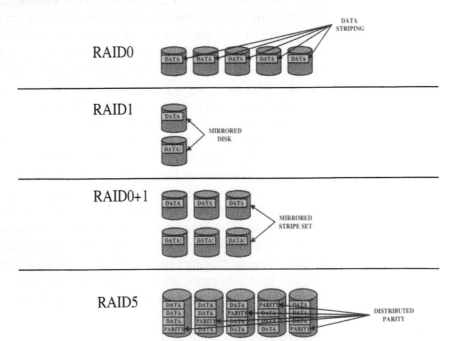

In later years, through marketing schemes and/or legitimate engineering work, additional RAID levels have emerged. The concept of RAID had three main objectives: increased performance, higher reliability, and lower cost. Each RAID level offers a different mix of performance, reliability, and cost. The objective that researchers at Berkeley had for RAID technology was to provide disk subsystems that yielded higher performance and reliability while at the same time reducing the overall cost. RAID levels 1 and 5 are the most commonly deployed. Table 6.3 presents the commonly known RAID levels, their functionality, characteristics, and trade-offs. In 1992, the RAID Advisory Board (RAB) was formed to define generally accepted RAID levels as well as to educate the industry. The RAB was formed by a group of interested users and vendors. Since that time, the RAB (www.raid-advisory.com) has evolved to a pseudo standards body for RAID technology, and it provides certification and conformance ratings (for a fee, of course) for vendors of disk technology seeking RAID conformance.

Table 6.3   *A Comparison of the Five Original RAID Levels*

RAID Level	*Implementation*	*Data and I/O Rate*	*Application Fit*	*Cost*
RAID0 (Striping)	A simple drive array. Technically not an official RAID level since there is no data protection.	Best. No redundancy overhead and high I/O concurrency.	All. No performance penalty for read or write.	Low: No redundancy requirements.
RAID1* (Drive mirroring)	Data is replicated to a redundant drive set that can be used for both performance and data protection gains. Most vendors implement RAID1 with RAID0 (striped mirroring).	Best for read operations but includes overhead of redundant write operation.	All. Slight performance penalty for write.	High: Twice the number of disks required for redundancy.

Table 6.3   *A Comparison of the Five Original RAID Levels (continued)*

RAID Level	Implementation	Data and I/O Rate	Application Fit	Cost
RAID2	Data is striped across all disks with parity (ECC) on multiple disks.	Adequate for read operations but substantial penalty for write operations. No advantage over RAID3 and was superseded by RAID3.	Applications that are mostly read oriented and are not heavily impacted by slower write performance.	Medium: Multiple parity disks.
RAID3	Data is spread across all data drives in one I/O operation with parity data (ECC) stored on a dedicated drive.	Adequate for read and write but not as high as RAID0, 1, and 5.	Applications that are mostly read oriented and are not heavily impacted by slower write performance. Best for single user, single threaded I/O.	Low: One parity disk.
RAID4	Data is spread across disks in large stripes with a dedicated parity disk. Overlapped I/O for reads but not for writes.	Adequate for read but poor for write due to lack of overlapped I/O on write.	Applications that are mostly read oriented and are not heavily impacted by slower write performance.	Low: One parity disk.
RAID5*	Data and parity is distributed across all disks in the array.	Best for read but poor for write due to the requirement of four physical I/Os for every logical write.	Applications that are mostly read oriented and are not heavily impacted by slower write performance.	Low: No dedicated parity disk required.

*Recommended for Exchange servers

Many vendors have improved or combined the various RAID levels to achieve even greater performance and reliability. For example, most controllers combine RAID0 (striping) and RAID1 (drive mirroring) to provide striped mirroring (often called RAID0+1 or RAID 10). Table 6.4 highlights some of the RAID levels that have emerged since the original RAID concept materialized in 1988.

Table 6.4   *A Comparison of RAID Levels Beyond the Original Five Introduced in 1988*

RAID Level	Implementation	Data and I/O Rate	Application Fit	Cost
RAID6	Similar to RAID5 but includes a secondary parity distribution scheme that offers higher fault tolerance. No commercial implementations available.	Best for read but poor for write due to the requirement of four or more physical I/Os for every logical write per parity scheme.	Similar to RAID5.	Medium: Specialized controller for dual parity schemes.
RAID7	"Computer in the disk" approach in which a real-time OS and high-speed proprietary bus provide many characteristics of a separate stand-alone computer as an array.	Best for both read and write.	All. Typically only specialized or proprietary applications.	High: RTOS and high-end hardware requirements.
RAID10 (Drive Mirroring with Striping)	Data is replicated to a redundant drive set that is a RAID0 stripe set and that can be used for both performance and data-protection gains. Most vendors implement RAID1 with RAID0 (striped mirroring).	Best for read operations but overhead of redundant write operation. However, gains are achieved because of striped mirror sets.	All. Slight performance penalty for write but not as substantial as RAID levels 2–5.	High: Twice the number of disks required for redundancy.
RAID53 or 35	An array of stripes in which each stripe is a RAID3 array.	Higher performance than RAID 3 or 5 by taking the best of both.	Applications that are mostly read oriented and are not heavily impacted by slower write performance. Similar to RAID5.	Medium: Specialized controller and more disks for RAID3 stripes.

6.1.1   Hardware vs. Software RAID

The argument of hardware- versus software-based RAID configurations may be moot since most understand the nonviability of software-based RAID in mission-critical environments. However, it is important to discuss this subject since most operating systems like Windows NT/2000 provide software-based RAID, and many system managers are tempted to cut corners and implement it in place of superior hardware-based RAID. Technically, RAID technology can be software-based, hardware-based, or a combination of both. In general, the only time software-based RAID is combined with a hardware-based solution is for controller duplexing. With controller duplexing, two hardware-based RAID controllers can be mirrored, eliminating the controller as a single point of failure. However, since many vendors now provide hardware-based redundant controller configurations, the more risky controller duplexing via software is less often used.

Windows NT/2000 supports RAID1 and RAID5 via the operating system. This is implemented with an NT filter driver that intercepts I/O requests and redirects them according to the RAID configuration. Software RAID, in general, uses more system resources since the operating system or device driver must handle the processing overhead that a RAID configuration requires. This is most severe in a RAID5 environment in which parity encoding and decoding must occur on the fly. The main advantage to software RAID is that there is no expensive controller to purchase. Software RAID may have a lower cost than hardware RAID, but the real cost may be in lost processor cycles that could be spent doing application work. In my experience, I have seen software-based RAID perform very well in comparison to hardware-based RAID. This is particularly true with the fast processors available in today's PC servers. The main problem with software-based RAID (besides stealing processor cycles) comes when recovery is required. With software-based RAID, configuration data and intelligence is stored in the operating system of device driver. If you can't get the system to boot, it does you no good. To illustrate my point, take a look sometime at what is required to recover your system disk for a Windows 2000 server using software RAID1. Having to resort to my emergency repair disk and editing the BOOT.INI is not my idea of a clean recovery (although this is better in Windows 2000). While software-based RAID may be tempting for your Exchange server, just say no if a mission-critical system is your goal.

Hardware-based RAID offloads the overhead required to encode and decode parity information and other RAID overhead to the hardware controller. Most hardware-based RAID controllers are really just a computer system on a board running a real-time operating system complete with a high-speed processor, RAM, and ROM. This hardware device dedicated to the task of providing data protection frees the system processor(s) from having to manage the disk subsystem and complex processing tasks like parity generation. To further enhance performance, most controllers provide a cache that can be configured as read-ahead, write-back, or a combination of both. Of course, hardware-based RAID does come at some cost. This is the main reason some system managers may shy away from investing in this technology. However, if your interest is in mission-critical Exchange servers, hardware-based RAID must be a part of that equation.

I am not aware of any corporation that has deployed Exchange Server without RAID disk subsystems (although, I am sure many exist in the realm of small and medium business deployments). By applying RAID to our original single drive (with 98.2% reliability) example from earlier, we see can how RAID can drastically improve our Exchange Server reliability by making the most unreliable subsystem more reliable. Taking the formulas from Table 6.1 for reliability of parallel and series systems, we can see the effect that RAID has on the reliability of the four-drive disk subsystem in Table 6.5.

Table 6.5   *Reliability Impact of RAID*

RAID Level	*Reliability Impact*
No RAID—single drive	Failure rate (β) = 1/500,000 = .000002 Reliability (R) = $e^{-(.000002 \times 8760)}$ = 98.2%
RAID0 —series system	Failure rate (β) for each drive = (1/500,000) = .000002 Reliability (Rs) = .982 × .982 × .982 × .982 = 92.9%
RAID 0+1—series and parallel system	Failure rate (β) for each drive = (1/500,000) = .000002 Reliability (Rs) for each mirror set = .982 × .982 = 96.4% Reliability (Rp) for subsystem (RAID 0+1): = 1 - [(1- .964) × (1--.964)] = 99.87%

As you can see in Table 6.5, the reliability of a disk subsystem is greatly enhanced through the use of RAID technology (with the exception of nonredundant RAID0). With the addition of other features that server and controller vendors have added such as redundant controllers, hot-plug drives, online sparing, and online volume growth, RAID technology is further improved. However, keep in mind that, in an Exchange Server, the disk subsystem is not the only subsystem in a server. In addition, hardware failures are only part of the cause of Exchange Server downtime. Within the context of this chapter, however, hardware—and specifically the disk subsystem—is our focus.

6.1.2   RAID Controllers

The market for RAID controllers in the PC server space has been going strong for over 10 years now. First, there were the PC server vendors themselves. Compaq, IBM, and others entered into this market early to provide high-performing and reliable disk subsystems for their servers. Third parties like Adaptec and DPT soon followed with server-neutral RAID controllers for the masses. When selecting a RAID controller, four key characteristics come to mind—performance, data protection, manageability, and vendor support.

- *Performance*—For applications like Microsoft Exchange Server, the controller must be capable of handling high levels of I/O throughput and provide maximum bandwidth and capacity. This requires that a controller be architected in such a way that RAID overhead is easily managed by on-board intelligence and that delivery of data to the host is fast and efficient by design. This requires a streamlined controller architecture that utilizes the last SCSI specifications to provide multiple channels for SCSI devices to attach. Many controllers available today provide up to four channels of Wide Ultra2 SCSI (80MB/s). The controller must also consist of a high-speed processor capable of handling the intensive operations that RAID technology requires. Many controllers utilize high-speed RISC processors for this task.

  Another important implementation point is how the controller manages RAID operations. Some vendors have invested huge amounts of R&D into developing silicon-based ASICs (application specific integrated circuits) specifically for the task of managing RAID operations. Others rely on the controller processor, real-time OS, or in worse cases, device drivers to handle RAID operations. Optimized firmware is another key feature of a hardware-based RAID controller. A controller's firmware is the source of its intelligence. This intelligence includes complex algorithms that are tuned to allow the controller to provide optimal performance as well as data protection. Features such as write coalescing, tagged command queuing, and others are implemented in the controller firmware.

The cache is not only important to a RAID controller's overall performance, but a well-designed controller cache will also aid in complex RAID operations such as RAID5 parity generation. The cache also has a significant impact on data protection, which I will discuss more in the next section. As I mentioned earlier, most controllers provide a cache that can be configured as read-ahead, write-back, or both. Most vendors also allow this cache to be configured on a per-volume basis as well. The size of the cache is not as important as you may think. From a marketing standpoint, it seems that "more is better" has won the argument. Most performance benchmarks I have seen indicate that, after a certain point, the size of the cache does not matter that much. As the number of devices and channels on a controller increases, the size of the cache will also need to increase to provide maximum performance benefit. In the early days when Compaq first shipped its SMART-2 controller, the size of the cache was 4MB. Benchmark data revealed that a larger cache size did not impact performance significantly enough to justify the additional cost. The final performance factor for a RAID controller will be the overall controller data path design and the host bus attachment. Certainly, PCI has become the host bus attachment of choice in the Intel server space. However, many controller vendors also have complex internal controller bus designs that get the data from the disk drives to the host bus in the most fast and efficient manner. All of these points are important performance options you should look for when selecting a controller for your Exchange server that provides optimal performance and scalability. Whether you are using locally attached RAID, controller-based storage, or SAN-based RAID controller, check out how well your vendor of choice fares on these points.

- **Data protection**—Obviously, it doesn't matter how fast your controller is if it doesn't protect your data. When looking at data-protection features that are important for a RAID controller, several come to mind. First and foremost, since it is a RAID controller, what RAID levels does a controller offer? Most controllers on the market do not offer all of the RAID levels shown in Tables 6.3 and 6.4. Most offer only a subset such as RAID0, RAID1, RAID4, and RAID5. One of the most popular controllers on the market (with shipments in excess of 1 million units)—the Compaq SMART (includes SMART-2, SMART 3100, 3200, 4200)—offers RAID levels 0, 1, 0+1, 4, and 5. For Exchange 2000, the recommendation is RAID 0+1 (striped mirroring—more on this later), so you want to make sure your controller supports it.

  Another key data-protection point is the controller cache. When the cache is configured for read-ahead, there is no data-protection issue since the cache is only being used for caching read requests from disks. For write-back caching, however, a good cache design is critical to data protection. In fact, a fair amount of misinformation has circulated regarding using write-back caching with Exchange Server (see the sidebar for addition information). A cache design that ensures data protection should meet three criteria: memory protection, battery backup, and being removable. To provide proper protection, a controller cache should use either ECC (error checking and correction) or mirrored configurations. Some vendors provide both options. For example, a cache of 4MB may actually be 5MB in a RAID5 memory configuration. It may also be 8MB in a mirrored configuration. Often, a vendor would most likely select the former due to cost considerations. Controller cache must also be battery backed. Batteries should be able to maintain cache data in the event of a power failure for several days (if you haven't corrected the situation by then, you aren't concerned about building mission-critical systems). In addition, batteries should be rechargeable and replaceable. As a side note, a UPS (uninterruptible power supply) does not constitute battery backup for a controller cache. Finally, the cache memory itself should be contained on some sort of daughtercard that can easily be removed in the event that the controller fails. Obviously, the daughtercard should also include the batteries (or what good is a daughtercard?). In the event that the system loses power or the controller fails, data can be maintained in the cache and/or transported to a new controller. Once a failure condition is resolved, the data maintained in cache will be properly written out to the drive array for which it was originally intended. The RAID level and cache design are the two most important points for ensuring data protection. Make sure you consider these points as you select hardware for your deployment.

Write-Back Caching and the Infamous Exchange Server −1018 Error

In my role at Compaq Computer working on-site with the Exchange development team, I have been working (and suffering with) −1018 errors since 1996 when, before Exchange 4.0 shipped, Microsoft's internal IS organization was (and still is) having these issues. Since that time, there have *never* been any documented cases from either Compaq or Microsoft of −1018 errors being caused by controller-based WB caching. Early on, however, a misguided but valiant effort was made by Microsoft PSS to explain −1018 errors as being a result of controller WB caching (actually mistaken for drive WB caching, which is different). Unfortunately this was bogus, as PSS had no data to backup its claims. Compaq responded at the time by asking Microsoft to fix the PSS Knowledgebase Q article and Microsoft obliged. Unfortunately, the Microsoft field staff received the mistaken and misguided information and began to recommend that WB caching be disabled. Based on case statistics and my experience, turning off WB caching does not impact (i.e., reduce) the incidents/occurrence rate of −1018 errors whatsoever—it only makes your Exchange servers run *really* slow.

In December 1998, the Exchange Server development team recognized that −1018 errors were as much an issue of how Exchange was responding to hardware errors as an issue of hardware errors. While −1018s are usually caused by hardware (although, up until Exchange 5.5, Exchange was the leading cause of its own database corruption), the software can instrument in such a way that errors can be recovered from. Exchange 5.5 SP2 was a result of this work and included retry code to retry on −1018 errors up to 16 times. At the same time, Compaq began working with Microsoft and customers directly to look deeper into −1018 errors and to capture customer cases. This was *not* because Compaq hardware caused −1018 errors but because Compaq was (and still is) the only hardware vendor working in the Exchange development team and was willing to help Microsoft look closer at this issue. Again, this has nothing to do with WB caching. Compaq also recognized that one of the main issues was that some customers were not practicing good configuration management and did not upgrade firmware, drivers, and service packs as often as they should. In most cases of −1018 errors reported, the customer has not upgraded to a version of firmware or software that specifically addresses drive or controller issues leading to data corruption. Compaq is also working harder to make its software and firmware upgrades easier to apply (which is the main reason that customers do not upgrade).

Since releasing the Compaq service advisory on −1018 errors (which documents the correct software/firmware versions and practices) and Microsoft's release of EX 5.5 SP2, both Compaq and Microsoft have seen a reduction in the occurrences of −1018 errors. However, they have not been eliminated. Compaq and Microsoft are continuing to work together to look at this issue closer. Because Compaq has about 60% of the installed base of Exchange servers in customer sites, Compaq is the hardware vendor that −1018 errors are most often reported on. However, don't be fooled; I have documented cases of −1018 errors on every other hardware vendor on the market and am confident that this is not a Compaq-specific issue. However, Compaq and Microsoft are the best combination to address the issue and to look into it further. Those efforts will have absolutely nothing to do with looking at WB caching as a source of the problem. Here's one additional note: We are starting to postulate that, since most of the occurrences of −1018s are on RAID5 configurations, RAID5 could be part of the issue. It is important to point out that I have seen −1018s with any or no RAID. However, deploying RAID1 (0+1) configurations only may further reduce occurrences. Microsoft's internal IS group (ITG) is so convinced that the problem is RAID5 that they are deploying only RAID0+1 configurations for Exchange 2000.

The bottom line here is that the recommendation to disable WB caching on Exchange or SQL servers is outdated. Provided a controller has a battery-backed, memory-protected, and removable WB cache, there will be no issues. Compaq and Microsoft recommend that customers take full advantage of WB caching for optimal performance. Furthermore, organizations should invest in solid configuration management practices to ensure that, when there are known software or firmware fixes, they are applied in a timely manner. Hardware devices will always fail, software bugs will continue to plague us, and we may never totally eliminate Exchange −1018s. However, let us at least pursue the right path and not go after red herrings such as WB caching.

- **Manageability**—Being able to easily manage and configure your RAID controller may not be the most important criterion for selecting a RAID controller. However, in my opinion, this point makes mission-critical servers a nearer reality. Manageable RAID controllers have four characteristics. First is the simple fact that a vendor provides rich configuration options. As mentioned earlier, some vendors allow the cache configuration to be modified and set to read-ahead, write-back, or both. Compaq's SMART controllers let you select a percentage between read-ahead and write-back, as illustrated in Figure 6.2.

In addition, many vendors let you select which arrays (defined as logical drives) on the controller to enable the cache for. In the case of Exchange 2000, for example, you may select to enable write-back caching for an array that holds a particular storage group or database but disable write-back caching for an array holding the other database for a particular storage group. To have this flexibility, the RAID controller needs a high degree of manageability.

Figure 6.2
Cache management settings of the Compaq SMART controllers

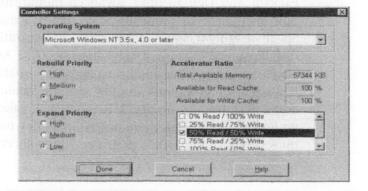

Besides having many configuration options available for a controller, you need to have the ability to control some of these options online. Some controllers require the system to be rebooted to a BIOS-level configuration utility in order to modify any controller options or run controller diagnostics. Some vendors provide the ability to do both. System administrators can use the BIOS-level utilities when the server is offline, but they are also able to manage their drive arrays while the server is up and running using Win32 utilities running on the Windows NT/2000 server console. One example of this may be tuning the cache configuration (read-ahead vs. write-back) on the fly based on application requirements. My third criterion for manageable RAID controllers is support for online capacity expansion. Since our Exchange deployments are constantly growing (more data and more users), the ability to dynamically grow storage while the server is online servicing users becomes paramount.

In my discussions of SAN technology later in this chapter, we will look at this more closely. However, for locally attached, controller-based storage, many vendors offer online capacity growth options as well. In addition, Microsoft has added support for capacity growth in Windows 2000 Server. Previous versions of Windows NT did not support online capacity expansion and required the server to be restarted for additional storage to be recognized. The last important criterion for manageable controllers is the ability to monitor and manage these devices remotely. Server vendors like Compaq, IBM, Hewlett-Packard, and Dell all offer advanced monitoring instrumentation of their RAID controllers via standard methods such as SNMP or WBEM. Figure 6.3 provides an illustration of Compaq Insight Manager's view of the Compaq SMART Array Controller. There are many other minor management capabilities for RAID controllers that various vendors support. While a manageable controller may be a luxury, it certainly will make life much easier for Exchange Server administrators as they manage the complex storage designs that Exchange 2000 will create.

Figure 6.3
Array controller and management with Compaq's Insight Manager

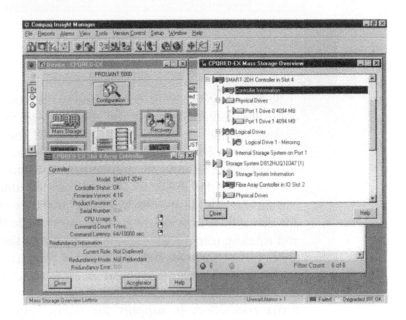

- *Vendor support*—Regardless of how well your RAID controller performs or how easily it can be managed, vendor support can have real impact of the reliability of your system. Vendor support is more than just a 7×24 toll-free number you can call when you have problems. It also includes how often the vendor updates key controller technology like firmware and device drivers. As I stated earlier, many data-corruption issues I have seen have been the result of firmware or driver bugs. The degree to which a vendor will take responsibility and provide a timely fix is very important. Of course, once a fix is provided, you still need to apply that fix. Besides bug fixes, thorough online and offline diagnostic utilities and easy updates are also important features that a controller vendor can provide. Sticking with top-tier vendors usually is the best bet here. There are many RAID controller vendors with products available. Choosing the vendor that can best support you will ensure maximum uptime for your Exchange system.

6.2   Drive Technology

6.2.1   Small Computer Systems Interface

When Compaq and other vendors introduced RAID controllers into the PC server marketplace in 1989, their drive technology of choice initially was IDE. At the time, IDE was the best choice for several reasons. Remembering back to the preceding section, I pointed out that the objective of RAID technology was to increase performance and reliability but to reduce cost. At the time, the SCSI (Small Computer Systems Interface) standards were just emerging and becoming solidified. SCSI drives for the PC server market still did not provide a good balance between performance, reliability, and cost. Supplies of SCSI drives were not ramped up either. IDE drives, on the other hand, were in good supply due to their popular usage in desktop computers. As a result, vendors initially chose IDE technology for the first RAID controllers available. SCSI technology did not stay behind for long, however. Drive manufacturers and customers quickly began to pressure vendors to switch to SCSI-based RAID technology. This resulted in IDE being relegated to the desktop and portable computer market where we now see IDE (and evolutions of IDE such as Ultra DMA or Ultra ATA). As drive manufacturers quickly ramped up production and customers and vendors began demanding SCSI drives, SCSI technology quickly surpassed IDE, and SCSI-based RAID technology controllers began to emerge from the leading server vendors and third parties. Overall, SCSI provides many benefits over IDE, but these could not be realized until the early 1990s when vendors like Compaq and IBM first began to transition their RAID controllers to SCSI technology. According to Dataquest, 95 percent of all high-end disk drives shipped today are SCSI.

SCSI technology, in my opinion, has evolved as a specification rather than as a standard. The difference is that a standard requires complete compatibility and conformance, whereas a specification is more of a "menu" of technology implementation options. Initially, one of the problems with SCSI technology was the lack of compatibility between different vendors' SCSI products. A drive from vendor A would not work with a controller from vendor B. This was mainly due to the fact that, when the SCSI specifications emerged, vendors simply selected which features they wanted to include with their products. In my experience as a network manager and IT guy back then, the fact that SCSI products were not interoperable lead to a slow adoption of SCSI products. Once vendors began to see the impact on their differing implementations of the SCSI specifications, they made attempts to design a bit more commonality into their products. Since an in-depth discussion of SCSI technology is really beyond the scope of this book, I provide Table 6.6 as an overview of the SCSI technology evolution over the last 10 years.

Table 6.6   *The Evolution of SCSI Specifications*

| SCSI Specification | Throughput | Bus Width | Maximum SCSI Bus Length (meters) | | | Maximum Devices (Including Host) |
			Single-Ended	Differential	LVD	
SCSI-1	5MB/s	8-bits	6	25	N/A	8
Fast SCSI	10MB/s	8-bits	3	25	N/A	8

Table 6.6   *The Evolution of SCSI Specifications (continued)*

| SCSI Specification | Throughput | Bus Width | Maximum SCSI Bus Length (meters) | | | Maximum Devices (Including Host) |
			Single-Ended	Differen-tial	LVD	
Fast Wide SCSI	20MB/s	16-bits	3	25	N/A	16
Ultra SCSI	20MB/s	8-bits	1.5	25	N/A	8
Ultra SCSI	20MB/s	8-bits	3	25	N/A	4
Wide Ultra SCSI	40MB/s	16-bits	N/A	25	N/A	16
Wide Ultra SCSI	40MB/s	16-bits	1.5	N/A	N/A	8
Wide Ultra SCSI	40MB/s	16-bits	3	N/A	N/A	4
Ultra2 SCSI	40MB/S	8-bits	N/A	25	12	8
Wide Ultra2 SCSI	80MB/s	16-bits	N/A	25	12	16

Source: SCSI Trade Association, 1999

The main benefit of SCSI over IDE technology is performance and design flexibility. SCSI technology is essentially a network protocol for disks. SCSI devices are attached to a channel where they can communicate with the host controller independently of one another. This allows for overlapped or interleaved processing of commands and I/O requests between the controller and all devices on the SCSI channel. For applications like Exchange Server and other database applications, this provides maximum I/O performance for the small 2–8KB I/Os that are common for these types of applications. In a RAID environment, SCSI technology also allows vendors more design flexibilities than IDE. While initially SCSI did not compete with other drive technologies in terms of reliability and cost, SCSI technology now measures up well. Most SCSI drives on the market today have MTBF ratings of 500,000 hours or more—well beyond what other technologies are touting. With regards to cost, you only need look in your local newspaper or online computer shopping Web site to see how cost-effective SCSI technology has become. SCSI vendors are in the midst of a rush to yet another enhancement to the SCSI specification. This time the goal is a 160MB/s data rate without any changes to the cabling or connectors. The doubling in speed from 80MB/s to 160MB/s will be the result of double-clocking the data at the same 40MHz SCSI clock. One advantage will be that both 80MB/s Ultra2 SCSI and 160MB/s Ultra2 SCSI devices will be able to operate at their full data rates sharing the same bus. While I want to avoid religious arguments of SCSI vs. IDE or Fibre Channel, I think that the current state of technology and the market demonstrate that SCSI is the drive technology of choice for the near term.

6.2.2   Fibre Channel

As SCSI vendors reach for higher data rates in SCSI devices, Fibre (yes, for differentiation, Fibre is spelled this way by the ANSI Standard) Channel has the promise of features that SCSI will not be able to provide. With Exchange 5.5, we see average information store sizes in the 20GB–50GB range. With Exchange 2000, we will likely see total server storage be greatly increased due to enhanced storage allocation techniques and flexibility. As Exchange information stores grow, I am afraid SCSI will soon fall short as a large-scale Exchange Server storage technology. This will be proven on three fronts—performance, capacity, and manageability. While SCSI technology adequately provides for Exchange information stores less than 100GB, it will be Fibre Channel that meets the demands of large-scale Exchange 2000 deployments of the future. Most major computer and storage vendors have selected Fibre Channel as the next step for enterprise storage. These vendors are providing Fibre Channel as a standard disk interface soon. In the near future, storage vendors will not be taken seriously unless they offer Fibre Channel–based systems.

Fibre Channel, although discussed in this chapter as a storage technology, is really designed to be much more than that. Fibre Channel is really a network architecture that provides features for connectivity, increased distance, and even protocol multiplexing. While Fibre Channel works as a channel technology like SCSI, it also was designed to work as a transport mechanism—something that SCSI cannot provide. In using Fibre Channel as a storage interface, vendors are seeking to eliminate the distance, bandwidth, scalability, and reliability issues that have always plagued SCSI technology. Fibre Channel is a true integration of both channel and network technologies that supports active and intelligent interconnection between all connected devices. Unlike SCSI, Fibre Channel is actually an ANSI standard from Technical Committee T11. It is an I/O interface standard (X.3230-1994) that supports storage, video, networks, and even avionics interconnection. Table 6.7 provides a comparison of

SCSI and Fibre Channel technology. Note that, while Fibre Channel is intended to use fiber-optic technology as a medium, copper topology implementations are available from some vendors.

Table 6.7 *Comparison of SCSI vs. Fibre Channel as a Storage Technology*

	SCSI	*Fibre Channel*
Market	Desktop, workstation, server	Server, backbone, SAN
Cost	$$	$$$
Data rate	80MB/s (160MB/s future)	100MB/s (500MB/s + future)
Devices	Disk, tape, optical	Disk
Devices per port	16	128
Distance (meters)	12 meters	10KM (70KM with repeaters)

6.2.2.1 *Arbitrated Loop vs. Switched Fibre Channel*

Another important differentiation about Fibre Channel storage is that it comes in two flavors: Fibre Channel Switched (FCS) and Fibre Channel Arbitrated Loop (FCAL). Initially, there were only FCAL implementations available from most vendors because FCAL's simplicity made its time to market a little faster. Now most vendors are either offering both technologies or phasing out FCAL in favor of FCS products. The difference between FCAL and FCS is very much the same as the difference between a switched and a bus-based LAN architecture. In an FCAL-based storage implementation (Figure 6.4), all Fibre Channel devices share, and contend for, a common bus for communication and data-transfer purposes. Therefore, the 100MB/s channel is shared by all devices is a similar fashion to a SCSI bus. In addition, FCAL is limited in distance to 30 meters, making it not well suited as a backbone or SAN technology.

FCS, on the other hand, is a switched implementation in which each port on a Fibre Channel switch provides a full 100MB/s bandwidth to devices attached to that port. FCS systems can also be meshed into a Fibre Channel "fabric" architecture, as illustrated by Figure 6.5. This configuration is well suited for SAN scenarios that I will discuss in the next section.

Figure 6.4
FCAL-based
storage
configuration
scenario

Fibre Channel Arbitrated Loop (FCAL)

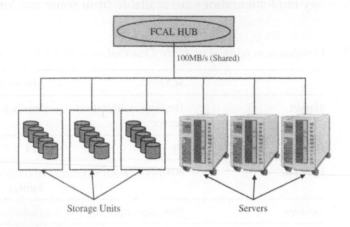

Figure 6.5
FCS storage
configuration
scenario

Fibre Channel Switched/Fabric

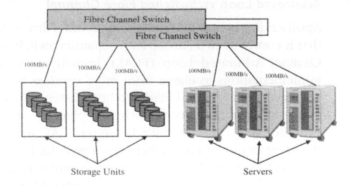

6.2.2.2   *Fibre Channel Stops Short of the Disk Drive*

An important point that should be cited before concluding our discussion on Fibre Channel as a storage technology is that, in most vendors' current implementations, Fibre Channel does not go all the way to the disk drive. Most implementations support a Fibre Channel connection between the host and the storage system, but internally to the storage system, the drives themselves are still based on SCSI technology (some vendors, like Data General, are offering Fibre Channel interfaces on disk drives, and the volumes will continue to ramp up). Most vendors accomplish this with an intelligent array controller that has a Fibre Channel interface on one side and hosts multiple SCSI channels on the other side. This array controller is often very similar technology to SCSI-based solutions and offers features such as RAID, cache, and many of the other features I discussed earlier. The reason for this is related to several factors. First, SCSI drives are very prevalent and cost effective. As I cited earlier, 95% of drives shipped are SCSI-based. Drive manufacturers have not yet ramped up substantial quantities of drives with Fibre Channel interfaces with which to meet market storage demands. This is partly due to cost constraints in producing disk drives with Fibre Channel interfaces, as the technology has not become ubiquitous enough to make it cost-effective. This is a similar analogy to new memory technologies—manufacturers await market demand and lower production costs before shifting production to new technologies. The other factor is performance. SCSI drives still offer adequate or even superior performance to Fibre Channel drives. After all, the bottleneck is really the mechanical media, not the channel itself. There has been much controversy over which technology (SCSI or Fibre Channel) performs better. At this writing, I am able to find no conclusive evidence to support either argument and feel it is beyond scope. However, it is safe to say that Fibre Channel will win in the high-end storage market as an interconnect method for reasons beyond performance.

For mission-critical servers of the future, my bet is on Fibre Channel as the storage architecture. It is the best solution to provide reliable and scalable storage at the lowest total cost of ownership. Despite the fact that we have only recently (since late 1998) seen the prevalence of Fibre Channel storage products on the market, the Fibre Channel standard is fairly mature, with work beginning in 1988 and the standard being finalized in 1994. Most importantly, in my opinion, is the fact that Fibre Channel is a standard, which brings a higher probability (but not a guarantee) of interoperability of Fibre Channel products. Also, since Fibre Channel is much more than a storage interface, the wide support of Fibre Channel in other applications such as video and avionics will further the development, progression, and acceptance of the technology. Many vendors are now offering Fibre Channel technology in their storage systems. Take a look at the top-tier vendors like Compaq, IBM, HP, EMC, and Network Appliance and investigate how they can help you build reliable and scalable storage solutions for your Exchange deployment.

6.2.3   Storage Area Networks

In the past, we have managed our data storage on a server-by-server basis. This host-based mentality has placed many limits on the manageability of that storage. We have traditionally married all storage decisions to the server. When configuring an Exchange server, we select how much storage we will attach to that server. The application (in this case, Exchange Server) is then optimally configured to use the storage provided by its host server. Another problem we face is reliably protecting our data. RAID technology does offer some protection against the loss of physical disk drives. Well-planned and executed disaster recovery policies and procedures can provide additional protection. However, human errors, software errors, data corruption, catastrophes, other losses still are a fact of life in most organizations. While all of the techniques we employ can aid in providing mission-critical services, they sometimes fall short because they are expensive, complex, or cumbersome to manage and implement. One major problem area for Exchange is the time it takes to restore data. This time continues to increase as the volume of data outpaces the technology available to back up and restore that data. storage area networks (SANs) were conceived with these issues in mind. The idea behind a SAN is to provide storage to the organization in a manner similar to the way a power or telephone company provides services—as a utility. Raw storage capacity can be added to the network and then virtualized for use by servers attached to the SAN. From the application point of view, storage should be a transparent service. Underlying a SAN can be many different technologies such as SCSI, Fibre Channel, or even ATM or gigabit ethernet. With storage as a utility, SANs move the focus from host-based storage to storage as a centralized and unified enterprise data store.

The three characteristics of SAN technology that are especially applicable to our Exchange Server deployments are scalability, manageability, and multiple host attachment. From a scalability point of view, SAN technologies will take us to the hundreds of gigabytes or even several terabytes to which we would eventually like to scale storage on our Exchange servers. When discussing scalability here, I am referring to capacity scalability. SCSI-based drive and array technology has served the industry well. However, in order to build large storage pools for our Exchange servers, simple SCSI arrays will not suffice in the long term. Fibre Channel–attached, SAN-based storage will be the key to large multiterabyte storage pools. What's more, these storage pools will also contain directly SAN-attached devices capable of providing disaster recovery for these large pools of storage. The scalability characteristics of SANs will provide the next step in storage technology that is required for Exchange Server consolidation projects as well. Scalability, in my mind, also includes the ability to access storage over greater distances. With SANs, a server can access storage many kilometers away as if it were locally attached to the server itself.

In terms of manageability, SAN technology offers many options that will benefit Exchange deployments. Storage manageability gives system managers the flexibility to plan, allocate, move, and expand storage within the context of the SAN. For example, if one server attached to the SAN is running low on storage capacity, that server can be allocated more storage from the overall pool. If a server no longer requires an increment of storage, it can be reallocated to other hosts within the SAN. In addition, if the overall storage pool in the SAN has reached capacity, more physical drives can be added to the SAN storage pool dynamically. The SAN storage pool can also be managed in terms of performance. A system manager may even choose to provide different services levels within the SAN. These service levels may be performance- or reliability-based and may be based on the level of each that an application or client device requires. The cornerstone of this great management flexibility in SAN technology lies in the concept on storage virtualization. With virtualization, the underlying physical devices are not as important and become simple building blocks. Groups of physical disks are combined into arrays, and these arrays become logical drives defined to host devices attached to the SAN interface. Virtualized storage allows for disks of differing capacities, performance characteristics, and data-protection levels (RAID) to be created from physical disk resources. Most SAN products on the market offer intelligent front-ends to aid the system manager in this process. The virtualization of storage within the SAN allows storage units to be dynamically allocated and assigned to any host attached to the SAN. The management functionality of SANs includes:

- Dynamic and transparent storage pool allocation
- Redistribution/reallocation of capacity
- SAN-attached backup and advanced disaster recovery techniques
- Improved monitoring for capacity planning, performance, and accounting

Multiple host attachment is an important SAN characteristic that makes this possible. SAN technology is really a paradigm shift from traditional PC server–based storage. Traditionally, we have looked at storage on a server as that which is attached to a controller (array or nonarray) residing in the server itself. In many cases, storage also was physically located in the server cabinet or at least an external cabinet nearby. With SAN technology, the array controller moves "out of the box" to the storage cabinet itself instead of the server, as illustrated in Figure 6.6.

This shift to external SAN/controller-based storage is a key concept that has not completely caught on in our industry yet. However, this concept is key to our ability to take advantage of the capabilities that SAN technologies offer. We have always looked at storage in terms of what is on the server itself. Now storage can be seen as a resource that the server can take advantage of. By moving storage management out of the server, we can truly begin to treat storage as a utility for our Exchange deployments. In fact, I look for the day when storage is managed as a totally separate IT resource from servers. Imagine application server managers who simply request allocations from an enterprise storage pool in which to store Exchange Server data. SAN technology and the detailed discussions around it are much more complex and extensive than I have time and expertise to discuss. In addition, an entire book on the subject of SAN technology could certainly be written. In fact, there are several good resources available on SAN technology. As an augment to this discussion for Exchange, take some time to do some in-depth research on SAN technologies. Also spend some time with your storage vendor of choice and identify product features that you would

Figure 6.6
The paradigm shift from host-based storage to SAN-based storage

Moving from Host-based to SAN-based Storage

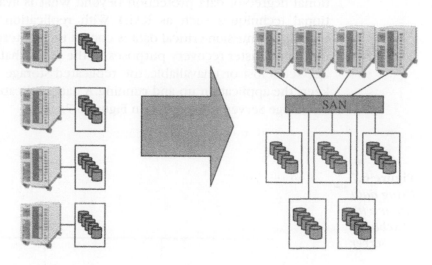

find useful for your Exchange deployments. For the purpose of this chapter, I will stick to the specific storage-technology capabilities that SANs can offer to mission-critical Exchange deployments.

6.3   Advanced Storage Functionality

As Exchange information stores hold increasing amounts of data, it will become increasingly difficult to backup, restore, and maintain that data using traditional methods. Beyond the ability to use SAN-based storage as a utility, the capabilities of storage virtualization, and the shift from host-based to SAN-based storage are the advanced capabilities of SAN technology to aid in issues such as disaster recovery and high availability. This involves functionality that SANs or other advanced storage technologies offer that provide additional tools beyond the traditional tape-based backup and restore capabilities we are used to. The key technologies that I believe will have the most impact on Exchange deployments are these:

1.   Data-replication technologies

2.   Snapshot and cloning technologies

3.   Network disk technologies

6.3.1   Data-Replication and Mirroring Technologies

Data-replication and mirroring technologies can provide an additional degree of data protection beyond what is available via traditional techniques such as RAID. With replication and mirroring techniques, mission-critical data is copied to an alternate storage set used for disaster recovery purposes. In the event that a primary storage set is lost or unavailable, the replicated storage can be used to keep the application up and running. A data-replication scenario for Exchange Server is illustrated in Figure 6.7.

Figure 6.7
Using data replication with Exchange Server

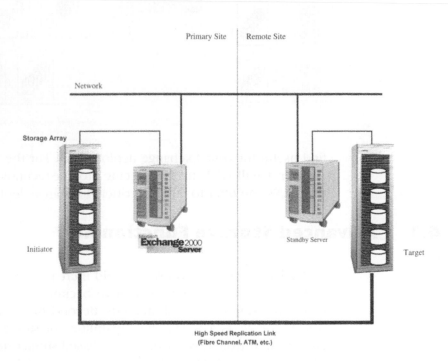

With data replication, there are basically two techniques: synchronous and asynchronous. These two techniques impact how data is copied (mirrored) between a primary data set and a backup copy set. Synchronous replication forces an update operation to be complete to the remote or backup copy set before the I/O is returned as complete to the application. With asynchronous replication, I/O completion is not dependent upon a successful operation to the backup set. Data-replication technology can be categorized into two flavors: hardware based and software based. Hardware-based data-replication products are usually made available by vendors of SAN products as an extension in functionality. Examples of hardware-based data-replication products include Compaq's StorageWorks Data Replication Manager (DRM) and EMC's Synchronous Remote Data Facility (SRDF). Hardware-based data-replication is certainly a superior technology to software-based solutions. This is due to the fact the hardware-based implementations have their functionality embedded in the storage controller and are usually transparent to the operating system. Hardware-based data-replication products also usually take advantage of other advanced technologies, such as Fibre Channel and ATM, as potential methods of extending the distance of data replication. Hardware-based solutions often rely on a software element to manage the replication activity. However, the software usually runs within the confines of a real-time operating system on the controller or the storage enclosure. The main factor in hardware-based solutions is that the functionality is implemented mostly in hardware and is not managed by and transparent to the operating system. Software-based solutions, on the other hand, usually rely on filter drivers. Filter drivers act as a "shim" layer between the operating system disk services layer and the device drivers. Filter drivers typically intercept I/Os destined for the disk subsystem and redirect them or perform some manipulation depending on the functionality configured.

Software-based data-replication products utilize filter drivers to perform the replication operations. As the software filter driver sees disk requests from the operating system, it can redirect them to meet the needs of the replication activity. For example, if the Exchange database engine sends an I/O request to write 4KB, this request will proceed down to the disk services layer and be intercepted by the filter driver. The filter driver would then perform a data-replication operation and attempt to ensure that the write occurred at both the primary data location as well as the replicated data location (see Figure 6.8 for an illustration). Although, most vendors of these solutions will tell you that they are completely safe, there is inherently more risk with a software implementation due to the fact that the operating system must carry the overhead and management of this functionality and because there are more opportunities for things to go wrong (with a hardware-based implementation, the activities would occur at a controller level and be transparent to Windows 2000 and Exchange Server).

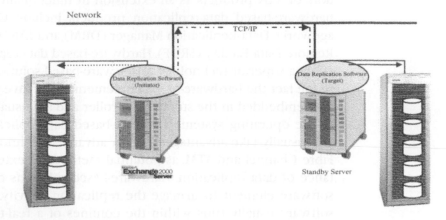

Figure 6.8
Implementation of software-based data-replication technology

Also, as a software component installed with the operating system, software-based implementations are subject to interaction and potential conflicts with other software components and their issues. As one would expect, software-based solutions to data replication tend to be less expensive than hardware-based solutions. One additional variant or implementation of data-replication technology is the concept of a "stretched" cluster. With a stretched cluster, cluster nodes are physically separated by large distances (supposedly unlimited with ATM), and cluster and application data is replicated. When a failure scenario occurs, the remote cluster node can failover the application and continue client service.

When investigating and potentially selecting data-replication technology for your Exchange deployment, the choice usually comes down to a cost/benefit analysis weighed against the risks of either implementation. To give you a head start, Table 6.8 provides a summarized look at some popular hardware- and software-based data-replication products.

Table 6.8 *Data-Replication-Technology Vendor Survey*

Vendor/Product	Implementation	Remarks
Compaq StorageWorks Data Replication Manager (DRM)	Hardware-based. Requires some software to be installed with the operating system. Supports Fibre Channel and ATM to increase replication distances.	Supported on high-end Compaq StorageWorks RA8000 and ESA12000-series storage systems. Supports "stretched" cluster concept.
EMC Synchronous Remote Data Facility (SRDF)	Hardware-based with some software running on the host and management system.	Largest installed based but tends to have cost prohibitions.
Veritas Vinca	Software-based. Implemented with NT filter driver. Uses either network or locally attached storage as the replication destination.	Not specific support for Exchange Server.
NSI DoubleTake	Software-based. Implemented with NT filter driver.	Supports clustered configurations.
Marathon Technologies Endurance 4000	Hybrid hardware- and software-based. Uses proprietary replication interconnect hardware and NT filter driver.	Could be viewed as a hybrid solution that is a combination of hardware and software.

6.3.1.1 Exchange and Data Replication

For an application like Exchange Server using data-replication technology, care must be taken to design a data-replication scenario that does not create problems for Exchange's Extensible Storage Engine (ESE) when writing transactions to the database files or transaction logs. To illustrate my point, suppose that Exchange performed a write operation to storage. With data replication configured, that write would need to be replicated to both the local data set and the remote copy set. In a hardware-based implementation, this would occur transparently to the operating system and Exchange. In the case of a software implementation, the operating system would have a filter driver performing the replication activity but would otherwise have no exposure to the data-replication function. The problem comes with transactional integrity. Since Exchange's database engine is performing transacted, oriented operations, there is no exposure of the transactional states and atomic units that Exchange uses to the data-replication function. The data-replication activity just occurs with NT I/O operations to disk and is none the wiser to whether these are simple I/O operations or transactional units. The real issue comes when the write that Exchange issues to the storage does not complete to both sides of the replication set or incurs a timing penalty to perform the operation. Since data-replication products may support asynchronous or synchronous modes of operation, the real key is whether they support synchronous replication (asynchronous provides no guarantee of successful simultaneous completion). This means that, when Exchange Server performs a write operation (regardless of whether it is to the transaction logs or the database files), there must be assurance that the operation completed at both the local data set as well as the remote replicated set. Synchronous replication ensures this since the I/O completion is not returned until the operation has completed at both locations (local and remote). Unfortunately, if the operation takes too much time, Exchange's ESE will fail the transaction and return an I/O error. This may be most likely in a scenario in which the connection for replication is via ATM or another medium (such as long distances over Fibre Channel) that could be subject to latency or timing issues. The idea behind using this technology with Exchange is that you could "mirror" or replicate your complete Exchange dataset to an alternate storage location that could be used to restore a downed Exchange server to operation if the primary location was lost or corrupted. Since you could replicate both the transaction logs and the Exchange database files, the complete transaction contents would be available to recover Exchange Server. It the future, as functionality such as log shipping emerges for applications like Exchange, data replication will become even more powerful due to application support from a transactional perspective.

From a Microsoft Product Support Services (PSS) and Exchange development perspective, I would not expect official support of this technology with Exchange Server since none of the products guarantee transactional integrity. If you have problems, Microsoft is unlikely to want to help you and will probably point you in the direction of the vendor from which you purchased the technology. That being said, I believe this technology can be successfully implemented in your Exchange deployments and have seen several organizations do so. My recommendation is the following. First, I would only deploy data-replication technology for Exchange that supports synchronous replication operations. Don't take chances—ensure that your I/Os are at both the initiator and target locations before completion. Next, ensure that you thoroughly plan, test, and pilot this technology in your Exchange deployment before putting it into production. There are many nuances, configuration choices, and implementation options that you will need to understand. Also, don't just test the replication—test the recovery. If you are deploying data replication over a wide area using ATM or another network technology, be sure you understand the impact bandwidth and latency problems can have on Exchange Server data availability and integrity. Finally, I would replicate your entire Exchange dataset (transaction logs and database files). This could be done on a per-storage-group basis or on a per-database basis. This combined with synchronous operation ensures that your Exchange data (uncommitted transaction logs and committed database files) is identical at both replication sets and can be recovered by the Exchange database engine. For some, data-replication technology may be a little "bleeding-edge." I am not advocating data replication but simply presenting it as another option that is complementary to your existing technologies and practices as you endeavor to build mission-critical Exchange deployments.

6.3.2   Cloning and Snapshot Technology

Another technology available to Exchange implementers and system managers is storage cloning and snapshot technologies. These technologies, while discussed together here, provide similar but different functionality. Rather than use the terms "clone" and "snapshot" (the later of which is actually an owned trademark of StorageTek), I would prefer to use the terms *BCVClone* and *BCVSnap* since they aren't owned by anyone, and I can avoid hurting anyone's feelings. First is the term BCV (Business Continuance Volume). The idea behind a BCV is a standalone data volume that can be used for recovery of an application for the purpose of continuing a business operation of function. The two variants of BCV that help us understand the use of this technology for Exchange across several products on the market are BCVClone and BCVSnap. For clarification, let's approach them separately and then unite the concepts later when we discuss their use with Exchange Server.

6.3.2.1   *BCVClone*

As the name implies, a clone is an exactly copy of an existing data set or volume. For vendors of BCVClone technology, implementations may slightly vary, but the idea and functionality are basically the same. To use our discussions on RAID from earlier in this chapter as a basis, a BCVClone is simply an additional RAID 0+1 mirror set member. For example, suppose your current SAN-base storage configuration (this technology usually only accompanies SAN product solutions) is a RAID 0+1 array for your Exchange database files. This provides a high degree of performance and data protection. Now suppose that, in addition to the two-member mirror set (RAID 0+1), you added a third member to your existing mirror set. Upon creation, data would be mirrored or normalized to that third member. The process of normalization is the most expensive part of using BCVClone technology since it is a complete mirroring of the production volume. Once normalized, the additional member would continue to stay in synch as an additional mirror of your production volume. At this point, this could be classified as a BCV or, more appropriately, a BCVClone. The BCVClone could either continue as a mirror set member or could be split off or "broken" from the existing mirror set. This broken-off member could be used for a variety of purposes including offline backup or as a readily available business continuance option. Using the BCVClone for backup purposes would help offload the primary storage array and provide a quicker and more efficient means of backup. (Keep in mind that this is considered an offline backup and does not have exposure to the necessary APIs and recovery steps needed for Exchange by itself.) The BCVClone could also be used as a quick recovery option in the event that the production copy of the data becomes corrupt. Additionally, the BCVClone could be merged back to the production data set as well. Most implementations of BCVClone technology have limits on the number of clones that can be created (a function of the controller and cache size). You could theoretically break off BCVClones at several points during your production periods as an additional means of disaster recovery and high availability for Exchange. Once BCVClones are no longer needed or become updated, they can be deleted or even joined back into the mirror set and renormalized to become a mirror set member once again.

6.3.2.2   BCVSnap

Like the BCVClone, the BCVSnap functions as a point-in-time copy of production data. However, a BCVSnap is not a mirror set member at any point. A BCVSnap is a business continuance volume that has been created from the production data, but the creation process is much different. The BCVSnap (snapshot) creates a virtual metadata map of the volume blocks on the production volume. As the name implies, it is a point-in-time picture of the volume blocks when the BCVSnap was created. Once a BCVSnap is created (which takes only a few seconds in contrast to minutes for a BCVClone), the production volume becomes a different animal. The original blocks of data comprising the BCVSnap continue to stay intact for the life of the BCVSnap. As the data blocks on the production volume change (i.e., an Exchange database engine transaction commits to the database files), these changed blocks are copied out to a new location allocated from the storage pool, and the production volume map is updated to reflect the copy-out data block. As more and more data on the production volume changes, more blocks are allocated from the pool and are copied out. Meanwhile, the BCVSnap continues to provide a map to the original set of production volume blocks that represent the point in time at which the BCVSnap was created. Thus, the production data volume is a combination of the unchanged blocks in the BCVSnap volume map and the copied-out data blocks resulting from changes to the production data as illustrated in Figure 6.9.

Figure 6.9
An illustration of BCVSnap technology

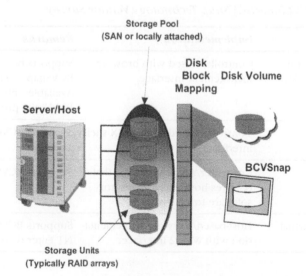

Like its close brother the BCVClone, a BCVSnap can be used for a variety of purposes that contribute to enhanced disaster recovery and high-availability capabilities and options for the system manager. Unlike a BCVClone, the BCVSnap incurs performance overhead because changed data in the production volume causes more copy-out operations to occur and overhead increases as the production volume spans both unchanged blocks in the BCVSnap and changed blocks in the copied out allocations in the storage pool. Whereas the BCVClone incurs its cost upfront when normalization is initiated and when the clone is split off, the BCVSnap's overhead is dependent upon the degree and intensity of changed data copy-out operations. Both BCVClone and BCVSnap technology can be a useful addition or complement (not a replacement) to your existing disaster recovery techniques for Exchange. This technology also comes in both hardware and software implementations. Like data replication, I prefer hardware-based solutions since the software-based choices are also implemented using NT filter driver technology. In the case of BCVSnap, you can see the potential issues that could be created with a software-based implementation. Table 6.9 provides a survey of BCVClone/BCVSnap technology product offerings to aid in your assessment of this technology for your own deployment.

Table 6.9   *BCVClone/BCVSnap Technology Vendor Survey*

Vendor/Product	Implementation	Remarks
Compaq StorageWorks Enterprise Volume Manager (EVM)	Controller-based with browser management interface.	Supports both BCVClone and BCVSnap. No merge capability. Available only with RA8000/ESA12000 products.
EMC TimeFinder	Controller-based with UNIX shell interface.	Supports BCVClone and merge capability.
Network Appliance Filer	Controller/software hybrid that requires host-based redirector software to access filter.	Supports BCVSnap functionality.
Compaq StorageWorks Virtual Replicator (SWVR)	Host-based/software implementation with Win32 interface.	Supports BCVSnap functionality. NT Filter driver-based.

Table 6.10 *A Comparison of BCVClone vs. BCVSnap Technology*

Functionality	BCVSnap	BCVClone
Persistence	Typically short-lived. Depends on for what purpose the BCV is used. BCVSnap is invalid if source volume is destroyed.	Longer-term. Again, depends on the purpose for which it is used. Can survive the loss of the source volume.
RAID support	Any RAID volume including RAID 0, 1 (0+1), and 5.	Limited to RAID 1 and 0+1.
Capacity overhead	Equal to the size of the source volume.	Equal in size to the source volume. However, BCVClone requires double overhead since a minimum of a three-member mirror set is required to create.
Initialization or normalization time	Instantaneous. Minimal time required for controller or software to create metadata volume block mapping.	Depends on the size of the source volume. Usually several minutes to an hour.
BCV creation (snapshot or clone split)	Instantaneous.	Instantaneous. Remerge requires time similar to normalization.
Source volume restore	Must copy BCVSnap to another volume and revert to the source volume.	Reverse normalization operation. Clone becomes mirror set source volume and is available immediately.
Performance impact	Source volume and copy-out snapshot data are both accessed during both read and write I/O operations.	Source volume and BCVClone are accessed as independent volumes both read and write I/O operations.

6.3.2.3 Using BCVClone/BCVSnap Technology with Exchange

When using this technology with Exchange Server, as in the case of data replication, several caveats exist. First, once again, Microsoft will not officially support this technology in Exchange 2000 until a later release of Exchange Server. This is, again, due to the fact that none of the vendor implementations available provides a guarantee of transactional integrity for the Exchange databases. However, both Compaq and EMC have worked extensively with the Exchange development team at Microsoft to ensure that their BCV solutions will work with Exchange 5.5 and Exchange 2000. The first issue arises when creating the clone or snapshot. When Exchange is running and services are online, the database files are open and do not represent the exact transactional state of the database. Remember from earlier discussions that the consistent state of the Exchange databases includes not only the database files but the transaction logs as well. The creation of a clone or snapshot of the Exchange database volume does not have exposure to this. Furthermore, all the implementations of either BCVClone or BCVSnap products require varying degrees of time for the snapshot or clone to be created. The snapshot will require the least amount of time and the clone will require more. Remember that the cloning or normalization will depend on the amount of data and the performance capabilities of the system. To make matters worse, during the time the BCV is being created, Exchange cannot access the disk subsystem. Because of this, Exchange services (in the case of Exchange 5.5) will need to be shutdown for the BCV to be created. For Exchange 2000, databases only need to be dismounted. Of the vendors that provide this technology, all have done some level of integration work for Microsoft Exchange Server. For Exchange Server 5.5, only Compaq and EMC have developed solutions that provide for the shutdown services and management of the transaction log files. Typically, only the Exchange database volume is the target of a clone or snapshot, and the transaction logs are managed separately.

Hopefully, in a later release, Microsoft will eventually provide direct API support. With this support, a vendor can utilize the ESE APIs to inform Exchange that a snapshot or clone is about to be taken. Once implemented, these APIs will allow Exchange to dismount the affected databases, allowing the operation to occur. During that brief period (which can be as long as several minutes), the Exchange users whose data is stored on the databases affected will not be able to access their data. When restoring the Exchange databases from a snapshot or clone, the forthcoming APIs will enable Exchange to treat the restored clone or snapshot the same as a restored database from a backup set. In this case, Exchange simply treats the BCV like a backup set and performs normal recovery by replaying the transaction logs that are required to bring the database up to a consistent state. Remember, as of this writing, these clone/snapshot APIs for Exchange Server are not available and will not be available until some time after the initial release of Exchange. 2000 therefore, to successfully implement BCVClone or BCVSnap for Exchange 5.5 or Exchange 2000, it must be treated as an offline mechanism, and the databases (or services shutdown, in the case of Exchange 5.5) must be dismounted. This means that you must rely on your vendor or your own expertise to properly manage the Exchange database files and transaction logs in a clone or snapshot environment. Microsoft has documented support for both Compaq and EMC's Exchange 5.5 solutions in KnowledgeBase article Q221756. I look for these vendors to add interim support (until the APIs are available) for Exchange 2000 in the near term. If you are considering implementation of this technology for your Exchange deployment, make sure you invest enough time planning and testing. More importantly, my recommendation is to not make the mistake of completely relying on this technology as your sole disaster recovery method. In the opinion of some, BCVClone/BCVSnap technology is a bit leading edge. Whether this is the case or not, this technology should only be treated as a complement to regular online backups and solid disaster recovery practices for Exchange. Properly respected and well-implemented, cloning and snapshot technology can be a valuable tool toward increasing the availability of your Exchange deployment.

6.3.3   Network-Attached Storage (NAS)

Another interesting technology that you may want to investigate for use in your Exchange deployments is network-attached storage (NAS), also known as network disk technology. As the name implies, a network disk is a virtual device made available over either a shared or dedicated network connection. Essentially, vendors or network disk products have implemented a disk block protocol over UDP or other networking protocol such as NFS, CIFS, or NCP. Systems that utilize the network disks do so via client software that allows them to see the network service as a disk device. Vendors of this technology for Windows NT/2000 typically either have a specialized proprietary device (i.e., Network Appliance) or use a host-based filter driver that provides other features such as virtualization and snapshots combined with a network disk capability (Compaq Storage-Works Virtual Replicator). The use of this technology with Exchange may not be that obvious. The first option is the utilization of network disks as primary storage for Exchange information stores, as shown in Figure 6.10.

In this scenario, an Exchange server runs the network disk client software or redirector and mounts network disk resources over the network for use as storage for the Exchange databases. The network disk software is transparent to applications like Exchange (because it is implemented as a filter driver) and makes the network disks

Figure 6.10
*Using network-
attached disks
with Exchange*

Using Network Attached Storage with Exchange

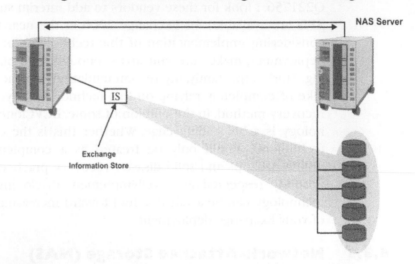

appear to the system as a local disk resource. With network disk-based storage, storage resources can be centrally managed as a utility similar to the SAN-based approach discussed earlier.

The immediate problem or challenge that comes to mind with network disk technology and Exchanges performance. In my first look at this technology, its viability was somewhat suspect. This was due to the fact that the capabilities of the disk subsystem are key to Exchange performance. The ability of the disk subsystem to deliver the I/O requirements that Exchange demands is more important than any other server subsystem (CPU, memory, etc.) in achieving maximum system performance. With NAS, the I/O requirements of Exchange must be delivered over the network and via several layers of software. For many Exchange servers, it is just not possible to deliver the required performance using network disk technology. It is for this reason that Microsoft does not officially support NAS for Exchange. Nevertheless, many organizations have still chosen to deploy network disks anyway. One use of network disk technology that seems to make the most sense is the combination of this technology with BCVs (either clone or snapshot). For example, using Compaq's StorageWorks Virtual Replicator product (which supports both snapshots and network disks), a snapshot of the Exchange database files is taken (of course, after properly shutting down Exchange services). The snapshot is then made available as a network disk, which is then mounted by an Exchange recovery server (nonproduction server used for recovery) as a recovered database, as shown in Figure 6.11.

Figure 6.11
*Mounting a
network-
attached
snapshot to a
recovery server*

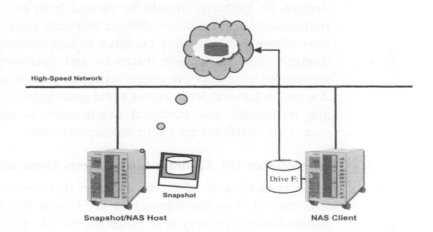

The recovery server can be used for individual mailbox or item recovery, or for other purposes. I do believe that network disks can have viable uses for Exchange deployments. However, I hesitate to recommend the use of this technology for Exchange because of performance issues. In particular, with the increased I/O requirements necessary for Exchange 2000's multiple storage groups and databases, I am doubtful that network disks will be adequate. For some smaller deployments in which the users per server are relatively low, NAS may be an excellent option. If you are considering this technology for your Exchange deployment, ensure that you understand and accept it limitations. Also, there are mostly likely many other creative ways in which this technology can be utilized.

6.3.4   Storage Designs for Exchange 2000

After a look at the various technologies and solutions available for Exchange storage, it is important that we drill down to an application and best practices level before concluding this chapter. In this final section, I would like to take the preceding discussions on storage technology and functionality as a foundation on which we can overlay Exchange 2000–specific storage designs. These storage designs for Exchange should be viewed from two perspectives— performance and reliability/disaster recovery. Since Exchange 2000 now allows for some fairly complex storage designs by supporting multiple database engine instances and databases, it would be impossible to discuss the entire matrix of possibilities. To keep the discussion focused, let's discuss some guidelines for leveraging storage technology and advanced functionality to maximize performance and reliability for Exchange deployments.

6.3.4.1   *Performance 101: Separate Random from Sequential I/O*

In previous versions of Exchange Server, this was an easy rule to follow. Since I/O to the transaction log files is purely sequential in nature (unless recovery is in progress), we can provide a dedicated volume for the transaction log files. Since I/O activity to the database files (only PRIV.EDB and PUB.EDB) in previous versions of Exchange was very random in nature, we could simply allocate a separate array for the database files as well. Now, in Exchange 2000, the same rule still applies. However, it is much more complex to implement. This is due to the innovation of multiple storage groups and databases. Technically, Exchange 2000 can support up to 15 configured storage groups (plus a 16th for recovery), each with a maximum of five databases. Because of the overhead required for each additional storage group, Microsoft will only support a maximum of four storage groups at initial release of Exchange 2000. Later, as further testing is done and technologies like 64-bit support (Win64) for Windows 2000 and Exchange 2000 are released, expect those numbers to increase. Since, in effect, previous versions of Exchange Server supported only one storage group with two databases, allocating and designing server storage was easier. Figure 6.12 illustrates how this rule may be applied for an Exchange 2000 server with four storage groups.

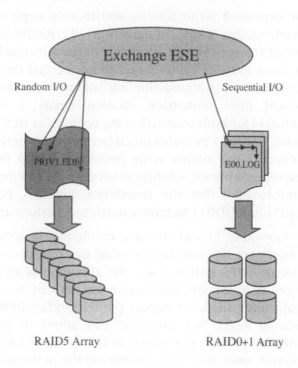

Figure 6.12
Optimizing performance: separation of random and sequential I/O

In Figure 6.12, each of the four storage groups has one database configured. A two-drive RAID1 volume is configured for each set of transaction logs (one set per storage group), and the transaction logs are placed on that volume. For the database files, a separate RAID1 volume is also configured for each of the four databases. Remember that Exchange 2000 database files are now a pair of database files—the properties store (*.EDB) and the streaming store (*.STM). If the streaming store files will see high activity (i.e., as in the case of Internet protocol clients), an additional performance-enhancing step may be taken by placing the STM files on yet another physical array since they have a highly large random I/O profile. There also may be difficult questions to answer about controller cache. For example, which volumes should use the cache and how should the cache be configured? In most cases, I believe we will see the same answers to these questions as in earlier versions of Exchange Server. When configuring the controller cache, choose the setting of 100% write-back (or the largest write-back ratio allowed) in order to maximize performance for expensive write activity and to help cope with the additional overhead that RAID configurations like RAID5 create. Next, configure all volumes to take advantage of the write-back caching provided on the controller (don't forget to ensure that the controller cache is protected). Both transaction log volumes and database volumes will benefit from write-back caching. Finally, I would recommend RAID0+1 for both transaction log volumes as well as database file volumes. RAID0+1 provides much better overall performance and is not subject to the intense write penalty of RAID5. However, if the best price/performance solution is sought, you can deploy RAID5 for the database files. For the transaction log files, however, stick with RAID1 or RAID0+1 to ensure maximum performance and protection.

Obviously, I speak of these configuration options and choices as if cost were no issue. Bear in mind that overall cost of configurations that are 100% RAID0+1 and the allocation of an individual array for every database and transaction log set can be quite expensive. In real-world practice, I expect the trade-offs will first be made in the area of RAID. Not everyone can afford to purchase 100GB of RAID0+1 storage per server. In the event that RAID0+1 is cost prohibitive, make sure you understand the performance and fault-tolerance trade-offs associated with RAID5 before selecting it as your best option. Another cost trade-off will be strict adherence to the rule. Must every sequential activity be separated from every random activity? In an ideal scenario, we could allocate an individual array for every transaction log set and database file. However, in practice, I expect that most configurations will combine the transaction logs from multiple storage groups onto one array. Since there is not sufficient performance data for Exchange 2000 available, time will tell if this trade-off can be tolerated. Based on data from previous versions of Exchange, I would conclude that this is not a huge performance factor. As with the design of any mission-critical system, there will be performance and cost trade-offs involved when designing storage for Exchange 2000 servers.

6.3.4.2   Using Advanced Storage Technology to Increase Exchange 2000 Reliability

When I discussed storage technology options and advanced capabilities earlier, I pointed to several key features that are of particular usefulness when deploying Exchange Server. Specifically, the most useful technologies are multiple-host attachment, BCVs, and data replication. What is most important from these discussions is not any one individual technology by itself but the combination and integration of all these technologies for your specific performance, reliability, and disaster recovery needs. Since every Exchange deployment is different, there are a variety of performance and reliability service levels that Exchange system managers must provide. The great opportunity afforded by all of the storage technologies available is that system managers can pick and choose from them based on their individual needs and risk assessments. In addition, these technologies can be combined with others like clustering to provide additional functionality. Using clustering as an example, the features of a clustered Exchange scenario could be combined with a technology like data replication to achieve what is known as the stretched cluster. In another example, since clustering requires a shared storage mechanism such as a SAN, the advanced features of SANs such as BCVs can be used in conjunction with clustering to add reliability and recovery options for an Exchange server. Figure 6.13 provides an unrealistic but illustrative view of how many different technologies could be combined and leveraged to drive Exchange deployments higher in terms of mission-critical capabilities.

Figure 6.13
Storage technologies combined to achieve the highest reliability

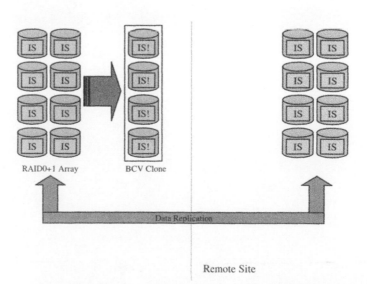

What is most important about all of the storage technologies we have discussed in this chapter is that there is no single solution for every Exchange deployment. System managers must arm themselves with the knowledge of what technologies are available. They must also understand if and how these technologies can be leveraged for their Exchange deployments. Furthermore, technology implementations and their integration with Exchange will vary by vendor. Each solution will need extensive testing and piloting before being put into production. Put into proper perspective and deployed in a conservative fashion, I believe that the tremendous capabilities available in today's storage technology can be one of your most valuable assets in building mission-critical Exchange deployments.

7

Leveraging Cluster Technologies for Exchange

In his book *In Search of Clusters*, Gregory Pfister defines a cluster as "a parallel or distributed system that consists of a collection of interconnected whole computers which are utilized as a single, unified computing resource." While the concept of clustering has been around in the computer industry for many years, the technology is relatively new to the Windows NT/Windows 2000 environment. In Microsoft's endeavors to make the Windows technology ever more reliable, clustering technology is one area to which they have turned. Microsoft's approach to clustering has differed from other operating system vendors. As organizations begin to take Windows NT/2000 technology more seriously and deploy more and more mission-critical applications on this platform, clustering will become increasingly important.

For Exchange 2000, clustering technology will offer significant reliability benefits for organizations willing to invest in this technology. As the Exchange Server platform becomes a basis for more application solutions and business-critical processes, the benefits of clustering will become quite necessary. In addition, as Microsoft strives to position Exchange 2000 as a platform for Internet service providers (ISP) and application service providers (ASP), high-availability technologies such as clustering will be a high-priority requirement. As such, it is necessary for us to spend some time discussing clustering technology available in Windows 2000 and how this technology can be leveraged to provide mission-critical capabilities for Exchange 2000 deployments.

7.1 High Availability Is A Key Concern

Organizations deploying messaging and collaboration applications face many challenges. Very often, implementers focus on performance and scalability. Questions such as "How many users per server can I deploy?" or "How do we do performance monitoring and tuning?" are among those most often heard. Equally important are the administrative and management aspects of deployment. Issues such as user administration, directory synchronization, database maintenance, and server management are common concerns. But it is disaster recovery and high availability that are at the forefront of the minds of implementers of Microsoft Exchange Server. Due to the mission-critical nature of messaging and collaborative applications, minimizing downtime and providing for rapid recovery are paramount. With the increasing size of information stores combined with the limits of current backup and restore technologies, disaster recovery issues can be the limiting factor when deciding the number of users per server to deploy. With tolerance for downtime low, keeping an Exchange Server constantly available is a key concern for IT organizations. The issue of high availability is a most important issue for Exchange Server deployments. When many look to increase availability and reliability for Exchange Server, cluster technology immediately comes to mind.

In this chapter, I will try to avoid an in-depth focus on clustering technology itself. My focus will be mostly on support and implementation of clustering in Exchange 5.5 Enterprise Edition and Exchange 2000 Enterprise Server. Since this book is geared toward Exchange 2000, I will spend the majority of my effort on Exchange 2000, other than to discuss the origins of clustering support for Exchange Server that were first supported in Exchange Server 5.5 Enterprise Edition. I will give a brief overview of the history and technology surrounding clustering technology as a foundation for later discussions. Next, I will spend some time focusing on support of clustering within the Windows 2000 operating system implemented as Microsoft Cluster Service. I will follow this with a close examination of how clustering support for Exchange 2000 is designed, implemented, and managed and will discuss deployment best practices. Finally, I will also look at some of the business and decision criteria that impact one's choice to implement cluster technology for an Exchange deployment. My goal here will be to give you a look at clustering technology for Exchange 2000 and how this technology can be leveraged to increase reliability for your Exchange deployment.

7.2   The Problems Clustering Does and Doesn't Solve

A common mistake made when employing cluster technology is to view clustering as the quintessential answer to all of the downtime problems an Exchange deployment faces. Proceeding with this notion is a fatal mistake, however. Clustering can only address issues within the domain of the cluster service technology. For example, if you have poor disaster recovery practices or software that is plagued with bugs, no magic clustering technology is going to save you. Clustering technology, especially that in Windows NT/2000, can only help solve issues it was designed to address. Stated simply, clusters most directly help you reduce single points of failure. A standalone server running Exchange has several points of failure. Hardware components like the system board, processors, power supplies with no redundancy, network cards, etc., may fail at some point in the life of a server. For example, industry-standard servers do not have any form of processor redundancy available, whereby a failed processor is lock-step fault tolerant and the system experiences zero downtime when a processor fails. This type of technology is only available in high-end systems such as Compaq's Himalayas. By deploying a cluster solution, many single points of failure can be eliminated. In some cases, software issues can even be thought of as single points of failure, and clusters may address some of these issues as well.

Another downtime problem that system operators often face is planned outages. Planned outages are often not "charged" against the availability of a deployment but are, nevertheless, downtime in which the system is not available for client access. These outages take the form of routine maintenance, rolling upgrades or block-points, configuration changes, and hardware or software upgrades. Deploying clustered Exchange servers can help address planned outages by allowing services running on one cluster node to be failed over to another node or nodes while maintenance activities are performed. The ability to fail services over to another node in the cluster can be invaluable. In most cases, you can perform comprehensive software or hardware upgrades and routine maintenance without users even knowing about it. The ability of cluster technology to assist with the problem of planned outages is perhaps the most important benefit of clustering available but is used, unfortunately, very infrequently. This benefit alone may be enough to justify an organization's investment in clustering Exchange Server. Clustering does not solve many other problems such as poor training, procedures, many software issues, or major catastrophes. In addition, clustering cannot help when there are infrastructure failures to services that directly support Exchange such as WINS, DNS, Active Directory, or network services. Clustering is not a replacement for sound disaster recovery practices.

Related to the implementation of Microsoft Cluster Service, every cluster is built on servers with shared storage such as shared SCSI or Fibre Channel. Shared storage presents an additional single point of failure that a cluster cannot protect you from. When all nodes in a cluster attach to the shared storage via a single controller installed in the individual node, that controller becomes a single failure point that the cluster cannot tolerate. Technologies such as Switched Fibre Channel and redundant paths can compensate for this by allowing redundant controllers in each cluster node that are attached to a separate switch fabric in the Fibre Channel SAN. Beyond reducing single points of failure and minimizing planned outages, clustering technology may not solve other key issues that cause downtime for our Exchange deployment. Clustering and the technologies it is built upon can add a significant degree of complexity to your environment. As you look further into clustering Exchange Server, it is important that you understand and evaluate whether or not clustering can address your key issues.

7.3   Windows NT/2000 Cluster Technology Fundamentals

Most people were first introduced to cluster technology via Digital Equipment Corporation's (now Compaq) Open VMS Cluster. Also known as a VAXCluster, this technology was introduced around 1984 and revolutionized the way we view computer systems. The VAXCluster (now called an OpenVMS Cluster) provides for a collection of systems to be connected to shared devices, and all systems can read or write to all of the devices. Two key attributes that many are looking for from a clustered environment is performance and scalability. You expect that, after investing extra money on the hardware and software required to support clusters, you will receive some additional performance and scalability benefits such as parallel processing capabilities, I/O shipping, or other techniques that can be gained from a group of systems operating as one. In some environments such as UNIX or OpenVMS, this can be a reality. However, the current truth in the Windows 2000 environment is that cluster services do not afford any of the true performance and scalability benefits you may desire. One benefit that Windows NT/2000 clustering can afford is availability. By allowing for applications and services to have failover and resiliency capabilities, clusters provide increased application availability. For applications like Exchange Server, clustering can provide protection from some specific causes of downtime like hardware failures.

The last thing you may expect cluster technology to provide for your system is increased manageability. Manageability can come in many forms. The most useful benefit for a clustered Exchange Server is the maintenance benefit of being able to move services and resources from one cluster node to another while maintenance operations like firmware, driver, operating system, service pack, and application updates are performed. Once the maintenance operations are complete, services and resources can be moved back to their original cluster node. When you connect a group of systems into a unified system and provide a single system image to clients requesting services, you enable the ability to share the load and the availability of those services across the entire system without the users of these services or even administrative staff having any knowledge of a cluster configuration. When one node experiences a failure, the other nodes can failover services or resources that the node owned. In most cases, this can be totally transparent to the clients. With the introduction of Windows NT Enterprise Edition in 1997, Microsoft included several optional components. Microsoft Cluster Server (MSCS) is one of these components. For Windows 2000, MSCS has been renamed Microsoft Cluster Service, a small but important differentiating detail. The goal of MSCS is to extend the operating system to include high-availability features seamlessly and support application without modification. Microsoft specifically excluded two features from MSCS. First, MSCS is not "lock-step" fault tolerant. This means it does not provide instantaneous "moving" of running applications. Also, applications running on Microsoft Cluster Service are very unlikely to achieve levels such as 99.99999% availability—about 3–4 seconds of downtime per year. Also, MSCS is not able to recover a shared state between client and server. In other words, work in progress during a failure scenario will most likely have to be repeated.

From a foundational architecture point of view, Microsoft Cluster Service is based on a shared-nothing model. In the world of clustering technology, there are two basic programming approaches to resource management—shared-nothing and shared-disk. The cluster architectural programming approach dictates how servers participating in a cluster manage and use both local and cluster devices and resources. A shared-disk implementation allows all cluster participants (nodes) to own and access cluster disk resources. This approach allows all applications running on all nodes to compete and have the same disks available. If two nodes in a shared-disk cluster need to access the same data, the data is either read separately by each node or must be copied from one node to another. Applications running in this model must have a method of synchronizing and serializing access to the shared data to prevent potential conflicts within the system (such as multiple processor access on an SMP system) or across the cluster. Usually, this is accomplished with a service that provides locking of the shared resource—a distributed lock manager. A distributed lock manager will track and provide access to cluster resources for all applications. The distributed lock manager can detect and resolve any conflicts in accessing the data. However, this operation does require additional overhead of system resources on each node in the cluster. In addition, a shared-disk typically requires special hardware configurations or support for multiple hosts to access the same devices. Since Microsoft Cluster Service does not implement the shared-disk approach, we will forgo further discussions on this approach. It is worth noting, however, that there are many advantages and disadvantages to both shared-disk and shared-nothing approaches that could entail quite a lengthy discussion. This is a bit of a "religious" argument, however, and is not germane to our discussion of Microsoft technology.

In the shared-nothing cluster, each server owns and manages local devices as specific cluster resources. Devices that are common to the cluster and physically available to all nodes are owned and managed by only one node at a time. For resources to change ownership, a complex reservation and contention protocol is followed and implemented by cluster services running on each node. Microsoft

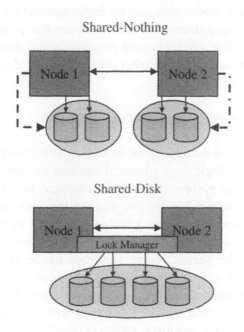

Figure 7.1
*Comparing
shared-nothing
to shared-disk
cluster designs*

Cluster Service is based on the shared-nothing clustering model. The shared-nothing model dictates that, while several nodes in the cluster may have access to a device or resource, the resource is owned and managed by only one system at a time. (In an MSCS cluster, a resource is defined as any physical or logical component that can be brought online and taken offline, managed in a cluster, hosted by only one node at a time, and moved between nodes.)

Each node has its own memory, system disk, operating system, and subset of the cluster's resources. If a node fails, the other node takes ownership of the failed node's resources (this process is known as *failover*). Microsoft Cluster Service then registers the network address for the resource on the new node so that client traffic is routed to the system that is available and now owns the resource. When the failed resource is later brought back online, MSCS can be configured to redistribute resources and client requests appropriately (this process is known as *failback*). Microsoft selected the shared-nothing model because developers felt it provided for easier management of resources and applications utilizing those resources. The shared-nothing model also can be implemented on industry-standard hardware configurations that don't require the proprietary hardware that a shared-disk model would require (again, this could be a point religiously argued by those who prefer the shared-disk approach over shared-nothing).

7.3.1 Resources and Resource Groups

The basic unit of management in a Microsoft cluster is the *resource*. Resources are logical or physical entities or units of management within a cluster system that can be changed in state from online to offline, are manageable by the cluster services, and are owned by one cluster node at a time. Cluster resources include entities such as hardware devices like network interface cards and disks or logical entities like server name, network name, IP address, and services. In a cluster, there are both physical and logical resources typically configured. Within the MSCS framework, resources are grouped into logical units of management and dependency called *resource groups*. A resource group is usually comprised of both logical and physical resources such as virtual server names, IP addresses, and disk resources. Resource groups can also just include cluster-specific resources such as the cluster time service or resources used for managing the cluster itself. The key in the shared-nothing model is that a resource group can only be owned by one node at a time. Furthermore, the resources that are part of the resource group owned by a cluster node must exist on (be owned by) that node.

The shared-nothing model prevents different nodes within the cluster from simultaneous ownership of resource groups or resources within a resource group. As mentioned earlier, resource groups also maintain dependency relationships between different resources contained within each group. This is because resources in a cluster very often depend on the existence of other resources in order to function or start. For example, a virtual server or network name must have a valid IP address in order for clients to access that resource. Therefore, in order for the network name or virtual server to start (or not fail), the IP address it depends on must be available. This is known as *resource dependency*. Within a resource group, the dependencies among resources can be quite simple or very complex. Resource dependencies (as shown later in Figure 7.5) are maintained in the properties of each resource and allow the cluster service to manage how resources are taken offline and brought online. Also, resource dependencies cannot extend beyond the context of the resource group to which they belong. For example, a virtual server cannot have a dependency on an IP address that exists within a resource group other than its own resource group. This restriction is due to the fact that resource groups within a cluster can be brought online and offline and moved from node to node independently of one another. Each resource group also maintains a policy that is available cluster-wide that specifies its preferred cluster node(s) (the node in the cluster it prefers to run on—*Preferred Owners*) and the *Possible Owners* node(s) (the node that it should fail over to in the event of a failure condition). Resource groups are the fundamental unit of management within a Microsoft Windows NT/2000 cluster. As such, it is important that you have a keen understanding of how they function and operate.

Figure 7.2
Basic two-node Microsoft Cluster Service configuration

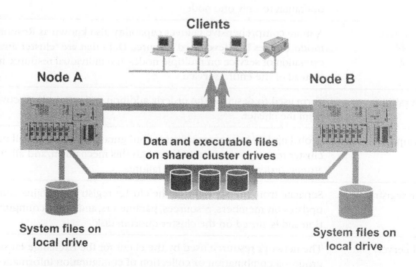

7.3.2   Key Cluster Terminology

There has been much confusion in the world of cluster technology, not just over basic terminologies but also architectural implementations. Table 7.1 highlights some key technology for Microsoft Cluster Service.

Table 7.1 *Microsoft Cluster Service Key Terminology*

Resource	The smallest unit that can be defined, monitored, and maintained by the cluster. Examples are physical disk, IP address, network name, file share, print spool, generic service, and application. Resources are grouped together into a resource group. The cluster uses the state of each resource to determine whether a failover is needed.
Resource group	A collection of interdependent resources that logically represents a client/server function. The smallest unit that can fail over between nodes.
Resource dependency	A resource may depend on other resources. A resource is brought online after any resource that it depends on. A resource is taken offline before any resources it depends on. All dependent resources must fail over together.
Quorum resource	Stores the cluster log data and application data from the registry used to transfer state information between clusters. Used by the cluster service to determine which node can continue running when nodes cannot communicate. Currently, in Windows 2000, the only quorum-capable resource is the physical disk.
Active/Passive	Term used for Service Failover mode in which the service is defined as a resource using the generic resource DLL. Failover Manager limits the application operation to only one node.
Active/Active	A more comprehensive failover capability also known as Resource Failover mode. Utilizes ISV-developed resource DLLs that are "cluster aware." Allows for operation of service on multiple nodes and individual resource instances failover instead of the entire service.
Membership	Term used to describe the orderly addition and removal of active nodes to and from the cluster.
Global update	Global update propagates cluster configuration changes to all members. The cluster registry is maintained through this mechanism, and all activities are atomic, ordered, and tolerant to failures.
Cluster registry	Separate from the NT registry, the cluster registry maintains configuration updates on members, resources, parameters, and other configuration information and is stored on the cluster quorum disk.
Virtual server	The network resource used by the client for the Exchange cluster resource group—a combination or collection of configuration information and resources such as network name and IP address resources. Can refer to an MSCS virtual server or a logical set of services provided by IIS.
Physical machine	The physical hardware device that comprises an individual cluster node. Can host multiple virtual servers and resources.

7.3.3 Microsoft Cluster Service Components

Microsoft Cluster Service is implemented as a set of independent and somewhat isolated components (device drivers and services). This set of components layers on top of the Windows NT/2000 operating system and acts as a service.

Figure 7.3
Microsoft Cluster Service architecture overview

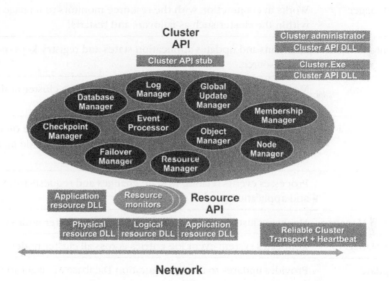

By using this design approach, Microsoft avoided many complexities that may have been encountered in other design approaches such as system scheduling and processing dependencies between the cluster service and the operating system. When layered on Windows NT/2000, Cluster Service provides some basic functions that the operating system needs to support clustering. These basic functions include dynamic network resource support, file system support for disk mounting and unmounting, and shared resource support for the I/O subsystem. Table 7.2 provides a brief overview of each of these components.

Table 7.2   *Microsoft Cluster Service Components*

Component	Role/Function
Node Manager	Maintains resource group ownership of cluster nodes based on resource group node preferences and the availability of cluster nodes.
Resource monitor	Utilizes the cluster resource API and RPCs to maintain communication with the resource DLLs. Each monitor runs as a separate process.
Failover Manager	Works in conjunction with the resource monitors to manage resource functions within the cluster such as failovers and restarts.
Checkpoint Manager	Maintains and updates application states and registry keys on the cluster quorum resource.
Communications Manager	Manages and maintains communication between cluster nodes.
Configuration Database Manager	Maintains and ensures coherency of the cluster database on each cluster node that includes important cluster information such as node membership, resources, resource groups, and resource types.
Event Processor	Processes events relating to state changes and requests from cluster resources and applications.
Membership Manager	Manages cluster node membership and polls cluster nodes to determine state.
Event Log Manager	Replicates system event log entries across all cluster nodes.
Global Update Manager	Provides updates to the Configuration Database Manager to ensure cluster configuration integrity and consistency.
Object Manager	Provides management of all cluster service objects and the interface for cluster administration.
Log Manager	Works with the Checkpoint Manager to ensure that the recovery log on the cluster quorum disk is current and consistent.

7.3.3.1   *The Cluster Service*

The Cluster Service (which is actually a group of subservices consisting of the Event Processor, Failover Manager, Resource Manager, Global Update Manager, and so forth) is the core component of MSCS. The Cluster Service controls cluster activities and performs such tasks as coordinating event notification, facilitating communication between cluster components, handling failover operations, and managing the configuration. Each cluster node runs its own Cluster Service. For discussions pertaining Exchange

Server, there are three key components in Microsoft Cluster Service to consider: the Resource Monitor, the Node Manager, and the Failover Manager.

7.3.3.2   *The Resource Monitor*

The Resource Monitor is an interface between the Cluster Service and the cluster resources, and it runs as an independent process. The Cluster Service uses the Resource Monitor to communicate with the resource DLLs. The DLL handles all communication with the resource, thus shielding the Cluster Service from resources that misbehave or stop functioning. Multiple copies of the Resource Monitor can be running on a single node, thereby providing a means by which unpredictable resources can be isolated from other resources. A resource monitor runs in a process separate from the Cluster Service; this protects the cluster service from resource failures. For Exchange 2000, the default cluster resource monitor process manages each Exchange virtual server running on the cluster. Via EXRES.DLL (the Exchange resource DLL), this resource monitor can communicate with the Exchange service components of the virtual server and can provide application-specific intelligence and instrumentation.

7.3.3.3   *The Resource DLL*

Closely related to our discussion of the Resource Monitor is the resource DLL. The Resource Monitor and resource DLL communicate using the MSCS Cluster Resource API, which is a collection of entry points, callback functions, and related structures and macros used to manage resources. Applications that implement their own resource DLLs to communicate with the Cluster Service and that use the Cluster API to request and update cluster information are defined as *cluster-aware applications*. Applications and services that do not use the Cluster or Resource APIs and cluster control code functions are unaware of clustering and have no knowledge that MSCS is running. These noncluster-aware applications are generally managed as generic applications or services. Both cluster-aware and noncluster-aware applications run on a cluster node and can be managed as cluster resources. However, only cluster-aware applications can take advantage of features offered by Cluster Service through the Cluster API. Cluster-aware applications can report status upon request to the Resource Monitor, respond to requests to be brought online or taken offline gracefully, and respond more accurately to IsAlive and LooksAlive requests issued by the cluster services. Cluster-aware applications should also implement Cluster Administrator extension DLLs, which contain implementations of interfaces from the Cluster Administrator extension API. A Cluster Administrator extension DLL allows an application to be configured into the Cluster Administrator tool (Cluadmin.exe). Implementing custom resource and Cluster Administrator extension DLLs allows for specialized management of the application and its related resources and enables the system administrator to install and configure the application more easily.

As discussed earlier, to the Cluster Service, a resource is any physical or logical component that can be managed. Examples of resources are disks, network names, IP addresses, databases, IIS Web roots, application programs, and any other entity that can be brought online and taken offline. Resources are organized by type. Resource types include physical hardware (such as disk drives) and logical items (such as IP addresses, file shares, and generic applications). Every resource uses a resource DLL, a largely passive translation layer between the Resource Monitor and the resource. The Resource Monitor calls the entry point functions of the resource DLL to check the status of the resource and to bring the resource online and offline. The resource DLL is responsible for communicating with its resource through any convenient IPC mechanism to implement these functions. Applications or services that do not provide their own resource DLLs can still be configured into the cluster environment. MSCS includes a generic resource DLL, and the Cluster Service treats these applications or services as generic, noncluster-aware applications or services. However, if an application or service needs to take full advantage of a clustered environment, it must implement a custom resource DLL that can interact with the Cluster Service and take full advantage of the full set of features provided by Microsoft Cluster Service.

7.3.3.4   The Node Manager

For our discussion of Exchange 2000 clustering, another key component is the Node Manager. The Node Manager runs on each node of the cluster and manages message traffic and heartbeats with other nodes in the cluster. This communication provides detection of node failures and a common view of cluster membership among all nodes in the cluster. When node failures occur, it is the Node Manager that initiates regroup events and determines which node a resource group should be moved to based on the Preferred Owner configuration for each resource group and the Possible Owner configuration for each resource.

7.3.3.5 *The Failover Manager*

The Failover Manager is the final important cluster component for our discussion. It manages the starting and stopping of resources and resource dependencies and works with the Node Manager in the failover of resource groups. The Failover Manager makes the final decisions about which node will own a resource group. All nodes that are capable of owning a resource group will negotiate for ownership. The negotiation process is based on node capabilities, current load, application feedback (if applicable), and the preferred ownership list for the resource group.

When a resource fails, it is up to the Failover Manager to restart it or take the resource offline (along with its dependencies). If Failover Manager takes the resource offline, it will recommend that ownership be changed to another node and restarted—known as failover.

7.3.4   Cluster Failover

With Microsoft Cluster Server, two types of failover are supported: resource failover and service failover. Both allow for increased system availability. More comprehensive in capabilities, the resource failover mode takes advantage of cluster APIs that enable applications to be "cluster aware." This is provided via a resource DLL that can be configured to allow customizable failover of the application. Resource DLLs provide a means for Microsoft Cluster Service to manage resources. They define resource abstractions, interfaces, and management. In a resource failover mode of operation, it is assumed that the service is running on both nodes of the MSCS cluster (also known as "Active/Active") and that a specific resource such as a database, a virtual server, or an IP address fails over—not the entire service. Many applications from independent software vendors (ISUs) as well as those from Microsoft do not have resource DLLs available that enable them to be cluster aware. To offset this,

Microsoft has provided a generic service resource DLL, which provides basic functionality to these applications running on Microsoft Cluster Service. The generic resource DLL provides for the Service Failover mode and limits the application to running on one node only (also known as "Active/Passive"). In a Service Failover mode, a service is defined to MSCS as a resource. Once defined, the MSCS Failover Manager ensures that the service is running on only one node of the cluster at any given time. The service is part of a resource group that uses a common name throughout the cluster. As such, all services running in the resource group are available to any network clients using the common name.

7.3.5   Cluster-Aware vs. Noncluster-Aware Applications

Cluster-aware applications provide the high levels of functionality and availability in a Microsoft Cluster Service environment. The applications and MSCS are aware of each other and can provide feedback that facilitates optimal operation. In this scenario, as much application state as possible is preserved during failover. Examples of cluster-aware applications are Microsoft SQL Server, SAP/R3, Baan, Peoplesoft, Oracle, and Exchange 2000 Enterprise Server. Noncluster-aware applications have several limitations that were discussed previously. The application and the cluster software cannot communicate with each other. Any communication that occurs is limited to that provided by the generic resource DLL provided with MSCS. Examples of noncluster-aware applications are NT file and print services, Microsoft Internet Information Server, and Microsoft Exchange Server 5.5 Enterprise Edition.

7.3.5.1   Active/Active vs. Active/Passive

The discussion on the failover types (service and resource failovers) as well as the differences between cluster-aware and noncluster-aware applications have been oversimplified into two basic terms— Active/Active and Active/Passive. When deploying cluster solutions with Windows NT/2000, the level of functionality and flexibility that an application can enjoy in a clustered environment directly relates to whether it supports Active/Passive or Active/Active configuration. Active/Active means that an application can run on all nodes in the cluster at the same time. This means that the application services are running and servicing users from each node in the cluster. To do this, an application must have support for communicating with the cluster services via its own resource DLL. Also, the application must be architected in such a way that specific resource units can be treated independently and failed over to other nodes. Per previous discussions, this requires specific support from the application vendor (whether Microsoft or third-party vendors) for the application to run in an Active/Active cluster configuration. For Active/Passive configurations, the application is either limited architecturally, has no specific resource DLL support, or both. In an Active/Passive configuration, the application runs on only one cluster node at a time. The application also has no awareness of the cluster software. The cluster software has no application awareness and simply understands that a generic service or group of services and resources must be treated as a failover unit.

Table 7.3 *Comparison of Active/Active and Active/Passive Clustered Applications*

Active/Active	Active/Passive
Services run on all cluster nodes simultaneously.	Services run on only one cluster node at a time.
Application-specific resource DLL	Generic resource DLL
Cluster API aware	No Cluster API awareness
Application-specific detection and failover	No application-specific detection and failover
Resource-level failover	Service-level failover
Extensive failover tuning and configuration	Minimal failover tuning and configuration

7.4   Cluster Support for Exchange 5.5

When Microsoft set out to provide clustering support in Exchange Server 5.5, the development team had two primary goals. First was to increase the availability of Exchange Server by adding clustering support. Second was to provide protection from hardware failures. Distributed processing, load balancing, and data backup were not part of these original goals. As a result, Exchange Server 5.5 provided only basic failover capabilities when paired with Microsoft Cluster Service. Exchange Server 5.5 Enterprise Edition implements support for MSCS using the Service Failover mode described earlier. One generic resource DLL is used for each Exchange service (i.e., Information Store, Directory Service, Message Transfer Agent, and System Attendant). This allows for individual services to be brought down without causing complete failover, and it also isolates services, which helps ease troubleshooting.

Functionality supported within Exchange Server 5.5 in a clustered environment can be classified into two categories: supported services and nonsupported services.

Supported services include those required to provide basic Exchange Server functionality such as the Information Store, Directory Service, Message Transfer Agent, and System Attendant. In addition, the Internet Mail Service and the Internet News Service support clustered functionality (with the exception of the dial-up mode of these services). These supported services provide automatic startup on failover, automatic recovery processing, and global registry updates when moving between cluster nodes. The remaining Exchange Server 5.5 functionality falls into the nonsupported category. The following table lists some of these services and provides known "gotchas" and tips if you desire to use this functionality.

Table 7.4 *Exchange Server 5.5 Enterprise Clustering Nonsupported Components*

Exchange 5.5 Component	Comments/Notes
Connectors	Site (supported) X.400—X.25 (not supported) X.400—TCP/IP (supported with caveats—see the Microsoft Knowledge Base article Q169113) Dynamic RAS (not supported)
MS Mail Connector	Must manually configure using cluster admin
CC:mail Connector	Manual configuration; will appear as offline until PO name is configured
Outlook Web Access (OWA)	Resource group must include Internet Information Server
Key Management Server	Manual restart on failover; manual configuration via cluster admin
Lotus Notes Connector	Not supported

Table 7.4   *Exchange Server 5.5 Enterprise Clustering Nonsupported Components (continued)*

Exchange 5.5 Component	*Comments/Notes*
IBM SNADS and PROFS Connectors	Not supported
Third-party gateways and connectors	Not supported (by Microsoft)

7.5   Cluster Support in Exchange 2000

The goal for Exchange 2000 Enterprise was to build on the initial clustering support provided in Exchange 5.5 Enterprise Edition and provide full application functionality in a clustered environment. Exchange 2000 Server supports Active/Active clustering. When any member resource of a resource group fails on a cluster node, the resource group will be failed over to another node in the cluster that will take over the services being provided by that resource group. One or more Exchange 2000 virtual servers can exist in the cluster, and each virtual server runs on one of the nodes in the cluster. Exchange 2000 can support multiple virtual servers on a single node. From an administrative perspective, all components required to provide services and a unit of failover are grouped (via a cluster resource group) into an Exchange virtual server (EVS) in Exchange 2000. An EVS, at a minimum, will include a storage group and required protocols plus any required cluster resources such as an IP address, network name, or physical disk. From the viewpoint of Microsoft Cluster Service, an Exchange Virtual Server exists as a collection of resources in each cluster resource group. If you have multiple Exchange virtual servers that shared the same physical disk resource (i.e., each has a storage group that resides on the same disk device), they must all exist within the same resource group and cannot be split into separate resource groups. This is done to ensure that the resources and virtual servers all fail over as a single unit, and it is an administrative restriction that ensures that resource group integrity is maintained. Clients connect to the virtual servers the same way they would connect to a standalone server. The cluster service monitors the virtual servers in the cluster. In the event of a failure, the cluster service restarts or moves the affected virtual servers to a healthy node. For planned outages, the administrator can manually move the virtual servers to other nodes. In either event, the client will see an interruption of service only during the brief time that the virtual server is in an online/offline pending state.

7.5.1   Supported Exchange 2000 Components

Clustering support differs according to the component. Not all components of Exchange 2000 are currently supported in a clustered environment. These components are the resources that comprise the resource group for an Exchange 2000 virtual server. The following table details which components are supported and, in some cases, the type of clustering they are capable of supporting:

Table 7.5   *Exchange 2000 Component Cluster Support*

Exchange 2000 Component	Cluster Functionality	Comments
Exchange System Attendant	Active/Active	Each Exchange virtual server is created by the System Attendant resource when configured.
Information Store	Active/Active	Each cluster node is limited to four storage groups (Exchange 2000 RTM Release).
Message Transfer Agent (MTA)	Active/Passive	The MTA will be in only one cluster group. One MTA instance per cluster.
POP3 Protocol	Active/Active	Multiple virtual servers per node.
IMAP Protocol	Active/Active	Multiple virtual servers per node.
SMTP Protocol	Active/Active	Multiple virtual servers per node.
HTTP DAV Protocol	Active/Active	Multiple virtual servers per node.
NNTP Protocol	Active/Active	Multiple virtual servers per node.
MS Search Server	Active/Active	One instance per virtual server
Site Replication Service	Active/Passive	Not supported in a cluster at Exchange 2000 RTM.
MS Mail Connector	Active/Passive	Not supported in a cluster at Exchange 2000 RTM.
cc:Mail Connector	Active/Passive	Not supported in a cluster at Exchange 2000 RTM.
Lotus Notes Connector	Active/Passive	Not supported in a cluster at Exchange 2000 RTM.
Novell GroupWise Connector	Active/Passive	
SNADS Connector	Active/Passive	Not supported in a cluster at Exchange 2000 RTM.

Table 7.5   *Exchange 2000 Component Cluster Support (continued)*

Exchange 2000 Component	Cluster Functionality	Comments
PROFS Connector	Active/Passive	Not supported in a cluster at Exchange 2000 RTM.
Active Directory Connector	Active/Passive	Not supported in a cluster at Exchange 2000 RTM.
Key Management Service	Active/Passive	Not supported in a cluster at Exchange 2000 RTM.
Chat Service/Instant Messaging	Active/Passive	Not supported in a cluster at Exchange 2000 RTM.

Exchange 2000 provides core features and support for Microsoft Cluster Service via two key components, as shown in Figure 7.4. These are the Exchange Cluster Administration DLL and the Exchange resource DLL.

Figure 7.4
*How Exchange
2000 interfaces
with Microsoft
Cluster Service*

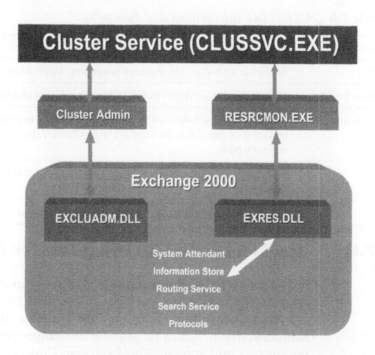

7.5.2   Key Component: Exchange Resource DLL

If you recall the earlier discussion of cluster-aware versus noncluster-aware applications, you'll remember that it is the existence of an application-specific resource DLL that is the key differentiator for cluster-aware applications. Also remember that Exchange 5.5 did not provide its own resource DLL and made use of the generic resource DLL provided with Microsoft Cluster Service. For Exchange 2000, Microsoft developers took the extra time and effort to guarantee full cluster functionality. The result of this effort is the Exchange resource DLL called EXRES.DLL. This DLL for Exchange 2000 is installed when the setup application realizes that it is operating in a clustered environment. EXRES.DLL acts as a direct resource monitor interface between the cluster services and Exchange 2000 by implementing the Microsoft Cluster Service API set. Table 7.6 shows the typical interactions and indications that EXRES.DLL will provide between Exchange resources and cluster services.

Table 7.6   *EXRES.DLL Interactions and Functions*

Interaction/Indicator	*Function*
Online/Offine	Exchange virtual server resource is running, stopped, or in an idle state.
Online/Offline Pending	The process or service is in the state of starting or shutting down.
Looks Alive/Is Alive	Resource polling functions to determine whether resource should be restarted or failed. Can be configured in Cluster Administrator on a per-resource basis.
Failed	The resource failed on the Is Alive call and was not able to be restarted (restart failed).
Restart	Resource has failed on the Is Alive call, and it directed to attempt to restart.

7.5.3   Key Component: Exchange Cluster Admin DLL

In order for Exchange resources to be configured and controlled by the Cluster Administrator, they must enable Exchange Services to communicate with the Cluster Administrator and for the Cluster Administrator program to provide Exchange-specific configuration parameters and screens. The Exchange Cluster Administration DLL (EXCLUADM.DLL), provides this support. The Exchange Cluster

Admin DLL provides the necessary wizard screens when configuring Exchange resources in Cluster Administrator and presents Exchange resources that can be added as resources in the cluster such as the Microsoft Exchange System Attendant. The cluster administration DLL is a key component in configuration and management Exchange services in the cluster. It is not required for resource monitoring and restart or failover actions. The Exchange Resource DLL (EXRES.DLL) performs this role.

7.5.4 Exchange 2000 Cluster Resource Dependencies

Figure 7.5 illustrates a tree structure of Exchange resource dependency. Exchange services must have certain resources as predecessors before they can be brought online as a cluster resource. By default, Exchange 2000 installs nine resources in the form of virtual servers into a cluster resource group that is being configured in the Cluster Administrator. Table 7.7 provides a brief description of each resource and its function.

Figure 7.5
Exchange 2000
Cluster
Resource
Dependencies

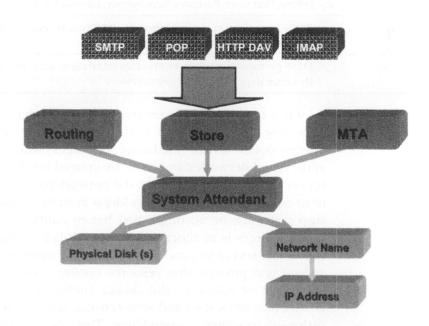

Table 7.7   *Exchange 2000 Default Cluster Resources (Services)*

Resource	Role
System Attendant	Foundation Exchange resource that must exist prior other resources being added to the cluster. Resource dependency: Network Name, Physical Disk
Information Store	Virtual server instance for the STORE.EXE process and its presentation to MAPI clients and other services. Resource dependency: System Attendant
Routing Service	Exchange 2000 Routing Service virtual server instance. Resource dependency: System Attendant
MTA Service	Message Transfer Agent virtual server. Exists only on one cluster node (Active/Passive). Provided for legacy messaging connector support and routing to Exchange 5.5 environments. Resource dependency: System Attendant
MS Search Service	Microsoft Search Engine virtual server instance. Provides Exchange content indexing service for clients. Resource dependency: Information Store
SMTP Service	SMTP virtual server instance. Provides Internet protocol client sendmail functionality and message routing. Resource dependency: Information Store
DAV Service	HTTP-DAV protocol virtual server. Provides Web/browser-based client access to information store. Resource dependency: Information Store
POP3 Service	POP3 protocol virtual server. Provides POP3 client access to information store. Resource dependency: Information Store
IMAP Service	IMAP protocol virtual server. Provides IMAP client access to information store. Resource dependency: Information Store

When configuring cluster resources for Exchange, four prerequisites must be satisfied. First, Exchange 2000 must be installed on the cluster nodes where Exchange resources will run. Next, an IP address and network name must be created for the Exchange virtual server being configured. Since the network name resource is dependent on the IP address, the IP address must be created first. The final step that must be accomplished before configuring Exchange-specific resources is to allocate the physical disk resources required by the virtual server you are configuring. At a minimum, there must be at least one physical disk resource configured for Exchange virtual servers to be added to the cluster configuration. When Exchange cluster resources start and stop (change states), they must do so in order of resource dependency. This means that, on startup, resources start in forward order of resource dependence (bottom to top in Figure 7.5). When resources are stopped (or a resource group is taken offline), resources are shut down in reverse order of dependence (top to bottom in Figure 7.5). When configuring cluster resources, having a firm grasp on the resource dependencies for Exchange 2000 clustering makes the task much simpler.

7.5.5 Exchange Virtual Servers: The Unit of Failover

The key unit of cluster management and failover is the virtual server. Virtual servers exist for several different Exchange 2000 services (as shown in Table 7.7). The virtual server is the mechanism by which clients, resources, and other services access individual Exchange services within the cluster. In Exchange 2000, there are virtual servers for the Internet clients (SMTP, IMAP, POP3, and HTTP-DAV), the Information Store (for MAPI clients), the MTA service (only configured in the first Exchange virtual server configured in the cluster), and the Microsoft Search Service. The virtual server takes on the name property of the network name resource that is configured prior to configuring Exchange resources. For example, if you configure the network name resource as "EXVS1," each Exchange virtual server resource configured in the cluster resource group for that virtual server will respond to that virtual server name when used by clients and other services and resources.

Figure 7.6
Configured
Exchange
virtual server
in Cluster
Administrator

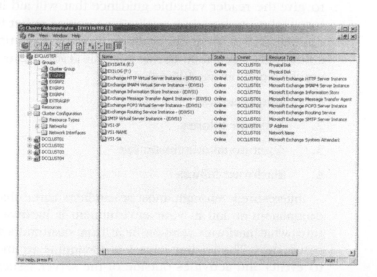

Since the virtual server is the unit of failover, Exchange 2000 virtual server resources will all fail over in the cluster as a managed unit. This means that the entire cluster resource group containing the virtual server resources will be failed over together from one node in the cluster to another. One or more Exchange information storage groups can be configured as part of an Exchange 2000 virtual server. However, a storage group can only belong to one virtual server. The virtual server is the key unit of client access, cluster management, and failover for Exchange 2000 services running in a clustered environment. When deploying Exchange 2000 clusters, ensure that you familiarize yourself with virtual servers and how they are used.

7.6   Decision Points for Deploying Exchange Clusters

When deciding whether to invest in a clustered Exchange Server environment, several issues must be considered and weighed in order to provide a return on investment (ROI) justification. Each organization will need to identify and analyze these issues introspectively. This section provides some decision points and questions an organization should consider before choosing to deploy Microsoft Exchange 2000 Server in a clustered environment. The intention is to give the reader valuable guidance that will aid in selecting clustered solutions based on qualitative thinking rather than technical or marketing hype. First, the leading causes of downtime must be considered. Most research shows that the leading causes of downtime can be ranked in the following order:

1.   Infrastructure

2.   Software failures

3.   Operational/administrative

4.   Hardware failures

Interestingly enough, most researchers agree that the least likely component to fail in your environment is hardware. This corroborates what hardware vendors hear from customers and from service return rates. The leading causes of downtime are more often related to events and activities outside of the server. Issues such as poorly trained personnel, building outages (power or air conditioning), or flawed backup and restore procedures typically account for more downtime than events such as hard-drive failures. In addition, software failures caused by the interaction of the operating system with third-party tools or drivers are often the downtime culprits as well. Regardless of what research indicates, it is important for each organization to determine the leading causes of down time on an organizational basis. It is important that this information be related to the actual causes of downtime for the Exchange Server environment. With this information in hand, we can step through several key decision points that will assist you in determining whether deploying Exchange Server clusters is right for your organization.

What are our availability requirements for Exchange Server?

Many organizations can tolerate hours or even days of downtime for their messaging and collaboration environment. Others need 99.999% availability. Since Microsoft Cluster Service can typically provide a maximum of 99.99% reliability (theoretically speaking), organizations requiring a higher degree of availability may find that their requirements cannot be met within the limits of current technology. The bottom line is that 99.999% availability is not a reality that is easy to achieve for Exchange Server deployments today.

Can we resolve most of our downtime issues by investment in other areas?

Hardware vendors provide many hardware technologies, such as RAID disk arrays and redundant power supplies and fans, that are either standard or optional across the entire server product line. However, many customers choose not to invest in or implement these features. The high-availability requirements of your organization may be attainable via investment in off-the-shelf technologies available from your server hardware vendor. Illustrating this point further, you may also choose to invest in personnel training or procedural redesign to alleviate problems in these areas that are causing down time. Looking to make investments in other areas may give you the opportunity to focus on the real issues for your deployment rather than simply throwing technology (i.e., clustering) at your downtime issues.

Does clustering solve our leading causes of downtime?

After evaluating the leading causes of downtime in your Exchange Server environment, you must determine whether the implementation of clustering would address these issues. The design goals for clustering support in Microsoft Exchange Server include protection from hardware failure and increased availability. If your organization's leading downtime causes are in areas such as operational/administrative, software failures, or infrastructure causes, investment in clustering technology may not reduce downtime. Exchange Server clustering can only protect you from issues such as hardware failures or localized outages and software errors (issues that would only affect the primary node in the cluster). As research indicates, hardware failures are often the least frequent cause of downtime. For example, if you choose to implement clustering as a means of protecting against all software failures, you are likely to be disappointed.

What is the effect of the increased levels of complexity that clustering introduces?

Since Microsoft Cluster Service is an additional software component and the additional hardware configuration issues create higher levels of complexity, can your operational staff tolerate the increased complexity, training requirements, and frustration factor? To administer a cluster, operators must be familiar with clustering concepts and learn to use the MSCS Cluster Administrator utility. In addition, procedures for failover and failback operations will also need to be developed. Clearly, Exchange Server is already a very complex environment. The question is whether your organization wants to increase that complexity by adding clustering to the equation.

Is the investment in clustering justified by the ROI?

This is the question that it all comes down to. After considering all the issues, most organizations have to answer this important question. Many organizations will decide that their messaging and collaboration environment is mission-critical in nature and warrants the utmost investment in every capability available to increase availability. Others will decide that investments in other areas make more sense. It really comes down to whether the additional availability achieved through clustering Exchange Server can be justified in your organization.

These decision points are only a beginning. Each organization should evaluate the question of high availability for Exchange Server based on organizational requirements and service-level agreements (SLAs) for its user/customer base. The issue is not whether clustering is good or bad technology but whether clustering addresses the leading causes of downtime within a particular organization. Selecting clustering technology with the assumption that it will solve all your downtime issues (including those not related to hardware failures) will only lead to disappointment based on false expectations.

7.7   Deploying Exchange 2000 Clusters

7.7.1   Storage Design Is the Key

One of the most challenging but most important parts of deploying Exchange 2000 clusters is storage planning. With Exchange Server 5.5 clusters, only one virtual server technically existed in the cluster, and storage allocation from the shared cluster storage was simplified. With Exchange 2000 Server, the support of multiple virtual servers and storage groups per node significantly complicates cluster deployment and management. Regardless of this challenge, storage design must be done right the first time for a successful implementation. The success and popularity of storage area network (SAN) technology as a shared storage mechanism for Windows 2000 Cluster Server will facilitate more learning and a faster progression on the learning curve of storage design and allocation in a clustered environment. When planning your deployment of Exchange 2000 in a cluster, ensure that you are familiar with the setup and configuration of SAN technology in a cluster as well as SAN features and options such as data replication and business continuance volumes.

When configuring Exchange 2000 in a clustered environment, you need to carefully plan the volumes you want to share between the member nodes in the cluster. In fact, "share" is not the most appropriate word because Microsoft clustering for Windows 2000 works in a shared-nothing model. This simply means that a volume can be owned, and therefore accessed, by only one member of the cluster at any point in time. The first step is to take a "backwards" approach to the hardware design and setup for a cluster. Start with the Exchange configuration and work backwards. For example, if you plan on deploying a four-node cluster (supported in a later release of Windows 2000) running Exchange 2000 Enterprise Server, decide the user-load requirements for the entire cluster first. As an example, suppose you want to support 10,000 users on a four-node Exchange 2000 cluster. Evenly dividing these users across the cluster would yield 2,500 users per node. You could then design each cluster node to meet the performance and scalability requirement for 2,500 users. The next step would be to determine the failover scenarios required by the user and cluster configuration. At initial release, Exchange 2000 will limit the number of storage groups per server to four. This means that each cluster node can never have more than four Exchange storage groups running on it at any time. This limit is particularly important in a cluster failover condition. If a failure has occurred and an Exchange virtual server has moved to another node, the total number of storage groups is still limited to four. Hopefully, this limitation will be removed in a later release of Exchange 2000 when technologies like 64-bit memory addressing are available. In the meantime, clusters must be designed with this limitation in mind. For our 10,000 user/four-node cluster example, failover rules must be configured in a manner that prevents any single node from exceeding the maximum four storage groups per node limitation.

Figure 7.7
Exchange 2000's multiple storage group and database architecture

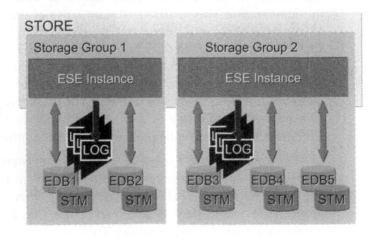

Once you have considered the per-node storage group limitations, you can determine how many users per storage group will be configured. Again, since one Exchange virtual server can contain multiple storage groups, care must be taken to ensure that the four-per-node rule is not exceeded during both normal and failover conditions. In the 10,000-user cluster example, let's keep it simple and plan for one virtual server per node and one storage group per virtual server (a ratio of 1:1). This means that one Exchange virtual server and a single storage group would service all 2,500 users on each node. Continuing to work backward, we can now begin to plan storage requirements and configuration for each cluster node. Using well-known best practices for maximizing disk I/O is the best approach here. The rule of thumb is to separate sequential from random I/O. An Exchange 2000 database actually consists of two files—the properties store (*.EDB) and the streaming store (*.STM). The properties store is a B-Tree database structured file that is accessed in a random I/O fashion. The streaming store is structured in clusters of 64KB runs and is typically accessed in a random manner. In addition, these files have different access characteristics depending on the type of clients that will be supported. For MAPI protocol clients, the streaming store is not utilized. For Internet protocol clients (such as IMAP, POP3, HTTP, and SMTP), the streaming store is the primary storage location with certain properties being stored in the properties store. Each Exchange storage group has one set of shared database transaction logs and can be configured with multiple database files (an *.EDB and *.STM pairing). Using our rule of thumb, each storage group should have a dedicated disk volume (preferable RAID1 or 0+1) in which to store the transaction log files (*.LOG) since they are accessed in a strictly sequential manner. Depending on the clients supported, you may also choose to separate the streaming store and the property store onto separate physical volumes as well. However, based on the cost-effectiveness of such a configuration, most deployments will typically choose to place both the property and the streaming store on the same volume (configured as RAID5 or 0+1 for maximum performance and data protection). Table 7.8 identifies each Exchange database component and the best practices that should be followed for optimal design.

Table 7.8   *Exchange 2000 Database Component Design Practices*

Database Component	Storage Design Best Practices
Storage group transaction logs	Sequential I/O: Dedicate a RAID1 or 0+1 array to each storage group for transaction logs.
Property store (*.EDB)	Random I/O (4KB): Dedicate a RAID1, 0+1, or 5 array to each storage group for the property store. Can be combined with streaming store if no or few Internet protocol clients are supported. For MAPI clients, combine with streaming store. For heavy I/O environments, a separate array for each property store in a storage group (up to five databases can be configured) may be necessary.
Streaming store (*.STM)	Mostly large (32KB) random I/O: Dedicate a RAID1, 0+1, or 5 array to each storage group for the streaming store. Can be combined with the properties store if no or few Internet protocol clients are supported. For MAPI clients, combine with property store. For Internet protocol clients in heavy I/O environments, a separate array for each streaming store in a storage group may be necessary. However, this may double storage requirements in a cluster.

When you have determined the number of users per node, the number of virtual servers per node, and the number of storage groups per virtual server, you can begin to design your cluster shared storage configuration using the storage design best practices, and the recommendations previously discussed. In Figures 7.8 and 7.9, respectively, consider two sample cluster designs based on our earlier example of a 10,000-user, four-node cluster and a 2,000 user, two-node cluster. These are only examples you will need to determine actual design for your deployment based on many factors.

NOTE: Upon initial release, Exchange 2000 Enterprise Server will only support a two-node cluster using Windows 2000 Advanced Server. Official support for four-node clustering with Windows 2000 will be added at a later time.

7.7.2   Windows 2000 Clustering Installation Requirements

Microsoft Windows 2000 does not provide a brand-new version of the clustering software, only an update to the Microsoft Cluster Server that shipped with Windows NT 4.0 Enterprise. In order to set up a cluster, you need to run the Windows 2000 Advanced Server

Figure 7.8
Example Exchange 2000 four-node cluster configuration for 10,000 users

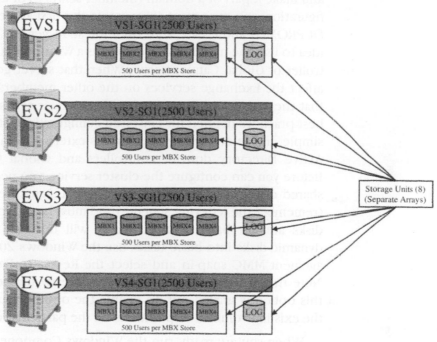

10,000-User, 4-Node Cluster Configuration

Figure 7.9
Example Exchange 2000 two-node cluster configuration for 2,000 users

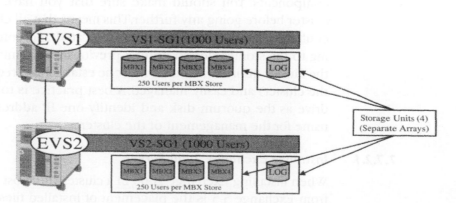

2,000-User, 2-Node Cluster Configuration

(two-node cluster) or Windows 2000 Data Center (four-node cluster) on all member servers. You need to install the first cluster member and make it part of a domain (member server). For a simple test configuration, you may want to promote the first node to a DC (using DCPROMO) and create your own forest. In general, it is not a good idea to use one member of a cluster as a Windows 2000 domain controller or Global Catalog server. When that server goes down, it can affect the Exchange services on the other members due to the fact that the Active Directory service is no longer available. The general best practices defined for clustered configurations still apply: keep it simple, and select one or two servers external to the cluster for the Active Directory domain controllers and Global Catalog servers. Before you can configure the cluster service, you need to enable the shared disk drives. The disks must have a signature and a partition (remember the lettering scheme) and must be of type "basic." If your disks are not basic, Cluster Server will not use them. To revert dynamic disks into basic disks, use the Windows 2000 storage management MMC snap-in and select the Revert to Basic disk option. Note that, if a partition or volume is already defined on the drive, this option is grayed out. To enable the option, you must wipe out the existing volumes or partitions on the particular disk.

When you are ready, run the Windows Component configuration to enable the cluster service to run on each of the cluster members. You will notice that the Cluster Administrator interface looks like that of Windows NT Enterprise version 4.0—it does not use MMC as the management console as is the case with most Windows 2000 components. You should make sure that you have an operational cluster before going any further. This means that all cluster nodes are configured and disk resources are allocated and configured according to the storage design criteria previously determined. In addition the cluster quorum resource must be established (required to create the cluster) and easily managed. A best practice is to identify the Q: drive as the quorum disk and identify one IP address and network name for the management of the cluster.

7.7.2.1   *Installing Exchange 2000 Server*

When installing Exchange 2000 in a cluster, the most notable change from Exchange 5.5 is the placement of installed files. It is no longer necessary to define a cluster group or to place files on a shared cluster disk. The reason is quite simple: Now that Exchange can run in active/active mode on all members of a cluster, it is necessary for each server in the cluster to have a local copy of the binary files. During installation, Exchange 2000 will discover the cluster configuration and proceed to install a "cluster-aware" version of the product on each cluster node locally.

Figure 7.10
Exchange 2000
setup senses
cluster
installation

Apart from this dialog box (to which you must agree), the installation proceeds as a normal installation and includes the schema update to the Active Directory, if this has not been done already (recommended). After that, you can install Exchange on the subsequent members of the cluster. As much as possible, you should attempt to select the same options that you used for the first member installation. Again, you will be forced by the setup program to install on the local system drive. During the installation, the Exchange setup will recognize the cluster configuration and the fact that the organization already exists. Do not attempt to run several installations at the same time. After the installation of Exchange 2000 on the cluster node is complete, the cluster node must be restarted before proceeding.

7.7.2.2   Creating Exchange 2000 Virtual Servers

Step 1: Creating the Exchange Resource Group

Before you can use the Exchange System Manager interface, you need to create a group that contains a minimum of:

- One IP Address.

- One network name. This is the name under which the Exchange Server will appear in the Exchange 2000 Organization.

- One or more disk resources that will be used to store transaction logs, databases, and temporary files.

- The Exchange System Attendant resource: In fact, adding the System Attendant resource will result in the creation of all the other resources need for an Exchange 2000 virtual server. These resources will be created by the Exchange Cluster Admin component (EXCLUADM.DLL) using Cluster Administrator.

Step 2: Adding the System Attendant Resource

It is imperative to create the System Attendant resource in order to get Exchange 2000 running in a cluster. You will be prompted for the resource dependencies of the System Attendant (the network name and any physical disk resources you desire the Exchange virtual server to utilize). In addition, the path of the data directory will also be required. Initially, the default drive and directory can be selected and changes can be made later to reflect the actual physical volumes on which transaction logs and database files will reside. Most important, all disk resources that the virtual server will utilize must be included as resource dependencies during creation of the System Attendant resource. Next, if more than one exists, you will be prompted for the administrative group and the routing group where the Exchange virtual server (named after the network name resource of the Exchange group) will belong.

Figure 7.11
Resource dependencies when adding the System Attendant resource

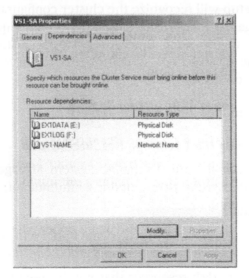

The Cluster Administrator will then proceed to create the rest of the Exchange resources and put them into the Exchange resource group. Once resources are created, you can bring the entire resource group online and thereby make the Exchange virtual server available to client. From this point on, you can use the Exchange System Manager MMC snap-into manage the Exchange virtual servers in the cluster. Using the Exchange System Manager interface, you should be able to view the Exchange virtual server and note that the default databases have been created on the common volume. You can then modify the configuration for the location of the storage group transaction logs or database files as necessary. Remember, only the physical disk volumes that were included as resource dependencies for the virtual server (at creation time) will be available for use. As with Exchange 5.5 clusters, you should not attempt to stop, pause, or start the services other than through the Cluster Administrator. Do not use the Services Control Panel, the Exchange System Manager, or the command-line interface. When connecting, clients (whether MAPI or Internet protocol–based) will be able to use the virtual server name when configuring the server option.

Figure 7.12
Exchange System Manager view of virtual servers

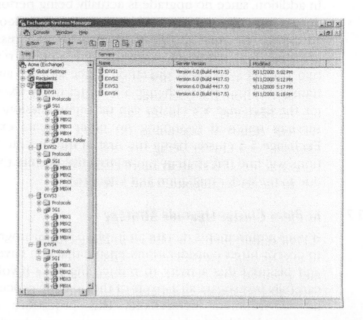

7.7.3   Migrating From Exchange 5.5 Clusters

If you have deployed Exchange 5.5 clusters and you want to be able to perform an in-place upgrade of your cluster configuration, Microsoft has provided a procedure to accomplish this. This procedure is discussed in the following sections. In some cases, such as hardware replacement and upgrade, you may not want to perform an in-place upgrade. For most scenarios, I recommend the mailbox-relocation strategy.

7.7.3.1   *Mailbox-Relocation Strategy*

With this strategy, an Exchange 2000 cluster is added to the same site as an existing Exchange 5.5 cluster. Since site replication services (SRS), which are required for an Exchange 2000 server to interact in an Exchange 5.5 site, are not supported, another Exchange 2000 server must already exist in the Exchange 5.5 site. After this is accomplished, user mailboxes and public information stores are moved from the Exchange 5.5 cluster to the Exchange 2000 cluster. This can be accomplished directly via the Exchange Administrator program (Move Mailbox) or via tools such as ExMerge. This strategy is preferable since it allows a phased or gradual migration from the Exchange 5.5 cluster environment to the Exchange 2000 cluster environment. In addition, since no upgrade is actually being performed, the procedure is less risky and requires a less complex "back-out" plan. The disadvantage to this approach is that it requires the additional investment of hardware, software, and support resources to have two parallel systems in operation. Once all user and public data is transferred from the Exchange 5.5 cluster to the Exchange 2000 cluster, the Exchange 5.5 cluster can be decommissioned and Exchange services removed (assuming no other caveats exist such as the Exchange 5.5 cluster being the first in the site, etc.). Most organizations will find this strategy more attractive despite the additional cost due to the easier migration and lower risk.

7.7.3.2   *In-Place Cluster Upgrade Strategy*

If your requirements dictate an in-place cluster upgrade strategy due to cost or other considerations, ensure that you have properly tested and planned this activity to reduce the risks involved. You should carefully investigate all aspects of the upgrade process and test it in a lab environment beforehand. This procedure should not be attempted without adequate preparation and the development of a back-out plan. The back-out plan will ensure that you can return the cluster to operational status without loss of user data in the event that the procedure fails.

When you perform an in-place upgrade of an Exchange 5.5 cluster to an Exchange 2000 cluster, the Exchange 5.5 system files are removed from the local drive, and then the Exchange 2000 system files are installed on the local drive. Exchange points to the existing user data that is preserved on the shared storage resource. When Exchange 2000 is in a clustered environment, it may coexist with earlier versions of Exchange as long as the two following conditions are met:

- The Exchange cluster is not the first Exchange 2000 instance within an Exchange 5.5 site.

- The Exchange cluster does not serve as a bridgehead to an Exchange 5.5 site.

Therefore, for every Exchange 5.5 cluster in a different site, before you upgrade the cluster, you must first join a nonclustered Exchange 2000 instance to the site.

Before upgrading the Exchange 5.5 cluster to Exchange 2000, Windows NT Enterprise 4.0 must be upgraded to Windows 2000 Cluster Server (either Advanced Server or Data Center Edition). For information about upgrading Windows NT 4.0 Cluster Service, see the Windows 2000 Advanced Server documentation. In addition, the Windows 2000 cluster nodes must be members of a Windows 2000 domain. This procedure also assumes that you have run the Active Directory Connector to populate Active Directory with the Exchange 5.5 mailbox information. Finally, it is recommended that Exchange 5.5 be running Service Pack 3 (SP3) before attempting this procedure.

The following nine-step procedure is taken from the Exchange 2000 documentation. Ensure that you have tested this procedure in a nonproduction environment before attempting to upgrade your production deployment.

To upgrade an Exchange Server 5.5 cluster:

1.   Back up all user and configuration data on the cluster. It is recommended that you perform this backup as an offline backup that includes the system state to ensure the ability to back out of this procedure.

2.   In Cluster Administrator, take the Exchange 5.5 cluster group offline.

3.   Go to the shared cluster drive holding Exchange data (EXCHSRVRmdbdata) and rename the mdbdata directory. If you do not rename this directory, the directory will be removed in Step 4.

4.   Remove Exchange 5.5 Server from both nodes by running Exchange 5.5 Setup and selecting Remove all on the Installation Options screen. This removes the Exchange 5.5 binaries. For more information about removing Exchange 5.5 Server, see the Exchange 5.5 documentation.

NOTE: If you are using the Active Directory Connector (ADC) as part of your migration process and have any connection agreements (CAs) pointing to the Exchange 5.5 cluster, these CAs must be deleted before proceeding.

---

5.   Go to the shared cluster drive and directory from Step 3 and rename the directory back to mdbdata.

6.   Install Exchange 2000 on both nodes of the cluster. After you finish installing a node, restart the node. Do not restart both nodes at the same time.

7.   Create a resource group (virtual server) in the same cluster group that the Exchange 5.5 virtual server was in, but do not bring the group online. For more information about creating resource groups, see the earlier section in this chapter.

8.   Go to the shared cluster drive and directory from Step 5. In the mdbdata directory, delete all the files except for Priv.edb and Pub.edb. Next, rename these files Priv1.edb and Pub1.edb, respectively.

9.   In Cluster Administrator, right-click the resource group and click Bring Online. The Exchange 2000 services will be started and the virtual server brought online. Once the virtual server is online, the database files will be converted as in the case of an in-place upgrade for a standalone Exchange 5.5 server. Note that since the streaming store (*.STM file) will not exist, it will be created during the conversion process.

7.7.4 Exchange 2000 Cluster Administration and Management Considerations

The important questions that get asked when deploying Exchange 2000 in a clustered configuration center around whether the Exchange administrator experience will be the same in a clustered environment as in standalone Exchange 2000. Administrators are justifiably concerned about the administrative and operational aspects of Exchange in a cluster. Realizing this concern, Microsoft designed Exchange 2000 clustering to have minimal administration and management differences as compared to a nonclustered configuration. The goal was to make management of Exchange 2000 in a cluster no different. With Exchange 2000's dependence on the Windows 2000 Active Directory, it is easier to accomplish this task. The administrative differences that are necessary become fairly intuitive to system managers. Roles such as adding and deleting users, managing storage, and other administrative tasks are no different in a clustered environment. Permissions, rights, etc., are also no different for cluster Exchange 2000. Disaster recovery for clusters, while leveraging the same mechanisms as nonclustered servers, requires some additional measures discussed in a later section. The major differences in managing Exchange 2000 in a cluster have to do with the cluster resource management of Exchange services running in the cluster. Cluster administration of resources does require some learning curve to successfully manage any application in a cluster. Prior to deploying Exchange 2000 clusters, you should ensure that your operations and system management staff understand the idiosyncrasies of Windows 2000 clusters and services. Also, clustering tends to complicate in direct proportion to the number of cluster nodes. Windows 2000 Advanced Server will support up to two nodes in a cluster, and Data Center Edition will support four nodes and beyond. At initial release, Exchange 2000 will not support more than two-node clusters. When Windows 2000 Data Center Edition is released at a later time, Exchange 2000 will support four-node clusters. When more than two cluster nodes are supported, the complexities of managing Exchange 2000 clusters will multiply. Specifically, managing, allocating shared storage, and planning for failover scenarios of four-node clusters will be most challenging. You can cope with this challenge and complexity with a thorough understanding Windows 2000 clustering, Exchange 2000 cluster planning, and advance testing and piloting of Exchange cluster before putting it into production use.

Management of the Exchange 2000 virtual servers is achieved via the Exchange System Manager Microsoft Management Console (MMC) snap-in. When opening the snap-in, virtual servers will appear the same as standalone servers. You can then create additional storage groups or databases by directly managing the virtual servers via the Exchange System Manager (ESM). Each of these virtual servers can run on each member of the cluster on which it has been authorized. Don't forget the per-node storage group limitations. By default, a single storage group is created for each virtual server, called "First Storage Group." Also, one mailbox store is created for each virtual server. One public store per cluster (created in the first Exchange virtual server configured in the cluster) is also created by default. Each storage group's databases, temporary files, and transaction logs are located on the disk resource configured at virtual server creation. As mentioned previously, the locations of all database files can be changed via ESM.

7.7.5   Exchange Cluster Load Planning

There are three basic strategies for load planning: Maximum Load—All Nodes, Maximum Load—Standby Node, and Balanced Cluster Loading. The strategy you choose depends, in part, on the role you are expecting the cluster servers to provide. For example, if you are setting up a cluster only to have a mechanism for planned outages, you may select a different strategy than if you want optimal performance in the event of an unexpected failure. In either case, you must plan intelligently to ensure that unplanned outages do not compound disaster by overworking your hardware. Your load-balancing strategy might also consider administrative overhead, hardware resources, and which Exchange components you want to host in a clustered environment. Depending on your needs, you can run Exchange clusters at varying loads. A *load* is the computing burden a system carries. Your server's optimal load depends on the elements that determine server performance: processor speed, RAM, disk-access speed, and so on. For cluster capacity planning, percentages are expressed relative to the load at which you achieve optimal performance from your hardware. In reality, your optimal load may use only 80% of the computing resources of your hardware. You should always plan to have spare resources available and never configure your hardware to run at 100% utilization for normal operation. There is not adequate "headroom" available, and cluster failures may result.

7.7.5.1 Maximum Load—All Cluster Nodes

You can configure a cluster to run a maximum load on both nodes of the cluster. On failover, the remaining active nodes would then be required to run at a higher load and suffer a decrease in performance. As an example, a two-node cluster supporting 2,000 users (1,000 per node) runs at 50% CPU operation under normal conditions. However, after a failover occurs, the remaining node will be running at near 100% CPU utilization and may result in slower (either perceived or real) response time for users. Configuring for a full load on both nodes is a good strategy if you have planned outages for updating and maintaining server software and hardware. Under these circumstances, you can choose to manually failover when there is little activity on your system. This strategy does not protect against unplanned outages. Failover when there is much activity may cause remaining servers to run at excessive loads and possibly fail. From an administrative perspective, this configuration is relatively simple to configure and manage, but in the unplanned outage, as the load increases on the remaining servers after a failover, the administrative costs increase.

7.7.5.2 Maximum Load—Standby Node

Also called N+1 Failover, this is the failover mechanism you would have used with Exchange 5.5 clustering since only an Active/Passive scenario was supported. As was the case with Exchange 5.5, you are able to run other applications such as file and print or Microsoft SQL Server on the idle cluster node. However, for simplicity's sake, you should not run other applications on the standby node. With this strategy, you configure a cluster with one node running at 80 % of the full load and one node is idle. On failover, the idle node assumes the load from the failed-over node and runs at the same load. This strategy sets the node preference list for all nodes to identify the standby node as the second in the preference list (the primary node is first) in the preference list for the resource group. Standby nodes are usually performing little or no work and can easily manage the additional load required upon failover.

7.7.5.3   *Balanced Cluster Loading*

With this strategy (available in two variants: cascading and distributed failover), you run nodes at a level such that remaining nodes in the cluster will always run at a maximum of optimal load after failover. With this strategy, a resource group may survive multiple node failures, each time cascading or failing over to the next node in its preference list. As an example, each node in a two-node cluster runs at 50% of optimal load so that, on failover, the remaining node runs at a full load. In a four-node cluster example, each node would be configured to run at approximately 25% utilization. This would ensure that even with the failure of three of the four cluster nodes, the remaining node would still be able to support the load with no perceptible performance degradation. Obviously, this is highly dependent on the number of virtual servers per cluster node and the number of storage groups configured per Exchange virtual server. As stated earlier, there can never be more that four storage groups running on any single cluster node. While this limit may change with later releases of Exchange 2000 and Windows 2000, it is best to plan for this limitation in your deployment. While this balanced-load approach may yield the optimal use of cluster resources, it is also complex to configure and manage. Careful performance analysis and capacity planning must be done as a prerequisite for this strategy to be successful. In addition, the cluster failover over parameters such as Preferred Node, Possible Nodes, and failover timings must be tediously configured. This strategy is safe in most cases, although it's more complex to configure. The additional administrative cost provides high availability and efficient use of hardware that may provide the best return on investment of all the strategies discussed. If you consider this strategy for your deployment, carefully consider all the issues and caveats before proceeding.

7.7.6   Disaster Recovery Considerations for Exchange Server Clusters

A solid and consistent tape-backup strategy should be an integral part of your high-availability strategy for deploying Exchange Server. In a cluster environment, there are additional cluster-specific configuration issues that should be addressed to help you choose the method that best suits your high-availability requirements. For example, backup of an Exchange virtual server on a cluster cannot be resumed "midstream" after a failover. Most of these issues result from noncluster-aware tape backup software and also relate to performing automated, scheduled backups. Since the recommended method for Exchange Server backup and restore is online (the backup software communicates with the information store via an API), disaster recovery scenarios for Exchange Server clusters can be more complex than standalone Exchange servers. In addition, whether the server is local or remote to the backup device and backup software can add other complexities to clustered Exchange Server environments. One scenario would be to provide the capability for both cluster nodes to perform local backup and restore operations. In this case, a backup device and software tool is installed on each cluster node. The benefit of this strategy is that backup performance is increased because the backup device is in the same server as the disks. In this scenario, whichever server is currently running the Exchange services can be backed up with a local agent or backup software tool such as NT Backup. However, since the backup software may not be cluster aware, errors will occur if the backup software attempts to back up an information store that is not on the local server (depending on which cluster node Exchange Server is currently running). Conversely, the backup software may not be configured to back up an information store that has been failed over from the other cluster node, resulting in a missed backup opportunity.

The other scenario is a LAN-based backup strategy. Here, the information store from the Exchange server in the cluster is backed up over the network via a backup agent (provided by the backup software vendor). The obvious drawback to this method is that performance may suffer due to the slower throughput capabilities of the network. The backup server could be one of the servers in the cluster, or it could be a separate server that accesses the cluster over the client LAN or dedicated disaster recovery LAN. If the backup server were not a member of the cluster, a failure of this server would cause all data backup from the cluster to fail. In addition, since the remote backup software tool does not have knowledge of which node Exchange services are running on, the backup could fail because the target information store was not available. If the server in the cluster being backed up fails, the tape backup software temporarily halts. However, because the autoreconnect feature to the backup agent may vary by vendor, the backup software may or may not be able to reconnect and continue with the backup of the Exchange Server information store once the cluster failover is complete. If the tape backup software is running on a cluster member and that server fails, the backup software agent may be able to be configured as a cluster group to failover to the other server. This presents problems that cannot be overcome by noncluster-aware tape software. Since the backup software is unaware of the cluster, the only behavior that can be configured after a failure is for the backup software to switch to the partner server and restart the backup from the beginning. One of the drawbacks of nonclusteraware tape software is that, if it is halted during a backup, it does not typically keep a log that can be used to restart the backup procedure in the middle of the backup, only from the very beginning. In order to provide the best disaster recovery scenario for Exchange Server on MSCS, consult with your backup software vendor regarding support for Microsoft Cluster Server and Exchange 2000.

7.7.7   Best Practices/Recommendations for Exchange 2000 Clustering

7.7.7.1   *Ensure Proper Security and Permissions Delegation*

Management and administration of Exchange 2000 in a clustered environment is more complex than in standalone configurations. Use care when configuring Exchange Admin accounts and privileges as well as cluster services accounts. When managing and creating Exchange 2000 virtual servers in a cluster, the privileges required are for an account to have Exchange Full Admin rights. This can be accomplished via the Exchange Delegation Wizard.

7.7.7.2   *Use Standardized and Simplified IP Addressing and Naming*

In a clustered scenario both, the cluster nodes as well as the services they host will require IP addresses and unique names. Microsoft Cluster Service requires that IP addresses allocated for the cluster, nodes, and services be static in nature (cannot be assigned via DHCP). All nodes and services must be preallocated IP addresses before the setup and installation is performed. These addresses should be structured in a manner that allows for simplified configuration and management of nodes and services. Likewise, naming for Exchange virtual servers and nodes should allow for simplified configuration and management. Table 7.9 illustrates a good strategy for IP addressing and naming for a four-node Exchange 2000 cluster. Notice that IP addresses for the node name and virtual server name are closely correlated.

Table 7.9   *Cluster IP Addressing and Naming*

Cluster or Node Name	Services	IP Address
FOUR-STOOGES	Cluster Manager	132.192.1.100
1-CURLY	VS1-NAME=EXVS1	1-CURLY: 132.192.1.10 EXVS1: 132.192.1.11
2-MOE	VS2-NAME=EXVS2	2-MOE: 132.192.1.20 EXVS2: 132.192.1.21
3-LARRY	VS3-NAME=EXVS3	3-LARRY: 132.192.1.30 EXVS3: 132.192.1.31
4-JERRY	VS4-NAME=EXVS4	4-JERRY: 132.192.1.40 EXVS4: 132.192.1.41

7.7.7.3   Resource Ownership and Failover

When configuring cluster resources, each resource will automatically be configured with all cluster nodes in Exchange 2000 installed as Possible Owners. However, if resources are created before all nodes have joined the cluster (or before Exchange 2000 has been installed), these nodes will not be listed as Possible Owners. If not manually configured, this will prevent resources from failover to these nodes. Care must be taken when configuring hardware (disk and network), addressing (IP and network name), and Exchange (System Attendant) resources to ensure that all nodes are included as Possible Owners. In addition, when configuring failover and failback scenarios, nodes must be listed in order in the Preferred Owners (for each virtual server resource group) dialog box in Cluster Administrator. This will ensure proper failover and failback operations.

7.7.7.4   Removing Exchange Virtual Servers and Binaries from a Cluster

When removing Exchange from a cluster, care must be taken to not interfere with the operations of other nodes. When removing an Exchange virtual server, the cluster group must be first taken offline. Next, the Exchange resources must be deleted. Removing the System Attendant resource will remove all other resources (based on dependency). Once the virtual server is removed from the cluster, the server can be deleted in Exchange System Manager. Finally, to remove the Exchange binary files from the cluster node, you must run the Exchange 2000 setup program and select the Remove option. When prompted, do not remove the Exchange cluster resources unless this is the last cluster node running Exchange services. Other important points here include:

- Do not delete the Exchange virtual server with the MTA instance unless it is the last node in the cluster. One virtual server in the cluster is created by default with an MTA instance for support of legacy options and connectors.

- If the Microsoft Search instance for a virtual server is deleted, the entire virtual server must be re-created in order for content indexing to function for the virtual server.

7.7.7.5 *Design Storage Before Configuring the Cluster*

With Exchange 2000's support for Active/Active clustering and multiple storage groups and databases, storage design can be quite complex. As discussed earlier in this chapter, consider all aspects before you configure your cluster. Since Exchange 2000 storage groups are a subset of an Exchange virtual server in a cluster, each storage group must fail over with the virtual server. This has implications for storage design. If you choose, based on performance considerations, to allocate a separate physical storage array for transaction log files and database files, each storage group will have a minimum of two arrays (one for logs and one for databases) that must provide the independence and granularity necessary to facilitate failover. For example, if you have two storage groups and they each share a common log file array (i.e., RAID1), they must be necessarily part of the same virtual server since the array will be the unit of failover as a cluster resource. The implications of granularity, failover, and virtual server-to-storage group mapping must be carefully planned. Another consideration for Exchange 2000 at initial release will be the four-storage-group-per-node limitation. Whether pre- or post-failover, each cluster node will only support a maximum of four storage groups. Failure to follow this rule will result in issues and potential failures for Exchange virtual servers.

The creation of disks and the allocation of databases to individual array sets is also a complex process. Microsoft Cluster Server supports only basic disks as cluster resources. Care must be taken to ensure that, once shared storage disk resources are configured, they must be initialized as the basic disk type before the first cluster node is configured. After creating the cluster, all shared disk resources must be managed by the cluster in order for Exchange to use them.

When creating Exchange virtual servers, only one option is given as the data location. In order to allocate databases and log files to specific physical array sets, you must use Exchange System Manager after the virtual server has been created. In the Exchange System Manager MMC snap-in, database and log file locations can be configured on each node. Ensure that you have included all necessary disk resources in the Exchange virtual server group in order to be utilized by Exchange. It is possible for cluster disk resources to be added to the resource group and configured for Exchange virtual servers at a later time. However, at a minimum, one disk resource must be available.

Exchange 2000 offers greatly improved clustering capabilities over previous versions. Clustering is now a viable option for significantly increasing availability and for server consolidation. While the new capabilities are worth investigating, they also create additional complexity. Care must be taken at every deployment phase—particularly in the planning and design phase. By starting with a solid understanding of how Microsoft Cluster is implemented and how Exchange 2000 leverages this, you have a foundation to build a successful deployment. With the acceptance and understanding of the limits of the technology available, you can successfully deploy Exchange Server on MSCS and significantly increase system availability and protect against hardware failures. Clustering Exchange Server can help your organization meet its high-availability requirements by protecting servers from critical failures that could not be tolerated in a nonclustered scenario.

8

Don't Overlook Security as a Powerful High-Availability Measure

For many Exchange deployments, proactive planning of security measures and protections for users, data, servers, and infrastructure are an afterthought. As we deploy Exchange, we focus on getting the messaging functionality in place and often don't have the extra cycles needed to properly investigate security issues. In addition, security is a topic that is very complex, and many do not have the training or expertise required to provide a secure Exchange environment. In some cases, a separate group or department from the Exchange deployment manages organizational security. This can create either a competitive environment or a knowledge gap in which Exchange system managers and security managers compete for resources, resulting in a lack of cooperation or knowledge transfer. Overall, this results in the security needs of the Exchange deployment being overlooked, improperly specified, or ignored altogether. Without going too far down this path (it's highly political in nature), it is safe to say that the users and the organization suffer the end consequences.

Because every organization's architecture and security requirements are different, there are many approaches you can take. In the course of this chapter, I will be discussing threats to Exchange security and the countermeasures available. You may choose to apply all or part of the topics covered depending on your scenario. Since the topics discussed will have a definite impact on the overall design of your organization's security infrastructure, you should read this chapter with this in mind and in conjunction with the "big picture" plan for your organization's security.

I begin this chapter by providing an overview of the threats to our Exchange servers, the users they service, and the data these servers are entrusted with. These concepts are generic enough in nature but will be applied specifically to an Exchange environment. Next, I will discuss Windows 2000 security features and how they greatly enhance our capabilities to keep Exchange 2000 secure through advanced authentication (Kerberos), directory services (Active Directory), public key infrastructure services (PKI, delivered with Certificate Services), application security (provided in access control and policies), and other enhancements such as IP Security (IPSec) and Encrypted File System (EFS). The remainder of the chapter will be focused on locking down our Exchange environment. Three key areas will be discussed—network security, anti-virus solutions, and message content security. Within these three "buckets," it is possible to gather all the things that ail our Exchange servers, users, and data. Network security addresses such topics as how Exchange authenticates users, protocols, firewalls, and SMTP virtual server security.

The section on anti-virus solutions discusses the virus threat, a three-perimeter approach, and how to select and implement an anti-virus solution. Message content security deals with the deployment of a PKI and using Certificate Services along with Exchange's Key Management Service to provide an architecture that allows users to encrypt and digitally sign messages. As your Exchange deployment matures and its uses become more diverse and business-critical, successfully guarding against theft, tampering, unauthorized access, or data destruction involves first understanding the threats. In the next sections, I will discuss four such threats: denial of service, viruses, unauthorized access, and forgery.

8.1   Threat: Denial of Service

The data and services in your infrastructure must be available for the people and business processes that rely on them. This applies not only to Exchange services but to the other services that support Exchange such as the Active Directory, DNS, and the underlying network services. Since mission-critical systems must process data at an ever-increasing pace while at the same time servicing large populations of users, these systems are most vulnerable to attacks that prevent users from accessing services or data. In a messaging system, each activity (send, receive, browse, delete, move, etc.) requires system resources such as either processor, memory, and disk or network bandwidth in order to complete. In addition, infrastructure services required by Exchange, such as DNS, Global Catalog service (Active Directory lookup), domain controllers (authentication), and the network itself, are also required. An attacker can target the Exchange server or any of these supporting servers by initiating a flood of activity against a particular server or device. Network bandwidth can be consumed, a DNS server can be disabled or flooded with requests, or malicious Internet users can overwhelm your Exchange servers with SMTP messages or connections to your Internet Message Access Protocol version 4 (IMAP4), Post Office Protocol version 3 (POP3), or Network News Transfer Protocol (NNTP) access to services. These attacks can debilitate your CPU and clog your virtual servers. Exchange allows you to accept or deny connections to your protocol virtual servers using lists of IP addresses and domain names that you specify. If your organization is continuously bombarded by an IP address or domain, you can explicitly deny access to that IP address or domain. Exchange uses reverse DNS lookup to check this list. All these scenarios could result in users and other services being denied access to services and data. The result could bring an Exchange organization to a halt.

Denial-of-service (DoS) attacks can come in many forms and don't always require a Ph.D. in computer science to instigate. Some of the most devastating attacks to date have required little expertise to produce. DoS attacks come at the network level as in the case of TCP "Syn" Flooding or ICMP attacks in which floods of network packets hit a server or router, preventing legitimate clients from accessing required services. Clients are also susceptible to DoS attacks and should not be ignored when planning countermeasures to this potential threat. DoS attacks against an Exchange server most likely come in two forms. The first form is a virus-borne attack that results in DoS through viral replication. The other form comes against Exchange SMTP services in which an SMTP (or other protocol) virtual server is tied up servicing bogus mail traffic while legitimate traffic cannot succeed. While this can occur against internal SMTP gateways, the attack is most common against external Exchange SMTP services that are directly exposed (although usually inside a firewall) to the Internet. We will discuss this threat and the measures available to address this scenario in more detail later in this chapter.

8.2   Threat: Viruses

Unsuspecting users may inadvertently execute programs they receive in e-mail. These programs can, in turn, infect systems and cause enormous amounts of damage that cost organizations dearly. According to Ferris Research, e-mail–borne viruses account for at least 95% of all attacks reaching the desktop computer. According to Gartner Research, macro viruses account for over 80% of these. The term "virus" has been used generically but actually only represents one form of the attack. There are actually four forms of viral threat— viruses, Trojans, worms, and mobile code. A virus is a piece of code that replicates by attaching itself to other programs or files. When these files are run, the virus is invoked and can further replicate itself. A Trojan horse is a piece of code embedded in a useful program for malicious purposes. A Trojan horse differs from a virus in that it does not try to replicate itself to other programs. A worm is a program that replicates by running copies of itself across a network. A virus can exhibit both virus and worm characteristics, as in the 1999 case of WormExplore.Zip. Mobile code comes in the form of links (URLs) embedded in Web pages and e-mail messages, which execute Java or ActiveX programs that can cause undesired results.

If you look at the most common types of viruses and Trojan horses (logic bombs, bacteria, worms, and macro viruses), you see a very important similarity: They are all applications or programs that need to be run. Because of the nature of messaging, the following realities apply. First, most viruses require the end user to run an application or open an e-mail attachment. Rarely does simply open-ing a message invoke a virus (this is certainly not far off, however). Second, most viruses are run on the local desktop. Third, e-mail is simply a transport for spreading viruses (as the floppy disk was prior to the global deployment of e-mail systems). We will discuss the viral threat and the methods available to counteract this threat later in the chapter.

8.3   Threat: Unauthorized Access

The data on your Exchange server and other servers must be main-tained in such a manner that no one can gain unauthorized access to the information. Such activities can be both malicious and acciden-tal. Mechanisms must be in place to protect data from sender to receiver. Our security measures for Exchange need to give users and management the assurance that only users who are authorized can access certain information. We need to provide a high degree of confidentiality as well. This means that only users who are supposed to have access to certain data should have permission to view it. Confidentiality can also mean blocking outsiders who are trying to gain access. For example, only specific employees in the human resources department should be able to view salary information. In a military application, only those with certain clearance levels should be able to read classified information. We need to have methods in place for controlling access to information among individuals or entire groups within the organization. Closely tied to the forgery threat (discussed in the next section), the unauthorized access threat can affect both servers and data. The measures available to prevent unauthorized access include access control, data encryption, and digital signing. Access control is provided by Exchange 2000 reliance on Windows 2000 and leverages mechanisms such as the Active Directory, access control lists (ACLs), access control entries (ACEs), and policy-based administration. Encryption ensures confidentiality by rendering intercepted or ill-gotten information unreadable. Likewise, digital signing ensures that there is no unauthorized access by rendering modified or altered information invalid through a failure of nonrepudiation. We will discuss access control, message encryption, and signing later in this chapter when we look at message content security.

8.4   Threat: Forgery

An attacker forging messages to appear as if they came from someone or somewhere else can spread false information throughout an organization or, in worse cases, trick users into releasing sensitive information. As an example, suppose you received a message from your boss instructing you to send the detailed plans and design of your network infrastructure to a third party. The message may appear authentic, and you mostly likely would simply follow your boss' instructions and forward the information to the outside party. Suppose this third party was actually a competitor instigating a forgery attack against your organization to get the information you just provided. In the early days of the Internet, basic SMTP/Sendmail servers made this quite easy. While this type of attack is more difficult today, the threat of forgery using this and other means is still very real. Therefore, we must also ensure that the system can guarantee a user's identity when sending and receiving messages. For organizations requiring the highest level of security, methods of nonrepudiation must be available. Nonrepudiation ensures that the message is from the source indicated and also ensures that the message has not been tampered with along the way. The most common method available to protect against this threat is digital signatures. Digital signatures validate a user's identity so that message recipients can be assured that message senders are who they claim to be. Digital signatures also provide further protection by ensuring that the message has not been tampered with during transit (the signature no longer would be valid if the message has been altered). We will discuss digital signatures later in the chapter as we focus on locking down our Exchange environment.

8.5   Threat: Mail Relaying

Exchange 2000 Server has a feature that prevents third parties from relaying mail through your server. Relay control allows you to specify a list of incoming remote IP address and mask pairs with permission to relay mail through your server. Exchange checks an incoming SMTP client's IP address against the list of IP networks allowed to relay mail. If the client is not allowed to relay mail, only mail addressed to local recipients is allowed. In addition, you can configure the Exchange server to match incoming SMTP clients against part of a domain name. Each time a message to be submitted through your SMTP virtual server is received, the FROM address is validated using reverse DNS lookup. Reverse DNS lookup verifies the sender's domain name and checks your list of approved relay domains. If the address is not authorized to relay mail, the server does not accept the incoming message. Internet users that send unsolicited mail can use the domain names of other organizations as the return address. SMTP does not always include verification of the FROM address in mail to be delivered. This makes it easy for those who wish to impersonate your domain by sending messages on behalf of your domain. Using an SMTP server to submit messages, these malicious Internet users can send hundreds or thousands of messages to users over the Internet using your domain name as the FROM address. These messages can be traced to your organization, even if a user in your organization did not send the mail.

The threats to our Exchange deployments are many. In this chapter, I hope to point out some of the most common threats and the measures we have at our disposal to protect against them. I am certain that an entire book could be devoted to this very subject (In fact, there are many). For our purposes, I will try to focus on the specific measures and technologies available to address Exchange-specific security concerns.

8.6   Windows 2000 Security Enhancements

This section explains the different features in Microsoft Windows 2000 and how Microsoft Exchange 2000 Server takes advantage of them. These new features are not found in previous versions of Microsoft Windows NT servers. They define a new environment in which the enterprise messaging and collaborative system operate. It is necessary to understand these features because users need to know how the systems behave in other platform environments.

These features in Windows 2000 can be broadly divided into two areas: core operating system features and additional security features. Windows 2000 integrates core operating system features that form the basis of a secured implementation. They are Active Directory, Kerberos authentication, the access control model, and Certificate Services. There are additional security features that can further enhance the security of the enterprise. These features are provided as part of the core operating system. They are IPSec, EFS, and the Security Configuration and Analysis (SCA) tool.

8.6.1   Active Directory

Unlike Exchange 5.5, Exchange 2000 does not have its own separate directory service. Exchange 2000 uses the Windows 2000 Active Directory to store its configuration and information about its mail entities. This has important management and security consequences. While an NT4 and Exchange 5.5 administrator had to manage two distinct objects (a user's NT account object and a user's Exchange mailbox object), a Windows 2000 and Exchange 2000 administrator now has to manage only a single object: the AD object. The two user objects have been unified into one AD object. The mailbox object of Exchange 5.5 is now stored as different properties of the AD user object. From a security point of view, this means that typical mail objects, such as a mailbox, now have a security identifier (a SID). This is simply because they are linked to an AD user object.

Table 8.1 shows the equivalents of the Exchange 5.5 directory objects in an AD Exchange 2000 world. It discusses whether they are security-, mail-, or mailbox-enabled. Security-enabled means you can use the object for any security-related operation (such as access control or delegation). Mail-enabled means that the object has a mail address to which you can send mail messages. Mailbox-enabled means the object has a mailbox on an Exchange 2000 server or another messaging system that utilizes the Active Directory.

The Active Directory database on a domain controller replaces the Security Accounts Manager (SAM) in Windows NT 4.0 as the security database. Every object in Active Directory that takes part in any security process needs to have a SID. A SID is a sort of random identifier that is a globally unique, 96-digit number to identify users and computers. There are two different sets of objects on Windows NT 4.0 and Exchange 5.5. The directory for Exchange 5.5 and earlier versions is separate from the directory (domain space) structure of Windows NT 4.0. However, these are unified in the Windows 2000 Active Directory, greatly reducing overall system administrative overhead as compared to managing two separate directory structures with NT 4.0 and earlier versions of Exchange. Essentially, the objects in Exchange 2000 and Windows 2000 are linked to a SID. Custom recipients in Exchange 5.5 are mail-enabled contacts in Exchange 2000 and do not have a SID. Distribution lists are changed to groups. There are security groups with a SID and distribution groups without a SID. When an object does not have a SID, the object cannot be placed in the access control list. Table 8.1 illustrates the differences between Exchange 5.5 recipients and Exchange 2000/Active Directory recipients and how they are mapped when migrated.

Windows 2000 defines various types of objects (shown in Table 8.2) that can be hosted in Active Directory and that Exchange 2000 can utilize.

Table 8.1   *Comparison of How Exchange 5.5 Objects Are Represented in the Active Directory with Exchange 2000*

Exchange 5.5 Recipient	*Windows 2000 Active Directory Representation*
Mailbox	A mailbox is a mailbox-enabled user. An e-mail address shows the Exchange server where the e-mail is to be routed. Mailboxes from Exchange 5.5 are replicated into Active Directory (using the Active Directory Connector) as users or contacts.
Distribution Lists	A distribution list is a distribution group or a security group in the Active Directory. Windows 2000 groups appear as distribution lists in an Exchange directory. The administrator can specify the group to be a security group, which allows the group to be placed in an access control list. Whether a security group or a distribution group in the AD, both are mail-enabled.
Custom Recipients	An AD mail-enabled contact is a custom recipient in an Exchange directory. It has an e-mail address associated with it but not an Exchange mailbox. It does not have a SID and cannot log on.

Table 8.2   *Active Directory Objects That Are Mail-Disabled, Mail-Enabled, or Mailbox-Enabled*

Windows 2000 Object	*Description*
Mail-Disabled	Has no e-mail capabilities. A security group like Domain Admins is an example.
Mail-Enabled	Has an e-mail address but no mailbox. A distribution group is an example.
Mailbox-Enabled	Has an Exchange mailbox associated with it. Only Windows user accounts can be mailbox-enabled.

Exchange 2000 extends Active Directory by adding auxiliary classes. The schema in Active Directory can be viewed by using the Active Directory Service Interfaces Edit Tool (ADSIEDIT) for Windows 2000. Active Directory includes entries specific to Exchange 2000 that are added when Exchange 2000 is first installed (alternatively, the schema can be extended as a separate standalone measure using the /forestprep setup option). Some of these entries include the Mail-Recipient Auxiliary Class, which enables e-mail and mailboxes on an object and provides e-mail addresses, protocol settings, and others; and the Mail-Storage Auxiliary Class, which enables mailboxes for users and provides store quotas, a home data-base, deleted-item retention, and others. When an administrator creates a new user in Exchange, a message asks if the user is to be mailbox-enabled (if Exchange 2000 is installed). The administrator can also enable the user later.

8.6.2   Kerberos Authentication

Kerberos is the new security protocol for Windows 2000, replacing NTLM authentication used in NT 4.0. It is provided natively within the Windows 2000 domain and is integrated into the administrative and security model. This is convenient since the administrator does not need to learn additional administrative tools to manage the infrastructure. Kerberos identifies the client through secured means to a domain controller. Kerberos authentication services are built into every Windows 2000 domain controller and Global Catalog server. When the user logs on, he authenticates to the Kerberos key distribution center (KDC). The KDC issues a ticket-granting ticket. The client then uses the ticket-granting ticket to access a service. A client who has the ticket to access the service can simply present the ticket for subsequent uses. All of the tickets are encrypted through public key technology, which is more secure than secret key encryption. Figure 8.1 shows the steps involved in Kerberos authentication with the Windows 2000 domain controller and member and an Exchange 2000 store server.

In the Kerberos authentication environment, Exchange 2000 is treated like a service. When the client needs to access Exchange, the client requests an Exchange service ticket from the KDC in the Windows 2000 domain controller. The service ticket is then used for authentication with the Exchange 2000 server. For subsequent access to Exchange 2000, the client uses the service ticket, and authentication is faster.

The Exchange services also use Kerberos to make a service logon to the domain controller through the local system account. The local system account uses computer credentials, which consist of the account and a password that is automatically changed every seven days. This provides better security compared with Exchange 5.5, which uses a site service account. The name of the Exchange 2000 Server is added to the Exchange Domain Servers Group, which is added to the ACL of the core objects. To facilitate the administration over what these accounts, and thus an Exchange

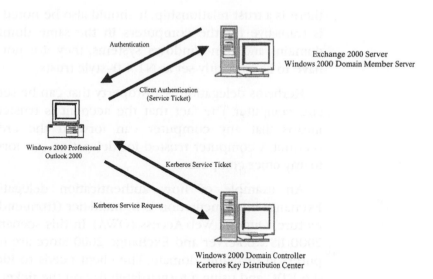

Figure 8.1
Client
authentication
to Exchange
2000 using
Windows 2000
Kerberos
authentication

server and its services, can do with other system, domain, and Exchange resources, Microsoft creates two groups during the Exchange 2000 installation process. The two groups are the global group Exchange Domain Servers and the domain local group Exchange Enterprise Servers. Both groups contain machine accounts of servers running Exchange 2000. The Exchange Domain Servers group contains all Exchange 2000 servers of a domain; it is updated automatically when a new Exchange 2000 server is installed in the domain. The Exchange Enterprise Servers group contains all Exchange Domain Servers groups from all domains in a Windows 2000 forest; it is updated by the Recipient Update Service (RUS). A member of the Exchange Enterprise Servers group can modify the properties of any mailbox- or mail-enabled object contained in its domain. Members of the Exchange Domain Servers group have read permissions to the Active Directory Exchange configuration container.

8.6.3 Authentication Delegation

If a client has already authenticated to Exchange 2000 server A, and server A needs to request another server B running on another computer, server A can request for the ticket on behalf of the client. This is possible because Kerberos supports authentication delegation. Authentication across different domains is also possible provided there is a trust relationship. It should also be noted that, while trust is transitive for the computers in the same domain, for external domains and non-Windows systems, they are not transitive. They have to be explicitly set as NT 4.0–style trusts.

Kerberos delegation is a property that can be set on the account and computer. The fact that the account is trusted for delegation means that any computer can forward the credentials of the account. A computer trusted for delegation can forward credentials to any other computers.

An example of how authentication delegation is used in Exchange implementation is in multi-tier (front-end/back-end architecture) Outlook Web Access (OWA). In this scenario, the Windows 2000 IIS 5.0 server and Exchange 2000 Store are on separate computers in the same domain. The client needs to identify himself to the KDC, and using a forwardable flag on the ticket to the Windows 2000 IIS 5.0 server, the client is authenticated through delegation when IIS needs to access the Exchange 2000 store on another computer. The ticket that IIS used has the authorization data of the user, not IIS. This is an improvement over NTLM, which does not support forwarding of credentials.

Figure 8.2

An example of Kerberos authentication delegation with Exchange 2000 front-end/back-end architecture

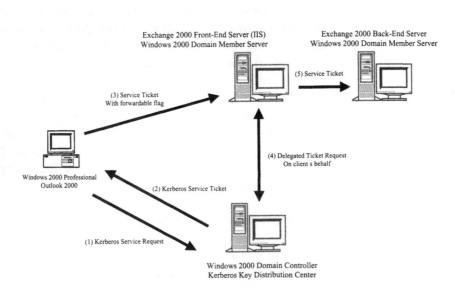

The only Microsoft client with Kerberos support is Windows 2000 Professional. For Windows 95 and Windows 98, Kerberos add-ons are available. However, these add-ons are not available for Windows NT 4.0.

8.6.4 Access Control with Exchange 2000

Although the architecture of the Windows 2000 access control model is very similar to the one used in NT4, it includes some critical new ACL extensions: property-based ACEs, object-type ACEs, better control over ACL inheritance, and the support for "deny" ACEs, *property sets*, and *extended rights*, When applied to Active Directory objects, these extensions enable *administrative delegation* or the ability to delegate AD administrative tasks to different administrators. I will come back to delegation later in this chapter.

The Exchange 2000 access control model is fundamentally different from the one implemented in Exchange 5.5: Exchange 5.5 used its own access control model; Exchange 2000 uses the Windows 2000 access control model. Every information store object now has a Windows 2000 security descriptor. Also, in Exchange 2000, due to the integration with AD, access control can be set on directory objects. Every directory object has an NTSecurityDescriptor containing a Windows 2000 security descriptor. If you open up a mail-enabled user-object in the AD Users and Computers MMC snap-in, you can examine both the AD security descriptor (in the Security tab) and the information store security descriptor (in the Exchange Advanced tab under Mailbox rights).

Compared to its predecessor in NT 4.0, the new authentication and access control model in Windows 2000 offers much more control over the inheritance of access control settings between parent and child objects. In Exchange 5.5, inheritance was fixed: if you set an ACL on the organization level, it was automatically inherited by all the sites in the organization. In Exchange 2000, an administrator can enforce and block inheritance. Obviously, enforcement always has precedence over blocking.

8.6.5 Public Folder Access Control

It is also worthwhile to look at how the new access control model affects the way access control is set on Exchange 2000 public folders. In Exchange 2000, Microsoft has grouped all public folder access control–related settings in the Permissions tab of a public folder's properties. The tab shows three pushbuttons: one to set client permissions, one to set public folder administrator permissions, and another one to set ACLs on the AD public folder object. The last one is a direct consequence of Exchange 2000's integration with AD. Similar to 5.5, the client permission button lets an administrator set client permissions using predefined roles (author, contributor, etc.). The roles mimic Windows 2000 object permissions; contrary to Exchange 5.5, they are now linked to security principals. The way public folder administrator permissions are set in Exchange 2000 offers much more granularity than in Exchange 5.5. Exchange 2000 includes permissions such as the ability to modify the public folder deleted item retention period and to modify the public folder quotas, etc. Public folder access control in Exchange 2000 involves three security descriptors: two on the public folder information store object (one for administrator, one for client permissions), and another one on the public folder AD object.

8.6.6   Exchange Administration Roles

Another access control mechanism is an Exchange role. An Exchange role is a link that contains the SID and the Exchange 2000 rights. They are essentially resource groups for Exchange 2000 administration. These roles are not defined in the directory but rather in the Exchange 2000 stores. These roles are application driven and are customizable by the developer. A developer can define roles as part of the application design and then populate at deployment time with actual users and groups. In an Exchange 2000 public folder store, the role-ACEs refer to the roles defined in the Exchange 2000 store. These roles are evaluated at run-time and the security system of the store queries the role definition table for the contents of the role when the user accesses the public folder. Therefore, the changes in the roles are instantly updated. These changes in the access-level control are reflected in the Exchange 2000 public folder ACEs interface. User-level permissions, default message permissions, permissions on the Active Directory object, and administrative permission on the objects contained in the store can be set.

8.6.7   Windows 2000 Policies

Policies are another useful feature in Windows 2000 that are utilized by Exchange 2000. A *policy* is a collection of configuration settings that you apply across objects. When a policy is changed, that change is propagated to every object to which the policy is applied. There are two types of policies that apply to Exchange 2000—system policies and recipient policies. System policies affect server-side objects such as mailbox stores, public folder stores, and individual servers. When making changes to system policies, you need to have permissions on all objects to which the system policy applies. Recipient policies are imposed on objects such as users and groups. Again, permissions are required when affecting changes to recipient policies. Policies are a powerful tool for Exchange 2000 because they can trigger changes across an entire organization. Policies can play a vital role in Exchange 2000 security measures.

8.6.8   Other Windows 2000 Security Enhancements

8.6.8.1   IP Security

While the Key Management Service with a PKI provides security on the application layer, IPSec provides security on the IP transportation layer (Network Layer 3). This enables protection with low overhead and can be deployed in different scenarios, such as workgroup, LAN, and remote access. Also, it provides protection in the IP and upper-layer protocols in the TCP/IP protocol suite, such as TCP, UDP, ICMP, and other protocols that send traffic at the IP layer. IPSEC uses the Diffie-Hellman algorithm to enable key exchange and provides the keying material for all other encryption keys. IPSec can automatically generate new keys during a communication. The communication can be sent in blocks of data, each block secured with a different key. This prevents an attacker from obtaining the entire communication with a single compromised key. Other security mechanisms that operate above Network Layer 3, such as the Secure Sockets Layer (SSL), can only provide security to applications that understand and know how to use SSL. An example of such an application is the Web browser. All other applications must be modified to protect communications with SSL. Security mechanisms that operate below Network Layer 3, such as link layer encryption, only protect the link but not necessarily all links along the data path. This makes link layer encryption unsuitable for end-to-end data protection on Internet or routed intranet scenarios. IP Security defines the protocol for network encryption at the IP protocol layer (Network Layer 3). The default IPSec authentication is Kerberos. However, if Certificate Service is made available, each domain member will have the appropriate certificate installed. Another method besides using Kerberos or Certificate Service is to use a preshared key. This is a simple method for authenticating computers not based on Windows 2000 or Kerberos in which the keys must be made available to both parties prior to the encryption exchange.

8.6.8.2   Encryped File System

The Encrypted File System (EFS) is a feature of Windows 2000 that allows users to encrypt data directly on volumes that use NTFS. It operates by using certificates based on the X.509 standard. If no certificate authority (CA) is available from which to request certificates, the EFS subsystem automatically generates its own self-signed certificates for users and default recovery agents. The EFS supports transparent encryption and decryption of files stored on an NTFS disk. A recovery policy is automatically implemented when users encrypt a file or folder for the first time. This ensures that users who lose their file encryption certificates and associated private keys are able to use a recovery agent to decrypt their files. The user must understand that, once the encrypted file leaves the hard disk, it is not encrypted. When a user sends a file as an attachment, via Exchange 2000, the file will not be encrypted. This is different from using the advanced security features of Exchange with KMS. The EFS encrypts files on the hard disk, and when the directory is opened for sharing, the files cannot be read. However, when a user is running an application that retrieves a file from the hard disk as the legitimate user, the file is decrypted. It should be emphasized that the EFS only addresses the encryption of data on disk. When data is transferred over the network, it will need IPSec, SSL, or other methods to ensure that data is encrypted over the network. The EFS is useful for mobile users who can encrypt directories, such as personal mail folders. In this way, if their portable computer is lost, the data cannot be read.

8.6.8.3   Windows 2000 Auditing

Auditing gathers security-relevant information. Two tools available are Event Viewer and the SCA tool. Event Viewer in Windows 2000 is extended to gather auditing information on several core operating system (OS) services including the directory service, DNS service, and file-replication service.

The SCA tool allows administrators to analyze the security of the system and reapply it. Both analysis and application are based on security templates that define values for a set of security-related system parameters. The administrative tool is also a snap-in. The security template is a set of predefined settings in terms of account policies, local policies, restricted groups, registry, file system, and system services. The settings are also classified into basic, compatible, secured, highly secured, and dedicated domain controller templates. These templates are later used to configure the SCA tool. The analyzer in the SCA tool is run to show whether there are discrepancies in the settings and templates. This is useful to check whether security policies are implemented and serve as another form of audit checking. This application has to be run on the local computer. Using SCA, you can analyze and configure file system and registry access control settings, system service startup parameters, membership of restricted groups, event log settings, account policies (such as password quality), and local policies (such as user rights). The SCA uses its proper database, secedit.edb, located in the %systemdrive%winntsecuritydatabase folder, and can also be run from the command prompt using secedit.exe.

Windows 2000 provides many new security enhancements compared to previous versions of Windows NT. Many of these security features require a significant amount of expertise in order to be properly leveraged and deployed. The administrator has to understand the different options available to enhance the overall security of the infrastructure. In an enterprise in which different platforms are available, it is necessary to also understand the level of security that can be implemented without causing interoperability issues. These features, found in both Windows 2000 Server and Professional, provide a secure environment for messaging and collaboration with Exchange 2000. These enhancements also provide a foundation for building additional levels of security into an Exchange 2000 deployment. In order to maximize these features, I recommend that you further delve into this technology to fully understand how it can be used with Exchange. In the next section, I will shift our focus to how we can lock down our Exchange deployments through improved network security, anti-virus solutions, and message content security.

8.7   Locking Down Exchange 2000

8.7.1   Network Security

Typically, we think of network security as protecting us from network intrusions and threats from outside sources. We look to measures such as firewalls, proxy servers, virtual private networks (VPNs), and network design as protection mechanisms against these threats. Starting with Exchange 5.0 in 1997, close integration with the Internet was provided. Further enhanced in Exchange 5.5, our awareness of the vulnerabilities of such great integration only surfaced in the last few years. It has only been in recent years that Exchange servers have been used as Internet gateways, handling inbound and outbound mail traffic for many organizations. With Exchange 2000, integration with the Internet and standard protocols such as SMTP, IMAP4, POP3, NNTP, and HTTP has grown to a level that makes it an attractive platform for companies using Exchange as a gateway to the Internet as well as for ISP/ASP using Exchange as a hosting platform for millions of users. This increased integration and versatility should serve as a warning of the increased need to protect Exchange Server from unauthorized access, denial of service, and other attacks. This section will look at the ways we should protect Exchange servers functioning as gateways to the Internet. We will overview methods available to protect Exchange and your network including monitoring and detection, firewalls and proxy servers, and securing Exchange SMTP virtual servers.

8.7.1.1   *Monitoring and Detection*

Since Exchange servers that are accessed externally via the Internet may support a wide variety of protocols, it is too simple a philosophy that only worries about SMTP. While SMTP access is the most common example, enhancements to Exchange 2000 OWA and the use of Exchange 2000 as a hosting platform for ISPs will bring other protocols like HTTP to the forefront. While we need to focus on locking down the points of access and limiting the protocols available (which we will cover later), we need to ensure that methods are available to track and monitor the access and use of the services that are exposed and vulnerable. Hopefully, your organization already has many of these tools and procedures in place, and you can simply ensure that they consider your Exchange deployment's needs. If not, we should look at some of the basics that you will want to consider to provide adequate monitoring and detection measures.

Detecting security incidents and attacks is not necessarily the rocket science it is sometimes made out to be. In fact, there are many tools built in to Windows 2000 that can get you started. Many times, the most useful tool can be the Windows 2000 system security log. This often-overlooked component of the system event logging process can be an invaluable tool for providing data about suspect security events. The following table lists some situations and scenarios that may be deemed suspect and may indicate a security breach.

Table 8.3   *Common Indicators of a Security Breach*

Common Indicator	Description
Unusual time of usage	Attackers often strike during off hours when there is a lower chance they will be detected or countermeasures will be applied. Security events logged during off business hours may need to be more closely scrutinized.
Unusual usage patterns	If a novice or nonadministrative user is performing functions or generating error codes that are atypical for this user, the account may have been compromised.
Irregular account usage	Windows 2000 comes with several default accounts such as Guest and Administrator. However, many installations change or add other default accounts used for privileged accesses. New and unfamiliar accounts on the system may also be suspect. In addition, activity in a previously inactive account could also be cause for concern.
Unexplained changes to permissions or files	Once an attacker gains access to your system, traces of the activity may need to be covered or new "back doors" added.
Gaps in system and security logs	System logs typically show patterns of activity for all hours. Missing time segments or drastic changes in activity recorded in logs may be a cause for concern.

For Exchange 2000 and Windows 2000, the system logs can be a valuable source of detection and monitoring information. However, this is most useful when other sources of information are available to collaborate events recorded in logs. Protocol Logging is another valuable tool. Exchange 2000 relies on IIS to support Internet protocols such as SMTP, IMAP, POP3, NNTP, and HTTP. For SMTP, NNTP, and HTTP, IIS comes with a utility for logging the commands made on IIS virtual servers hosting these protocols. These protocol logs track commands that the virtual servers receive from connections made from clients and other servers. When connecting to these virtual servers, clients and servers engage in a dialog of commands that, under normal circumstances, facilitate the flow of data over these protocols. For example, in earlier versions of SMTP (not Exchange), it was possible for an attacker to Telnet to an SMTP server, enter a string of characters, and terminate the connection, causing the SMTP service to fail. Protocol logging would provide some evidence in this type of attack that would be useful in tracking down the attacker. In conjunction with system event logs, protocol logging on services that are potentially exposed will provide strong evidence that will be useful for tracking attacks when they occur and preventing future attacks from occurring. In addition, you can use protocol logging to provide auditing for users and commands throughout your environment as an additional precautionary and preventative measure.

Once you have investigated and deployed basic measures, such as security event and protocol logging, you may want to go one step further and deploy full-blown intrusion-detection measures. More and more intrusion-detection tools are becoming available as many companies scramble to fill this market need. In the book *Internet Security for Business*, intrusion-detection tools are divided into four categories, as shown in Table 8.4.

Table 8.4   *Categories of Intrusion-Detection Tools*

Category	Description
Statistical tools	These tools are based on normal behaviors and access patterns for users and administrators. These patterns are measured by these tools over time and provide statistical norms upon which to based extraordinary evaluations. Deviation from the norms often indicates that intrusions have occurred.

Table 8.4   *Categories of Intrusion-Detection Tools (continued)*

Category	Description
Signature-based tools	Some user and administrative commands (the signature) are indicators of security breaches or unauthorized activities. These attack signatures are used to trigger alerts on security incidents.
State transition–based tools	These tools are based on the assumption that unauthorized changes in account states (i.e., to administrator or Domain Admin privileges) are based on predicable patterns and can be used to indicate breaches in certain types of services.
Expert system tools	Many of the leading intrusion-detection tools have these "expert" capabilities that use rules to evaluate system access data and patterns in the same way security experts do manually. These tools represent security intrusion-detection expertise packaged into a product.

Obviously, many tools combine these categories into one tool. There are many tools available today that provide network mapping, port scanning, and intrusion detection all rolled into one tool. If your organization has not looked at these tools and assessed what capabilities are needed to protect your Exchange environment, I recommend that you spend some time on this topic in order to protect your deployment. Monitoring and detection are important measures required for services such as Exchange SMTP virtual servers or OWA servers that are vulnerable and exposed to the Internet. In the next section, I will look at firewall technology and provide some suggestions on how this technology can complement your monitoring and intrusion-detection measures.

8.7.1.2   Firewall Technology

Typically, when we think of network protection and access control, we think of firewall technology. As the name implies, a firewall is designed to protect or minimize potential damage from security incidents and attacks. Firewall technology represents the best technology available to protect Exchange and other systems from attack from outside sources. For Exchange servers deployed throughout your intranet, firewall technology is not targeted at protecting these systems. The focus of this section will be on how firewall technology can help protect Exchange servers that are located at the perimeter of your network and are exposed or partially exposed to attack.

We should start by covering some firewall basics. While I do not intend to give you an in-depth tutorial on firewall technologies, I do want to lay a bit of groundwork for later discussions and application to Exchange. Firewall products available today provide a range of functions and features. These features can range from the simple packet filter to complex systems, that provide detailed analysis and management at the application later. The later acts as a protective relay for Exchange SMTP mail and other services between internal mail systems and hosts on the Internet. In addition, a firewall does not necessarily consist of a single computer but can be a collection of systems that together provide the functionality required to protect your internal network and services. There are several types of systems that fall into the category of firewall technology. Table 8.5 highlights several of the most common firewall protection mechanisms available.

Table 8.5   *Firewall Technologies*

Technology	Limitations	Description
Packet filter	• No application support • No authentication • Does not hide internal network	Typically implemented at the router, packet filtering scans incoming packet traffic for configured protocols and compares the traffic to a defined rule set of filters. A decision is then made whether to allow, drop, or reject the incoming packet.
Proxy servers	• Session overhead • Cost • Inconvenient	A dual-homed system, proxy servers adopt a store-and-forward design to terminate all connections at the firewall. Proxy servers work at the application level and act on behalf of clients inside the network perimeter and servers outside.
Circuit proxy	• Client configuration required • Nonapplication specific	A variant of a traditional proxy server, the circuit proxy goes beyond the traditional proxy and provides a transparent end-to-end virtual circuit between clients and servers.

Lest you get the impression that firewall technology is the complete answer, it is important to clarify some limitations of firewall technology. First, firewalls do not provide any data protection or integrity. For example, it is not the role of a firewall to eliminate viruses in the incoming traffic. This would be too great a performance burden on a typical firewall. Another limitation relates to authentication. Firewalls provide none since they only look at packets and application traffic. Thus, firewalls cannot prevent spoofing attacks. If you want data encryption and confidentiality of your data, firewalls can't provide this either. The final point is that firewalls do not protect you from internal attacks and are only one entry point into your network. There are several excellent firewall technology vendors on the market, such as Axent and Checkpoint (noted leaders), that apply a combination of the technologies discussed into their products. In addition, Windows 2000 comes with its own proxy server, which provides many of these features.

Firewall technology is a vital part of protecting your Exchange deployment (especially those Exchange servers exposed to the Internet), but it does not provide the complete solution. Proper authentication, monitoring, and intrusion-detection techniques are also required. By leveraging firewall technology with other measures, you can provide the needed protection for mission-critical Exchange systems.

8.7.1.3   Firewall Architectures for Exchange

There are many design methods and techniques for deploying firewall technology with Exchange 2000. In this section, I will look at three potential architectures that you may choose to implement (or already may have implemented in your organization). These designs are focused on Exchange-specific services, such as SMTP and HTTP, that are the most typical. However, these designs could be applied to a variety of other applications and protocols.

Architecture Alpha—Basic Packet Filtering/Screening Router Approach

One approach is to place a filtering or screening router as the first point of presence of your connection to the Internet. This router could be owned and managed by your organization or the ISP that provides your access to the Internet. The router acts as the first line of defense and provides packet filtering according to the rules configured. Only traffic matching the configured policies is allowed access internally. Services such as an Exchange SMTP virtual server or OWA server would be located behind this filtering router. Between the intranet and this host, another secondary router would

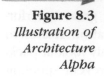

Figure 8.3
*Illustration of
Architecture
Alpha*

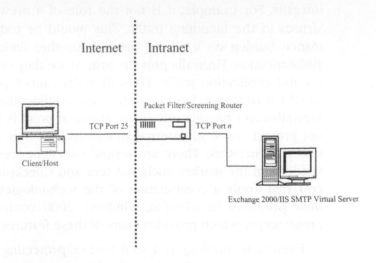

be located. The screening router will allow internal traffic to freely
flow in an outbound direction but only allow incoming traffic on
certain TCP/UDP ports, depending on the services supported. For
example, for Exchange 2000 SMTP virtual servers acting as an Internet mail gateway for the organization, TCP ports 25 (SMTP) and 465
(SMTP via SSL) would need to be enabled at the screening router.
The router would then allow incoming connections from other
SMTP servers on the Internet to establish connections and transfer
mail to your organization. The downside to this architecture is that
the screening router is really the only protection mechanism
between the outside network and your internal network. Of course,
most organizations deploying an architecture like this would most
likely want to place an additional router between the host running
external services such as SMTP or HTTP and the internal network.
This creates a buffer zone often called a DMZ as shown in the next
architecture.

Architecture Bravo—Screening Router with DMZ

Architecture Bravo builds on the previous architecture (Alpha) and
adds the concept of a "demilitarized zone," or DMZ. The DMZ acts as
an intermediate subnet that "insulates" the internal network from
the Internet. External services such as an organization's Web or FTP
server would reside on the DMZ subnet. In addition, a proxy server
host would be located on the DMZ and proxy other more sensitive
services on the internal network. The proxy server host would both

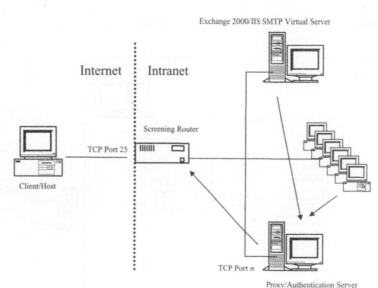

Figure 8.4
Illustration of Architecture Bravo

act as a gateway to the internal network as well as proxy functions. Alternatively, Exchange 2000 SMTP virtual servers could be located on the DMZ subnet along with other public servers (such as Web servers). The degree of protection is dependent on how complicated you want your design to be. Keep in mind that the more secure your design is, the more management and administration it requires. Additionally, this design could be further extended by adding a further degree of network separation, as shown in Figure 8.5.

Architecture Charlie—Highest Security

Architecture Charlie continues to build on the previous two and further extends the security barrier by placing the secondary screening router directly between the internal network and the DMZ. The principals are the same as in the two previous architectures: An external router filters packets and protects services exposed to the Internet such as SMTP. Instead of a proxy server acting as both the gateway and the proxy for internal networks, the functions of gateway and proxy are divided by adding an additional screening router as a gateway protecting internal networks and a separate proxy host dedicated to this role. In the book *Internet Security for Business,* the authors refer to this architecture as the "belt-and-suspenders" architecture. As the name implies, this architecture provides two ways to

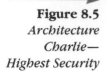

Figure 8.5
*Architecture
Charlie—
Highest Security*

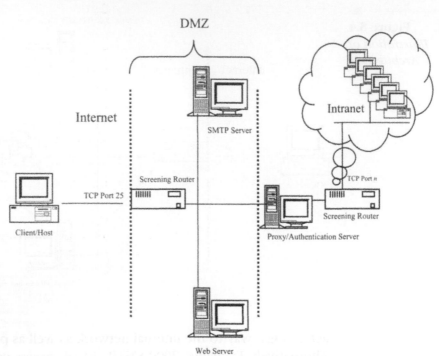

"keep your pants up." In the previous architecture (Architecture Bravo), one host provided both functions (proxy and gateway). In architecture Charlie, the additional router and separation of roles adds an additional line of defense that, while subtle, can be an important extra-added measure.

These architectures certainly don't represent the only design methods for protecting Exchange and other services exposed to the Internet. However, these architectures are fundamental, and most variants will be closely rooted to one of these approaches. Advances in firewall technologies are coming with each new release of vendor software. In addition, organizations with services exposed to the Internet are more cautious than they used to be. Regardless of which architecture your organization deploys for Windows 2000 and Exchange 2000, ensure that the one your organization has in place or is planning to deploy provides adequate protection for Exchange services like SMTP and HTTP. Also, don't forget to familiarize yourself with the protocols and TCP/UDP ports that Windows 2000 and Exchange 2000 utilize (refer to Appendix A).

8.7.1.4 Special Firewall Considerations for Outlook Web Access

When deploying SMTP services exposed to the Internet, you are mainly focused on allowing access for your mail gateway to connect and transfer mail to other SMTP hosts on the Internet and allowing those hosts to connect and transfer mail to you. The focus is on server-server connections for the purpose of mail routing. Additionally, the SMTP gateway acts as a store-and-forward host, and no internal access to systems is required.

When you want to provide OWA to incoming clients via the Internet, the focus is on client-server connections. Also, these clients are potentially able to access internal information contained in Exchange store servers. Since OWA and other Internet protocols for Exchange 2000 can be deployed in a front-end/back-end design (front-end protocol servers provide proxy access to back-end store servers), front-end servers must be exposed to the Internet. The front-end server accepts OWA requests from the client via HTTP and must send the requests to the appropriate back-end server where client data resides. Obviously, a firewall must separate front-end servers from their back-end counterparts in this scenario. Regardless of the architecture applied from these examples, special considerations are needed for OWA services exposed to the Internet. OWA services must either be secured by implementing VPN technology or via specific firewall configurations. In the case of a VPN, OWA clients connect securely through the firewall via an encrypted tunnel, and there is no reason for special firewall considerations (other than those required to support the VPN connection) for front-end/back-end designs. In the event that you choose to expose front-end servers to the Internet, your firewall architecture will need to provide access for several or all of the services listed in Table 8.6.

Table 8.6 *Outlook Web Access Services Firewall Configuration*

Service/Protocol/ Port	Description
HTTP TCP port 80	Default HTTP services access port required for clients to connect to OWA services inside the firewall perimeter.
HTTP TCP port 443	Optional: Use if you want to enable HTTP connections for OWA clients via SSL.

Table 8.6   *Outlook Web Access Services Firewall Configuration (continued)*

Service/Protocol/ Port	Description
LDAP TCP port 3268	Required for LDAP directory and Global Catalog access for OWA clients if the front-end OWA server is separated from the back-end server and the Global Catalog server by a firewall. TCP port 3268 must be allowed for clients to access the Active Directory via LDAP.
LDAP TCP port 389	Required for LDAP directory and Global Catalog access for OWA clients when searching the local domain.
LDAP TCP port 636	Required only in the event that front-end servers need to send LDAP requests via secure SSL connections as an extra security measure.
Kerberos TCP port 88	If clients such as Windows 2000 Professional are using Kerberos authentication, TCP port 88 must be enabled through the firewall for authentication to occur.
Kerberos UDP port 88	If clients such as Windows 2000 Professional/Internet Explorer 5.0 are using Kerberos authentication, UDP port 88 must be enabled through the firewall for authentication to occur.

NOTE: Although LDAP requests are typically passed on port 389 to a local domain controller, this only allows a client to search the local domain. Since most outside clients will need to search the entire Active Directory forest, TCP port 3268 is required.

The most secure firewall configuration for OWA places a firewall mechanism at either side of your front-end server (the front-end server is placed in the DMZ). In this configuration (shown in Figure 8.6), the OWA client request passes through the first firewall (external) and connects with the front-end server via TCP port 80 (or port 443 in the case of HTTP/SSL). Using LDAP, the front-end server queries the Global Catalog server through the second firewall perimeter via TCP port 3268. This enables the front-end server to locate the appropriate back-end server for the client requesting service. Once determined, the front-end and back-end servers communicate via TCP port 80 through the second firewall (internal). Inside the first firewall, HTTP via SSL access is not needed and is typically just added overhead. Therefore, even if the client is connecting from the outside via TCP port 443, the front-end need not communicate to the back-end server via SSL (unless specifically required in your organization). Depending on your clients needs and organizational security requirements, you may open additional ports on your firewall perimeters to allow services such as RPC communication or Kerberos authentication.

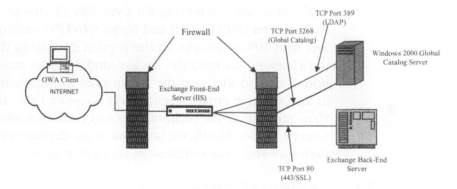

Figure 8.6
Optimal secure firewall Architecture for OWA

8.7.2 Anti-Virus Solutions

On Friday, March 26, 1999, several corporate networks across the world were stricken with a Microsoft Word macro virus referred to as "Melissa." Because of its unusual ability to propagate itself through electronic mail, the virus forced companies to disable portions of their e-mail systems to prevent further propagation both within and outside of their firms. Besides self-propagation, the virus sent inappropriate e-mail to addresses it found in personal address books on Microsoft Outlook mail clients. The virus used well-documented methods that provided a way for unsuspecting users to infect an entire organization. Melissa was a Word macro virus that was attached to an e-mail message. Once a user launched the attachment, the Word macro modified the standard template (NORMAL.DOT) by adding virus macro code. While not data-destructive, the virus code would replicate itself by sending copies of the virus to large blocks of recipients in the Global Address List (GAL). This often resulted in Exchange servers throughout an organization being choked as the amount of mail traffic grew exponentially as the virus replicated itself. While rather simple, the Melissa virus demonstrated clearly how vulnerable our Exchange systems are to a DoS attacks. Later attacks such as WormExplore.Zip and the "ILOVEYOU" virus have only reinforced this point.

Computer viruses are a particularly troublesome scourge that is growing in threat against e-mail systems. According to a 1999 Gartner Research advisory, e-mail is responsible for a large portion of viral infections, accounting for over 40% of attacks. Other services such as Web (HTTP), FTP, and News (NNTP) combined account for less than 10% of attacks. In the section discussing threats earlier in the chapter, I covered the background on virus attacks. In this section, I want to focus on the approaches to preventing virus attacks in an Exchange environment. I will discuss a three-tier approach to virus prevention: the technologies and vendors available and how to select a vendor. Finally, we will look at the deployment points or scenarios for anti-virus solutions in your environment.

8.7.2.1 Perimeters of Defense

When you view your organization with respect to viral infection, think of it as a fortress of services with limited access points. These access points are (1) the Internet (2) the server store, and (3) the client device. For an anti-virus solution in your organization to be complete, it will need to provide protection for these three perimeters of defense.

The first perimeter or tier of protection needs to protect the client device (usually a desktop PC). It is here that floppy disks can be accessed and viruses spread. Macro viruses also originate at the client PC as individuals connect to shared drives and access common files that can be infected with macro viruses as in the case of the Melissa virus. At the client perimeter, you have only one option: file-level antiviral solutions. These products provide real-time in-memory and file-based scanning for both local and attached network drives. Besides real-time scanning, manual scans are also available. Like all anti-virus solutions, these products rely on signature files that identify viruses and provide the ability to clean them from a system. The best practice for the client perimeter of defense is to implement scanning products and provide a secure desktop environment that limits current users' local client permissions to those that are nondestructive (since a virus program would run under the current context of the logged on user). While real-time and file-based scanning programs are a key part of a total anti-virus strategy, they are usually not the concern of the Exchange system manager. More recently,

Microsoft has looked closer at the specific vulnerabilities on the client side (Outlook) and has provided specific security enhancements for Outlook 2000 that limit the abilities of viruses targeted at Outlook vulnerabilities, as in the case of Melissa and ILOVEYOU.

The second tier or perimeter of defense for an organization is the servers where files and user data are stored. File servers are important servers for which to implement sound anti-virus solutions, but it is the Exchange information store that is the primary concern of Exchange system managers. Most messaging systems like Exchange store data in a proprietary database format such as Exchange's Extensible Storage Engine (ESE) discussed in Chapter 3. Traditional file server–based anti-virus scanning engines cannot scan these stores. In order to scan Exchange Server information stores, vendors of anti-virus solutions must access Exchange stores directly and provide scanning of e-mail attachments directly. This is accomplished in several ways. One method allows the A-V product to log on to the Exchange server as a privileged user and uses the MAPI protocol to open each individual mailbox and scan messages for attachments. The attachments that are infected can be cleaned and are typically replaced by a friendly notice indicating that the message contained a virus and was cleaned. Another approach to Exchange store scanning, implemented by vendors like Sybari, is a pseudo-reverse-engineering approach. This proprietary approach uses ESE APIs to connect with the Exchange database engine to gain access to the message attachments table and to provide real-time and manual scanning. This approach results in a very high-performance solution with less resource overhead as compared to the MAPI-access method.

Microsoft provides the last approach as a result of efforts from anti-virus vendors who reverse-engineered the access to the Exchange database engine. Provided in Exchange 5.5 Service Pack 3, the anti-virus API for Exchange provides vendors a supported interface in which to access the Exchange information store without having to use MAPI or engage in unsupported methods. This API is carried forward in Exchange 2000, and several vendors at the time of this writing have already announced and delivered support for the API. Eventually, most will adopt this approach and provide support in their A-V products for Exchange 2000. Products that address viral protection for this perimeter of defense are shown in Table 8.7, which provides a description of each product as well.

The final access point (and perimeter of defense) into your environment can also be protected from potential virus infection. This perimeter is the point of entry to your systems from the Internet. We discussed earlier in the chapter how this gateway can be protected via firewall architectures. However, I deferred specific discussions around anti-virus protection to this section. At this point of access into an organization, SMTP mail is delivered and routed throughout an Exchange environment. Most organizations have SMTP mail services that provide an access point exposed to the Internet as discussed earlier. SMTP mail traffic then either is routed directly to "home" servers where users reside or routed to an internal SMTP relay host for eventual routing to final destinations. It is at this entry point into the organization that many virus threats can be stifled. As SMTP-based mail enters into the organization, it can be scanned for viral content. This gateway/firewall-level protection scans attachments entering from the Internet and can remove viruses and other undesirable content before it enters the organization. This eliminates the propagation of such content and provides a method of containment. Most products on the market can capture a high percentage (95–99%) of unwanted files and content.

A complete protection scheme to prevent virus outbreaks in your Exchange deployment is an approach that combines gateway/firewall scanning with protective measures at the other perimeters of defense (client device and server store). Table 8.7 lists the leading and key vendors providing both store-based and gateway-based scanning products. Many of the vendors provide both capabilities within a single product family. Others have chosen to focus in only one area. The listing is by no means a recommendation or an exhaustive list of all products on the market. However, when selecting anti-virus solutions, many of these products will most likely end up on your short list. In the next section, I will address selection of an anti-virus solution.

Table 8.7 *Anti-Virus Solutions Vendor Listing*

Product/Vendor	Perimeter Coverage	Description/Remarks
Symantec Norton Anti-virus (NAV)	• Store • Gateway	The NAV line of products includes products for both store-based and gateway scanning. http://www.symantec.com/nav

Table 8.7 *Anti-Virus Solutions Vendor Listing (continued)*

Product/Vendor	Perimeter Coverage	Description/Remarks
Network Associates Inc. GroupShield	• Store • Gateway • Client	NAI sells both types of products in its Total Virus Defense (TVD) family and has a unique alliance device available for gateway scanning. http://www.nai.com
Computer Associates InoculateIT	• Store • Gateway	CA InoculateIT has options for store- and gateway-based scanning and can be managed via CA Unicenter TNG. http://www.cai.com
Trend Micro ScanMail/ InterScan VirusWall	• Store • Gateway • Client	Trend Micro has ScanMail for store-based scanning and VirusWall for SMTP gateways and integrates with HP OpenView. http://www.antivirus.com
Sybari Antigen	• Store • Gateway	Sybari is a relative newcomer but has a very innovative product that provides both store- and gateway-based scanning. http://www.sybari.com
Content Technologies MailSweeper (Integralis)	• Store • Gateway	MailSweeper is Content's main product and is a gateway scanner. Content has a unique add-on called SECRETSweeper that scans S/MIME messages. The company does have store-based technology available. http://www.integralis.com
Nexor Interceptor	• Gateway	Nexor provides an excellent, simple gateway scanning product. http://www.nexor.com
Nemx Anti-Virus for Exchange	• Store • Gateway • Client	Nemx has a small market presence but a solid product. http://www.nemx.com

The key motivating factor for deploying an anti-virus solution lies in the fact that virus creation and infection are on the rise and e-mail will become the primary source of infection. Support staffs will be buried in the administrative burden of virus control and disaster recovery unless an organization selects and deploys a solid anti-virus solution. The solution needs to address every perimeter of defense—client, store, and gateway. Unless organizations have these mechanisms of protection in place, virus infestations will continue to cause unwanted and unnecessary downtime for messaging systems.

When selecting from the myriad of anti-virus solutions vendors available, you are faced with a difficult decision on which product is right for your organization. You can select the product that has the "best" features, use one that you already own, or engage in a complex process of elimination that is based on certain criteria, performance, and functionality. This process and method of selection will vary for each organization according to its needs. The following table provides some important criteria I recommend when selecting an anti-virus solution.

Table 8.8   *Recommended Anti-Virus Vendor Selection Criteria*

Criteria	*Recommendation/Guideline*
Vendor focus	Does the vendor focus on anti-virus solutions that are full featured and provide a complete comprehensive solution? Or does it focus on a niche or one perimeter of defense? For example, does the vendor offer only a gateway scanning product or an entire suite that covers all three perimeters? I recommend a comprehensive solution.
Vendor support	Anti-virus technology is advancing at a rapid pace. How quickly does a vendor update its products? How soon are new technologies such as the Exchange ESE A-V API leveraged? In addition, how soon are service packs, hotfixes, and new virus signature files made available? Finally, when you need assistance installing or supporting a solution, how responsive is the vendor?
Heterogeneous support	If your organization is heterogeneous like most, Exchange and e-mail are not the only applications that need A-V protection. Often a vendor that supports multiple operating systems and applications can be a superior choice. Multiple platform support, such as Alpha processor or clustering, may also be important.
Performance impact	In particular, store-based scanning can be quite resource intensive for an Exchange server. Carefully evaluate and test the impact each vendor has on server system resources. Higher resource utilization does not necessarily equate to more effective scanning.
Multiengine support	One way to ensure effective scanning and to increase the chances of detection is to deploy multiple scanning engines. For example, an organization may deploy one engine at the gateway, another at the store, and still another at the client. Some products allow engines to be interchanged in order to serve this purpose.
Detection rates	Most vendors claim high virus- and content-detection rates for their products. You may want to investigate this further and establish a standardized testing and evaluation procedure for products as part of your selection process.

Table 8.8	*Recommended Anti-Virus Vendor Selection Criteria (continued)*
Criteria	**Recommendation/Guideline**
Manageability and administration	The whole reason to deploy an A-V solution is to minimize the support staff overhead of managing A-V incidents. Ensure that the product you select is easily managed, maintained, supported, and administered. Many products also provide integration with leading enterprise management applications such as HP OpenView, CA Unicenter, and Tivoli TME.

It is clear that deployment of a good anti-virus solution for your organization is of paramount concern for mission-critical systems. If you have not invested in this sometimes-overlooked area of protection, take steps now to select, pilot, and implement a comprehensive A-V solution organization-wide. Implementing scanning at your gateways, server stores, and clients covers the key perimeters of defense. In addition to implementing a good A-V strategy, don't forget the basics such as good security measures, monitoring and intrusion-detection techniques, and solid disaster recovery practices and procedures. Also conduct thorough pilot testing before rolling out an anti-virus solution in order to minimize risks involved. This vital area can be a key to maintaining a highly available Exchange deployment.

8.7.2.2   *User Education Is Key*

I can't emphasize strongly enough how far a little user education will go in these instances. Scanning on your incoming SMTP gateway is an excellent method to protect your organization against the likes of attackers like Melissa, WormExplore, and ILOVEYOU. Scanning for attachment content at the SMTP service is the best way to protect your organization. While this is effective, it can't stop everything. That is why user education is the other pillar that good protection must stand on. For me, it seems rather simple: If you don't know the person who is sending you an attachment with an *.EXE, *.COM, *.VBS, or other extension, *don't open it!* However, not all users know that every VBS file is a potential bomb. Users of our Exchange services must be educated on these finer points and be encouraged to practice the default rule of not opening any attachment they aren't sure of. In recent outbreaks such as the ILOVEYOU virus, the users who were savvy enough not to open up the suspect messages and instead hit the Delete key went about their business as usual. This is a key point. It is not anti-virus software by itself that can protect you from these attacks. It is a combination of a well-implemented gateway and store-based scanning process combined with some solid user education practices. Microsoft Outlook is a very rich and powerful client tool. With this richness and power come some vulnerabilities that have been exploited by attacks like Melissa and ILOVEYOU. Only through this two-pronged approach can you ensure that your organization is protected. After all, user education is relatively cheap by comparison.

8.7.3   Message Content Security

Message content security is the final point is this chapter's complete security strategy for Exchange deployments. Unauthorized access and forgery are the threats of concern when we discuss message content security. Based on an organization's security requirements, message content security may be satisfied with the mechanisms provided by the Windows 2000 and Exchange 2000 access control features discussed earlier in this chapter. However, if further measures are required, message content security must rely on techniques such as message encryption and digital signatures. In the final section, I will discuss the basics of a PKI (required to utilize encryption and signing), Certificate Services, Exchange 2000 Key Management Service, and how encryption and signing are used to protect against severe threats of unauthorized access and forgery.

8.7.3.1   Public Key Infrastructure

The subject of public key infrastructures (PKIs)could warrant many books and papers on its own. In the context of our discussion, I want to provide an overview with emphasis on why is it fundamental to providing message content security for an Exchange environment.

Simply put, a PKI is a system of managing secure keys that provides a robust trust mechanism throughout an enterprise, multiple enterprises, or business partners. A PKI functions to provide a process for issuing, distributing, and validating keys and certificates. The important aspects of message content security for Exchange are encryption and digital signing. Secure Multipurpose Internet Mail Extensions (S/MIME) address this aspect and require such an infrastructure to be in place. Specifically, S/MIME is a standard (S/MIME version 3 in its current form) that secures e-mail transmissions in an interoperable fashion using X.509 version 3 certificates and that provides authentication and privacy via digital certificates. The digital certificates used by S/MIME enable e-mail to be signed and encrypted so that only the desired recipient can read the message. The signature also provides nonrepudiation of the sender. Of course, there are many third-party free or fee-based products that will provide variants of encryption and signing capabilities for Exchange clients such as Entrust, VeriSign, and freeware-based Pretty Good Privacy (PGP).

In a recent report on PKIs, the Radicati Group suggests five key properties for a successful PKI:

1. Applications and users need certainty of which key pairs belong to given entities.

2. The integrity of key pairs must be maintained with safeguards that reduce the risk of key compromise.

3. If a key pair is compromised or revoked, methods must exist to invalidate the key pair and publish this fact.

4. Methods must exist to back up, protect, and restore critical keys.

5. Encryption/signature technology needs to match legal requirements and restrictions.

Thus, a PKI is a collection of entities that are providing the preceding functions. Figure 8.7 provides a look at a typical PKI design for an Exchange deployment. Leveraged for Exchange message content security, a PKI controls issuance, management, revocation of keys and certificates.

8.7.3.2   Certificate Services

A *certificate* is an electronic credential that authenticates a user on the Internet and on intranets. Certificates ensure the legitimate online transfer of confidential information or other sensitive materials by means of public encryption technology. If someone in your organization connects to a Web site or a server in another company and that server has a certificate signed by an authority you trust, you can be confident that the company the certificate identifies actually operates the server. Likewise, servers can use certificates to verify a client's identity. In either case, you safeguard your intranet against forgery or impersonation by an outside party. Also consider that, by

Figure 8.7
*A public key
infrastructure
for Exchange*

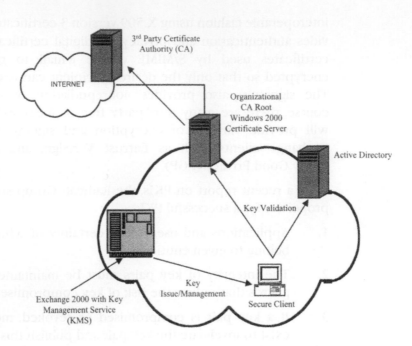

issuing certificates to employees, coworkers, and internal resources, you can verify a user's identity internally as well.

Certificates are an integral part of message content security because they also allow users to generate digital signatures and encrypt e-mail. Digital signatures not only validate the sender's identity, they ensure that the message contents have not been altered. No one can tamper with a digitally signed message without detection. When the sender encrypts a message, only the recipient is able to decrypt it and read its contents.

Windows 2000 Server Certificate Services allows an organization to act as its own CA or as a subordinate CA in a larger CA hierarchy. A CA is an issuer of digital certificates; it provides and assigns the unique strings of numbers that make up the keys digital certificates use. A CA can issue its own certificates to clients and servers and can revoke certificates when the private key associated with the certificate is compromised or when the subject of the certificate leaves an organization. Certificate Services issues X.509 version 3 certificates. Key Management Service, which can issue X.509 version 1 certificates for backwards compatibility, is discussed later in this chapter.

8.7.3.3   Certificates and Public Keys

Public keys must be certified by a CA. Any x.509v3-compatible CA can issue certificates to an Exchange organization. A certificate binds the user's public key to his or her mailbox. Each X.509 certificate includes:

- A unique serial number

- The distinguished name of the CA

- The name of the user, which is referred to as the subject of the certificate

- The validity period of the certificate

- Version 3 extensions

   Version 3 extensions are the standard certificate format that Windows 2000 Server certificate-based processes use. They can include information related to key identifiers, key usage, certificate policy, alternate names and attributes, certification path, constraints, and enhancements for certificate revocation.

8.7.3.4   Certificate Trust List

With a certificate trust list, an organization can ensure that the CA issuing the certificate can be trusted, even if the CA is in another organization. This is the most secure way to verify the source of messages sent from another organization. It is also transparent to users—they don't need to perform any additional steps to send a digitally signed message to a user in a trusted organization. Because certification establishes trust between CAs, security keys sent between users in certified organizations are automatically trusted. On the other hand, if a user receives a digitally signed message from a CA not on his or her certificate trust list, the recipient cannot rely on that signature. Key Management servers in Exchange 2000 now use the Windows 2000 Server Certificate Services to maintain certificate trust lists.

8.7.3.5   Certificate Revocation

Revocation checking warns users when they verify signed messages that contain a revoked certificate. Revoking a user's advanced security is not the same as deleting a user, and you should do this only if the security of the user is compromised; for example, you should consider revoking advanced security if it appears that someone is signing messages on behalf of another user or if someone has gained access to the user's security file and password. You can enable security again by assigning another temporary token to the user. A revocation list contains the serial number and expiration date of each revoked user's certificate. The Key Management server stores the revocation list in the key management database and then writes it to Active Directory. The revocation list in the directory is then cached on the client and updated daily. You should limit the use of revocation since, as the revocation list grows larger, the client's advanced security performance degrades because each time the client verifies a message's signature, it must check the revocation list.

8.7.3.6   *Exchange 2000 Key Management Service*

Exchange 2000 Server uses advanced security, provided by the Key Management Service, to deliver several benefits:

1.   Sender-to-recipient authentication ensures that a signer's identity is authentic.

2.   Encryption ensures that only intended recipients can read the message.

3.   Digital signatures ensure that the content of a message hasn't changed since the message was signed.

4.   Storage of all keys in an encrypted database and backup database protects certificates.

5.   Support for the Data Encryption Standard (DES), CAST encryption algorithms, and the S/MIME messaging format provides compatibility with other systems.

6.   Support for X.509 version 1 certificates, which are compatible with Outlook 97 and earlier clients.

Every user of Exchange Key Management Service has at least two certificates. One is the encryption certificate that contains the public encryption key and is an attribute of the user object in Active Directory. The other is the signing certificate that contains the public signing key and is stored locally in a secure location on the client.

Key Management Service is closely integrated with Windows 2000 Server Certificate Services and other operating system utilities such as Group Policy. In addition, Key Management Service features give administrators greater flexibility without compromising the security and reliability of the service. Earlier versions (Exchange Server 5.5) of the Key Management Service managed the certificate trust list. A certificate trust lists keeps track of all trusted CAs, even those that are outside your organization. The Windows 2000 CA Server now maintains the certificate trust list for Key Management servers. Now Exchange administrators can import external certificates to Windows 2000 Server Group Policy objects, and from there, certificates are published to Active Directory. Any computer in the forest running Windows 2000 Server can download a certificate and trust it. Windows 2000 Professional clients find the certificate trust list on their domain controllers. For clients running earlier versions of Windows, the Key Management server publishes the certificate trust list so that Outlook clients can access it whenever encryption is used in messaging. Windows 2000 Server or Key Management Service manages the certificate trust list without intervention in either case.

With Exchange 2000, Key Management servers work in conjunction with Active Directory to enable or recover multiple users at once. Administrators are no longer confined to enabling or recovering only one person or an entire recipient container of users. Unlike Exchange 5.5, each session requires you type the administrative passwords only once. With Exchange 2000 Server, you can now have one Key Management server for every administrative group in your organization. With Exchange 5.5, you can have one Key Management server for each Exchange site.

Another feature of Key Management Service in Exchange 2000 Server is the capability to import or export users from one Key Management server to another. If you have a large organization with multiple administrative groups and someone is transferred to another department, you may need to move the user to another administrative group. That may entail moving that user's keys to a different Key Management server. The export and import feature makes it possible for you to move one or more person's keys securely and without risk of misdirection.

Important: Because a user can exist on only one Key Management server, you must first export a user or group of users before you can import them on another server.

8.8   Putting Security Together

Deploying and managing a secure Exchange environment involves many areas disciplines, and levels of expertise. In this chapter, we have just scratched the surface and overviewed the "big picture" of Exchange security. The most important points are two—that we understand the threats to our Exchange environments and that we are aware of and understand the technology available to us to address these threats.

The threats we discussed were denial of service, unauthorized access, viruses, forgery, and mail relaying. It is possible that your organization will never be a target for any of these threats. However, the first incident that occurs will usually bring painful awareness to the fact that protective measures are required. As an example, look at how the outbreak of the Melissa virus in 1999 changed our outlook on anti-virus solutions. For each of these threats, we have overviewed the most common means of protection.

For the denial-of-service attack, the most common point of attack for an Exchange server is via the SMTP service, where an attacker floods or crashes the SMTP server, thereby denying those services to legitimate users. We also saw with the Melissa virus how a virus attack can lead to a denial-of-service situation. To protect against unauthorized access, several protection mechanisms are available such as Windows 2000 and Exchange 2000 access control methods like the Active Directory, Kerberos authentication, access control entries and lists, policies, permissions, and Exchange roles. Digital encryption and signing provided with a well-designed and managed PKI can also be an added measure against unauthorized access.

For virus threats, there are many products and solutions from a range of vendors that help cover the three perimeters of defense—the client, server store, and gateways. A comprehensive solution coupled with good security measures will counteract most viral infection threats. For organizations threatened by potential forgery of messages and other content, the most common measure available for both internal and external threats is encryption and signing.

The final threats affecting SMTP services exposed to the Internet are unwanted mail relaying and unsolicited commercial e-mail (UCE—a.k.a. SPAM) These threats can be addressed by a superior firewall design and implementation of Exchange Server's own features provided to protect against this nondestructive but annoying threat.

Many technologies exist to lock down our Exchange environments, and Exchange 2000 improves upon its already excellent built-in security features. Take some time to assess your environment and the threats that are most likely to occur. Careful research, planning, pilot testing, and deployment of rock-solid security measures will help ensure that your Exchange deployment provides maximum reliability.

Bringing It All Together With Proactive Management

Over the last several years, as I have met with organizations deploying Exchange Server, one fundamental concept continues to be driven home to me. It may seem obvious to some of you, but proactive management is one of the most important yet underutilized techniques for increasing system availability. This point was illustrated by one organization that I have dealt with quite often. This organization was facing severe pressures from senior management and their client base because of unacceptable levels of downtime for the Exchange deployment. This organization's cause of downtime was not hardware or environment; it was the result of frequent Exchange information store corruption. Since it was impossible to solve this issue and guarantee that it would never occur again, the organization chose to overcome the problem through proactive management practices. By simply deploying a management application that was Exchange-aware and by putting in place some problem notification, tracking, and resolution/response procedures, they were able to significantly reduce the user impact of this issue. In the short term, the number of occurrences did not significantly change (although Microsoft and the hardware vendor diligently continued to work the issue). However, the system management staff's alerting, notification, and procedures for handling the issue did change. Instead of reacting to an occurrence of database corruption (which caused several hours of downtime), support staff was immediately alerted to the condition and was able to immediately move mailboxes from the server experiencing the error to a spare standby server. This served to minimize the actual downtime a user experienced, while support staff could troubleshoot the problem server. Since this organization measured downtime in terms of lost client opportunity (versus actual hours of server downtime), availability metrics improved, and the organization was successful in meeting its reliability service-level agreements. Senior management and users cheered, and in the long run, Exchange system managers were heroes. This was all accomplished without actually solving the cause of downtime (this organization continues to experience the same issue although less frequently). It was proactive management that virtually eliminated the issue (in the eyes of clients anyway).

9.1   Proactive vs. Reactive Management

Every system manager has a choice to make when he takes on the job. You can choose to manage problems after they occur ("flying by the seat of your pants" or reactive management), or you can make a conscious choice to build a foundation and set a precedent by trying to manage problems before and when they occur and even being able to anticipate their occurrence (proactive management).

For some, this choice has already been made for you based on budgetary constraints or legacy practices. After all, proactive management is more expensive. More training is required, more planning and development are needed, and the tools necessary for proactive management are costly. In fact, the staffing, training, and tools necessary to provide proactive management for your Exchange deployment could very well be one of the most costly components of the overall messaging system. The choice must be made with this in mind. Also, organizational management (the people who will pay for it) needs to buy into a proactive management strategy from the beginning. They will have to be educated on why the extra staff, training, and tools are required. Everyone should have an understanding of the trade-offs involved as well. Without proactive management, you may need to commit to lower levels of service for the messaging system. If the organization understands and accepts this, all is well. You, as the system manager, however, will have to work hard to understand these trade-offs in cost and service and adequately communicate this to your customers and management. To some, proactive management is not a requirement but a luxury (although the point could be argued extensively). If the messaging system is not a business-critical tool for an organization, the costs of proactive management may not be justified.

Let me give you a scenario with two possible outcomes to illustrate my point. Suppose an Exchange server supporting 1,500 users has three 20GB information stores (each in a separate storage group and each supporting 500 users). Suppose one of these 20GB information stores became corrupt. In the case of a proactive management approach, the corruption would be reported during a daily full backup and logged to the application log on the server. Proactive measures would be in place to scan the event log and backup log for errors. These errors would be reported to support staff who would immediately take action and either restore the database from tape or perform some other proactive measure such as moving user mailboxes from that database to a spare database reserved for this purpose. Most likely, in this case of proactive management, the problem would be corrected and/or alleviated before the users even became aware of the problem. The result: minimal or no impact on service-level achievement.

Now, let's turn to the case of reactive management. Taking our scenario with a corrupt 20GB database, daily full backups would still report the corrupted database. However, since no proactive measures are in place to alert support staff, the error goes unnoticed and continues to occur for several weeks. All along, the database is never backed up (because a corruption error will terminate backup). After several weeks, the users begin reporting lost messages or corrupted mailboxes. Eventually, the Exchange database engine dismounts the database and reports that it is corrupt. The 500 users on this database are now without service. Support staff now scrambles to begin repair and/or recovery operations for this 20GB database. Upon closer examination, they determine that the last good backup was taken several weeks ago. Depending on several factors, the recovery operation could take several hours to complete, and in the worst-case scenario, users may have lost several weeks of e-mail or other content. In the meantime, users are unhappy and management is disappointed because 500 users were without service for an extended period—a miserable failure to meet service-level agreements.

Hopefully, I have convinced you that proactive management is the best approach. I do realize that not all organizations have the resources available to implement every aspect of a complete proactive management strategy. However, if you are able to take some key insights and ideas from this chapter, I am confident you will improve service-levels for your Exchange deployment.

In this chapter, I will focus on the aspects of proactive management that can have a significant impact on your Exchange deployment. In my thinking, proactive management has three key components:

- **Performance management**—This involves the monitoring and management of system performance and capacity characteristics to ensure that performance and delivery service-levels are achieved. It involves establishment of performance baselines in order to compare observed statistics. Performance management also includes the capacity planning functions critical to anticipating growth.

- **Configuration management**—This involves the documentation, monitoring, and management of system hardware, software, firmware, and configuration data to ensure the highest levels of homogeneity among Exchange servers within a deployment. Configuration management facilitates troubleshooting and minimizes the occurrences of anomalies across a deployment. Configuration management also establishes guidelines and a means for managing change across a population of servers.

- **Fault management**—This establishes the process, procedures, and tools required for alerting and notification, action and decision-making, resolution, and reporting of system faults and anomalies. The goal of fault management is to identify and resolve error conditions before they impact the end user.

After drilling down to greater detail in each component area, I will also discuss some popular tools available that provide these features and support Exchange Server and Windows NT/2000. Closely tied to proactive management is the establishment of service-level agreements.

Since I believe that service levels must be established in order to determine the level of proactive management necessary, I will first devote some time to the definition and establishment of service-level agreements for your messaging system. By chapter's end, I hope to give you some excellent tools and practices that you can implement in your own deployment. While I can't guarantee availability and reliability for your deployment, I can promise that proactive management techniques can cover a multitude of downtime woes.

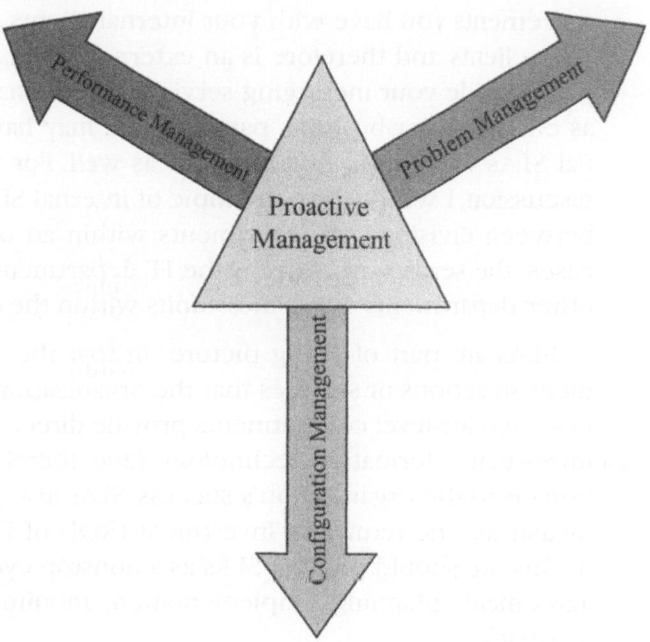

Figure 9.1
Three-pronged approach to proactive management

9.2   Establishing Service-Level Agreements

In discussions regarding service-level agreements, we should start by defining exactly what the term SLA means. In a generic sense, an SLA is an agreement between a service provider and a client about the quality or degree of service that the client requires from the service provider. As I have discussed previously, the service levels can cover a range of topics such as performance, delivery, availability, reliability, etc. Most service-level agreements tend to focus on the responsibilities of the service provider. However, I would encourage you to include the responsibilities of the end user as well as the messaging system when defining your SLAs for your Exchange deployment. Also, I should probably distinguish an external SLA from an internal SLA. An external SLA for your messaging system is a contract or agreement between the messaging system staff and an external service provider. For example, suppose you rely on an ISP for your Internet mail (SMTP) connectivity for your Exchange deployment. The messaging IT organization may have service levels and agreements defined with that ISP with the messaging system as client.

While this external SLA directly affects the internal service-level agreements you have with your internal clients, it is not an SLA with your clients and therefore is an external SLA. As another example, if you provide your messaging services to external organizations such as customers or business partners, you may have established external SLAs with those organizations as well. For the purposes of this discussion, I will stick to the topic of internal SLAs. Internal SLAs are between divisions or departments within an organization. In most cases, the service provider is the IT department, and the clients are other departments or business units within the company.

SLAs are part of a "big picture" in that they establish a commitment to actions or services that the organization requires to do business. Service-level commitments provide direct evidence of just how important information technology (and therefore, the IT organization) is to the organization's success. SLAs also provide a method of measuring the return on investment (ROI) of IT resources. Because of this, we should think of SLAs as a nonstop cycle or loop of dialog, agreement, planning, implementation, monitoring, reporting, and feedback.

According to a 1998 Ferris Research report, approximately 40% of large organizations have SLAs in place for their messaging systems. Of the organizations that did not have messaging system SLAs in place, about two-thirds of these either are developing them or have plans to do so. There is an obvious trend toward the establishment of internal SLAs for messaging systems. This is due to the fact that e-mail and collaborative applications have become an essential business tool, and the need to manage and monitor messaging system performance has become absolutely critical to an organization's success. SLAs provide a fundamental construct for defining system requirements and evaluating the performance of the messaging service provided. For a messaging system like Exchange Server, SLAs provide a means to establish the service necessary to conduct business and provide assurance that messaging services are available when needed.

Cost is another driving factor behind service-level agreements. Organizations will always demand the highest levels possible but are often tempered by the costs involved. The process of establishing and maintaining SLAs provides a cost factor and justification required for the service expectations of users. The "holy grail" is found when business units and IT staff find a "sweet spot" between cost and service level resulting from trade-offs between critical business services and tools and the reasonable cost of those services.

There are four factors that will typically motivate you to develop SLAs for your Exchange deployment. The first is the realization that messaging and collaboration is a mission-critical resource. When outages occur, they usually do not go unnoticed. In fact, in the last several years, messaging system downtime has risen to the levels of many line of business (LOB) applications such as ERP, MRP, etc. (some would say that the importance of messaging services has even surpassed these applications). Like LOB applications, when the messaging system in down, the organization will suffer productivity losses. Cases in which e-mail is a primary means of product or service delivery, the losses far exceed simple productivity losses.

The gap between client expectations and services provided is another motivating factor for establishing messaging system service-levels. As SLAs are developed, the process helps users understand the real challenges (in technology, costs, and other areas) that IT staff members face in providing services. This awareness brings users down to a level of more realistic expectations for the characteristics and qualities of the services being provided. When an SLA has been developed and established, it functions both as a measure of performance and as a measure of the real value of services being provided.

Migration or architecture changes are often another significant factor that drives the need for establishing SLAs. Since the technology (both software and hardware) has such as outrageous rate of change, there are always new "feeds and speeds" calling out to users and technologists alike. The need for better performance, reliability, and new technologies are examples of this. Since Exchange Server has only been around since 1996, the quick rise to fame of Exchange is an example of how organizations with legacy messaging systems jumped on a new technology bandwagon that resulted in major architectural changes and IT investments. Since senior management is not always willing to sign blank checks for technology investments, SLAs have provided a great method of documenting the return on investment for these investments.

The final motivator for SLAs may be a change is the IT organization's status within the organization. Since IT has always been a source of revenue loss (a cost center instead of a P&L business unit), many IT organizations have found themselves to be last in line when corporate funds are distributed. As a result, IT organizations have had to find methods of reducing costs and even methods of making money called *chargebacks*. Chargebacks to business units who use IT services are a method of both controlling costs and of providing a soft-dollar revenue stream to the IT organization. With these practices in place, IT can not only provide justification for its existence but also a legitimate flow of funds back into its coffers that offsets the expense of the IT organization. Service-level agreements are an ideal method of supporting these chargeback policies.

Whatever your motivations, it is clear that establishing SLAs for your Exchange deployment will be critical to your success as a planner or implementer. In the next section, let's take a look at the process of developing SLAs and provide some guidelines that will help you with this foundational piece of implementing proactive management.

If you thought the process of developing service-level agreements for your Exchange deployment was going to be easy, consider the process first. Of course, you could choose to develop SLAs in a vacuum (i.e., without including the client or customer), but I am most certain that, in the long run, you would fail. When done right, the establishment of service-level agreements should take a fair amount of time and be the result of cooperative efforts and negotiations among all involved parties (service provider and clients). Much of the time involves communication, compromise, and getting a handle on the organization's expectations and value for the messaging system. Northeast Consulting Resources, Inc., provides some commonly referenced generic guidelines for establishing service-level agreements as shown in the following sidebar.

Guidelines for Establishing a Service-Level Agreement

A service-level agreement (SLA) defines the responsibilities of an IT service provider and the users of that service. Typically, an SLA will include the following components:

1. Definition of the service provided, the parties involved, and the effective dates of the agreement.

2. Specifications of the hours and days during which the service will be offered, including testing, maintenance, and upgrades.

3. Specifications of the numbers and locations of users and/or hardware for which the service will be offered.

4. Explanation of problem-reporting procedures, including conditions of escalation to the next higher level of support. It should also include a definition of the expected response time to a problem report.

5. Explanation of change-request procedures. It may include expected times for completing routine change requests.

6. Specification of target levels of service quality such as availability, reliability, response time, throughput, and average and experienced reporting of these metrics. The specification should also include explanations of how these metrics are calculated and the frequency of reporting.

7. Specification of charges associated with the service. Charges may be a flat rate or based on different levels of service quality provided.

8. Specification of the user responsibilities under the SLA, such as training, configuration, or circumvention of change-management procedures.

9. Description of procedures for resolution of service-level disagreements.

10. A defined process for feedback and amending the service-level agreement.

Source: 1998, James Herman and Theo Forbath of Northeast Consulting Resources, Inc.

Developing and establishing SLAs is a process, not simply a document that is written by IT staff and handed to a client. You need to have a consensus between service provider and client about exactly what services will be provided and the quality of those services. When developing and establishing service-level agreements for your Exchange deployment, I recommend that you use a four-step process.

9.2.1 STEP 1: Service-Level Agreement Planning

The process of planning service-level agreements for your messaging system should be seen as a process and a "setting of the stage." The goal of the planning step should be to assemble the right people and other resources necessary to make the SLA development process successful. The process is successful when agreement is reached regarding both the services the messaging system will provide and the quality of those services.

The first task of the SLA planning phase is to get buy-in and cooperation from all the groups within the organization that will be involved as either a client or a provider of the services. The important part here is that client representation (which often is not involved in the process) must be part of the team from the beginning. If you move forward in the process without the involvement of your messaging system customers, the entire process will fail because service-level agreements will not meet the business needs of the clients.

Another task in the planning process will be to gather the data necessary for the establishment of the SLAs. Messaging system cost is one of the important data points that is necessary for determining trade-offs between the degree of service and quality versus overall cost. The following sidebar provides an example of some of the cost components of a typical messaging system deployment like Exchange Server.

Example Messaging System Component Annual Cost Breakdown

Cost Component

Installation costs

> Planning and research
> Server hardware
> Server software
> Client software
> Outside consulting
> Management software and utilities
> Implementation and rollout

Annual Operating Costs

> Server hardware support contracts
> Server software support contracts
> Client software support contracts
> Messaging system WAN charge
> Messaging system IT staff
> Application development staff
> Outside consulting
> Staff training
> Client training
> Help desk staff

The final key task in SLA planning is the assembly of the SLA development team. Once you have buy-in and cooperation from all necessary parties, you need to build a team of individuals representing these parties who are knowledgeable in their respective areas. All members of the team should have the same goal in mind: to develop cost-effective service-level agreements that meet the business needs for which the messaging system was implemented. You will need experts in technology as well as individuals who understand the business the organization is in. You should also include representation from the accounting and finance disciplines that can assist in the tedious cost-benefit and return-on-investment calculations. Also, don't forget your attorneys. As part of the SLA development process for areas such as messaging retention/deletion and archival, it is a good idea to understand the legal implications that an SLA can have on the organization. I am sure someone at Microsoft possibly wishes that SLAs for message retention would have prevented some of those incriminating e-mail messages from getting into the hands of U.S. Department of Justice lawyers in the recent antitrust proceedings.

Overall, you need to use the planning step in SLA development as the cornerstone of the process. The people and resources you bring together at this juncture will determine the long-term success of service-level agreements you establish for your Exchange deployment. Takes the steps necessary to ensure that the right individuals with the right skills are assembled and have the same goal in mind.

9.2.2   STEP 2: Service-Level Agreement Development

The first task of this step is to get a handle on the true business needs of the organization. The SLA development team needs to have an understanding of the various business activities and processes that occur within the organization. You need to know how e-mail and collaborative applications impact these activities and processes as well as how individual employees utilize these services in their everyday jobs. When doing this research in your organization, make sure you talk with the different departments including cost centers, profit and loss centers, support and administrative centers, and those business groups that are on the front lines and have critical deadlines or risks. Talk to groups that are high producers and low producers as well as those with high costs and low costs. You need to have a good understanding of how the business works and how the services your Exchange deployment provides can positively or negatively impact each key department in the organization. As your team learns about your organization's key business activities try to identify just how the e-mail and collaborative applications provided by Exchange Server are used in the day-to-day tasks of conducting business. This can also be a great opportunity and exercise for your messaging system staff to determine possible future uses and applications they may be able to deploy. As part of this process, determine what happens when the messaging system fails. For example, if the sales department uses e-mail or a custom-developed application for submitting sales orders, what happens when Exchange is down for eight hours (and how much does this cost the company)? Don't forget to factor in user perceptions and overall satisfaction with the current system. Using this information, you can start to get an idea of the most critical aspects and services of your messaging system and to which business units they are most critical. This, in turn, will give you a starting point for selecting which metrics (such as delivery time, system availability, etc.) you should begin to focus on. You can begin to monitor these metrics immediately and establish baselines for the performance of these metrics for the various services your Exchange deployment offers. You can gather these statistics over a period of several months in order to establish empirical data on which to base further decisions in your SLA development process.

At the same time as you begin to gather data on metrics being driven by the business activities, begin to look closer at statistics and other data that the IT organization may already be gathering for the messaging system. You may already have help desk data on the types of problems that occur most frequently or information regarding client satisfaction and perceptions. For your Exchange servers, you may be already gathering data on performance metrics such as message volume, size, delivery times, and error rates. You may have data on the causes of downtime or outages and capacity planning information documented as well. While many of the metrics that an IT organization maintains internally are not directly tied to business activities and goals, these metrics are useful data and should be included in the SLA development process. Both the business-driven metrics and these are a vital part of ensuring that realistic and measurable service-level agreements are developed.

Once you have a clear understanding of how the business works and how certain key business activities need the support of service-level agreements for your Exchange deployment, you can set out on the next task in the SLA development process. That task is the identification of potential service-levels. The idea is to get many potential SLA candidates on the table and narrow it down from there. As the team brainstorms, many ideas for possible SLAs may be conceptualized. The important point at this stage is to select service levels that support the ability of your organization to meet its business objectives. There is not a wrong or right type of SLA. However, the following table lists some important qualities for potential SLA candidates.

Table 9.1   *Qualities of Service-Level Agreements*

Quality	Description
Business-based	An SLA should support specific business objectives and not be implemented for the sake of attainment.
Realistic	Service-levels should be achievable. For example, setting a goal of 99.999% availability for your messaging system may be unattainable.
Measurable	SLAs must be measurable to ensure that they are achieved. If you are not capable of measuring a particular SLA metric, there is no point in its definition. Also, do not establish SLAs that are beyond your control to affect.
Cost-effective	Service-level definition, management, and attainment can be a costly endeavor. An SLA and the resulting business benefit should not be more costly to achieve than the business impact if it is not achieved.
Consensus-based	All parties involved should agree on all aspects of an SLA. An SLA without mutual consensus is doomed to failure.

As part of the process of defining SLAs, you will also need to determine how they will be measured. This may involve the development or purchase of new tools and facilities with which to do so. If tools are not available to monitor and measure an SLA, I would recommend against establishing the SLA in the first place (see the "Measurable" quality in Table 9.1). Part of the SLA development step is selecting the right tools that will provide monitoring and reporting of the various levels of service you desire to achieve. Having a tool available can be a major decision point for determining whether or not a service level is feasible. If your organization cannot afford such tools, you will have to justify the cost of these tools against the business objectives and their criticality. Later in this chapter, we will overview some of the many tools available that can aid in proactive service-level management.

9.2.3   STEP 3: Service-Level Agreement Deployment

Once you have invested the effort in planning and developing your SLAs, you need to provide a mechanism of converting the service-levels agreed upon by business units and IT staff into tangible units of management activity. Before this step begins, ensure that the necessary facilities and infrastructure are in place. This includes the necessary training and tools required to monitor and report on the service-level agreements that will be deployed. I suggest that you do not try to do this and deploy an SLA in parallel. Take the time to allow for steep learning curves and familiarity with the tools and practices to develop. The utilities and practices will take some "tweaking" before they are ready for prime time. The client/customer of the service-level agreements may need an adjustment period as well in order to grow accustomed to the new levels of service. Also, the new SLAs may call for specific requirements or deliverables from the client as well. The best way to assist customers in this phase is to provide some sort of training or orientation on the service-level agreement. This would provide education on why the SLAs are important to them and the organization and what must be done on their part to make them successful. For maximum impact, I would recommend that this occur throughout the entire SLA process to ensure stronger support from the business units that require these service-levels. If the SLA team did a good job of working and cooperating with the business units through the entire process, it will be evidenced by strong support and acceptance during the final SLA deployment phases.

9.2.4   STEP 4: Service-Level Review and Feedback

As you are developing and documenting your service-level agreements for your Exchange deployment, you need to ensure that there are mechanisms in place to allow for the SLAs to be reviewed. I recommend that you include a periodic review process or feedback loop. This process would provide for customer feedback on how effective the SLAs are in furthering business objectives. This would also evaluate how clients and service levels impact each other. This will provide you with an opportunity to fine-tune service-level agreements if they are not meeting business needs. It also may be a point at which customer expectations can be a reconsidered or reset. Along the way, this review process can also serve as a means of determining requirements for technology enhancements. I recommend that you review your service-level agreements frequently to ensure that they are meeting business objectives and are being administered adequately by your IT staff. Most organizations review their SLAs for the messaging system at least once per year. However, I tend to lean toward a more frequent review cycle such as semiannual or quarterly reviews. Many times, organizations will rely on major milestones or technology inflection points as a determinant of when reviews are required. For example, a migration from Exchange Server 5.5 to Exchange 2000 may be one such point at which an organization performs a complete review of all service-level agreements associated with the messaging system. Other reasons may include business or IT reorganization/consolidation, a merger or acquisition, an outsourcing decision, or a major outage event. Regardless of what motivates you to review your service-level agreements, the process must take place in order to ensure that your SLA are serving the purpose for which they were developed and deployed.

There are many issues and decision points that go into the service-level agreement implementation process. These include those that are both technical and nontechnical in nature and can form equal barriers and stumbling blocks during the process. At any point in the process, issues such as inappropriate user expectations or misunderstood business processes can interfere or sabotage your effort to implement sound service-level agreements. For the nontechnical issues, the cause usually boils down to perceptions, communication, politics, and money. On the technical side there are not usually as many issues. While there may always be technical issues encountered, they are usually not specific to the SLA process. Issues such as network bandwidth and design, heterogeneous environments, and the unpredictability of external systems are among the top technical issues that trouble the deployment and management of service-level agreements. Organizations are working harder and harder to develop SLAs for messaging systems that support business objectives, are meaningful to users, and are manageable for the IT organization. When setting out on the path of implementing SLAs for your Exchange deployment, ensure that you have a process in place that will provide a step-by-step means of success.

9.3   Performance Management

As I stated earlier, performance management involves the monitoring and management of system performance and capacity characteristics to ensure that performance and delivery service levels are achieved. This involves establishment of performance baselines in order to compare observed statistics. Performance management also includes the capacity-planning functions critical to anticipating growth. Performance management of your Exchange deployment is a critical part of ensuring mission-critical reliability. You may have taken all possible disaster recovery measures to ensure that your messaging system is up and running, but if you are not aware of how your system is performing, you can leave yourself open for a myriad of downtime woes. Performance management involves three key activities:

1.   Performance monitoring and data collection

2.   Performance baseline definition

3.   Performance detection, diagnosis, and correction

9.3.1   Performance Monitoring and Data Collection

In this activity, key performance indicators for both the operating system (Windows NT/2000) and the application (Exchange Server) are monitored and collected in a management repository. To understand exactly how user demands on a system like Exchange are translated into server load, you must collect performance data. This process is usually carried out over an extended period of time over all or a sampling of the servers in your Exchange deployment. Once collected, this data must be analyzed in order to explain how the Exchange server responds to user activities. I recommend that you carry out your monitoring on a scheduled and periodic basis that allows you to identify tends in server performance. The data collection process should continue throughout the life of your Exchange deployment. For an Exchange 2000 server, there are several critical areas for which monitoring and data collection need to occur. Table 9.2 lists the server hardware subsystems and describes their importance to achieving optimal performance for Exchange 2000. Table 9.3 lists and describes the key monitoring points for Exchange Server.

Table 9.2 *Key Monitoring and Data Collection Points for Server Subsystems*

Server Subsystem	Windows 2000 Object	Counter	Description	Guideline
System memory	Memory	Pages/sec	Pages/sec is the number of pages read from or written to disk to resolve hard page faults. It is the sum of Memory: Pages Input/sec and Memory: Pages Output/sec.	Avg. < 10
		Page Faults/sec	Page Faults/sec is the overall rate at which the processor handles faulted pages. It is measured in numbers of pages faulted per second.	Dependent upon application and system characteristics
		Available Bytes	Available Bytes is the amount of physical memory available to processes running on the computer, in bytes. It is calculated by summing space on the Zeroed, Free, and Standby memory lists.	
		Committed Bytes	Committed Bytes is the amount of committed virtual memory, in bytes.	Avg. < 80% of physical memory
Disk subsystem	PhysicalDisk	Avg. Disk Queue Length	Avg. Disk Queue Length is the average number of both read and write requests that were queued for the selected disk during the sample interval.	Avg. < 50% of the number of spindles
		Current Disk Queue Length	Current Disk Queue Length is the number of requests outstanding on the disk at the time the performance data is collected.	Difference between queue and number of spindles should not exceed 2
		Avg. Disk Sec/ Read	Avg. Disk Sec/Read is the average time in seconds of a read of data from the disk.	Avg. < 20ms
		Avg. Disk Sec/ Write	Avg. Disk Sec/Write is the average time in seconds of a write of data to the disk.	Avg. < 10ms

Table 9.2   *Key Monitoring and Data Collection Points for Server*
                  Subsystems (continued)

Server Subsystem	Windows 2000 Object	Counter	Description	Guideline
		Disk Reads/sec	Disk Reads/sec is the rate of read operations (I/Os) on the disk.	Dependent upon spindles in disk volume
		Disk Writes/sec	Disk Write/sec is the rate of write operations (I/Os) on the disk.	Dependent upon spindles in disk volume
		Split IO/sec	Split IO/Sec reports the rate at which I/Os to the disk were split into multiple I/Os.	Dependent upon application and system characteristics
Processor subsystem	System	Processor Queue Length	Processor Queue Length is the number of threads in the processor queue.	Avg. < 2
		Context Switches/sec	Context Switches/sec is the combined rate at which all processors on the computer are switched from one thread to another.	Dependent upon application and system characteristics
	Processor	% Processor Time	% Processor Time is the percentage of time that the processor is executing a non-idle thread. This counter was designed as a primary indicator of processor activity.	Avg. < 80%
		Interrupts/sec	Interrupts/sec is the average number of hardware interrupts the processor is receiving and servicing in each second.	Dependent upon application and system characteristics
Network subsystem	Network interface	Bytes Total/sec	Bytes Total/sec is the rate at which bytes are sent and received on the interface, including framing characters.	Dependent upon application and system characteristics
		Current Bandwidth	Current Bandwidth is an estimate of the interface's current bandwidth in bits per second (bps).	Avg. < 60% total bandwidth
		Output Queue Length	Output Queue Length is the length of the output packet queue (in packets).	Avg. < 2

When you are monitoring Exchange Server, there are many different objects and counters available that provide important data for characterizing the function and load of your server. Table 9.3 shows key performance indicators that can provide a summary view of server health. To be sure, there are many more indicators available than are presented in the table. The intent here is to provide a list of those most commonly used in evaluating Exchange Server performance.

Table 9.3   *Key Exchange Server Monitoring and Data Collection Points*

Exchange Server Object	Counter	Description	Guideline
Epoxy	Client Out Queue Length	Length of queue from epoxy client to store	Dependent upon application and system characteristics; monitored on a per protocol basis
	Store Out Queue Length	Length of queue from epoxy store to client	Dependent upon application and system characteristics; monitored on a per protocol basis
Microsoft ExchangeIS Transport Driver	Requests Pending Transport Ack	Current number of requests pending acknowledgment from SMTP transport	BASELINE Per Store Instance (SG)
MSExchangeTransport Store Driver	Store Requests Pending Ack	Current number of requests pending acknowledgment from the Store	BASELINE Per Store Instance (SG)
MSExchange OLEdb Resource	Transactions Committed Rate	The number of transactions successfully committed/sec	BASELINE
MSExchangeIS	RPC Requests	The number of client requests that are currently being processed by the Store process	Avg < 10 Peak ≤ 20
MSExchange IS Mailbox	Folder Opens/sec (per information store database)	The rate at which requests to open folders are submitted to the information store	BASELINE Per database

Table 9.3   *Key Exchange Server Monitoring and Data Collection Points (continued)*

Exchange Server Object	Counter	Description	Guideline
	HTTP/DAV Notify Requests/sec (per information store database)	The rate at which the store sends HTTP Notify requests	BASELINE Per database
	Message Opens/sec (per information store database)	The rate at which requests to open messages are submitted to the information store	BASELINE Per database
	Messages Submitted/min (per information store database)	The rate that messages are submitted to the information store by clients	BASELINE Per database
	Send Queue Size (per information store database)	The number of messages in the information store's send queue	BASELINE Per database

Perhaps the most important process on your Exchange Server is the information store process (STORE.EXE). STORE.EXE provides both the underlying Exchange database engine (Extensible Storage Engine, or ESE) and the interface between user and data. Therefore, it is critical that performance of the information store be constantly monitored and managed. Problems with performance here will result in slower response times and increasing message delivery times. It is vital that this process be online and operating at optimum performance.

Important to server performance monitoring and data collection is an understanding of response time versus throughput. A user's perception of server performance could be viewed as response time. For example, how long does a user have to wait after double-clicking a mail message until the message opens for reading? If a server is heavily loaded and has had diminished resources, the response time will be longer, which furnishes a direct correlation between server resource bandwidth and server load conditions. Response time is an important measurement for servers that are directly supporting user functions such as mail, scheduling, and public folder applications.

Throughput, on the other hand, is typically important for servers performing background activities such as message routing as replication. For example, in a bridgehead server environment, throughput measurements such as messages per second or bytes per second are more relevant measurements of server performance than response time. Throughput can also be an important performance measurement for mail servers supporting heavy user loads.

As you are monitoring server performance, it is important to understand bottlenecks. Bottlenecks occur in server subsystems such as processor, memory, and disk. They are, simply, the resource subsystem with the high demand. Bottlenecks are often closely interrelated since the presence of one bottleneck only masks the resource with the next highest demand. Furthermore, a bottleneck in one resource may prevent another resource from being fully utilized. For example, the processor subsystem will be delayed from completing tasks by a disk subsystem being taxed beyond its capacity. The result is low processor utilization as the processor waits for disk I/O to be completed.

Use of a performance-monitoring tool such as System Monitor or third-party management applications is critical to successful performance management activities. Make sure you know how to use these tools. System Monitor, for example, will often cause valuable information to be missed as a result of improper capture or monitoring intervals. For example, when logging or graphing performance characteristics of disk queue length or reads per second for a disk subsystem, you may capture the update interval for time periods that do not present a true picture of disk subsystem performance. With an interval of 30 seconds, for example, the data may appear to be well within subsystem capacities (such as disk queue length is below 2). When the capture interval is changed to five seconds, however, it may be revealed that the resource is experiencing peak periods of utilization that are masked by the longer 30-second update interval. Resources such as the disk subsystem often experience "spikes" due to such things as load or write-back cache "flushing." Thought should be given to the scale used when analyzing server performance. A graph scale that misrepresents the actual performance data has misled many an analyst.

Two rules of thumb are:

1.   Performance data ("counters") should be viewed alongside similar data. For example, comparing processor utilization

measured in percentages with system memory consumption measured in bytes could be confusing since different scales are represented.

2. Performance data should be viewed with a proper understanding of the sampling period (graph time) as well as the graph time window. When looking at time-related performance data, careful consideration of the time period sampled is important to proper analysis of the data. For example, when viewing a counter such as messages per minute, it is important to have a sample period of sufficient extent to support justified conclusions.

The process of performance monitoring and data collection needs to be an established practice for your Exchange deployment. Without it, it is difficult to provide proactive management of your environment. The mistake that some organizations make is to only monitor servers after they experience performance problems or on an exception basis. Make this an established operation that takes place for every server in your Exchange deployment. Using the data you collect, you can make critical decisions that will impact your ability to provide the levels of service required by the business objectives of your organization.

9.3.2 Performance Baseline Definition

Once you have collected performance-monitoring information for your server subsystems, operating system, and Exchange Server, the process of defining baseline performance thresholds in support of your service-level agreements and healthy system operation can be defined. These thresholds are based on the server workload characteristics observed for the collected performance data. You will need to make decisions about what thresholds are necessary based on both client- and server-side measurements. Most likely, it will be obvious if these thresholds are set incorrectly. Performance thresholds that are set too low will generate necessary alerts for your operations staff as they are attempting to proactively manage the performance of Exchange servers. The more important concern is thresholds that are set too high, which will most often result in performance problems remaining undetected. By the time system managers become aware of the problems, it will be too late and performance management will shift to a reactive mode. When Microsoft or an alternate source of expertise provides no threshold, you will need to conduct the monitoring and data-collection process on your own to set logical thresholds for your specific deployment. The level of system performance for your Exchange servers that you consider acceptable when your system is handling a normal workload becomes your baseline. A baseline is a very subjective standard and may correspond to a range of measurements and values.

9.3.3 Performance Detection, Diagnosis, and Correction

Once performance management baselines have been established, you will need to devise methods to monitor and alert you to impending problems and to provide rapid resolution before these problems impact system users. Once a performance problem has been detected, quick identification of the root cause is necessary in order to resolve the issue. Just as you establish processes and procedures for disaster recovery, so should you develop and implement them for performance management. Again, this may require some additional investment in the time and expertise to develop these procedures as well as an investment in training for your operations staff. Using the thresholds you have defined based on your data collection and characterization exercises, you must use the tools at your disposal and configure performance alerts and notifications based on those thresholds. For example, if you baseline a particular monitoring point such as messages per second, you need to determine both high and low thresholds that will signal system problems. A low rate of messages per second through an SMTP connector may point to other problems such as network bandwidth issues. A high rate may just be an indication of increased system activity or could be a warning of a denial-of-service attack (citing an extreme case). Regardless of the thresholds you set, they must be well thought out and not generate unnecessary alarms or let potential early warning signs go unnoticed.

The tools you employ may cost a fee or be free. There are many great third-party management tools for Windows 2000 and Exchange 2000 that come with built-in "knowledge scripts" or "knowledge modules." These built-in components give you a head start and take the guesswork out of performance-management threshold definition. Of course, most of these tools also allow you to customize the configuration based on the needs and service levels for your Exchange deployment. Windows 2000 provides its own means to give you some of the same functionality of these tools but does not come close to the features provided in third-party tools such as NETIQ AppManager. Windows 2000 provides this functionality by combining the Computer Management MMC snap-in (in previous versions of Windows NT, this was provided as a separate application—Windows NT Performance Monitor) and the System Monitor tool. The Computer Management snap-in provides the Performance Logs and Alerts system tool. Within this tool, three objects are available—counter logs, trace logs, and alerts. Within the System Monitor (Perfmon.exe), you can view real-time system performance data or utilize data from counter and trace logs defined in Computer Management (shown in Figure 9.2). These tools can be used as a compliment to third-party management tools.

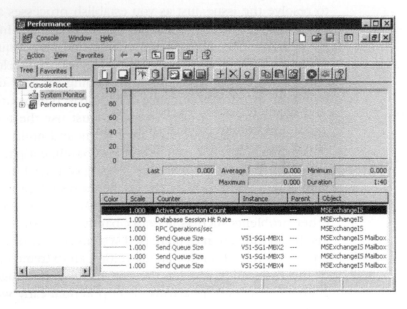

Figure 9.2
Windows 2000 System Monitor for Exchange 2000 monitoring

The final phase of the performance management and monitoring process is the correction of performance problems. Problems that are correctable fall into two categories: online and offline corrections. Online corrections are those that can be completed while the system is up and running. Examples of online performance corrections are those such as stopping services, processor affinity tuning

(Windows 2000 Process Monitor), or dynamic memory allocation (Exchange Server uses dynamic buffer allocation). Offline performance corrections are those that require the server to be shut down in order to perform hardware upgrades or reallocation operations that will address the performance issue. These include adding additional processors, memory, and disk drives.

For Exchange Server, the most common performance bottleneck is disk I/O. By identifying "hot" volumes via performance monitoring and diagnosis, you may decide to add more spindles to a particular volume. Whatever your approach to performance problem resolution, you need to ensure that you have a clear understanding of how each individual server subsystem impacts Exchange Server performance. This requires personnel with expertise in both hardware as well as Exchange Server. When you are planning for performance management of your Exchange servers, don't forget to address every aspect including performance monitoring and data collection, performance baseline definition, and performance detection, diagnosis, and correction.

9.4 Configuration Management

I get very frustrated when I have a group of systems all seemingly configured the same and one of those systems exhibits a particular problem that none of the others seem to experience. The problem exhibited may be performance related or be as severe as frequent system crashes. In my travels and discussions with Exchange system managers, I can't tell you how often I hear stories of system problems that, upon further diagnosis, are caused by dissimilarities in configuration. There are literally thousands of configurable parameters throughout Windows NT/2000 alone. Exchange Server adds a further dimension to this. A deviation from the standard of one parameter on a particular server can wreak havoc on a deployment and may go undiscovered until it causes severe problems. In addition, configuration parameters are not the only cause of configuration-management issues. In fact, configuration-management problems are usually software or hardware related. Table 9.4 lists the most common software and hardware causes of configuration-management problems I have commonly seen in Exchange deployments.

Table 9.4   *Software and Hardware Configuration Management Challenges*

Configuration Management Point	Remarks
Windows NT/2000 service pack	Service packs for Windows NT/2000 that include bug fixes and enhancements are released on a regular basis and are a constant challenge to keep current across an entire deployment. Furthermore, service packs require a reboot of the operating system and are sometimes challenging to schedule.
Application service packs (Exchange Server)	Exchange Server service packs are also released regularly and have similar challenges to operating system service packs.
Third-party application updates and service packs	Invariably, most Exchange Servers must run some degree of third-party software such as management applications and agents, backup agents, and anti-virus software. Ensuring homogeneity among third-party software can also be a challenge.
Hardware Device Drivers	Most hardware vendors have specific device drivers for devices such as network interface cards and disk controllers.
Hardware Firmware (ROMs)	Most hardware vendors have firmware that is frequently updated to address issues. Within a server, the system, disk controller, and other devices such as tape drives and disk drives all contain firmware that must be maintained with current versions.

Solid configuration management practices are key to a mission-critical Exchange deployment. You will need to establish practices and guidelines for maintaining the highest degree of homogeneity across your Exchange deployment. Once you develop and establish the degree and means of enforcement, you will need to determine the tools you will employ to monitor, troubleshoot, and resolve configuration-management issues. Tools in Windows NT/2000 such as the Registry Editor, Windows Diagnostics, Hardware Device Manager, and Resource Kit utilities will assist in configuration management without additional investments. However, I also recommend that you invest in a third-party management application that is strong in configuration management capabilities for both the operating system and Exchange Server. Look specifically for applications with change management or control features. Tools such as Microsoft Systems Management Server (SMS), NETIQ's AppManager, or BMC's Patrol provide excellent configuration management features. Don't forget about your hardware vendor in all of this. Most top-tier server vendors provide excellent server management tools such as Compaq's Insight Manager (CIM). CIM (shown in Figure 9.3) provides some of the best configuration management available in terms of the hardware, device driver, and firmware version control.

Figure 9.3
Compaq Insight Manager's version control feature

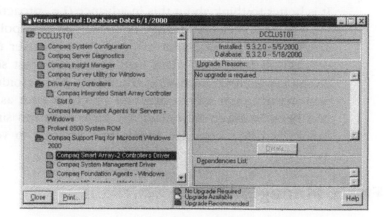

The best method to get a handle on configuration management across your Exchange deployment is the practice of *blockpointing*. Blockpoints are manageable units of change that you can roll out to your entire server population on a regular basis. Blockpoints are packages that are tested and certified for deployment. Blockpoints may include all the components listed in Table 9.4 or just a subset. In practice, your system operations and deployment staff set a schedule for blockpoints for your deployment. Typically, I have seen organizations set specific time periods for blockpoints such as quarterly or semiannually. One popular timing method for blockpoints is to tie them to operating system service pack updates. Once you have determined a blockpoint schedule, you will need to set up a process for blockpoint qualification and certification. This usually involves methods for determining what components will be part of blockpoints and the process in which they will be tested and certified for deployment. The process typically involves gathering all required components and testing them together in a lab environment that mirrors your deployment environment. Here you will determine any incompatibilities or "gotchas" and devise methods for how the blockpoint will be applied.

The final step will be to schedule the blockpoint process for your deployment. For large deployments, it may not be possible to apply the blockpoint across the entire deployment over a weekend. The time required as well as the impact on users will need to be considered. You should also determine a course of action (a backout plan) in the event that a blockpoint fails and renders a server unavailable. It is better to think about this in advance (i.e., proactively) and have your fallback measures readily available. The blockpoint approach to configuration management can truly be a lifesaver that maximizes reliability. I have seen many instances in the past several years of Exchange Server outages that could have been avoided if configuration management monitoring and practices such as blockpointing had been in place. If you do not have measures similar to blockpoints in place, consider adding this practice to your operations portfolio.

9.5   Fault Management

While configuration management is focused on problem avoidance, fault management focuses on the notification and disposition of problems that occur. No matter how excellent your management practices and processes are, you will encounter fault conditions. Fault management is the process of addressing these problems when they occur. Most management applications and practices divide fault management into three segments: fault detection, fault notification, and fault resolution.

In an Exchange environment, fault management typically is available from three primary sources: Windows NT/2000 built-in tools, Exchange management tools, and third-party applications. Windows 2000's primary built-in tools are the System Monitor and the Event Log. System Monitor can provide threshold alerting and notification for both system events and performance counters. The Event Log is used by the operating system as well as applications like Exchange Server to record informational and critical events that occur during runtime. For Exchange, server and link monitors are available as additional tools that can provide a mechanism for detection and notification of critical problems such as service failures or link outages. It is third-party applications that provide the most functionality in this area, however.

While it is possible to set up comprehensive detection and notification mechanisms using only Windows NT/2000 and Exchange Server's built-in tools, I would not want to be responsible for any sizable deployment without the benefit of specialized tools like NETIQ AppManager or BMC's Patrol. Once a problem is detected, most tools provide a wide range of mechanisms to ensure that personnel are notified. Most of these tools can not only detect and provide notification of fault, they also can provide rudimentary artificial intelligence techniques for beginning the process of fault resolution. Some feature innovative approaches that assist support staff in the resolution process. Many tools also provide integration with help desk, trouble-ticketing, and enterprise management applications as well.

Given that all vendors have access to the same interfaces and techniques for monitoring Exchange and Windows NT/2000, the main differences between third-party applications lie in their user interfaces, reporting, customization capabilities, scalability, platform support, and integration with other applications and tools. Many vendors also try to further differentiate by adding preconfigured Exchange knowledge modules or scripts that take the guesswork out of managing an Exchange deployment. Table 9.5 provides an overview of the more popular third-party application management tools that are available for Exchange Server. The table is merely a sampling of the most commonly seen (and thus, the market share leaders) and the author's experiences and humble opinions. Certainly, these tools are being improved and innovated with each new version available. Like the race for backup software (discussed in Chapter 5), this is very much a leap frog game. In addition, there are frequent new players rushing into the market for application management tools. I recommend that you not take my word for it and evaluate these products on your own. Each product comprises a unique combination of features, strengths, and weaknesses. You will find that the best management tool for your Exchange deployment is the one that meets your organization's unique set of needs.

Table 9.5   *Survey of Application Management Products for Exchange*

Product	Strengths	Weaknesses	Comments
NETIQ App Manager	• User interface • NT centric	• Lack of heterogeneous environment support • Lack of enterprise management application integration	One of the most popular application managers for Microsoft BackOffice and Exchange. NETIQ has great support and is a favorite of many organizations. However, reporting features and customization tend to be weaker than competitors'. NETIQ's merger with mission-critical software will enhance their offerings significantly.
BMC Patrol	• Strong heterogeneous environment support • Good enterprise application integration • Customization capabilities	• Support • Patrol server agents noted to be problematic at times	BMC Patrol is perhaps the pioneer management application to support Exchange Server. While early versions of BMC Patrol had some issues with server agents such as system crashes and memory leaks, later versions have proved much more reliable and stable.
Tally Systems Veranda/Mailcheck	• Service-level and usage analysis capabilities	• Niche player • Little integration and multiplatform support	Tally Systems' Mailcheck and Veranda team to provide specific messaging system–management features such as end-to-end connectivity monitoring and probing and delivery tracking. Veranda focuses more on reporting and analysis of messaging activities.
CA Unicenter TNG for Exchange	• Enterprise management application integration • Heterogeneous environment support	• May be overkill for application management • Cost	Unicenter TNG offers a great enterprise-wide management platform. The TNG for Exchange component is simply an extension to the base product. One downside may be the investment required to accomplish simple management tasks for Exchange.
Tivoli TME for Exchange	• Enterprise management application integration • Reporting	• May be overkill for Exchange application management • Cost	Like CA Unicenter TNG, Tivoli TME for Exchange provides an excellent add-on component for a well-established enterprise management tool. However, again, this may be overkill for organizations simply desiring an Exchange application manager.

Table 9.5 *Survey of Application Management Products for Exchange (continued)*

Product	Strengths	Weaknesses	Comments
MessageWise InLook	• "Touchless" agent architecture • Strong reporting and configuration management capabilities	• NT centric • Lack of enterprise management application integration	MessageWise's product has strengths in that founders of the company came from real-world Exchange environments and sought to build a product to address their perceived shortcomings for managing Exchange deployments. Despite this focus, the product has not been established as one of the more popular tools and lacks market share.
BindView	• "Touchless" agent architecture	• Interface difficult to navigate • Little customization available • "Me-too" product	BindView has moved from its roots in the NetWare directory management space to application management. With their recent acquisition of Entevo, they should probably stick with directory management and tools.
Appliant AppVisor for Exchange	• "Touchless" agent architecture	• Interface difficult to navigate • Little customization available • "Me-too" product	AppVisor is a relative newcomer to Exchange management. One highlight of the product is that, like the MessageWise and BindView products, AppVisor does not install an agent on the Exchange Server.

9.6 WBEM—The Future of Management

The enterprise and application management community is experiencing a definite shift in paradigms. Strong efforts are underway to unify the existing management technologies for application, network, and enterprise systems management into a consistent model of access leveraging Web-based technologies. The Internet and Web-based applications using the HTTP protocol have become so ubiquitous, and the protocol is so lightweight in nature. This and the challenges often encountered when deploying traditional enterprise management solutions using either proprietary protocols or SNMP have led to the WBEM initiative. WBEM stands for Web-based enterprise management, and it was conceived in 1996 by five vendors—Compaq, Microsoft, Cisco, BMC, and Intel. However, more than 60 other vendors are now endorsing and involved in the initiative.

WBEM defines an architecture that is simplified to overcome traditional issues such as scalability, functionality, and cost of deployment. It leverages HTTP and browser-based interfaces to provide a common base for application, network, and systems management. The goal is to provide an easy-to-use, cost-effective, proactive, and automated technology for accessing and presenting management data in a consistent manner. With WBEM technology, the paradigm shifts from focusing on the infrastructure of the network and devices to a focus on content and processes. Administrators need to be able to track network, server, and application problems and faults from the user level to the application level. Based on industry standards, WBEM provides this capability by combining traditional management techniques and elements and presents this information to a browser via HTTP. Unlike previous methods of management (a console and a managed device or application), WBEM uses a three-tier architecture (shown in Figure 9.4) consisting of a management server, managed applications and devices, and a Web browser.

Figure 9.4
WBEM architecture diagram

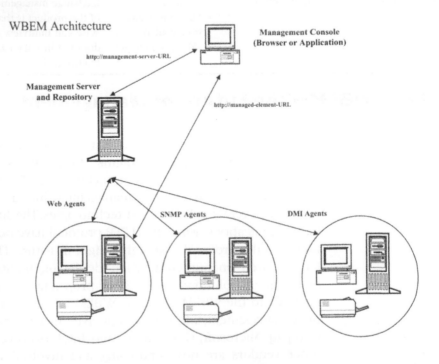

The WBEM architecture replaces the traditional management console with a browser, which can access either the management server or the managed devices and applications. The management server provides a clearinghouse for access to managed applications and devices that are accessed via HTTP as well as traditional methods such as SNMP (Simple Network Management Protocol) and DMI (Desktop Management Interface) agents. Web agents for devices and applications like Exchange Server use common methods and techniques to provide registration, discovery, security, HTTP communications, and HTML rendering and provide a home page for management browsers to use as a starting point when performing management tasks. If you would like more information on the WBEM initiative, you can visit `http://www.dmtf.org`. As a management access method for managing Exchange Servers, I look for WBEM to be a key technology going forward. In fact, most of the leading application management vendors for Exchange, like BMC and NETIQ, have already begun moving in the direction of WBEM. In particular, BMC already enables Web-based access to management agents. This is also evidenced by Microsoft's embracing of this technology in Windows 2000. Windows 2000's Windows Management Interface (WMI) is based on WBEM. As you are evaluating your management strategy for your Exchange deployment, get current on WBEM and understand how it fits into your plans. Furthermore, find out how your application management vendor is planning to support WBEM and whether it is leading or following.

9.7 Putting It All Together—Mission-Critical Exchange

As we come to the end of our project of building mission-critical Exchange deployments, it is not an end but a beginning. In a way, I have had the easy task. Yours is the more challenging project. You must glean the key points from this book and other sources and apply them to your own environment. As Microsoft's latest and greatest, Exchange 2000 is not yet widely deployed. In the years to come, we will both have much to learn about deployment, high availability, disaster recovery, administration and management, and other operational issues for Exchange 2000 and future versions. The goal of this book was to point out the key issues that we face, the technology limitations, and possible techniques and solutions for overcoming them.

We started our journey by looking at high availability and our need to eliminate as much downtime as possible in our Exchange deployments. As Exchange Server becomes more of a cornerstone platform for Microsoft technologies such as knowledge management, the need for more "nines" of availability will escalate. We need to be aware of what our organizational availability requirements are and understand what role the importance of the Exchange deployment has in meeting business and organizational objectives. We need to take Exchange and Windows NT/2000 seriously as a mission-critical application in order to meet these objectives. We can start by analyzing and understanding downtime and outages in our Exchange environments today and the impact those outages have on business.

9.7.1   Downtime

We must look inside of the black box of downtime and understand its components. Whether poor management, tools, training, hardware, software, environment, or operational and procedural issues, we need to understand where the most significant downtime charges are occurring. Once identified, we can concentrate and focus on these areas and apply sound principals, practices, and technology to reduce or eliminate them.

9.7.2   Understand the Technology

A key step and foundation of mission-critical systems is to understand the technology we are working with. This is not Exchange 2000 alone but Windows 2000 and all the components that Exchange is built on. In Chapter 3, I devoted a significant amount of time to Exchange Server database technology. This is not because the database engine is the only part of Exchange Server that matters but because the database engine and its underlying technologies are at the core of high-availability issues. Issues such as storage allocation and design, disaster recovery, clustering, and proactive management all begin at Exchange's database technology. While other components and technologies in Exchange Server should not be overlooked in the quest for mission-critical messaging systems, in my opinion, the way Exchange Server stores and manages data is the most important in our efforts.

9.7.3 Disaster Recovery Technology and Best Practices

Building on Exchange database technology, we can also add disaster recovery technology. Understanding how Exchange Server provides backup and restore of data is key to maximizing system availability. The degree to which we understand the technology for backup and restore operations in Exchange will determine the success we have in planning, designing, and implementing solid disaster recovery procedures. Our operations staffs must train tirelessly in this area to ensure that, when real-world disaster recovery crises arise, minimal downtime will be incurred with zero data loss. Key to success is the development of top-notch procedures and best practices. Selecting the best disaster recovery technology available (for both hardware and software) is also paramount. As you are wading through the sea of vendors, you need to have established selection criteria that will allow you to select technologies that ensure mission-critical system capability at the lowest total cost of ownership. Throwing money at disaster recovery technology does not guarantee success when procedures, practices, and training are inferior. You can make a difference here by taking the time and investing wisely to establish disaster recovery methods for your Exchange deployment that are best suited to your business requirements.

9.7.4 Storage Technology

Once you have invested in understanding the technology and developing sound practices for data management and disaster recovery, it is worthwhile to investigate how certain technologies can further your goals. Storage technology is where to start. As I have stated, I believe that storage technology (primary and secondary storage) is the most important component to mission-critical systems. Not only is storage key to holding, protecting, and managing your data, it is also the key to performance and scalability of an Exchange environment. No single component can have such a drastic impact on these areas as storage technology. In Chapter 6, I discussed storage technologies from a core technology point of view (i.e., SCSI vs. Fibre Channel). More importantly, I also discussed some exciting new technology in storage area networks (SANs) and the level of performance, scalability, data management, and flexibility that SAN technology offers. If you are evaluating the future direction for storage in your Exchange environment (whether Exchange 5.5 or Exchange 2000), I can't imagine leaving out SAN technology.

Long-term, we will see the evolution from server-centric storage (host-based) to controller-based storage that is independent of the server platform. The goal is an enterprise storage "utility" in which performance, capacity, disaster recovery, and other storage-management concerns are hidden from the view of application implementers and support staff. It is SAN technology that will deliver this in the near future. Alternative high-availability storage technologies such as data replication, business continuance volumes (cloning and snapshots), "server-less" backup (direct SAN-attached device backup and restore), and clustering are also enabled by SAN technology. All of these technologies can be valuable complements to your tried and true disaster recovery and high-availability techniques. In your search for technology areas that have the most impact on your Exchange Server reliability, start with storage technology.

9.7.5   Clustering

Clustering technology will also play a more important role in Exchange 2000 reliability. While clustering features in Exchange 5.5 did not give us much to be excited about, Exchange 2000 promises and delivers much more robust clustering options. The key point here will be how we can leverage an Active/Active Exchange cluster to provide increased availability and to facilitate server consolidation activities. After all, it is only after we are sure that more feature-rich high-availability options like clustering are available for Exchange Server that we will venture down the path of server consolidation efforts that will increase the number of users per server. While the number of users per server may not drastically increase with Exchange 2000, the number of users per cluster certainly brings more possibilities. At initial release, Exchange 2000 will only support two-node clusters. With the Data Center release of Windows 2000, four-node support further enhances this availability option.

While clustering does not promise to heal all that ails your Exchange Server, it does provide additional options. Many large deployments for both corporate messaging environments as well as deployments in Internet or application service providers (ISP/ASP) will require clustering as a means to achieve the degrees of scalability and server density required in these environments. For the first time (delivered in Exchange 2000), clustering in Exchange Server provides a high-availability option with an adequate return on investment that should not be overlooked when building mission-critical systems.

9.7.6 Security

Another often overlooked facet of high availability is security. When not overlooked, many Exchange system managers neglect the close tie that security has to maximizing system availability and protecting data. Many times, we look to other departments or groups within IS to provide this vital function for our Exchange deployment. However, in building mission-critical systems, we must take responsibility locally for the security of the Exchange environment. Security in Exchange Server encompasses many issues such as the public key infrastructure (PKI), encryption, digital signatures, etc. Most often, we think of security for Exchange as it relates to virus protection and measures for preventing attacks of e-mail–borne viruses that result in data loss and corruption, denial-of-service attacks, or minor inconveniences. As a system manager, you may not have sole responsibility for security in your organization, but you must find a way to ensure that the security issues impacting Exchange are at the forefront of your organization's security measures. Whether it is protecting Exchange servers acting as SMTP mail gateways, implementing store-based scanning, or using other measures, you must play an active role in ensuring that the perimeters of penetration (gateways, servers, and clients) are protected from attack. Based on our experiences over the last several years with e-mail–based virus attacks like Melissa and WormExplore.Zip, we are painfully aware of how devastating these attacks can be on system availability. Many times, these attacks do not destroy data but prevent users from accessing the system. The bottom line is that system availability is impacted. We cannot afford to neglect security when planning and building bulletproof Exchange deployments.

9.7.7 Proactive Management

If forced to limit this book to two key topics that would have the most drastic impact on Exchange Server availability, I would choose storage technology and proactive management. Since this final chapter is focused on proactive management and its benefits, I won't harp on the subject. However, I should reiterate the importance of building your proactive management strategy on business objective-based service-level agreements. Without SLAs, it is difficult to understand to what end your proactive management efforts have met. Proactive management has three key components that are mutually inclusive—all three need to be in place to have a sound strategy. These are performance management, configuration management and fault management. You need to define each of these based on your service-level requirements. These components cannot be handled on your own—you must carefully choose the right tools that will help you implement them. The upside is that the market for Exchange application management tools is rich and competitive with many vendors desiring to "ride the Exchange wave." The right tools do not always come at a high price. Many tools such as System Monitor and Event Logging come for free in Windows 2000. Take the fee-based and free tools and build a management environment that is uniquely suited to your Exchange environment and that provides maximum reliability through proactive management.

Armed with these concepts and tools, my hope is that this book has provided you with some insights and knowledge that will aid you in your quest for mission-critical Exchange deployments. The next steps are up to you. Exchange Server is a key Microsoft technology that many future products will leverage. Success here and now with Exchange as a messaging platform will ensure that you can build mission-critical systems for messaging, collaboration, knowledge management, and future applications that Microsoft will deliver. Take heart. We are pioneers, and mission-critical Exchange is within our grasp!

A

Supplemental Information and Documentation

This appendix is provided for the purpose of supplying key supplemental information and documentation. Most of the information supports key concepts or material contained in the text, particularly in Chapters 4 and 5, concerning disaster recovery. Much of the information is provided as a template for your actual disaster recovery procedures for Exchange 2000. As always, you should evaluate your own needs based on the specifics of your Exchange deployment and the service-level agreements you have in place with your customers. The procedures provided in this appendix should be thoroughly tested in a nonproduction environment and accessed for applicability within your own deployment. These procedures are an accumulation of information obtained from a variety of sources, including Microsoft Product Support Services and Compaq Global Services.

A.1 Recovery Procedures—Exchange 2000 Server

A.1.1 Single Mailbox Recovery

Exchange consolidates the contents of mailboxes into a small number of database files. This design provides excellent performance and operating efficiency, but means that in order to recover data from a single mailbox, you must restore an entire database. You do not have to take down your live Exchange system in order to recover mailbox data. Exchange allows you to bring up Information Store databases from one server on a different server. In Exchange 5.5, a recovery server was usually installed with the same logical organization and site naming as the live server, but was not joined to the live site. Databases could be transferred to and started on the recovery server. Since the recovery server had a "blank" directory database, it was necessary to create directory mailbox objects linked to the mailboxes in the database before they would be accessible. This could be done by creating a new mailbox in Exchange Administrator, with the same directory name as the mailbox you wanted access to. The new mailbox entry in the directory would link itself to the existing mailbox in the database. If you needed to recover multiple mailboxes, creating entries one by one could be a tedious task. The DS/IS Consistency Adjustor tool in Exchange 5.5 Administrator came to the rescue by automatically generating directory entries for all mailboxes in the database. With mailboxes now linked back to the directory on the recovery server, you could run an ordinary client such as Outlook to access mailbox data, or use a tool such as EXMERGE to recover multiple mailboxes to .PST files.

Exchange 2000's requirements for building a recovery server are similar in principle, but somewhat different in implementation. The first and most important difference is that you must install a recovery server to a different Active Directory forest. This requirement is due to the fact that there can be only one Exchange organization per forest, and all servers installed in the forest must join that organization.

This requirement is not as tough as it may first seem. Windows 2000 servers are more flexible in the roles they can take than are Windows NT 4 servers. Using the DCPROMO utility, a server can be promoted to domain controller of its own forest, then demoted again and rejoined to another forest as a workstation without having to reinstall it.

You do not have to match any naming between the "recovery forest" and the original forest. Therefore, Exchange 2000 recovery servers can exist on the production network without interference. An Exchange 5.5 server had to match up the organization and site names between live servers and recovery servers. In Exchange 2000, you must match the organization and administrative group names. An Exchange 2000 administrative group has many of the same features and functions as an Exchange 5.5 site.

Along with matching these names, you must also match the logical storage group and database names of the original server. In Exchange 5.5 this was not an issue because there was only a single (unnamed) storage group, and database names were always the same across all servers. Because Exchange 2000 lets you have up to 20 databases on a server, and allows you to arrange them and name them any way you wish, you have to remember what you named them and where you put them in order to recover them.

What happens if you don't know the names of my databases and storage groups, or you get them wrong? When trying to start the databases, you will get errors that will include the correct names. You can then rearchitect the recovery server appropriately. It's not a disaster to not know the names, but it is a significant inconvenience. There is one additional name you must match between the original server and the recovery server, and getting this one right can be difficult. The legacyExchangeDN is an attribute carried by almost all Active Directory objects that have anything to do with Exchange 2000. The legacyExchangeDN is essential to interoperability between Exchange 2000 and Exchange 5.5. It identifies Exchange 2000 objects in a way that matches Exchange 5.5 naming conventions. A typical legacyExchangeDN value is of the form: /O=organization/OU=site/CN=container/CN=object.

In Exchange 5.5, you could not rename a site after installing the first server into it. Exchange 2000 gives you much greater naming flexibility, allowing you to rename administrative groups, storage groups, and even databases at will. Such renaming does not change existing legacyExchangeDN values. If it were to do so, all replication and message flow between Exchange 5.5 and Exchange 2000 would stop, and you would have to tear down and rebuild all connections between the two versions.

When you install the first Exchange 2000 server into a forest, the legacyExchangeDN "root," the part of it that defines the /O= and /OU= values, is set in one of two ways:

1.   If you are upgrading an Exchange 5.5 site, the root of the legacyExchangeDN is based on the Exchange 5.5 organization and site names.

2.   If you are installing an Exchange 2000 server without upgrading, then the legacyExchangeDN reflects the organization name you choose during setup, and the "site" part of it will be First Administrative Group.

Exchange 2000 does not allow you to choose the administrative group name during SETUP, although you may change it afterward if you wish. But even if you change the name later, the legacyExchangeDN still includes /OU=First Administrative Group, not the new administrative group name. Usually, this behavior doesn't matter, unless you are building a recovery server for a database that was upgraded from Exchange 5.5. In this case, you will usually install your recovery server to a new forest as the first server in a "native" Exchange 2000 organization. The legacyExchangeDN will therefore include /OU=First Administrative Group. But the legacyExchangeDN from the original organization will be /OU=Exchange 5.5 Site Name. Until you match up the legacyExchangeDN values, the database can't run on the recovery server. You will also run into this problem if you are recovering a database in an Exchange 2000 organization with more than one administrative group. The legacyExchangeDN values for all administrative groups created after the First Administrative Group will match the names you give them at creation time.

There are three ways you can get the right legacyExchangeDN values inserted in a recovery system discussed below. For more information and assistance, please consult Microsoft product support services.

LegacyExchangeDN Value Fix—Method 1

1.   After installing your first Exchange recovery server, create a new administrative group in Exchange System Manager, a group whose name matches the /OU= value of the original legacyExchangeDN.

2.   Install a second member server into your recovery server forest.

3.   Install Exchange 2000 on the second server, placing it in the new administrative group.

4.   If, in the original system, you changed the display name of the administrative group after creating it, you must also change it on the second recovery server before beginning database recovery.

5.   Restore your database to the second server, following the procedures already outlined in this paper.

LegacyExchangeDN Value Fix—Method 2

1.   After creating your recovery forest, install Exchange 5.5 instead of Exchange 2000, using the same organization name, and a site name that matches the legacyExchangeDN desired. Note that when installing Exchange 5.5 on a Windows 2000 server, the Exchange 5.5 service account must have local computer Power User rights if installing to a

member server, or Server Operator rights if installing to a domain controller. For simplicity's sake, in a recovery environment, make the Administrator account the Exchange 5.5 service account.

2. If you have installed to a domain controller, which will usually be the case, change the LDAP port from 389 to 390, to avoid LDAP conflicts between Exchange 5.5 and Active Directory. This change is made in Exchange 5.5 Administrator on the LDAP Site Settings in the Protocols container under Configuration. If you did not make the account you are logged on as the Exchange 5.5 service account, grant your logon account Service Account Admin permissions on the organization, site, and Configuration containers.

3. Install the Active Directory Connector from the Exchange 2000 installation disk, and configure a connection agreement to the Exchange 5.5 server. The Active Directory Connector administrator program is installed by default in the Microsoft Exchange group in the Start menus. This connection agreement can be a one way from Exchange to Windows Agreement, and you may accept most defaults. This agreement is prerequisite to upgrading Exchange 5.5 to Exchange 2000. When configuring the Connections property sheet, be sure to change the Exchange 5.5 LDAP port listed to 390 to match the LDAP settings you previously altered in Exchange 5.5 administrator.

4. Upgrade to Exchange 2000, and restore your database, following the procedures outlined from Microsoft and Exchange 2000 documentation.

LegacyExchangeDN Value Fix—Method 3

1. Switch the Exchange 2000 installation on the recovery server to Native Mode. To do this, right-click the organization object at the top of the tree in Exchange System Manager, and mark the check box on the General page.

2. Rename the First Administrative Group object to match the display name on your original server.

3. Do an LDIFDE export of all the Microsoft Exchange objects in the Configuration container in Active Directory.

A.1.2 Restoring an Information Store to a Recovery Server

The process for starting a public information store database is the same as for starting a mailbox database. Public information store data recovery in Exchange 2000 is very similar to the processes used in Exchange 5.5.

1. Record

   - All the logical names needed to recover the database
   - The Exchange 2000 organization name
   - The Administrative Group name to which the database belongs
   - The Storage Group name to which the database belongs
   - The logical database name
   - The legacyExchangeDN value of the Administrative Group to which the database currently belongs

2. Run DCPROMO on a Windows 2000 server and create a new forest.

   Install and configure DNS if necessary. If appropriate SRV records are not available in DNS for your domain controller, Exchange installation may fail with errors such as "Setup is unable to access the Windows 2000 Active Directory" or "Failed to look up the Windows 2000 site to which this computer belongs."

3. Install Exchange 2000, using the same Organization name as in the production system.

4. Create a Storage Group with the exact same logical name as the storage group from which the database was originally taken. If the database was taken from the default First Storage Group, you do not have to rename or create another storage group.

   Create logical database names in the storage group matching the original ones. You can rename existing databases by right-clicking them and choosing Rename. For example, if the database you are restoring was called "Mailbox Store (PRODSVR)," and a database exists on the recovery server named "Mailbox Store (RECSVR)," you can just change

(RECSVR) to (PRODSVR), rather than create a new database in the storage group. (Creating a new database will also work)

You do not have to match actual database filenames unless you are restoring offline backups. Even differences in log file prefixes will be handled when restoring an online backup. When restoring offline backups, you should match up physical database names exactly, and this will require creating new databases rather than renaming existing ones.

An offline backup consists of the .EDB and .STM files for a database, with no log files. These files, if the database was shut down cleanly before they were copied, can be started without the presence of their original log files, and they will generate new log files. If restoring an offline backup, delete all log and database files preexisting on the recovery server before restoring the .EDB and .STM files.

In Exchange 2000, because there can be several storage groups, and thus several sets of log files, log files are no longer named EDBnnnnn.LOG. Instead, the first storage group has logs prefixed with E00 instead of EDB. A log file that would have been EDB12345.LOG in Exchange 5.5 would be E0012345.LOG in Exchange 2000. If you create a second storage group, the prefix is E01 (E0112345.LOG), and so on.

5.   Dismount the database(s) to be restored. Then, in Exchange System Manager, mark the check box for "This database can be overwritten by a restore" on the properties of the database(s) you are restoring.

6.   Restore your backup set(s), being careful to mark the Last Restore Set check box when restoring the last online backup set. If you fail to mark this check box, hard recovery will not be run automatically after restoration. In this case, you must either restore again, marking the check box this time, or you can run ESEUTIL /CC while standing in the temporary folder where RESTORE.ENV has been created.

Until hard recovery has been run, the database will not start. This is different from Exchange 5.5, where hard recovery was run as part of starting the Information Store service. If you are restoring offline backup files, hard recovery is not necessary, because the database files are already Consistent.

7.   Mount the database(s).

8.   In Exchange System Manager, right click the Mailboxes object for the database, and run the Cleanup Agent. After it runs, the mailboxes for the database will have red X marks next to them, indicating that they are not currently linked to an Active Directory account.

A.1.3   Recovering Mailbox Data to an Offline Recovery Server

Before you can access a mailbox in the database, you must associate the mailbox with an Active Directory account. Because you have restored the database to a "blank" Active Directory, the mailboxes are all in a disconnect state, and there are few Active Directory accounts to associate them with.

If you need to recover only one or a few mailboxes, the easiest way to associate them with appropriate Active Directory accounts is to do the following:

1.   Create as many Active Directory accounts as may be needed.

2.   In Exchange System Manager (ESM), go to the Mailboxes object. The mailboxes should already be displayed with red X's next to them, indicating that they are not associated currently with any Active Directory account.

3.   Right-click a mailbox, and choose Reconnect. Select the Active Directory account desired.

4.   Access the mailbox contents with an ordinary client (such as Outlook) or by using other utilities such as EXMERGE.

What if you want to recover all the mailboxes in a database? It could take a long time to manually create hundreds or thousands of Active Directory accounts, and to then link them one by one to each mailbox. This was a job that was done for you in Exchange 5.5 by the DS/IS Consistency Adjustor tool.

In Exchange 2000, the Mailbox Reconnect Tool (MBCONN.EXE) comes to the rescue. Not only will it read the Mailboxes table and generate an LDIF import file to create Active Directory accounts matching each mailbox, it will automatically link up all the mailboxes to the newly imported accounts. Refer to the documentation for MBCONN for step-by-step details.

EXMERGE is the most popular utility for exporting mailbox data en masse after mailboxes have been linked up to directory accounts again. To use EXMERGE or MBCONN, you must have rights to access all mailboxes as if you were the owner. In Exchange 5.5, you could get such access by granting yourself Service Account Admin permissions on the site object. In Exchange 2000, Active administrators are, by default, explicitly denied access to mailbox contents. While a full directory administrator can still change this default, the default denial does make it easier to audit unauthorized access by administrators, and to implement policies protecting user privacy.

As the domain Administrator account, or as a member of the Domain Admins or Enterprise Admins group, you cannot get access to Exchange mailboxes by adding yourself to Exchange administrative groups. This means that you cannot just add your administrative account as a member of the Exchange Domain Servers group and get access to all mailboxes. Ironically, if you don't have these domain administrative rights, adding yourself to the Exchange Domain Servers group will give you access to all mailboxes.

A.1.4   Backup and Recovery of the Exchange 2000 SRS Database

The Site Replication Service (SRS) is used for directory replication in a mixed site (one containing both Exchange 5.5 and Exchange 2000 servers). Typically, you will configure the SRS to run on a single Exchange 2000 server in each mixed site, although it is possible to have multiple SRS servers.

The contents of an SRS database are very similar to those in a normal Exchange 5.5 directory database. In fact, Exchange 5.5 servers in a site think the SRS server is just another Exchange 5.5 server. Exchange 5.5 servers replicate information with the SRS database during normal intrasite replication cycles. You can even connect to the SRS database with the Exchange 5.5 administrator (but you should avoid making administrative changes while connected to the SRS database with the Exchange 5.5 administrator).

Like other Exchange 2000 data stores, the SRS database can be backed up online with NTBACKUP. While the contents of the SRS database are similar to those of an Exchange 5.5 directory database, the database itself is an Exchange 2000 database, and shares the same general backup and recovery characteristics as other Exchange 2000 databases.

The SRS is a directory database, and there are two main differences between backing up a directory and backing up an Information Store database that you should keep in mind. First, in most organizations, there is more than one server with a copy of each directory database. These extra replicas serve as "automatic" backups to each other. It is thus not so critical that your backups be completely up to date. If you must restore an older backup of a directory database, other servers with up-to-date replicas of the database can backfill changes that have occurred since the time of backup. This principle applies to Exchange 5.5, Active Directory, and the SRS database.

Next, it is critical that you have at least one good backup of each directory database, and that backup must be recent enough that it contains sufficient configuration information for the database to reestablish communication with other replicas in the system. If a directory database is destroyed with no good backup, complete reinstallation of the server or service is usually required. This is different than the case with an Information Store database. When an Information Store database is completely lost, starting the service with no database present will cause a new one to be created. While existing user information may be lost in this case, there is no effect on the configuration or functionality of the rest of the system.

Two recovery scenarios for the SRS are important for planning purposes:

1.   Restoration of the SRS when you have a good backup of the database.

2.   Recreation of the SRS service when you have no backup.

A.1.4.1   *Restoration of the SRS Database from Backup*

In the Exchange 5.5, there was no distinction made between starting a database service and mounting the database. In Exchange 2000, because you can have numerous databases, starting the service and mounting particular databases are separate operations (although you can set individual databases to automatically mount on service startup). This is true not just for the Information Store, but also for all other Exchange 2000 databases.

In Exchange 5.5 and in Exchange 2000, the database service must be running and the database mounted in order to take an online backup (in Exchange 5.5, starting the service and mounting the database always happened together in a single operation). In Exchange 5.5, to restore an online backup, it was necessary to stop the service, so that the database could be dismounted and overwritten. In Exchange 2000, the service must be started, but the database dismounted in order to restore a backup. There is no option when starting the SRS service to mount the database afterward; starting the service and mounting the database are a single operation, as with an Exchange 5.5 database. But you must somehow be able to get the service into a state where it is running but the database is not mounted before you can restore the database.

The way this is accomplished is by starting the database in semi-running mode. If the existing SRS database is damaged or is not present, the service will still start, but it will not attempt to mount the database or create a new one. This gives you the opportunity to restore from backup. This behavior is very different from that which Exchange 5.5 administrators have come to expect. The Key Management Server restoration process has a similar mode, with differences that will be described later in this appendix. In order to get the SRS started in semi-running mode, you must remove all the existing database, checkpoint, and log files from the DSADATA folder(s) before starting the service, or the database must be so damaged that it is not mountable. The Application Log will record an Event at SRS startup confirming that you are indeed in semi-running mode.

The steps in the NTBACKUP interface for restoring the SRS are almost identical to those for the Information Store. You specify a temporary folder, into which the RESTORE.ENV transaction logs and patch files for the restoration are copied, and then mark the "Last Restore Set" check box to signal the SRS service to begin hard recovery after restoration. The ESEUTIL /CC switch can even be used to trigger hard recovery if you forget to mark the check box. To perform a simple restoration of an SRS database, the following steps are necessary:

1. Stop the SRS service, if it is running, and remove all files from the SRSDATA folder(s). WARNING: Do not delete existing SRS files; simply move them to a safe location.

2.   Start the SRS service.

You can verify that SRS is in semi-running mode by examining the Application Log for an event similar to this:

Event Type:	Warning	Date:	3/23/2000
Event Source:	MSExchangeSRS	Time:	2:38:14 PM
Event Category:	Internal Processing	User:	N/A
Event ID:	1400	Computer:	BIGBOY

Description: The Microsoft Exchange Site Replication Service could not initialize its Exchange database (EDB) and returned error 1. The Site Replication Service will wait in a semi-running state so the database can be restored from backup and the SRS can mount it.

3.   Restore a previous backup of the SRS service, marking the "Last Restore Set" check mark in NTBACKUP. It's not essential that you restore the most recent backup. As long as the organization topology has not changed so much that the restored database doesn't know where to find its replication partners, the database will be updated automatically by ordinary replication. In all cases, an SRS database will have other replication partners. In a pure Exchange 2000 site, where the SRS is still being used as a 5.5 directory replication bridgehead, it will repopulate itself from both Active Directory and Exchange 5.5 servers in other sites. Where the SRS is being used in a mixed Exchange 2000 and Exchange 5.5 site, the same is true.

A.1.4.2   Complete SRS Server Recovery

If you've been forced to run a /disasterrecovery SETUP to recover from complete loss of an Exchange server, the SRS service will be disabled after SETUP completes, and there will be no SRS database created. After you have finished recovery of the Information Store and other databases, you can restore the SRS. After SETUP /disasterrecovery finishes, there will be three files in the SRS folder: lconfig.map, rconfig.map, and srstempl.edb. These are template files used in generating new SRS databases. If you inadvertantly delete these files, you can get new copies of them from the setupi386exchangesrsdata folder on the installation CD. They are needed if you are configuring an SRS server any time other than during upgrade of a 5.5 server.

This scenario assumes that all Active Directory and Active Directory Configuration information has survived the disaster intact—the only thing still missing is the SRS database itself. To restore it:

1. Enable the SRS service from the Services administrative console.

2. Remove any existing files from the SRSDATA folder (except the three template files, lconfig.map, rconfig.map, and srstempl.edb).

3. Start the SRS service. It should start in "semi-running" mode.

4. Start NTBACKUP and restore a backup of the SRS database, marking the "Last Restore Set" check box. It's not necessary to mark "Mount database after restore"; hard recovery will automatically mount the database for you. If you start NTBACKUP before you have started the SRS service, you may receive the following error:

    The specified computer is not a Microsoft Exchange server or its Microsoft Exchange services are not started. To get past this error, restart NTBACKUP after the SRS service has been started. Starting the service and trying again in the same NTBACKUP session will not work.

5. Verify that the database has started successfully by examining the Application Log. Remember that the SRS service may start, even though its database fails to mount. Successful startup of the service does not necessarily imply successful startup of the database.

    Restarting the SRS service after restoration without first allowing hard recovery to run will create transaction log and checkpoint files in the SRSDATA folder that do not match the restored files in the temporary folder. These newly created files must be removed before hard recovery will succeed.

    If you forget to mark the "Last Restore Set" check mark, and then try to start the SRS service before hard recovery has succeeded, you will find an error like this in the Application Log:

Event Type:	Error	Date:	3/28/2000
Event Source:	ESE98	Time:	7:15:53 PM
Event Category:	Logging/Recovery	User:	N/A
Event ID:	619	Computer:	BIGBOY

Description: MSExchangeSRS (1280) attempted to attach database 'D:ExchsrvrSRS-DATAsrs.edb' but it is a database restored from a backup set on which hard recovery was not started or did not complete successfully.

A.1.4.3   Re-creating an SRS Database When No Backup Is Available

If you have no backup of the SRS, you can delete and recreate the entire SRS service, as long as you have another Exchange 2000 server in the site. If you haven't yet installed a second Exchange 2000 server, you may install one temporarily, and then remove it after recovery has finished. The reason that you need another Exchange 2000 server is that you are not permitted to delete the last SRS service in a site until all servers in the site have been upgraded from Exchange 5.5 to Exchange 2000. This safeguard prevents you from severing the links between the Exchange 5.5 and Exchange 2000 servers in the site. But if you are going to start over with a fresh SRS database on a server, you need to completely remove the existing service first. Adding a second Exchange 2000 server to the site neatly solves this dilemma, because you are allowed to delete any SRS service desired if there is more than one present in the site.

To recreate an SRS service:

1.   Install a second Exchange 2000 server into the site, if necessary.

2.   Start ESM from the console of the other Exchange 2000 server. You cannot run ESM remotely when creating a new SRS database, although you may attach to the server with a Terminal Services session, which has all the required characteristics of an actual local console session.

3.   Expand Tools to expose the Site Replication Services container.

4.   You should see each SRS in your organization listed as "Microsoft Exchange Site Replication Service (Server

Name)." If, instead, you see "Directory Replication Service (Administrative Group Name)," select Site Replication Service View from the console View menu.

5. While focused on the Site Replication Services container object, select Action, New, Site Replication Service.

6. Creating a new site replication service performs directory updates similar to those done when joining a new server to a site. Be patient as it may take several minutes or even longer for the process to complete.

7. After the new SRS has been created, you may delete the original SRS service on the first server.

8. To move the SRS back to its original server, run through steps 2 through 5 again, reversing the server on which each action is performed.

A.1.4.4 *Offline Backup of the SRS*

The SRS is not a critical Exchange service, in the sense that end users aren't affected if it is stopped for a short period of time. After a new SRS has been configured, you may wish to stop it and make a file copy of the SRS.EDB file. Because the SRS database can be back-filled from other directory databases, restoring an offline copy after a disaster may be an even simpler operation than restoring from online backup. To restore an offline copy of the SRS, simply stop the service, remove all files from the SRSDATA folder, copy back the SRS.EDB, and restart the SRS service. Be sure to update the offline copy of the file if you make topology changes which would affect the ability of the database to find replication partners for backfill after restoration. In most cases, such drastic changes would make preservation of this database irrelevant anyway.

A.1.5 Backup and Recovery of the IIS Metabase

Exchange 2000 uses SMTP as its native transport protocol, while Exchange 5.5's Message Transfer Agent (MTA) was based on the X.400 protocol. Exchange 2000 still supports X.400 communication for backward compatibility with Exchange 5.5 and interpretability with other X.400 systems. The SMTP transport stack used by Exchange 2000 is the native Windows 2000 stack included with the Internet Information Service (IIS). To install Exchange 2000 on a server, you must have already installed the IIS components of Windows 2000, specifically, the NNTP and SMTP protocols.

IIS stores most of its configuration information in the metabase. The metabase is a hierarchically organized configuration database for all the protocols managed by IIS. The preferred way of reading from and writing to the metabase is through the various administrative consoles provided for each protocol. There is also a Windows 2000 Resource Kit utility called METAEDIT that gives you raw access to the metabase, in much the same way that REGEDIT gives you raw access to the Windows Registry.

In Exchange System Manager, when you make configuration changes in the Protocols container for a server, most of those changes are written to the metabase. Some of the same information is also kept in Active Directory. When a /disasterrecovery SETUP is done, and the previous metabase no longer exists, Exchange will reconstruct as much as possible the settings that should be in the local metabase. Not all information in the metabase is present in Active Directory, and so you cannot count on using Active Directory as a substitute for backing up the metabase. But in many cases, especially if you have not changed protocol settings away from their defaults, you will not notice any loss of configuration information or functionality.

There are two ways you can back up the metabase. You should do both kinds of backups, because they are useful for different purposes.

First, *backup the IIS metabase* alone from the Internet Services Manager console. If you right-click the server object in Internet Service Manager, you are presented with a Backup/Restore Configuration option. This allows you to backup and restore the metabase.bin file while IIS services are online. By default, this file is stored in \winnt\system32\inetsrv. Backups are stored in the \metaback folder under this file path.

While a metabase backup occurs "online," the metabase is not an Exchange database. There are no transaction logs, and there is no "roll forward" capability. The backup is an exact file copy of the metabase.bin file at the time it is taken. You should store copies of metabase backups in a secure location off the server.

A metabase-only backup should be done before and after significant configuration changes are made to any IIS protocols. For

Exchange, these protocols include HTTP, POP3, IMAP, NNTP, and SMTP. If the metabase is damaged or destroyed, the most recent backup can be restored. If the metabase is missing or damaged, IIS protocol services will not be able to start,

Second, backup the server *System State*, which includes the metabase and installation-specific server security keys needed to start the metabase. If the entire server installation is destroyed, having the metabase alone won't do you any good, because it is linked to security keys that are specific to the server installation. Restoring the previous System State will restore the metabase and its needed keys.

If a problem in the metabase prevents Exchange or IIS protocol services from starting, and there is no backup available, the following procedure may be necessary:

1. Uninstall and Reinstall all IIS services, using the Add/Remove Windows Components function in the Add/Remove Programs utility in Control Panel.

2. Run Exchange SETUP with the /disasterrecovery switch. This will cause Exchange to read information from the Active Directory that will be used to reconstruct previous metabase information as much as is possible.

3. Reconfigure missing metabase settings manually. For example, NNTP virtual directory changes you have made will need to be redone.

A.1.6   Recovery of the Active Directory

As an Exchange administrator, you have a vital interest in whether Active Directory is properly backed up and safeguarded. How will you recover Exchange if Active Directory is completely lost? A single mailbox recovery, as described earlier, is an Exchange recovery as if Active Directory had been completely lost. If you know how to do single mailbox recoveries, you know how to recover from destruction of Active Directory. (Encrypted messages cannot be recovered, however, if Active Directory is lost.) Best practices and recommendations for backing up Active Directory are available in Windows 2000's online help and in white papers published by Microsoft.

In any case, there are some general principles every Exchange administrator should understand about preserving Active Directory information. Contrasting and comparing Active Directory with the Exchange 5.5 will illuminate those principles. In an Exchange 5.5 site with more than one server, directory information is automatically replicated between all servers. When replication is up to date, most of the information on each server is identical. Suppose the directory database on one server were destroyed. Recovery can be done in one of two ways, depending on whether or not you have any backup copy of the directory:

- If there is a backup copy, even one that is very out of date, you can restore it, and backfill replication from the other servers will soon bring the database completely up to date.

- If there is no backup copy, then you must go into Exchange Administrator and remove the server from the site. After that, you can rejoin the server to the site to generate a new directory database. When you remove the server from the site, all objects "owned" by the server are necessarily deleted. Therefore, before removing the server, you should connect to another server in the site and export all the directory information for mailboxes belonging to the damaged server. After reinstallation, you can reimport the mailbox data.

In Exchange 5.5, directory databases act as only partial backups for each other—if one database is destroyed, it cannot be recreated in its entirety from another one in the site. In Active Directory, however, each domain controller in the domain is a complete backup of all the others. This is because no objects are "owned" by specific domain controllers—objects are owned by the domain or the forest as a whole. Removing a replica of Active Directory does not remove any objects from the directory (unless it is the last domain controller existing for a domain).

Replica placement is at least as important to your Active Directory disaster recovery strategy as are your backup procedures to each domain controller. This does not mean that you should dispense altogether with making backups of Active Directory, however, and rely on having several replicas. Replicas back each other up with up-to-date copies of directory information. There are times when you may need out-of-date information, such as after inadvertently deleting an important container, or after installing a rogue application. If you don't have copies of Active Directory from before the time that a regretted change was made, you may find it difficult or impossible to back out from the issue. Both Exchange 5.5 and

Active Directory have authoritative restoration capabilities that allow you to put older information back on top of newer information when necessary.

Even in the smallest organizations, it is a very good idea to have at least two domain controllers, providing two replicas of the Active Directory database. The typical recommendation for larger organizations is that there should be no fewer than three domain controllers per domain. Backup copies of Active Directory for each domain should be stored offsite in a safe location, especially if all domain controllers are geographically close to each other. As a minimum backup plan, you should at least one backup per domain both before and after significant changes are made to the directory.

If you have more than one replica of Active Directory, your disaster recovery efforts are greatly benefited in two ways. First, service to clients is not interrupted by destruction of one of the directories, and so the restoration process does not have to be treated as an emergency. Second, you have more options for recovering from the failure. You can restore from backup; you can rebuild the server and join it to the domain again as a domain controller, or you can bring up a third server as a replacement domain controller.

Preserving Active Directory information is critical to the survival of your network. Because of the replicated nature of the directory, it is easy to provide online redundancy, and recovery of a lost directory can be accomplished by several means and without undue time pressure—if you have an intelligent replica topology, and carry out sensible periodic backup procedures.

A.1.7 Backup and Recovery of the Key Management Server Database

In versions of Exchange prior to Service Pack 1 for Exchange 5.5, the Key Management Server (KMS) acted as its own Certification Authority (CA). This meant that it was a self-contained, independent unit within Exchange. While its administration and maintenance were thus very simple, it couldn't communicate with or establish trust with other CAs. In Service Pack 1, the KMS was modified to allow it either to act as its own CA for X.509 Version 1 certificates, or to rely on a Windows NT CA to generate X.509 Version 3 certificates. In Exchange 2000, the KMS uses a Windows 2000 CA to generate certificates in all cases. This means that if the Windows CA is destroyed, the KMS database is useless. You must now think of KMS as a system encompassing the CA Server, the Active Directory database, and the KMS database.

Perhaps no other Exchange data are as critical to safeguard as your security certificate and KMS information. This is because losing security information may affect not just one server, but may mean the loss of critical mail on every server in your organization. If you lose even one of the components that make up your security infrastructure, all the rest become useless. You must keep copies of all the following key components in order to recover Exchange keys and ensure that encrypted email remains readable:

A. The CA certificates for each of your Certification Authority servers (*.P12 files). These certificates may exist in a chain that must be reconstructed in its entirety. Each certificate is linked to the server name, and so if you must reinstall entire servers, you must give them the same names they previously had. The CAs are not inherently linked to any particular Active Directory installation.

B. The passwords that protect each .P12 certificate file.

C. The Active Directory database containing user accounts that have been granted administrative permissions over the KMS database. KMS can be configured to allow different administrators different privileges, and to even require that two administrators log on at once in order to perform some operations. You must have access to at least one "full" administrative account. Note that while the account used to validate access to a KMS database is a Windows account, the password required is not the Windows account password. If you forget the KMS password, it cannot be recovered or reset.

D. The KMS database startup password. This can be stored in a plain text file, and read automatically at KMS service startup, or entered manually on the properties of the service at each startup.

E. The KMS database itself, which can be backed up online with NTBACKUP. The KMS database must be backed up to a local device; it cannot be backed up from a remote NTBACKUP installation.

You should have secure backups of your CA certificate(s) for every Certification Authority. Backing up the issued certificate database (also called the issued certificate log) is also highly recommended, although not absolutely essential to restoring KMS. But losing the database may cause problems with other entities on your network.

A.1.7.1   KMS Backup

The recommended way to back up a CA server is to back up the entire server, including the System State, using NTBackup. You can also back up only the most critical CA information from the Certification Authority management console following these steps:

1.   Start the Certification Authority management console.

2.   Click Action, All Tasks, Backup CA. This will present you with the backup wizard.

3.   Mark Private key and CA certificate for backup. You must have a backup of the CA certificate that includes its private key in order to restore KMS.

4.   Usually, you should also backup the certificate log. The certificate log database is an ESE database, and is backed up through an online backup procedure similar to that for an Exchange Information Store.

5.   When prompted to select a password for the backup, choose a strong password and safeguard it well. If you forget the password, the backup will be useless. Even more important, if the backup is stolen and restored by an unauthorized person, your entire certification chain of trust has been compromised. Your CA certificate private key is literally the key to everything in your certificate system.

After backup completes, you will have a small .P12 file in your backup folder and a \Database subfolder containing the certificate issue database. The .P12 file can be imported to another CA, and if this is done, that CA can mimic signing of certificates as if it were your own CA. Safeguard the .P12 file as one of your most valuable corporate assets.

A.1.7.2 Remote Offline Backup of the KMS Database

The KMS service is not involved in day-to-day security operations between users. If the service is stopped or the KMS server is taken offline, this normally has no effect on users who have already been enrolled in Advanced Security. The server is needed only to enroll new users or to recover lost keys.

For security reasons, NTBACKUP works only against a local KMS database. You cannot backup the KMS database online from across the network using NTBackup, because the KMS database is invisible when someone runs NTBackup remotely. This makes it more difficult for unauthorized personnel to discover the location of the server.

It is recommended that you secure your KMS server even against most Exchange and network administrative personnel, and you may even wish to leave it offline most of the time if enrollment is not a frequent task in your environment. Nonetheless, if it is necessary to back up KMS from a remote location, it can be done as follows:

1.   Install Terminal Services or another remote client on the KMS server.

      NOTE: Terminal Services, in order to accommodate multiple simultaneous administrative sessions, shrinks the pool of some memory resources allocated by default to the console session. Do not install Terminal Services on an Exchange server that you expect to be under heavy memory pressure, such as a mailbox server with several hundred users. Instead, use a more "lightweight" remote console client that provides access to only a single client session such as NetMeeting.

1.   Run NTBACKUP from inside the remote console session, and back up the KMS database to a file, instead of to tape.

2.   Remotely back up the .BKF file created to tape.

This process can be automated by scheduling NTBACKUP to run under the Task Scheduler service on the KMS server.

A.1.7.3 Restoring the KMS Database

If every server in your organization were to be destroyed, you would need all of the following backups and passwords to restore KMS functionality:

1. CA certificate .P12 file backup and password

2. Active Directory backup containing KMS administrator account(s)

3. KMS database backup and database startup password.

4. KMS administrator password(s)

In overview, you must perform the following steps to provide complete recovery of Key Management Services for Exchange 2000:

1. Restore Active Directory

2. Restore the Certification Authority server(s)

3. Restore the KMS database

A.1.7.4   *Restoring the Certification Authority*

The only two pieces of information absolutely essential to restoring a Certification Authority are the CA certificate and the original CA server name. You don't even need the previous Active Directory forest (but you do need the Active Directory to restore KMS). You must restore a CA to a server with the same name as the original. To restore the CA:

1. Using Control Panel's Add/Remove Programs utility, select the Add/Remove Windows Components option, and mark Certificate Services for installation.

2. In the setup wizard, select a CA type that matches the original CA's type. If you are installing a subordinate CA, you must first install all upstream CAs in the chain.

3. Mark Advanced Options, and click Next.

4. Click the Import button, and import your .P12 backup of the CA certificate. You will be asked to supply the password. After importing, click Next.

5. Verify that the CA Identifying Information page displays the correct information for your previous CA, and then click through the rest of the wizard, modifying paths and other configuration information as desired.

6. In the Certification Authority console, change the Policy Settings to issue the three additional certificates required by Exchange.

After installation of the CA has finished, you may restore your issued certificates database through the Certification Authority console.

A.1.7.5   Restoring the KMS Database

You may restore a previous KMS database to a new KMS service installation by the following method:

1.   Install Key Management Services from the Exchange 2000 Setup CD. It is not strictly necessary to reinstall KMS to an Exchange server with the previous name, but it may be preferable to do so.

2.   If you chose to put the KMS startup password in the kmserver.pwd file, move this file to a safe location.

3.   Stop the KMS service, and move all files in the exchsrvrkmsdata folder to a safe location.

4.   Copy the previous kmserver.pwd file into place, if it exists.

5.   Start the KMS service. If no kmserver.pwd file was used, you must enter the startup password in the Start Parameters for the service. As with the SRS service, starting KMS with no database in place causes it to start in "semi-running" mode to await restoration of a backup.

6.   Using NTBackup, restore the previous KMS database.

7.   Stop and restart the KMS service.

It may take some time for the KMS service to receive the system certificates it needs from the Certificate Authority. Until this happens, you may be unable to perform some administrative tasks. You may or may not have to recover keys for users, depending on whether Active Directory information was lost in the disaster, and whether any user workstations were involved.

ESEFILE

ESEFILE is a utility written by the Exchange ESE development team although it contains no JET code. ESEFILE has a range of miscellaneous uses; here each use is described.

A.1.7.6   Large and Fast File Copy

ESEFILE /C can copy a file of any size. Copying a file this way is very fast. For large (>100MB) files it can be twice as fast as COPY/XCOPY.

Usage

ESEFILE /C source destination

The file is opened un-cached so we can copy files larger than can be opened in cached mode. There are several caveats:

- Wildcards are not accepted.

- Only one file can be copied at a time.

- The destination file cannot be on a networked drive.

- File timestamps are not preserved.

A.1.7.7   Checksumming an Entire Database

To checksum all the pages in a database while it is offline you can use ESEFILE.

Usage

ESEFILE /S *database* (ESE format—Exchange 5.5)

ESEFILE /X *database* (EDB format—Exchange 4.0/5.0)

This is not a substitute for the integrity check. Logical verification is not done by ESEFILE. If you use /X on an ESE format database, or /S on an EDB format database, you will get a checksum error on every page.

A.1.7.8   Checksumming an Individual Page

To verify the checksum of an individual page use ESEFILE /d.

Usage

ESEFILE /D database pageno

Output

00000000 2a c3 aa 89 01 00 00 00 01 00 00 00 00 00 00 00 *..............

00000010 00 00 00 00 00 00 00 00 01 00 00 00 c4 0f 00 00 ....

...The binary value of the page ...

checksum: 0x5477CEA7 (1417137831) (INCORRECT)

A.1.7.9   *Large File Deletion*

To delete a file larger than can be deleted using explorer or any of the command line utilities provided with Windows use ESEFILE /u.

Usage

ESEFILE /U filename

A.2   Supplemental Exchange 2000 Security Information

A.2.1   Key Protocols and Ports for Exchange 2000 Security Configuration

The following is a list of protocols and ports used by Windows 2000 servers and Exchange 2000 servers. It is important to go through them to customize the firewall you are using.

Table A.1   *Ports and Protocols for the Services in Windows 2000/ Exchange 2000*

PORT	TCP/UDP	Name of Service
25	TCP	SMTP
42	TCP	WINS Replication
47	TCP	GRE for PPTP
53	UDP	DNS Name Resolution
53	TCP	DNS
67	UDP	DHCP Lease (BOOTP)
68	UDP	DHCP Lease
80	TCP	HTTP
88	UDP	Kerberos
102	TCP	MTA—X.400 over TCP/IP
110	TCP	POP3
119	TCP	NNTP

Table A.1 *Ports and Protocols for the Services in Windows 2000/ Exchange 2000 (continued)*

PORT	TCP/UDP	Name of Service
135	TCP	*Location Service* • RPC • RPC EP Mapper • WINS Manager • DHCP Manager • MS DTC
137	UDP	*NetBIOS Name Service* • Logon Sequence • Windows NT 4.0 Trusts • Windows NT 4.0 Secure Channel • Pass Through Validation • Browsing • Printing
137	TCP	WINS Registration
138	UDP	*NetBIOS Datagram Service* • Logon Sequence • Windows NT 4.0 Trusts • Windows NT 4.0 Directory Replication • Windows NT 4.0 Secure Channel • Pass Through Validation • NetLogon • Browsing • Printing
139	TCP	*NetBIOS Session Service* • NBT • SMB • File Sharing • Printing • Logon Sequence • Windows NT 4.0 Trusts • Windows NT 4.0 Directory Replication • Windows NT 4.0 Secure Channel • Pass Through Validation • Windows NT 4.0 Administration Tools (Server Manager, User Manager, Event Viewer, Registry Editor, Diagnostics, Performance Monitor, DNS Administration)
143	TCP	IMAP
389	TCP/UDP	LDAP

Table A.1   *Ports and Protocols for the Services in Windows 2000/*
Exchange 2000 (continued)

PORT	TCP/UDP	Name of Service
443	TCP	HTTP (SSL)
465	TCP	SMTP (SSL)
500	TCP/UDP	ISAKMP/Oakley negotiation traffic (IPSEC)
522	TCP	User Location Store
563	TCP	NNTP(SSL)
636	TCP/UDP	LDAP (over TLS/SSL)
750	UDP	Kerberos Authentication
750	TCP	Kerberos Authentication
751	UDP	Kerberos Authentication
751	TCP	Kerberos Authentication
752	UDP	Kerberos Password Server
753	UDP	Kerberos User Registration Server
754	TCP	Kerberos Slave Propagation
888	TCP	Logon and Environment Passing
993	TCP	IMAP4 (SSL)
995	TCP	POP3 (SSL)
1109	TCP	POP with Kerberos
1723	TCP	PPTP Control Channel (IP Protocol 47—GRE)
1720	TCP	H.323 CALL SETUP
1731	TCP	AUDIO CALL CONTROL
2053	TCP	Kerberos de-multiplexor
2105	TCP	Kerberos encrypted rlogin
2980	TCP/UDP	INSTANT MESSAGING SERVICE
3268		Global Catalog
3269		Global Catalog
3389	RDP	Terminal Services

A.2.2   Security Schemes and Encryption Strength

With the various security features available, the administrator has to consider the lowest common denominator to ensure the operability of Exchange across different levels of security work. The following is a summary of some of the encryption and authentication and keys used in the United States and Canada. For other countries, it would be advisable to seek clarification from the Microsoft representative on the length of key permitted.

Table A.2   *Windows 2000/Exchange 2000 Security and Encryption*

Service	Method Used	U.S./Canada
IPSEC	Encryption	DES 128-bit
	Authentication	MD5 128-bit
	Integrity	SHA 160-bit
		Kerberos
KMS	Encryption	DES, 3DES 128-bit
	Digital Signature	RSA 512-bit
EFS	Encryption	DESX 128-bit

B

Exchange Backup/Restore API (ESEBCLI2.DLL) Reference

In Chapters 4 and 5, detailed information on backup and restore process as well as best practices are provided. The information contained in this appendix is supplemental information as provided by Microsoft to software developers desiring to utilize the ESE98 APIs in their own products (Backup, Archival, and Storage Management software). Readers who will benefit from this information are those who desire another viewpoint of the Exchange 2000 (ESE98) backup and restore process from a programmatic point of view. The ESE backup API has gone through several evolutions during the last several years paralleling the releases of Exchange Server (from 4.0 to 2000). In Exchange 2000, with the advent of a more complex storage model (multiple storage groups and databases), the backup API has been enhanced greatly.

NOTE: This information has been provided as a courtesy of the Exchange Development team at Microsoft. This information is considered Microsoft proprietary and is subject to change as the product technology continues to be enhanced.

B.1   Multi-Instance External Backup/Restore for Exchange 2000 (ESE98)

The Exchange Storage Engine (ESE) is a general database engine. The new eseback2.dll and esebcli2.dll are phasing out the old eseback.dll and edbcli.dll, which are Exchange centric, to provide backup/restore capabilities. The new APIs are designed for generic ESE applications. In this version of ESE (ESE98), ESE supports multi-instance capability, and allows each database engine instance to run independently. One instance can perform a backup while other instances can perform restores. All the instances are running within one application process; throughout the rest of this document, the application that uses ESE will be Exchange. There are three different types of databases in Exchange 2000 that use ESE98: Information Store, Site Replication Service (SRS), and Key Management Service (KMS). For Exchange, each storage group represents an instance of ESE; they are synonymous.

The following APIs deal with backing up and restoring an ESE database, and they perform some application-specific interaction required by Backup/Restore Clients. eseback2.dll and esebcli2.dll communicate with the application through callback DLLs. For example, **HrESEBackupSetup**() calls **ErrESECBPrepareInstanceForBackup**() to allow applications to have a chance to do pre-backup action such as disallowing shutdown.

B.1.1   Advantages

DLLs supply a unified way to communicate between ESE server applications and Backup/Restore Clients. When both server application and other Backup/Restore Clients are on the same machine, it passes the backup data through shared memory. The unified interface also allows the Backup/Restore Client to work with future applications that implement ESE APIs.

B.1.2   New Requirements for ESE Applications and Backup/Restore Clients

The new APIs allow the user to restore a subset of the databases in the backup set of an instance of ESE. However, since all databases in a storage group share the same logs, the storage group should be considered the unit of backup/restore. Since the new APIs require a list of databases to backup before copying anything to tape, Backup/Restore Clients may want to store the list of databases at the beginning of tape. This will allow the Backup Restore Clients to show the list of databases available in a backup set at the beginning of a restore, which will allow the user to choose a subset of the databases to restore.

B.1.3   New Improvements—Clean APIs and Simplified Restore

The APIs are cleaned up and are generic to all ESE applications. Currently most applications do 3-phase restore:

1.   Copy files from tape to disk.

2.   Do an ESE level restore to bring database to a consistent state.

3.   (Optional) Make the data in the database consistent with the application level.

The three phases of restore are easier with the new APIs. When a client calls to prepare restore, a callback function to the server application starts, and the server application can start a thread to wait for the existence of first phase indication, say, restore.env file. At the end of the first phase, the restore.env is created, and the server application can start the second phase right away. This avoids the current implementation in which the second phase restore is done implicitly in the next restarting of a service. This also means NTDS can do ESE restore before reboot. Now we use callback functions to do this.

B.2   General Information

B.2.1   Access Rights

The account that the Backup/Restore Client runs under must have Windows 2000 Backup Restore privledges.

B.2.2   Filenames

All filenames that are passed to and from the Backup/Restore functions include the entire path.

B.2.3   Error Handling

All functions will return an error code of type HRESULT, which will have one of three values:

- 0—success

- ESE specific errors, which can be found in esebkmsg.h

- Win32 or RPC errors

The errors specific to ESE can be formatted using **FormatMessage()**. The resulting string is the error message. There are two generic errors: hrErrorFromESECall and hrErrorFromCallbackCall. In these two cases, you can get a more specific error using **GetLastError**(); the error message string has the placeholder for the error number.

```
hr = HrESEBackupX();
HRESULT hrLast = GetLastError();

FormatMessage
(
    FORMAT_MESSAGE_FROM_HMODULE |
    FORMAT_MESSAGE_FROM_SYSTEM |
    FORMAT_MESSAGE_IGNORE_INSERTS |
    FORMAT_MESSAGE_ALLOCATE_BUFFER,
    hesebcli2,
    hr,
    MAKELANGID(LANG_NEUTRAL, SUBLANG_DEFAULT),
            // Default language
    (LPSTR) &lpMsgBuf,
    0,
    NULL )
);

// Display the string.
if ( hrErrorFromESECall == hr || hrErrorFromCallbackCall == hr )
    wprintf( (LPSTR) lpMsgBuf, hrLast );
else
    wprintf( (LPSTR) lpMsgBuf );
```

See the MSDN section on **FormatMessage**() for more information.

B.3   General Functions

Generally the first thing that a Backup/Restore client will do is get a list of the servers in the domain that are ready for backup/restore operations by using **HrESEBackupRestoreGetNodes**(). Once the server has been selected for backup/restore, then the client can access the node to find out what type of applications are available for backup with **HrESEBackupRestoreGetRegistered**(). Both functions must have their parameters freed before the process terminates.

B.3.1   HrESEBackupRestoreGetNodes

This function allows the Backup/Restore Client to get a tree of computer nodes in the domain available for backup/restore operations. Only some of the nodes in the tree are actual servers; the other nodes are virtual ones only. All nodes will have a node name, flags (currently used to indicate if the node is a server node, BACKUP_NODE_TYPE_MACHINE), and an optional icon. The basic tree structure at the present time is

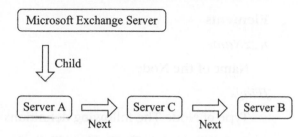

There are no plans to modify the tree structure in the future, but this may change.

The tree structure returned must be freed after use by calling **ESEBackupRestoreFreeNodes**().

```
HRESULT HrESEBackupRestoreGetNodes (
    WCHAR *              wszComputerName,
    BACKUP_NODE_TREE     pBackupNodeTree
)
```

Parameters

wszComputerName

Input parameter. This is the server to start getting the tree information from. To start with the local computer, `wszComputerName` should be `NULL`.

ppBackupNodeTree

Output parameter. Pointer to a tree structure of type **BACKUP_NODE_TREE**, described below.

```
typedef struct _BACKUP_NODE_TREE
{
    WCHAR *                        wszName;
    unsigned long                  fFlags;
    ESE_ICON_DESCRIPTION           iconDescription;

    struct _BACKUP_NODE_TREE *     pNextNode;
    struct _BACKUP_NODE_TREE *     pChildNode;
} BACKUP_NODE_TREE;
```

BACKUP_NODE_TREE is a structure that contains the tree of servers available for backup.

Elements

wszName

Name of the Node.

fFlags

Type of Node. The following definitions are OR ed together:

- BACKUP_NODE_TYPE_MACHINE—indicates that the node is a server.

- BACKUP_NODE_TYPE_DISPLAY—indicates that the node is a virtual node in the tree. For Exchange, this will be the top node.

iconDescription

Icon for this node.

pNextNode

Next node on the same level.

pChildNode

Link to the next level in the tree.

B.3.2   ESEBackupRestoreFreeNodes

Used to free the tree structure returned by **HrESEBackup-RestoreGetNodes**().

```
void ESEBackupRestoreFreeNodes
(
    BACKUP_NODE_TREE *      pBackupNodeTree
)
```

Parameters

pBackupNodeTree

Input parameter. Pointer to tree structure obtained with **HrESE-BackupRestoreGetNodes**().

B.3.3   HrESEBackupRestoreGetRegistered

This function returns an array of server applications registered for backup/restore on a particular server. The applications returned can be filtered based on wszDisplayName and fFlags. In the case of Exchange, there is only one application, Exchange. After this call, the returned values must be freed by a subsequent call to **ESEBackupRestoreFreeRegisteredInfo**().

```
HRESULT ESEBACK_API HrESEBackupRestoreGetRegistered
(
    WCHAR *               wszServerName,
    WCHAR *               wszDisplayName,
    unsigned long         fFlags,
    unsigned long *       pcRegisteredInfo,
    ESE_REGISTERED_INFO ** paRegisteredInfo
);
```

Parameters

wszServerName

Input parameter. Points to the name of the server.

wszDisplayName

Input parameter. Returns only applications with certain Display Names. If NULL, do not filter based on this field.

fFlags

Input parameter. This is a combination of

- ESE_REGISTER_BACKUP,

- ESE_REGISTER_ONLINE_RESTORE, and

- ESE_REGISTER_OFFLINE_RESTORE.

If 0, it means all the registered applications will be returned.

pcRegisteredInfo

Output parameter. Count of the elements in the paRegisteredInfo array.

paRegisteredInfo

Output parameter. Array of elements describing the existing registered applications.

ESE_REGISTERED_INFO contains information about a backup/restore enabled application.

```
typedef struct _ESE_REGISTERED_INFO
{
    WCHAR *                 wszDisplayName;
    WCHAR *                 wszEndpointAnnotation;
    unsigned long           fFlags;
    ESE_ICON_DESCRIPTION    iconDescription;
} ESE_REGISTERED_INFO;
```

Elements

wszDisplayName

Application display name or product name. For Exchange, this will be "Microsoft Exchange Server." NOTE: The Information Store, SRS, and KMS will have the same value for wszDisplay Name("Microsoft Exchange Server").

wszEndpointAnnotation

Application annotation name:

- Information Store is "Microsoft Information Store."
- SRS is "Microsoft Site Replication Service."
- KMS is "Microsoft Key Management Service."

fFlags

The flags that the application registered with

- ESE_REGISTER_BACKUP,
- ESE_REGISTER_ONLINE_RESTORE, and
- ESE_REGISTER_OFFLINE_RESTORE.

iconDescription

The icon of the application.

```
typedef struct _ESE_ICON_DESCRIPTION
{
    unsigned long       ulSize;
    void *              pvData;
} ESE_ICON_DESCRIPTION;
```

ESE_ICON_DESCRIPTION is the icon description structure.

Parameters

ulSize

The icon data size.

pvData

The icon data.

B.3.4   ESEBackupRestoreFreeRegisteredInfo

This function is used to free the memory returned by **HrESEBackupRestoreGetRegistered**().

```
void ESEBACK_API ESEBackupRestoreFreeRegisteredInfo(
    unsigned long           cRegisteredInfo,
    ESE_REGISTERED_INFO *   aRegisteredInfo
);
```

Parameters

pcRegisteredInfo

Input parameter. Count of the elements in the paRegisteredInfo array .

paRegisteredInfo

Input parameter. Array of elements describing the existing registered applications.

B.4   Backup Functions

The backup applications use the following APIs to backup a set of databases and their log files. The Backup/Restore client should find that the servers and applications may be backed up using the General functions. To backup, the client will perform the following calling sequence.

1.   **HrESEBackupPrepare**()—to establish an RPC to the server application and get information about the databases. The client will connect to the server and specify which service it is going to backup (e.g., "Microsoft Information Store"). The server will return the number of instances of

ESE that are running on the server and a pointer to structures for each one. The structure will contain

- Instance ID,
- Name of the Instance (Storage Group),
- Number of databases in this instance,
- Database GUIDs, and
- Icon information.

2. **HrESEBackupSetup()**—to tell server which instance to backup. None of the databases in the ESE instance can be mounted or unmounted during the backup. The client passes in

- ESE instance ID and
- Type of backup.

3. **HrESEBackupOpenFile()**—to open the database for read.

4. **HrESEBackupReadFile()**—to read the database.

5. **HrESEBackupCloseFile()**—to close the database.

6. Loop back to step 5) until all database files are read for each database that will be backed up. (NOTE: for databases with a STM file, both files must be backed up separately in two different open/read/close sequences.)

7. **HrESEBackupGetLogAndPatchFiles()**—to get a list of log file names and patch file names.

8. **HrESEBackupOpenFile()**—to open the log/patch file for read.

9. **HrESEBackupReadFile()**—to read the log/patch file.

10. **HrESEBackupCloseFile()**—to close the file.

11. Loop until all log/patch files are read.

12. **HrESEBackupTruncateLog()**—to delete logs after backup.

13. **HrESEBackupInstanceEnd()**—to end the backup for the instance.

14. **HrESEBackupEnd()**—to disconnect from the server application.

Note that the backup API is based on instances of ESE (Storage groups in Exchange terminology). Currently, only one backup per ESE instance is allowed at one time. There may be backups of different instances of ESE occurring at the same time, but only one database in an instance of ESE may be backed up at a time. (Multiple databases may be backed up during a backup session, but only one at a time.)

Allowing a multiple-instance backup at the same time will help speed up tape backup. To backup multiple instances in parallel the backup application will be required to open multiple backup sessions. To restore multiple instances in parallel also requires multiple sessions. For a **multi-instance restore**, the server must have additional ESE instances available. The store.exe process in Exchange 2000 can have at most four ESE instances or storage groups mounted at a time while clients are accessing databases in those four instances. However, ESE supports up to 16 instances on a server. The additional 12 instances may be used *for restore only*.

B.4.1 HrESEBackupPrepare

The Backup/Restore Client establishes the connection to the server (using server name and application annotation). The server returns a set of hierarchy information that the client can use to allow user to select an instance for backing up.

```
HRESULT HrESEBackupPrepare
(
    wchar *                   wszBackupServer,
    wchar *                   wszBackupAnnotation,
    unsigned long *           pcInstanceInfo,
    INSTANCE_BACKUP_INFO *    paInstanceInfo,
    HCCX *                    phccxBackupContext
);
```

Parameters

wszBackupServer

Input parameter. This is name of the server to backup.

wszBackupAnnotation

Input parameter. This is the backup server's application annotation:

- Information Store is "Microsoft Information Store."

- SRS is "Microsoft Site Replication Service."
- KMS is "Microsoft Key Management Service."

pcInstanceInfo

Output parameter. Number of instances of ESE corresponding to the number of elements in the *paInstanceInfo* and *phccxBackup-Context* array.

paInstanceInfo

Output parameter. Pointer to an array of structures allocated inside in this function.

phccxBackupContext

Output parameter. Client side context handle for backup.

INSTANCE_BACKUP_INFO is the structure for each running instance. For each instance we have, the structure contains

```
typedef struct _INSTANCE_BACKUP_INFO
{
        __int64                   hInstanceId;
        RPC_STRING                wszInstanceName;
        unsigned long             ulIconIndexInstance;
        unsigned long             cDatabase;
        DATABASE_BACKUP_INFO *    rgDatabase;
        unsigned long             cIconDescription;
        ESE_ICON_DESCRIPTION *    rgIconDescription;
} INSTANCE_BACKUP_INFO;
```

Elements

hInstanceId

Instance ID.

wszInstanceName

The name of the instance.

ulIconIndexInstance

Index into rgIconDescription array that represents the icon of the instance.

cDatabases

Number of databases used by the instance.

rgDatabase

Structure that contains information about the databases. See below.

cIconDescription

Size of rgIconDescription.

rgIconDescription

Array of icons.

The icon corresponding to the instance is given as an index in this array by ulIconIndexInstance. For each database, the corresponding element of the array rgIconIndexDatabase is an index in the icon description array.

DATABASE_BACKUP_INFO is the structure that represents each database in the ESE instance.

```
typedef struct _DATABASE_BACKUP_INFO
{
    WCHAR **                    wszDatabaseStreams;
    WCHAR **                    wszDatabaseDisplayName;
    GUID *                      rguidDatabase;
    unsigned long *             rgIconIndexDatabase;
} DATABASE_BACKUP_INFO;
```

Elements

wszDatabaseStreams

Arrays of filenames corresponding to the database files (EDB and STM), double-zero terminated.

wszDatabaseDisplayName

In the case of Exchange, the first string will be the database file name and the second one (if present) will be the STM file name display name.

rguidDatabase

GUID of the database.

rgIconIndexDatabase

Index into the Icon array (rgIconDescription) for the ESE instance.

The returned pointer must be freed with **ESEBackupFree InstanceInfo()**.

B.4.2   ESEBackupFreeInstanceInfo

Function for user to free the buffers returned by **HrESEBackup Prepare**().

```
void ESEBACK_API ESEBackupFreeInstanceInfo
(
        unsigned long              cInstanceInfo,
        INSTANCE_BACKUP_INFO *     aInstanceInfo
);
```

Parameters

cInstanceInfo

Input parameter. Information to free.

aInstanceInfo

Input parameter. Pointer to be freed.

B.4.3   HrESEBackupEnd

Release all the resources held for backup. If **HrESEBackupInstance End**() has not been called, it will be called with ESE_BACKUP_ INSTANCE_END_ERROR.

```
HRESULT HrESEBackupEnd
(
        HCCX                       hccxBackupContext
);
```

Parameters

hccxBackupContext

Client side context handle for backup.

B.4.4   HrESEBackupSetup

Prepare to backup an instance. This function also checks whether there has been a full backup before attempting an incremental backup. If no full has been done, then the function will not put the instance into backup mode. The function will forbid any database attachment/detachment operations until the backup is finished. The actual databases from the instance that will be part of the backup will be determined by using **HrESEBackupOpenFile**().

```
HRESULT HrESEBackupSetup
(
    HCCX                    hccxBackupContext,
    __int64                 hInstanceId,
    unsigned long           btBackupType,
);
```

Parameters

hccxBackupContext

Input parameter. Client side context handle for backup.

hInstanceId

Input parameter. Instance id for backup.

btBackupType

Input parameter. This can be

- BACKUP_TYPE_FULL—a full backup,

- BACKUP_TYPE_FULL_WITH_ALL_LOGS—a full backup and all the logs since last full backup. Not supported yet (but planned for a future release), or

- BACKUP_TYPE_INCREMENTAL—incremental backup, with backup logs only.

B.4.5   HrESEBackupInstanceEnd

Ends the backup procedure for an instance, started by **HrESeBack-upSetup()**.

```
HRESULT HrESEBackupInstanceEnd
(
    HCCX                    hccxBackupContext,
    unsigned long           fFlags
);
```

Parameters

hccxBackupContext

Input parameter. Client side context handle for backup.

fFlags

Input parameter. Flag to inform calling process about whether the backup was successful or not. Possible values are

- ESE_BACKUP_INSTANCE_END_SUCCESS, or

- ESE_BACKUP_INSTANCE_END_ERROR.

B.4.6   HrESEBackupGetLogAndPatchFiles

Call to get the log and patch file list for backup.

```
HRESULT HrESEBackupGetLogAndPatchFiles
(
      HCCX                          hccxBackupContext,
      wchar *                       pwszFile
);
```

Parameters

hccxBackupContext

  Input parameter. Client side context handle for backup.

pwszFile

  Output parameter. A buffer holding a list of log files and patch files to backup. The file names in the list are separated by '\0'. The last file name is followed by "\0\0".

B.4.7   ESEBackupFree

Function to free the buffers return by **HrESEBackupGetLogAnd-PatchFiles()**. Also used by restore client to free buffers returned by **HrESERestoreAddDatabase()** or other functions.

```
void ESEBackupFree
(
      void                          *pvBuffer
);
```

Parameters

pvBuffer

  Input parameter. Buffer to be freed.

B.4.8   HrESEBackupOpenFile

Only databases specified in **HrESEBackupPrepare()** or returned from **HrESEBackupGetLogAndPatchFiles()** can be opened with this function. No more databases can be opened after **HrESE-BackupGetLogAndPatchFiles()** is called. **HrESEBackupOpen-File()** opens a database in number of sections specified in cSessions.

NOTE: cSections should be one. Only one section is supported at this time. There are no plans to support more than one section; however, this may change in the future.

```
HRESULT HrESEBackupOpen
(
    HCCX                        hccxBackupContext,
    wchar                       wszFileName,
    unsigned long               cbReadHintSize,
    unsigned long               cSections,
    void **                     rghFile,
    __int64 *                   rgliSectionSize
);
```

Parameters

hccxBackupContext

Input parameter. Client side context handle for backup.

wszFileName

Input parameter. The file to read.

cSections

Input parameter. The number of sections the function should return (should be one).

cbReadHintSize

Input parameter. Used for local backup. Typically this should be multiple of 64k: (NT IO unit) * number of drives the databases are on.

rghFile

Output parameter. An array of handles of each section for read. This will always be one.

rgliSectionSize

Output parameter. An array of the size of each section to read. The size must be one.

B.4.9   HrESEBackupReadFile

Read data into user's buffer.

```
HRESULT HrESEBackupReadFile
(
        HCCX                            hccxBackupContext,
        void *                          hFile,
        void *                          pvBuffer,
        WORD                            cbBuffer,
        WORD *                          pcbRead
);
```

Parameters

hccxBackupContext

Input parameter. Client side context handle for backup.

hFile

Input parameter. File handle of a section (should be only one section) of a file to read from.

pvBuffer

Input parameter. The buffer to read into.

cbBuffer

Input parameter. Size of pvBuffer.

pcbRead

Input parameter. Actual number of bytes read into the buffer.

B.4.10 HrESEBackupCloseFile

Close section handle opened with HrESEBackupOpenFile

```
HRESULT HrESEBackupCloseFile
(
        HCCX                            hccxBackupContext,
        void *                          hFile
);
```

Parameters

hccxBackupContext

Input parameter. Client side context handle for backup.

hFile

Input parameter. Handle of the section of the file to be closed.

B.4.11 HrESEBackupTruncateLogs

ESE will check all attached databases and find the smallest genHigh in the backup information in each database header. genHigh is the earliest log that can be deleted for this instance of ESE. Then ESE deletes all logs up to genHigh. At the end of backup, the database header is updated such that the backup info shows the log files in the backup set (genLow and genHigh).

```
HRESULT HrESEBackupTruncateLogs
(
        HCCX                        hccxBackupContext
);
```

Parameters

hccxBackupContext

Input parameter. Client side context handle for backup.

B.5   Restore Functions

Typically, restoring databases involves three steps:

1.   Load files from another media.

2.   Bring the database to an ESE level of consistency.

3.   Perform application level fix-up, such as reference count between tables.

There are two possible restore sequences:

1.   Restore to a server *with services* running. The process that mounts the databases is running on the server. For Exchange, this will be store.exe.

2.   Restore to a server *without services* running. This restore method is not used by Exchange, but it is included for general purposes.

The restore environment can be accessed several different ways. **HrESERestoreSaveEnvironment()** should be called to save a restore session before calling **HrESERestoreClose()** or **HrESE RestoreComplete()**. On subsequent calls to continue restoring (**HrESERestoreReopen()**), the restore environment will be loaded automatically. To view the restore data, either **HrESERestoreGetEnvironment()** or **HrESERestoreLoadEnvironment()** can be called to return the restore environment, **HrESERestoreGetEnviro nment()** can be called for the current restore session, and **HrESER estoreLoadEnvironment()** can be called for any restore environment.

Table B.1 *Model I(a) - Restore to a Server with Services Running (from a Full Backup)*

Backup Client Side	*Server Side*
Reading from the head of the tape, the client gets a list of databases to restore. This allows user to pick the databases from the list to be restored.	
HrESERestoreOpen(). The client can specify a destination directory or can ask the server to do that.	Provide a temporary destination directory for the restore process if requested. This will be used to store the log files, the patch file, and the restore environment for this particular restore session. If there will be multiple restores happening, then the temporary destination directories must be different.
HrESERestoreAddDatabase() is called multiple times for each database to be to be restored.	The server will return the destination of the database files (EDB and STM).
Restore the files to the destination specified. A call to **HrESERestoreOpenFile()** is recommended for all files. Files that do not return the error hrRestoreAtFileLevel will require calls to **HrESEWrite File()** and **HrESECloseFile()** to copy the data. Files that return the error code should be restored at the file system level in the restore directory. (All files that Exchange uses will return the error code.)	
Restore the log and patch files (returned by **HrESE BackupGetLogAndPatchFiles()**). A call to **HrESERestoreOpenFile()** is *required* for all log and patch files. This call will fail with the error hrRestoreAtFileLevel, but the call is needed to build log sequence information.	
HrESERestoreSaveEnvironment() will save the restore environment (database mapping, log range, etc.) into a file (in the restore directory).	
HrESERestoreComplete()	All the needed files are restored and the restore environment is saved. The server can start recovery (**HrESERecoverAfterRestore()**).
HrESERestoreClose()	

→

Table B.2 *Model I(b) - Restore to a Server* with Services *Running (Full Backup Plus an Incremental Backup)*

Backup Client Side	Server Side
By reading from the head of the tape, the client gets a list of databases to restore. This allows user to pick the databases from the list to be restored.	
HrESERestoreOpen() the client can specify a destination directory or can ask the server to do that.	Provide a temporary destination directory for the restore process if requested. This will be used to store the log files, the patch file, and the restore environment for this particular restore session. If there will be multiple restores happening, then the temporary destination directories must be different.
HrESERestoreAddDatabase() is called multiple times for each database to be restored.	The server will return the destination of the database files (EDB and STM).
Restore the files to the destination specified. A call to **HrESERestoreOpenFile()** is recommended for all files. Files that do not return the error hrRestoreAtFileLevel will require calls to **HrESEWriteFile()** and **HrESECloseFile()** to copy the data. Files that return the error code should be restored at the file system level in the restore directory. (Most ESE known files will return the error code.)	
Restore the log and patch files (returned by **HrESEBackupGetLogAndPatchFiles()**). A call to **HrESERestoreOpenFile()** is *required* for all log and patch files. This call will fail with the error hrRestoreAtFileLevel, but the call is needed to build log sequence information.	
HrESERestoreSaveEnvironment() will save the restore environment (database mapping, log range, etc.) into a file (in the restore directory).	
HrESERestoreClose()	**ErrESECBRestoreClose()**
HrESERestoreReopen()	**ErrESECBRestoreOpen()**— when fRestore parameter set to true the backup client is reopening a restore process, the restore environment is specified using the restore directory provided as parameter to the callback.

Table B.2   *Model I(b) - Restore to a Server* with Services *Running*
              (Full Backup Plus an Incremental Backup) (continued)

Backup Client Side	Server Side
Restore the log and patch files (returned by **HrESE-BackupGetLogAndPatchFiles**()). A call to **HrESERestoreOpenFile**() is required for all log and patch files. This call will fail with the error hrRestoreAtFileLevel, but the call is needed to build log sequence information.	
HrESERestoreSaveEnvironment() will save the restore environment (database mapping, log range, etc.) with the new information.	
HrESERestoreComplete()	All the needed files are restored and the restore environment is saved. The server can start recovery (HrESERecoverAfterRestore()).
HrESERestoreClose()	

Table B.3   *Model II - Restore to a Server* Without Services *Running*
              (NOT APPLICABLE IN MOST CASES)

Backup Client Side	Server Side
Reading from the head of the tape, the client gets a list of databases to restore. This allows user to pick the databases from the list to restore.	
Call **HrESERestoreOpen**() with the directory destination of the log and path files.	
HrESERestoreAddDatabaseNS() is called multiple times, one call for each database to be restored.	
Restore the files to the destination specified. A call to **HrESERestoreOpenFile**() is recommended for all files. Files that do not return the error hrRestoreAtFileLevel will require calls to **HrESEWriteFile**() and **HrESECloseFile**() to copy the data. Files that *return* the error code should be restored at the file system level in the restore directory. (Most ESE known files will return the error code.)	

Table B.3   *Model II - Restore to a Server Without Services Running (NOT APPLICABLE IN MOST CASES) (continued)*

Backup Client Side	*Server Side*
Restore the log and patch files (returned by **HrESE-BackupGetLogAndPatchFiles()**). For each file call **HrESERestoreOpenFile()**. A call to **HrESE RestoreOpenFile()** is *required* for all log and patch files. It will fail with the error hrRestoreAt-FileLevel, but the call is needed to build log sequence information.	
HrESERestoreSaveEnvironment() will save the restore environment (database mapping, log range, etc.) with the new information.	
HrESERestoreComplete()	This means that all the needed files are restored and the restore environment is saved.
HrESERestoreClose()	Server can call.
HrESERecoverAfterRestore() at any time. The function will load the restore environment from a directory specified as a parameter and will start the recovery process with the information. The recovery instance that will run will have the system and log file path specified as a parameter of this function.	

B.5.1   HrESERestoreOpen

Restore *with services*:

wszServiceAnnotation is not NULL. Setup the RPC connection between the server application and the client (*with services*). The server will return a destination (directory) for the log and patch files if it is not provided by the client (wszRestoreLogPath is NULL). This destination will contain recovery information specific to this instance of ESE.

Restore *without services*:

wszServiceAnnotation is NULL. Prepare the restore process for the case where no restore server is involved (*without services*). The Backup/Restore Client simply restores the files from media and does nothing. The restore environment will be saved in wszRestoreLog-Path by calling **HrESERestoreSaveEnvironment()**.

```
HRESULT HrESERestoreOpen
(
        WCHAR *                 wszServerName,
        WCHAR *                 wszServiceAnnotation,
        WCHAR *                 wszSrcInstanceName,
        wchar *                 wszRestoreLogPath,
        HCCX *                  phccxRestoreContext
);
```

Parameters

wszServerName

Input parameter. Name of the server to restore to.

wszServiceAnnotation

Input parameter. The restore application annotation name for the restore RPC call entries of the application (e.g., "Microsoft Information Store"). Each ESE application has different annotation. It must be NULL to restore *without services*.

wszInstanceName

Input parameter. The name of the instance using the databases at backup time.

wszRestoreLogPath

Input parameter. The path where the restore environment file will be stored. If it is not provided by the client (NULL), then this path must be provided by the server. The store will provide this path in the case of Exchange.

phccxRestoreContext

Output parameter. The client side context for restore.

B.5.2   HrESERestoreReopen

Restore *with services*:

wszServiceAnnotation is not NULL. Restablish the RPC connection between the server application and the client. The restore process is identified by the restore directory (wszRestoreLogPath). The restore environment is loaded from this directory. The restore environment should have been previously saved with **HrESERestoreSaveEnvironment()**.

Restore *without services*:

wszServiceAnnotation is NULL. In this case no annotation is needed because no RPC connection is involved.

```
HRESULT HrESERestoreReopen
(
            WCHAR *                    wszServerName,
            WCHAR *                    wszServiceAnnotation,
            WCHAR *                    wszRestoreLogPath,
            HCCX *                     phccxRestoreContext
);
```

Parameters

wszServerName

Input parameter. Restore server name.

wszServiceAnnotation

Input parameter. The application annotation name of the application to be restored. Each ESE application has different annotation. It must be NULL to restore *without services*.

WszRestoreLogPath

Input parameter. Location of a previous restore environment to load.

phccxRestoreContext

Output parameter. The client side context for restore.

B.5.3   **HrESERestoreClose**

```
HRESULT HrESERestoreClose
(
      HCCX                      hccxRestoreContext,
      unsigned long             fRestoreAbort
);
```
Parameters

hccxRestoreContext

Input parameter. The client side context for restore. This function also calls **ErrESECBRestoreClose()** to notify the server application that restore from media is done if the restore process is *with services*. Note that this does not mean that the recover process can be started; for this purpose, **HrESERestoreComplete()** must be used.

fRestoreAbort

Iutput paramter. This can be

- RESTORE_CLOSE_NORMAL or
- RESTORE_CLOSE_ABORT.

depending on whether the termination is a normal one or the restore process is canceled.

B.5.4   **HrESERestoreAddDatabase**

This function must be called for each database to be restored when restoring *with services*. The function will return the destination file names for the database and streaming files (EDB and STM).

```
HRESULT HrESERestoreAddDatabase
(
    HCCX                    hccxRestoreContext,
    WCHAR *                 wszDatabaseDisplayName,
    GUID                    guidDatabase,
    WCHAR *                 wszDatabaseStreamsS,
    WCHAR **                pwszDatabaseStreamsD
);
```

Parameters

hccxRestoreContext

Input parameter. The client side context for restore.

wszDatabaseDisplayName

Input parameter. The database that the user chooses from a backup set to restore.

guidDatabase

Input parameter. The GUID for the database (get at backup time from the server).

wszDatabaseStreamsS

Input parameter. A list of source streams double '\0' terminated (the databases filenames [EDB and STM] and other streams).

pwszDatabaseStreamsD

Input parameter. List of corresponding destination streams (double '\0' terminated). The returned names must be freed by **ESEBackupFree()**.

B.5.5   HrESERestoreAddDatabaseNS

This is the "no server" (*without services*) case for **HrESERestore-AddDatabase**(). In this case the caller must provide the destination of the files.

```
HRESULT HrESERestoreAddDatabaseNS
(
        HCCX                        hccxRestoreContext,
        WCHAR *                     wszDatabaseDisplayName,
        GUID                        guidDatabase,
        WCHAR *                     wszDatabaseStreamsS,
        WCHAR *                     wszDatabaseStreamsD
);
```

Parameters

hccxRestoreContext

   Input parameter. The client side context for restore.

wszDatabaseDisplayName

   Input parameter. The databases that user chooses from a backup set to restore.

guidDatabase

   Input parameter. The GUID for the database (get at backup time from the server).

wszDatabaseStreamsS

   Input parameter. List of source streams for the database.

wszDatabaseStreamsD

   Input parameter. A list of corresponding destination streams.

B.5.6   HrESERestoreOpenFile

Must be called for each file to be restored. If it returns a certain error (hrRestoreAtFileLevel), it means that the restore of the files must be done at file system level, and the call of **HrESERestoreWriteFile**() and **HrESERestoreCloseFile**() is not needed for that file. The call will fail for most of the known ESE files (*.edb, *.stm, *.log, *.pat, etc.) but must be included for the log files as it allows the log sequence information to be built. The **HrESERestoreWriteFile**() and **HrESERestoreClose**() calls are primarily intended for the restore of application-specific data files that ESE might not be aware of. Exchange 2000 does not have any of the specific data files that require this.

```
HRESULT HrESERestoreOpenFile
(
        HCCX                        hccxRestoreContext,
        WCHAR *                     wszFileName,
        unsigned long               cSections,
        void **                     rghFile
);
```

Parameters

hccxRestoreContext

Input parameter. The client side context handle for restore.

wszFileName

Input parameter. The file to be restored.

cSections

Input parameter. The number of sections that the file will be formed of (should be one).

rghFile

Output parameter. The array of handles of each section. Currently there is only one.

B.5.7   HrESERestoreWriteFile

Writes data into the opened file (or section).

```
HRESULT HrESERestoreWriteFile
(
        HCCX                        hccxRestoreContext,
        void *                      hFile,
        void *                      pvBuffer,
        unsigned long               cbBuffer
);
```

Parameters

hccxRestoreContext

Input parameter. The client side context handle for restore.

hFile

Input parameter. The section handle of a file for to be written in.

pvBuffer

Input parameter. The buffer to write.

cbBuffer

Input parameter. The size of pvBuffer.

B.5.8   HrESERestoreCloseFile

Close section handle opened with HrESEBackupOpenFile.

```
HRESULT HrESERestoreCloseFile
(
    HCCX                    hccxRestoreContext,
    void *                  hFile
);
```

Parameters

HccxRestoreContext

Input parameter. This the client side context handle for restore.

hFile

Input parameter. The handle of a section of a file to be closed.

B.5.9   HrESERestoreSaveEnvironment

This function will save the in-memory restore environment to disk. This function must be called before **HrESERestoreClose**(), if **HrESERestoreComplete**() has not been called. For example, this is the correct calling order for the Restore functions:

- ...

- HrESERestoreSaveEnvironment

- ...

- HrESERestoreClose

- ...

- HrESEReopen

- ...

- HrESERestoreComplete

```
HRESULT HrESERestoreSaveEnvironment
(
        HCCX                          hccxRestoreContext
);
```

Parameters

hccxRestoreContext

The client side context for restore.

B.5.10 **HrESERestoreComplete**

The function informs the application that the files are back, and recovery can be started at any time to bring the databases to a consistent state. In the restore *with services* case the server is informed about this with the callback function **ErrESECBRestoreComplete**(). The server application can start recovery from this callback, eventually.

```
HRESULT HrESERestoreComplete
(
        HCCX                          hccxRestoreContext,
        wchar *                       wszCheckpointFilePath,
        wchar *                       wszLogFilePath,
        wchar *                       wszTargetInstanceName,
        unsigned long                 fFlags
);
```

Parameters

hccxRestoreContext

Input parameter. The client side context for restore.

wszCheckpointFilePath

wszLogFilePath

Input parameters. The checkpoint and log files path for the ESE instance that will perform the recovery. Those values will be stored in the restore environment. At recovery time, they will be read from the restore environment (or they can be overwritten by the **HrESERecoverAfterRestore**() call).

wszTargetInstanceName

Input parameter. The name of a running instance. This will be used to find log files generated after the backup moment that need to be replayed against the recovered database in order to bring it as up to date as possible. This value will be stored in the restore environment. At recovery time this will be read from the restore environment (or they can be overwritten at **HrESERecoverAfterRestore**() call).

fFlags

Input parameter. These flags may be OR'ed together and passed into **HrESERestoreComplete**():

- ESE_RESTORE_COMPLETE_NOWAIT—the recovery process will start asynchronously (i.e., this call will return right away, and not wait until recovery has ended). The result is logged in the Event Log on the server side.

- ESE_RESTORE_COMPLETE_ATTACH_DBS—Passed to the server in order to specify if we want to mount the databases after a restore.

- ESE_RESTORE_KEEP_LOG_FILES—Normally, after a restore and a successful recovery, log files that are not needed anymore are deleted (i.e., restored log files and log files created during recovery). Specifying this flag will not delete any log files.

B.5.11 HrESERestoreGetEnvironment

Returns the in-memory restore environment. The returned value must be freed with the **ESERestoreFreeEnvironment**() function.

```
HRESULT HrESERestoreGetEnvironment
(
    HCCX                    hccxRestoreContext,
    RESTORE_ENVIRONMENT **  ppRestoreEnvironment
);
```

Parameters

hccxRestoreContext

Input parameter. The client side context for restore.

ppRestoreEnvironment

Output parameter. Returned environment.

B.5.12 HrESERestoreLoadEnvironment

This is primarily a utility function to allow viewing of the restore environment. This function loads a restore environment into memory. The restore environment is loaded from a certain server and path. It can be called from the server or from the client. The returned restore environment must be freed after use with the function **ESERestoreFreeEnvironment**().

```
HRESULT HrESERestoreLoadEnvironment
(
    WCHAR *                   wszServerName,
    WCHAR *                   wszRestoreLogPath,
    RESTORE_ENVIRONMENT **  ppRestoreEnvironment
);
```

Parameters

wszServerName

Input parameter. Server name.

wszRestoreLogPath

Input parameter. Path on the server to the environment.

ppRestoreEnvironment

Output parameter. The restore environment information.

The restore environment has the following format:

```
typedef struct _RESTORE_ENVIRONMENT {
WCHAR *             m_wszRestoreLogPath;
WCHAR *             m_wszSrcInstanceName;

WCHAR *             m_wszCheckpointFilePath;
WCHAR *             m_wszLogFilePath;
WCHAR *             m_wszTargetInstanceName;

unsigned long       m_cDatabases;
WCHAR **            m_wszDatabaseDisplayName;
GUID *              m_guidDatabase;
WCHAR **            m_wszDatabaseStreamsS;
WCHAR **            m_wszDatabaseStreamsD;
unsigned long       m_ulGenLow;
unsigned long       m_ulGenHigh;
WCHAR *             m_ m_wszLogBaseName;

time_t              m_timeLastRestore;
RECOVER_STATUS      m_statusLastRecover;
```

```
HRESULT            m_hrLastRecover;
time_t             m_timeLastRecover;
WCHAR *            m_wszAnnotation;
} RESTORE_ENVIRONMENT;
```

Elements

m_wszRestoreLogPath

The path where the restore environment is loaded from.

m_wszSrcInstanceName

The name of the instance that was backed up.

m_wszCheckpointFilePath

wszLogFilePath

The checkpoint and log files path for the ESE instance that will perform the recovery.

m_wszTargetInstanceName

The name of a running instance. This will be used to find logs generated after the backup that need to be replayed against the recovered database in order to bring it as up to date as possible.

m_cDatabases

The number of databases restored.

m_wszDatabaseDisplayName

Array (m_ cDatabases elements) of pointers to strings representing the database display names.

m_guidDatabase

Array (m_ cDatabases elements) of database GUIDs for the databases.

m_wszDatabaseStreamsS

Array (m_ cDatabases elements) of pointers to a list of strings double '\0' terminated representing the source stream names: file names for database file and optional STM file, other files, and/or data streams.

m_wszDatabaseStreamsD

Array (m_ cDatabases elements) of pointers to list of strings double '\0' terminated representing the corresponding destinations for source streams.

m_ulGenLow

m_ ulGenHigh

m_wszLogBaseName

The range of log files restored and the base name of the logs.

m_timeLastRestore

The time when the environment was saved.

m_statusLastRecover

Informs about the last operation on the restore environment. It can have one of the following values:

- recoverInvalid
- recoverNotStarted
- recoverStarted
- recoverEnded

m_hrLastRecover

Error code of the last recover (if statusLastRecover is recoverEnded).

m_hrLastRecover

Time of the last recover (if statusLastRecover is recoverEnded).

m_wszAnnotation

Annotation used at **HrESERestoreOpen()**, which created the restore environment.

B.5.13 **ESERestoreFreeEnvironment**

This function is used to free the memory for the restore environment structure returned from a **HrESERestoreLoadEnvironment()** call.

```
void ESERestoreFreeEnvironment
(
      RESTORE_ENVIRONMENT *    pRestoreEnvironment
);
```

Index

Printed and bound by CPI Group (UK) Ltd, Croydon, CR0 4YY

03/10/2024

01040340-0017